Social Implications of Data Mining and Information Privacy:
Interdisciplinary Frameworks and Solutions

Ephrem Eyob
Virginia State University, USA

 **INFORMATION SCIENCE REFERENCE**

Hershey · New York

Director of Editorial Content:	Kristin Klinger
Director of Production:	Jennifer Neidig
Managing Editor:	Jamie Snavely
Assistant Managing Editor:	Carole Coulson
Typesetter:	Jennifer Neidig
Cover Design:	Lisa Tosheff
Printed at:	Yurchak Printing Inc.

Published in the United States of America by
Information Science Reference (an imprint of IGI Global)
701 E. Chocolate Avenue, Suite 200
Hershey PA 17033
Tel: 717-533-8845
Fax: 717-533-8661
E-mail: cust@igi-global.com
Web site: http://www.igi-global.com

and in the United Kingdom by
Information Science Reference (an imprint of IGI Global)
3 Henrietta Street
Covent Garden
London WC2E 8LU
Tel: 44 20 7240 0856
Fax: 44 20 7379 0609
Web site: http://www.eurospanbookstore.com

Library of Congress Cataloging-in-Publication Data

Social implications of data mining and information privacy : interdisciplinary frameworks and solutions / Ephrem Eyob, editor.

    p. cm.

  Includes bibliographical references and index.

  Summary: "This book serves as a critical source to emerging issues and solutions in data mining and the influence of social factors"-- Provided by publisher.

  ISBN 978-1-60566-196-4 (hardcover) -- ISBN 978-1-60566-197-1 (ebook)

  1. Data mining--Social aspects. 2. Information technology--Social aspects. 3. Data protection. I. Eyob, Ephrem, 1954-

  QA76.9.D343S64 2009

  005.74--dc22

                              2008030773

British Cataloguing in Publication Data
A Cataloguing in Publication record for this book is available from the British Library.

Editorial Advisory Board

Table of Contents

Detailed Table of Contents

Chapter I
Philip Brey, University of Twente, The Netherlands

Cultural differences among Western and non-Western societies may have impacts on the attitudes of information privacy. It covers whether information ethics, and by inference, information privacy is culturally relative. The author argues that there must be concepts and principles of information ethics that are universally valid.

Chapter II
Thomas M. Chen, Swansea University, UK
Zhi (Judy) Fu, Motorola Labs, USA

Protecting privacy when surfing the Internet is an ongoing challenge to end-users and system administrators. Chapter II provides a taxonomy for regulatory and technological solutions to protect user privacy.

Chapter III
Peter Danielson, University of British Columbia, Canada

Regulatory bodies have not adapted to the moral norms and models used in data mining technology. Building ethical data mining usage is a framework argued by sketching three models of game theory: pure conflict, pure collaboration, and a mixed motive cooperation game.

Information privacy and security can be compromised in applications such as customer relations management (CRM). Virtual relationships must be carefully managed between customers and businesses in order to add value and minimize unintended consequences that may harm the relationship. Based upon a customer's requirements of privacy and an enterprise requirement to establish markets and sell goods and services, there is a value exchange relationship. Chapter IV covers a model of an integration of spheres of customer privacy, security, and their implementations.

From an urban information perspective, emerging trends on information networked individualism via the Internet is the topic of Chapter V. The chapter presents a framework of an urban cohesive social network in the dynamics of their existing communicative ecology, and social behavior of urban dwellers. It challenges the accepted view that providing technology application support only, is not adequate to meet the location and proximity requirements in urban neighborhoods information seeking perspectives.

Using variables like user training, security culture, policy relevance, and policy enforcement, a theoretical model was tested to see the influence of these variables on security effectiveness. Both qualitative and quantitative data was used to analyze the survey response using structural equation modeling. Evidence was found supporting the hypothesized model . Furthermore, it explores a higher factor version of the model that provided an overall fit and general applicability across various demographics of the collected data.

Information sharing from data mining applications is controversial and protected by privacy regulations and ethical concerns. It introduces a method for privacy preserving clustering, called Dimensionality

Reduction-Based Transformation (DRBT). The method relies on random projection to hide the underlying attribute values subjected to cluster analysis. The authors argue that this method has advantages with little overhead cost in CPU intensive operations, and has a sound mathematical foundation

The classification of Web pages using machine learning techniques is the focus of this chapter. Different techniques are used to classify Web pages using the most efficient algorithms by search engines to provide accurate results to the user. Additionally, machine learning classifiers can be trained to preserve privacy from unauthenticated users.

Chapter IX

Issues related to U.S. Federal data mining programs are expounded in this part. The authors argue that in the context of 9/11, intelligence gathering within and outside United States is one of the primary strategies of the U.S. Homeland Security Agency. These activities have raised a number of issues related to privacy protection and civil liberties of citizens and non-citizens.

Chapter X

Legal rights and privacy in the United States as related to data mining in contemporary society are covered in this chapter. It covers the legal frameworks of data mining and privacy which historically lags to technological developments. The author argues that legal rights as related to privacy in the United States is not keeping pace with the data mining activities of businesses, governments, and other entities.

Chapter XI

Significant advances in telecommunications and GPS sensors technology are enabling the users of these technologies to track down objects and individuals with remarkable precision. As useful as these technologies are, without strict safeguards on privacy it becomes problematic in the hands of malevolent users. It reviews state-of-the-art work on trajectory data privacy. Furthermore, the authors share views regarding the current state and future trend in trajectory data privacy.

Web pages are classified on content or imbedded contextual information. The pages can contain irrelevant information that may reduce performance of the Web classifiers. The accessed data can be mined to predict user authentication and hide personal details to preserve privacy. This chapter covers comprehensively the feature selections techniques used by researchers in Web classification.

Collection of data related to agricultural produces and subsequent data mining of it can improve production, handling, and public health safety. It deals with recent advances in technology application in agriculture such as uses of RFID and bar coding to trace backward and forward information of fresh produce on production, handling, storage, repackaging, and final sale to consumer. The authors discuss the promises of these technologies in agriculture and potential benefits to business, government, World Health and food safety monitoring organizations in order to increase safety and service, and reduce costs of such products.

Chapter XIV

A case study involving research into the science of building teams is the focus of this chapter. Accomplishment of mission goals requires team members to not only possess the required technical skills but also be able to collaborate effectively. The authors describe a research project which aims to develop an automated staffing system. Any such system requires a large amount of personal information about the potential team members under consideration. Gathering, storing, and applying this data raises a spectrum of concerns, from social and ethical implications, to technical hurdles. The authors hope to highlight these concerns by focusing on their research efforts which include obtaining and using employee data within a small business.

The final chapter gives a summary of data types, mathematical structures, and associated methods of data mining. Topological, order theoretical, algebraic, and probability theoretical mathematical structures are introduced in Chapter XV. The n-dimensional Euclidean space, the model used most for data, is defined; it notes that the treatment of higher dimensional random variables and related data is problematic. Examples are given for topological clusters and topological discriminant analyses and their implications on preserving privacy issues.

Foreword

The last several years have been characterized by global companies building up massive databases containing computer users' search queries and sites visited; government agencies accruing sensitive data and extrapolating knowledge from uncertain data with little incentive to provide citizens with ways of correcting false data; and individuals who can easily combine publicly available data to derive information that – in former times – was not so readily accessible.

"Social Implications of Data Mining and Information Privacy: Interdisciplinary Frameworks and Solutions" addresses precisely these issues. Cultural differences can possibly lead to differing expectations of how information is handled and ideas of to whom information belongs. European countries, most notably Germany, Austria, and Switzerland, share the view that personal information belongs to the person in question, whereas in the United States, information belongs to the company who generated or collected it.

Establishing an ethics-framework for data mining is crucial. Politics often uses drastic examples of relatively rare crimes, such as terrorism or child pornography, to introduce legislation that may later be extended to cover minor crimes or to surveil political opposition. In the corporate world, effective CRM may very well infringe on personal privacy; it is, however, needed to provide customers with the services they expect. While many complain about "companies that know everything about their costumers," we expect call centers, for instance, to know about our entire previous communication, about payments, and so forth. When companies morph into corporations and jointly offer services, we want them to provide services for which they are required to share our data. We resent however, the idea that they exchange data or might use it for other purposes.

Data privacy and integrity gain in importance because many people use computers almost continuously and – more importantly – computers remain connected to the Internet all the time. In cities, Internet access is a commodity infrastructure similar to water or power. Jurisdiction needs to take these changes into account, too. Legal frameworks react and evolve as society changes. Such frameworks must reflect the standards that citizens expect and fit them, as such, into the context of existing laws.

I wish all readers many enjoyable and fascinating hours with this book and congratulate the editor and authors on their excellent work!

Dr. Edgar Weippl
Austria

Edgar R. Weippl (CISSP, CISA, CISM) is science director of Secure Business Austria and university assistant at the Vienna University of Technology. His research focuses on applied concepts of IT-security and e-learning. Edgar has taught several tutorials on security issues in e-learning at international conferences, including ED-MEDIA 2003-2007 and E-Learn 2005. In 2005, he published Security in E-Learning *with Springer. After graduating with a PhD from the Vienna University of Technology, Edgar worked for two years in a research startup. He then spent one year teaching as an assistant professor at Beloit College, WI. From 2002 to 2004, while with the software vendor ISIS Papyrus, he worked as a consultant for an HMO (Empire BlueCross BlueShield) in New York, NY and Albany, NY, and for Deutsche Bank (PWM) in Frankfurt, Germany.*

Preface

Data mining is the extraction of readily unavailable information from data by sifting regularities and patterns. These ground breaking technologies are bringing major changes in the way people perceive these inter-related processes: the collection of data, archiving and mining it, the creation of information nuggets, and potential threats posed to individual liberty and privacy. This edited book, *Social Implications of Data Mining and Information Privacy: Interdisciplinary Frameworks and Solutions*, brings a collection of chapters that analyze topics related to competing goals: the need to collect data and information for disparate operational objectives, and the necessity to preserve the integrity of the collected data to protect privacy. Currently, scores of data mining applications technologies exist in marketing products, analyzing election results, identification of potential acts of terrorism, and prevention of such threats; uses of data mining in agricultural, in healthcare, and in education among many others.

The warehousing and data mining of data serve the public interest by improving service, reducing costs, and ultimately satisfying customers. The uneasiness on the use of these technologies arise from the fact that data are collected for different purposes, say, credit card charges for purchases of goods and services, the information provided for the transactional purposes are massaged and analyzed for unrelated uses that deviate from the original purposes. All these seemingly disparate data are collected, warehoused, and mined to find patterns. Aggregated data provides useful information for marketing goods and services to a segment of population. The aggregation of data can provide privacy whereas micro targeting mining does not. Data in the hands of unsavory characters can harm the victims and cause overall negative perceptions in providing personal information to conduct business transactions.

The significance of understanding data mining and the confusion it generates due to the misuse of collected data are explored in this edition. Addressing these concerns both legally and ethically by examining the implications of data mining as it impacts privacy and applications on these issues are explored in the various chapters of this edited book. The objective of the book is to provide the most comprehensive, in-depth, and recent coverage of information science and technology in data mining and information privacy disciplines. Various privacy problems are addressed in the public debate and the technology discourse. The chapters address what problems are critical and suggestions to address the solutions. Furthermore, which forms of privacy policy are adequate and the ramifications involved are covered. Carefully selected chapters in this edition include: information ethics, information privacy on the Web, models for data mining metaphors, information privacy in customer relations management, electronic networking in urban neighborhoods, theory of information security empirical validation, electronic collaboration and privacy preservation, machine learning for Web classification and privacy, U.S. federal government and data mining applications in Home Land Security Agency, legal framework for data mining and privacy, data mining and trajectory applications, data mining in agriculture, data mining principles, and building teams for project management.

In order to provide the best balanced coverage of concepts and issues related to the selected topics of this book, researchers from around the world were asked to submit proposals describing their proposed coverage and the contribution of such coverage to the book. All proposals were carefully reviewed by the editor in light of their suitability, researcher's records of similar work in the area of the proposed topics, and the best proposal for topics with multiple proposals. The goal was to assemble the best minds in the information science and technology field from all over the world to contribute entries to the book. Upon the receipt of full entry submissions, each submission was forwarded to at least three expert external reviewers on a double-blind, peer review basis. Only submissions with strong and favorable reviews were chosen as entries for this encyclopedia. In many cases submissions were sent back for several revisions prior to final acceptance.

The following paragraphs provide a brief synopsis on the chapters covered.

Cultural differences among Western and non-Western societies may have impacts on the attitudes of information privacy. Chapter I covers whether information ethics, and by inference, information privacy is culturally relative. The author argues that there must be concepts and principles of information ethics that are universally valid. It analyzes the normative implications of information ethics in a cross-cultural context. It posits the position between moral absolutism and relativism, which are based on intercultural understanding and mutual criticism that could be helpful in overcoming differences and misunderstandings between cultures in their approach to information and information technologies.

Protecting privacy when surfing the Internet is an ongoing challenge to end-users and system administrators. Chapter II provides taxonomy for regulatory and technological solutions to protect user privacy. Information can be collected either overtly or covertly and the protection and the integrity of the information is an going problem that is baffling technological solution due to the open architecture design of the World Wide Web.

Regulatory bodies have not adapted to the moral norms and models used in data mining technology. Building ethical data mining usage is a framework argued in Chapter III. This is done by sketching three models of game theory: pure conflict, pure collaboration, and a mixed motive cooperation game.

Information privacy and security can be compromised in applications such as customer relations management (CRM). Virtual relationships must be carefully managed between customers and businesses in order to add value and minimize unintended consequences that may harm the relationship. Based upon a customer's requirements of privacy and an enterprise requirement to establish markets and sell goods and services, there is a value exchange relationship. Chapter IV covers a model of an integration of spheres of customer privacy, security, and their implementations.

From an urban information perspective, emerging trends on information networked individualism via the Internet is the topic of Chapter V. The chapter presents a framework of an urban cohesive social network in the dynamics of their existing communicative ecology, and social behavior of urban dwellers. It challenges the accepted view that providing technology application support only, is not adequate to meet the location and proximity requirements in urban neighborhoods information seeking perspectives.

Using variables like user training, security culture, policy relevance, and policy enforcement, a theoretical model was tested to see the influence of these variables on security effectiveness. Both qualitative and quantitative data was used to analyze the survey response using structural equation modeling. Evidence was found supporting the hypothesized model in Chapter VI. Furthermore, it explores a higher factor version of the model that provided an overall fit and general applicability across various demographics of the collected data.

Information sharing from data mining applications is controversial and protected by privacy regulations and ethical concerns. Chapter VII introduces a method for privacy preserving clustering, called dimensionality reduction-based transformation (DRBT). The method relies on random projection to hide the underlying attribute values subjected to cluster analysis. The authors argue that this method has advantages with little overhead cost in CPU intensive operations, and has a sound mathematical foundation.

The classification of Web pages using machine learning techniques is the focus of Chapter VIII. Different techniques are used to classify Web pages by means the most efficient algorithms with search engines to provide accurate results to the user. Additionally, machine learning classifiers can be trained to preserve privacy from unauthenticated users.

Chapter IX covers issues related to U.S. Federal data mining programs. The authors argue that in the context of 9/11, intelligence gathering within and outside United States is one of the primary strategies of the U.S. Homeland Security Agency. These activities have raised a number of issues related to privacy protection and civil liberties of citizens and non-citizens. The chapter extensively discusses relevant issues on the gathering of intelligence for national security and the war on terror and privacy protection of individuals.

The next chapter explores the legal rights and privacy in the United States as related to data mining in contemporary society. It covers the legal frameworks of data mining and privacy which historically lags to technological developments. The author argues that legal rights as related to privacy in the United States is not keeping pace with the data mining activities of businesses, governments, and other entities which is the topic of Chapter X.

Significant advances in telecommunications and GPS sensors technology are enabling the users of these technologies to track down objects and individuals with remarkable precision. As useful as these technologies are, without strict safeguards on privacy, it becomes problematic in the hands of malevolent users. Chapter XI reviews state-of-the-art work on trajectory data privacy. Furthermore, the authors share views regarding the current state and future trend in trajectory data privacy.

Web pages are classified on content or imbedded contextual information. The pages can contain irrelevant information that may reduce performance of the Web classifiers. The accessed data can be mined to predict user authentication and hide personal details to preserve privacy. Chapter XII comprehensively covers the feature selections techniques used by researchers.

Collection of data related to agricultural produce and subsequent data mining of it, can improve production, handling, and public health safety. Chapter XIII deals with recent advances in technology application in agriculture such as uses of RFID and bar coding to trace backward and forward information of fresh produce on production, handling, storage, repackaging, and final sale to consumer. The authors discuss the promises of these technologies in agriculture and potential benefits to business, government, and world health and food safety monitoring organizations in order to increase safety and service, and reduce costs of such products.

Chapter XIV highlights a case study involving research into the science of building teams. Accomplishment of mission goals requires team members to not only possess the required technical skills, but also be able to collaborate effectively. The authors describe a research project that aims to develop an automated staffing system. Any such system requires a large amount of personal information about the potential team members under consideration. Gathering, storing, and applying this data raises a spectrum of concerns, from social and ethical implications, to technical hurdles. The authors hope to highlight these concerns by focusing on their research efforts which include obtaining and using employee data within a small business.

The final chapter gives a summary of data types, mathematical structures, and associated methods of data mining. Topological, order theoretical, algebraic and probability theoretical mathematical structures are introduced in Chapter XV. The n-dimensional Euclidean space, the model used most for data, is defined. It notes that the treatment of higher dimensional random variables and related data is problematic.

Since topological concepts are less well known than statistical concepts, many examples of metrics are given. Related classification concepts are defined and explained. Possibilities of their quality identification are discussed. One example each is given for topological cluster and for topological discriminant analyses and their implications on preserving privacy.

The coverage of these chapters provide strength to this book for both information science and technology researchers and also decision makers in obtaining a greater understanding of the concepts, issues, problems, trends, challenges, and opportunities related to this field of study. It is my sincere hope that this publication and its vast amount of information and research will assist researchers, teachers, students, and practitioners in enhancing their understanding of the social implications of data mining usage and information privacy and the frameworks and solutions applied.

Acknowledgment

I am indebted to the many people who helped in many ways to put this edited book together. Particularly, I am deeply appreciative of the assistance of a number of people at IGI Global. Without their dedicated guidance and feedback, this book would not have been completed successfully. First and foremost, Kristin M. Roth, Development Editor at IGI helped me stay on track and gave many positive feedbacks during the development stage. Julia Mosemann was instrumental in finding answers to-day-day problems related to the book project.

I would also like to thank the editorial advisory board team who gave their valuable time, effort, and counsel to improve the final product, and they are:

- Professor Ari-Veikko Anttiroiko, University of Tampere, Finland
- Professor Adeyemi A. Adekoya, Computer Information Systems, Virginia State University
- Dr. Ljiljana Brankovic, Faculty of Engineering, The University of Newcastle, Australia
- Professor Floriana Esposito, Dipartimento di Informatica, Universita' di Bari, Italy
- Professor Marc Holzer, Dean, School of Public Affairs, Rutgers University, Newark New Jersey
- Dr Paul Henman, The University of Queensland, Brisbane, Australia
- Dr. Stephen Marsh, Research Scientist, Information Security NRC, Inst. for Information Technology, Toronto Canada
- Professor Emmanuel Omojokun, Department of Computer Information Systems, Virginia State University, USA

The following reviewers are thanked for their hard work, dedication, and for their meticulous reviews and comments to the authors. Without their constructive suggestions, the overall quality of the book would not have reached its potential for contribution in this field. The reviewers include:

- Majid Amini, Virginia State University
- Ari-Veikko Anttiroiko, University of Tampere , Finland
- Xue Bai, Virginia State University
- Tom Chen, Southern Methodist University
- Peter Danielson, University of British Columbia, Canada
- Floriana Esposito, Universita' di Bari Italy
- Zhi (Judy) Fu , Motorolla Corporation
- Anil Gurung, Kansas State University
- Dawit Haile, Virginia State University

- Paul Henman, The University of Queensland, Australia
- Mark Holzer, Rutgers University
- Jane Lindquist, IBM
- Fidelis Ikem, Kutztown University
- Robert Liu, California State University
- Xin Luo, Virginia State University
- Stephen Marsh, Institute for Information Technology Canada
- Robert McCormack, Aptica Corporation
- Stanley Olivera, Embrapa Informática Agropecuária, Brazil
- Emmanuel Omojokun, Virginia State University
- Nancy Pouloudi, Athens University, Greece
- Robert Sprague, University of Wyoming
- Shahid Shahidula, Virginia State University
- Selbkuberan K, Innovative Labs, India
- Vassilios R. Verykios, University of Thessaly, Greece
- Shuting Xu, Virginia State University
- Yaquan Xu, Virginia State University

I would also like to thank my wife Zaid, our children Simon, Estelle and Aaron for their support and understanding when I was busy with the editing tasks of this book.

Finally to all that I have missed to list, I would like to express my heartfelt gratitude for your efforts and assistance.

Ephrem Eyob
Chesterfield, Virginia USA

Chapter I
Is Information Ethics Culturally Relative?

Philip Brey
University of Twente, The Netherlands

ABSTRACT

In this chapter, I examine whether information ethics is culturally relative. If it is, different approaches to information ethics are required in different cultures and societies. This would have major implications for the current, predominantly Western approach to information ethics. If it is not, there must be concepts and principles of information ethics that have universal validity. What would they be? I will begin the chapter by an examination of cultural differences in ethical attitudes towards privacy, freedom of information, and intellectual property rights in Western and nonwestern cultures. I then analyze the normative implications of these findings for doing information ethics in a cross-cultural context. I will argue for a position between moral absolutism and relativism that is based on intercultural understanding and mutual criticism. Such a position could be helpful in overcoming differences and misunderstandings between cultures in their approach to information and information technologies.

INTRODUCTION

Information ethics[1] has so far mainly been a topic of research and debate in Western countries, and has mainly been studied by Western scholars. There is, however, increasing interest in information ethics in nonwestern countries like Japan, China and India, and there have been recent attempts to raise cross-cultural issues in information ethics (e.g., Mizutani, Dorsey and Moor, 2004; Ess, 2002; Gorniak-Kocikowska, 1996). Interactions between scholars of Western and nonwestern countries have brought significant differences to light between the way in which they approach issues in information ethics. This raises the question whether different cultures require a different information ethics and whether concepts and approaches in Western information ethics can be validly applied to the moral dilemmas of nonwestern cultures. In other words, is information ethics culturally relative or are there concepts and principles of information ethics that have universal validity? The aim of this essay is to arrive at preliminary answers to this question.

MORAL RELATIVISM AND INFORMATION ETHICS

In discussions of moral relativism, a distinction is commonly made between descriptive and metaethical moral relativism. *Descriptive moral relativism* is the position that as a matter of empirical fact, there is extensive diversity between the values and moral principles of societies, groups, cultures, historical periods or individuals. Existing differences in moral values, it is claimed, are not superficial but profound, and extend to core moral values and principles. Descriptive moral relativism is an empirical thesis that can in principle be supported or refuted through psychological, sociological and anthropological investigations. The opposite of descriptive moral relativism is *descriptive moral absolutism*, the thesis that there are no profound moral disagreements between societies, groups, cultures or individuals. At issue in this essay will be a specific version of descriptive moral relativism, *descriptive cultural relativism*, according to which there are major differences between the moral principles of different cultures.

Much more controversial than the thesis of descriptive moral relativism is the thesis of *metaethical moral relativism*, according to which the truth or justification of moral judgments is not absolute or objective, but relative to societies, groups, cultures, historical periods or individuals.[2] Whereas a descriptive relativist could

make the empirical observation that one society, polygamy is considered moral whereas in another it is considered immoral, a metaethical relativist could make the more far-reaching claim that the statement "polygamy is morally wrong" is true or justified in some societies while false or unjustified in others. Descriptive relativism therefore makes claims about the values that different people or societies actually have whereas metaethical relativism makes claims about the values that they are justified in having. Metaethical moral relativism is antithetical to *metaethical moral absolutism*, the thesis that regardless of any existing differences between moral values in different cultures, societies, or individuals, there are moral principles that are absolute or objective, and that are universally true across cultures, societies or individuals. Metaethical moral absolutism would therefore hold that the statement "polygamy is morally wrong" is either universally true or universally false; it cannot be true for some cultures or societies but false for others. If the statement is true, then societies that hold that polygamy is moral are in error, and if it is false, then the mistake lies with societies that condemn it.

The question being investigated in this essay is whether information ethics is culturally relative. In answering this question, it has to be kept in mind that the principal aims of information ethics are not descriptive, but normative and evaluative. That is, its principal aim is not to describe existing morality regarding information but rather to morally evaluate information practices and to prescribe and justify moral standards and principles for practices involving the production, consumption or processing of information. A claim that information ethics is culturally relative is therefore a claim that metaethical moral relativism is true for information ethics. It is to claim that the ethical values, principles and judgments of information ethics are valid only relative to a particular culture, presumably the culture in which they have been developed. Since information ethics is largely a product of the West, an affirmation of the cultural relativity of information ethics means that its values and principles do not straightforwardly apply to nonwestern cultures.

But if the cultural relativity of information ethics depends on the truth of metaethical relativism, does any consideration need to be given to descriptive relativism for information ethics? This question should be answered affirmatively. Defenses of metaethical relativism usually depend on previous observations that descriptive relativism is true. If descriptive relativism is false, it follows that people across the world share a moral framework of basic values and principles. But if this is the case, then it seems pointless to argue for metaethical moral relativism: why claim that the truth of moral judgments is different for different groups if these groups already agree on basic moral values? On the other hand, if descriptive relativism is true, then attempts to declare particular moral principles of judgments to be universally valid come under scrutiny. Extensive justification would be required for any attempt to adopt a particular moral framework (say, Western information ethics) as one that is universally valid. In the next section, I will therefore focus on the question whether there are good reasons to believe that there are deep and widespread moral disagreements about central values and principles in information ethics across cultures, and whether therefore descriptive cultural relativism is true for information ethics.

THE DESCRIPTIVE CULTURAL RELATIVITY OF INFORMATION–RELATED VALUES

In this section, I will investigate the descriptive cultural relativity of three values that are the topic of many studies in information ethics: privacy, intellectual property and freedom of information. Arguments have been made that these values are distinctly Western, and are not universally accepted across different cultures. In what fol-lows I will investigate whether these claims seem warranted by empirical evidence. I will also relate the outcome of my investigations to discussions of more general differences between Western and nonwestern systems of morality.

How can it be determined that cultures have fundamentally different value systems regarding notions like privacy and intellectual property? I propose that three kinds of evidence are relevant:

1. **Conceptual:** The extent to which there are moral concepts across cultures with similar meanings. For example, does Chinese culture have a concept of privacy that is similar to the American concept of privacy?
2. **Institutional:** The extent to which there is similarity between codified rules that express moral principles and codified statements that express moral judgments about particular (types of) situations. For example, are the moral principles exhibited in the laws and written rules employed in Latin cultures on the topic of privacy sufficiently similar to American laws and rules that it can be claimed that they embody similar moral principles?
3. **Behavioral:** The similarity between customs and behaviors that appear to be guided by moral principles. This would include tendencies to avoid behaviors that are immoral regarding a moral principle, tendencies to show disapproval to those who engage in such behaviors and to show disapproval to those who do not, and tendencies to show remorse or guilt when engaging in such behaviors. For instance, if a culture has a shared privacy principle that states that peeking inside someone's purse is wrong, then it can be expected that most people try not to do this, disapprove of those who do, and feel ashamed or remorseful when they are caught doing it?

It is conceivable that in a particular culture a value or moral principle is widely upheld at the behavioral level, but has not (yet) been codified at the institutional and conceptual level. But this is perhaps unlikely in cultures with institutions that include extensive systems of codified rules, which would include any culture with a modern legal system. It is also conceivable that a moral value or principle is embodied in both behavioral customs and codified rules, but no good match can be found at the conceptual level. In that case, it seems reasonable to assume that the value or principle at issue is embodied in the culture, but different concepts are used to express it, making it difficult to find direct translations.

A full consideration of the evidence for descriptive moral relativism along these three lines is beyond the scope of this paper. I only intend to consider enough evidence to arrive at a preliminary assessment of the cultural relativity of values in contemporary information ethics.

Privacy

It has been claimed that in Asian cultures like China and Japan, no genuine concept or value of privacy exists. These cultures have been held to value the collective over the individual. Privacy is an individual right, and such a right may not be recognized in a culture where collective interest tend to take priority over individual interests. Using the three criteria outline above, and drawing from studies of privacy in Japan, China and Thailand, I will now consider whether this conclusion is warranted.

At the conceptual level, there are words in Japanese, Chinese and Thai that refer to a private sphere, but these words seem to have substantially different meanings than the English word for privacy. Mizutani, Dorsey and Moor (2004) have argued that there is no word for "privacy" in traditional Japanese. Modern Japanese, they claim, sometimes adopt a Japanese translation for the Western word for privacy, which sounds like "puraibashii", and which is written in katakana, which is the Japanese phonetic syllabary that is mostly used for words of foreign origin. According to Nakada and Tamura (2005), Japanese does include a word for "private," "Watakusi", which means "partial, secret and selfish". It is opposed to "Ohyake", which means "public". Things that are Watakusi are considered less worthy than things that are Ohyake. Mizutani, Dorsey and Moor (2004) point out, in addition, that there are certainly behavioral customs in Japan that amount to a respect for privacy. There are conventions that restrict access to information, places or objects. For example, one is not supposed to look under clothes on public streets.

In China, the word closest to the English "privacy" is "Yinsi", which means "shameful secret" and is usually associated with negative, shameful things. Lü (2005) claims that only recently that "Yinsi" has also come to take broader meanings to include personal information, shameful or not, that people do not want others to know (see also Jingchun, 2005 and McDougall and Hansson, 2002). This shift in meaning has occurred under Western influences. As for institutional encoding of privacy principles, Lü maintains that there currently are no laws in China that protect an individual's right to privacy, and the legal protection of privacy has been weak and is still limited, though there have been improvements in privacy protection since the 1980s.

Kitiyadisai (2005), finally, holds that the concept of privacy does not exist in Thailand. She claims that the Western word privacy was adopted in the late nineteenth or early twentieth century in Thailand, being transliterated as "pri-vade," but this word gained a distinctly Thai meaning, being understood as a collectivist rather than an individual notion. It referred to a private sphere in which casual dress could be worn, as opposed to a public sphere in which respectable dress had to be worn. In the Thai legal system, Kitiyadisai claims, there has not been any right to privacy since the introduction of privacy legislation in

1997 and a Thai constitution, also in 1997, that for the first time guarantees basic human rights. Kitiyadisai argues, however, that Thai privacy laws are hardly enacted in practice, and many Thais remain unaware of the notion of privacy.

It can be tentatively concluded that the introduction of a concept of privacy similar to the Western notion has only taken place recently in Japan, China and Thailand, and that privacy legislation has only taken place recently. In traditional Japanese, Chinese and Thai culture, which still has a strong presence today, distinctions are made that resemble the Western distinction between public and private, and customs exist that may be interpreted as respective of privacy, but there is no recognized individual right to privacy.

Intellectual Property Rights

In discussing the cultural relativity of intellectual property rights (IPR), I will limit myself to one example: China. China is known for not having a developed notion of private or individual property. Under communist rule, the dominant notion of property was collective. All means of production, such as farms and factories, were to be collectively owned and operated. Moreover, the state exercised strict control over the means of production and over both the public and private sphere. A modern notion of private property was only introduced since the late 1980s. Milestones were a 1988 constitutional revision that allowed for private ownership of means of production and a 2004 constitutional amendment that protects citizens from encroachment of private property.

The notion of intellectual property has only recently been introduced in China, in the wake of China's recent economic reforms and increased economic interaction with the West. China is currently passing IPR laws and cracking down on violations of IPR in order to harmonize the Chinese economic system with the rest of the world. But as journalist Ben Worthen observes, "[t]he average citizen in China has no need and

little regard for intellectual property. IPR is not something that people grew up with … and the percent of citizens who learn about it by engaging in international commerce is tiny." Worthen also points out that Chinese companies "have no incentive to respect IPR unless they are doing work for Western companies that demand it" and that "since most of the intellectual property royalties are headed out of China there isn't a lot of incentive for the government to crack down on companies that choose to ignore IPR."[3] All in all, it can be concluded that China's value system traditionally has not included recognition of intellectual property rights, and it is currently struggling with this concept.

Freedom of Information

Freedom of information is often held to comprise two principles: freedom of speech (the freedom to express one's opinions or ideas, in speech or in writing) and freedom of access to information. Sometimes, freedom of the press (the freedom to express oneself through publication and dissemination) is distinguished as a third principle. In Western countries, freedom of information is often defined as a constitutional and inalienable right. Law protective of freedom of information are often especially designed to ensure that individuals can exercise this freedom without governmental interference or constraint. Government censorship or interference is only permitted in extreme situations, pertaining to such things as hate speech, libel, copyright violations and information that could undermine national security.

In many nonwestern countries, freedom of information is not a guiding principle. There are few institutionalized protections of freedom of information, there are many practices that interfere with freedom of information, and a concept of freedom of information is not part of the established discourse in society. In such societies, the national interest takes precedence, and an independent right to freedom of information either is not recognized or is made so subordinate to national interests that it hardly resembles the Western right to freedom of information. These are countries in which practices of state censorship are widespread; mass media are largely or wholly government-controlled, the Internet, databases and libraries are censored, and messages that do not conform to the party line are cracked down upon.

Let us, as an example, consider the extent to which freedom of information can be said to be a value in Chinese society. Until the 1980s, the idea of individual rights or civil rights was not a well-known concept in China. Government was thought to exist to ensure a stable society and a prosperous economy. It was not believed to have a function to protect individual rights against collective and state interests. As a consequence of this general orientation, the idea of an individual right to freedom of information was virtually unknown. Only recently has China introduced comprehensive civil rights legislation. In its 1982 constitution, China introduced constitutional principles of freedom of speech and of the press. And in 1997, it signed the International Convention on Economic, Social, and Cultural Rights, and in 1998 the International Convention on Civil and Political Rights (the latter of which it has not yet ratified).

Even though the Chinese government has recently come to recognize a right to freedom of information, as well as individual human rights in general, and has introduced legislation to this effect, state censorship is still rampant, and the principle of upholding state interest still tends to dominate the principle of protecting individual human rights. Internet censorship presents a good example of this. Internet traffic in China is controlled through what the Chinese call the Golden Shield, and what is known outside mainland China as the Great Firewall of China. This is a system of control in which Internet content is blocked by routers, as well as at the backbone and ISP level, through the "filtering" of undesirable

URLs and keywords. A long list of such "forbidden" URLs and keywords has been composed by the Chinese State Council Information Office, in collaboration with the Communist Party's Propaganda Department. This system is especially geared towards censorship of content coming from outside mainland China (Human Rights Watch, 2006).

Rights-Centered and Virtue-Centered Morality

A recurring theme in the above three discussions has been the absence of a strong tradition of individual rights in the cultures that were discussed – those of China, Japan and Thailand – and the priority that is given to collective and state interests. Only very recently have China, Japan and Thailand introduced comprehensive human rights legislation, which has occurred mainly through Western influence, and there is still considerable tension in these societies, especially in China and Thailand, between values that prioritize the collective and the state and values that prioritize the individual.

Various authors have attempted to explain the worldview that underlies the value system of these countries. In Japan and Thailand, and to a lesser extent China, Buddhism is key to an understanding of attitudes towards individual rights. Buddhism holds a conception of the self that is antithetical to the Western conception of an autonomous self which aspires to self-realization. Buddhism holds that the self does not exist and that human desires are delusional. The highest state that humans can reach is Nirvana, a state of peace and contentment in which all suffering has ended. To reach Nirvana, humans have to become detached from their desires, and realize that the notion of an integrated and permanent self is an illusion. In Buddhism, the self is defined as fluid, situation-dependent and ever-changing. As Mizutani et al. and Kitiyadisai have noted, such a notion of the self is at odds with a Western notion of privacy and of human rights in general, notions which presuppose a situation-independent, autonomous self which pursues its own self-interests and which has inalienable rights that have to be defended against external threats.

In part through Buddhism, but also through the influence of other systems of belief such as Confucianism, Taoism and Maoism, societies like those of China and Thailand have developed a value system in which the rights or interests of the individual are subordinate to those of the collective and the state. To do good is to further the interests of the collective. Such furtherance of collective interests will generally also benefit the individual. The task of government, then, is to ensure that society as a whole functions well, in a harmonious and orderly way, and that social ills are cured, rather than the ills of single individuals. In other words, government works for the common good, and not for the individual good.

Only recently have countries like China and Thailand come to recognize individual human rights and individual interests next to collective interests. But according to Lü (2005), the collectivist ethic still prevails:

Adapting to the demands of social diversity, the predominant ethics now express a new viewpoint that argues against the simple denial of individual interests and emphasizes instead the dialectical unification of collective interests and individual interests: in doing so, however, this ethics points out that this kind of unification must take collective interests as the foundation. That is to say, in the light of the collectivism principle of the prevailing ethics, collective interests and individual interests are both important, but comparatively speaking, the collective interests are more important than individual interests. (Lü, 2005, p. 12)

If this observation is correct, then the introduction of human rights legislation and property rights in countries like China is perhaps not motivated by a genuine recognition of inalienable individual

human rights, but rather a recognition that in the current international climate, it is better to introduce human rights and property rights, because such principles will lead to greater economic prosperity, which is ultimately to the benefit of the collective.

The dominant value systems prevalent in China, Thailand and Japan are examples of what philosopher David Wong (1984) has called virtue-centered moralities. According to Wong, at least two different approaches to morality can be found in the world: a *virtue-centered morality* that emphasizes the good of the community, and a *rights-centered morality* that stresses the value of individual freedom. Rights-centered morality is the province of the modern West, although it is also establishing footholds in other parts of the world. Virtue-centered morality can be found in traditional cultures such as can be found in southern and eastern Asia and in Africa. Wong's distinction corresponds with the frequently made distinction between individualist and collectivist culture, that is found, amongst other, in Geert Hofstede's well-known five-dimensional model of cultural difference (Hofstede, 1991). However, this latter distinction focuses on social systems and cultural practices, whereas Wong makes a distinction based in differences in moral systems.

In Wong's conception of virtue-centered moralities, individuals have duties and responsibilities that stem from the central value of a common good. The common good is conceived of in terms of an ideal conception of community life, which is based on a well-balanced social order in which every member of the community has different duties and different virtues to promote the common good. Some duties and virtues may be shared by all members. The idea that human beings have individual rights is difficult to maintain in this kind of value system, because recognition of such rights would have to find its basis in the higher ideal of the common good. But it seems clear that attributing rights to individuals is not always to the benefit of the common good. The recognition of individual property rights, for example, could result in individual property owners not sharing valuable resources that would benefit the whole community. In virtue-centered moralities, the ideal is for individuals to be virtuous, and virtuous individuals are those individuals whose individual good coincides with their contribution to the common good. Individual goods may be recognized in such communities, but they are always subordinate to the common good. Individuals deserve respect only because of their perceived contribution to the common good, not because they possess inalienable individual rights.

Conclusion

The discussion of privacy, intellectual property rights and freedom of information has shown that a good case can be made for the descriptive cultural relativity of these values. These values are central in information ethics, as it has been developed in the West. Moreover, it was argued that the uncovered cultural differences in the appraisal of these values can be placed in the context of a dichotomy between two fundamentally different kinds of value systems that exist in different societies: rights-centered and virtue-centered systems of value. Information ethics, as it has developed in the West, has a strong emphasis on rights, and little attention is paid to the kinds of moral concerns that may exist in virtue-centered systems of morality. In sum, it seems that the values that are of central concern in Western information ethics are not the values that are central in many nonwestern systems of morality. The conclusion therefore seems warranted that descriptive moral relativism is true for information ethics.

METAETHICAL MORAL RELATIVISM AND INFORMATION ETHICS

In the first section of this article, it was argued that descriptive moral relativism is a necessary

condition for metaethical moral relativism, but is not sufficient to prove this doctrine. However, several moral arguments exist that use the truth of descriptive relativism, together with additional premises, to argue for metaethical relativism. I will start with a consideration of two standard arguments of this form, which are found wanting, after which I will consider a more sophisticated argument.

Two Standard Arguments for Metaethical Relativism

There are two traditional arguments for metaethical moral relativism that rely on the truth of descriptive moral relativism (Wong, 1993). The one most frequently alluded to is the *argument from diversity*. This argument starts with the observation that different cultures employ widely different moral standards. Without introducing additional premises, the argument goes on to conclude that therefore, there are no universal moral standards. This argument rests on what is known in philosophy as a naturalistic fallacy, an attempt to derive a norm from a fact, or an "ought" from an "is". The premise of the argument is descriptive: there are different moral standards. The conclusion is normative: no moral standard has universal validity. No evidence has been presented that the truth of the premise has any bearing on the truth of the conclusion.

A second, stronger, argument for moral relativism is the *argument from functional necessity*, according to which certain ethical beliefs in a society may be so central to its functioning that they cannot be given up without destroying the society. Consequently, the argument runs, these ethical beliefs are true for that society, but not necessarily in another. However, this argument is also problematic because it grounds the truth of ethical statements in their practical value for maintaining social order in a particular society. Such a standard of justification for ethical statements is clearly too narrow, as it could be used to justify the moral beliefs of societies whose beliefs and practices are clearly unethical, for instance fascist societies. If a society operates in a fundamentally unethical way, then the transformation of some of its social structures and cultural forms would seem acceptable if more ethical practices are the result.

Wong's and Harman's Argument for Metaethical Relativism

More convincing arguments for moral relativism have been presented by David Wong (1984, 2006) and Gilbert Harman (1996, 2000). Their argument runs, in broad outline, as follows. There are deep-seated differences in moral belief between different cultures. Careful consideration of the reasons for these moral beliefs they have shows that they are *elements of different strategies to realize related but different conceptions of the Good.* No good arguments can be given why one of these conceptions of the Good is significantly better than all the others. Therefore, these moral beliefs are best explained as different but (roughly) equally valid strategies for attaining the Good.

This is a much better argument than the previous two, since it puts the ball in the metaethical absolutist's court: he will have to come up with proof that it is possible to provide good arguments for the superiority of one particular conception of the Good over all other conceptions. Metaethical absolutists can respond to this challenge in two ways. First, they may choose to bite the bullet and claim that a rational comparison of different conceptions of the Good is indeed possible. Different conceptions of the Good, they may argue, rely on factual or logical presuppositions that may be shown to be false. Alternatively, they may argue that there are universally shared moral intuitions about what is good, and these intuitions can be appealed to in defending or discrediting particular conceptions of the Good. For instance an individual who believes that physical pleasure is the highest good could conceivably be persuaded to abandon this belief through exposure to arguments that purport to demonstrate that there are other goods overlooked by him that are at least as valuable. Such an argument could conceivably rely on someone's moral intuitions about the Good that could be shown to deviate from someone's explicit concept of the Good.

Second, a mixed position could be proposed, according to which it is conceded that individuals or cultures may hold different conceptions of the Good that cannot be rationally criticized (*pace* metaethical relativism) but that rational criticism of individual moral beliefs is nevertheless possible (*pace* metaethical absolutism) because these beliefs can be evaluated for their effectiveness in realizing the Good in which service they stand. After all, if moral beliefs are strategies to realize a particular conception of the Good, as Wong and Harman have argued, then they can be suboptimal in doing so. A belief that Internet censorship is justified because it contributes to a more stable and orderly society can be wrong because it may not in fact contribute to a more stable and orderly society. Empirical arguments may be made that Internet censorship is not necessary for the maintenance of social order, or even that Internet censorship may ultimately work to undermine social order, for example because it creates discontentment and resistance.

In the existing dialogue between proponents of rights-centered and virtue-centered systems of morality, it appears that both these approaches are already being taken. Western scholars have criticized the organic conception of society that underlies conceptions of the Good in many Asian cultures, while Western definitions of the Good in terms of individual well-being have been criticized for their atomistic conception of individuals. Rights-based systems of morality have been criticized for undervaluing the common good, whereas virtue-based systems have been criticized for overlooking the importance of the individual good. In addition, both rights-centered and virtue-centered systems of morality have been criticized for not being successful by their own standards. Western individualism has been claimed to promote selfishness and strife, which results in many unhappy individuals plagued by avarice, poverty, depression and loneliness. Western societies have therefore been claimed to be unsuccessful in attaining their own notion of the Good, defined in terms of individual well-being. Virtue-centered cultures have been claimed to have difficulty in developing strong economies that serve the common good, because good economies have been argued to require private enterprise and a more individualist culture. In addition, strong state control, which is a feature of many virtue-centered cultures, has been argued to lead to corruption and totalitarianism, which also do not serve the common good.

In light of the preceding observations, it seems warranted to conclude, *pace* metaethical absolutism, that rational criticism between different moral systems is possible. It does not follow, however, that conclusive arguments for universal moral truths or the superiority of one particular moral system over others are going to be possible. Critics of a particular moral system may succeed in convincing its adherents that the system has its flaws and needs to be modified, but it could well be that no amount of criticism ever succeeds in convincing its adherents to abandon core moral beliefs within that system, however rational and open-minded these adherents are in listening to such criticism.

Conclusion

I have argued, *pace* metaethical relativism, that it is difficult if not impossible to provide compelling arguments for the superiority of different notions of the Good that are central to different moral systems, and by implication, that it is difficult to present conclusive arguments for the universal truth of particular moral principles and beliefs. I have also argued, *pace* metaethical absolutism, that is nevertheless possible to develop rational

arguments for and against particular moral values and overarching conceptions of the Good across moral systems, even if such arguments do not result in proofs of the superiority of one particular moral system or moral principle over another.

From these two metaethical claims, a normative position can be derived concerning the way in which cross-cultural ethics ought to take place. It follows, first of all, that it is only justified for proponents of a particular moral value or principle to claim that it ought to be accepted in another culture if they make this claim on the basis of a thorough understanding of the moral system operative in this other culture. The proponent would have to understand how this moral system functions and what notion of the Good it services, and would have to have strong arguments that either the exogenous value would be a good addition to the moral system in helping to bring about the Good serviced in that moral system, or that the notion of the Good serviced in that culture is flawed and requires revisions. In the next section, I will consider implications of this position for the practice of information ethics in cross-cultural settings.

INFORMATION ETHICS IN A CROSS-CULTURAL CONTEXT

It is an outcome of the preceding sections that significant differences exist between moral systems of different cultures, that these differences have important implications for moral attitudes towards uses of information and information technology, and that there are good reasons to take such differences seriously in normative studies in information ethics. In this section, I will argue, following Rafael Capurro, that we need an intercultural information ethics that studies and evaluates cultural differences in moral attitudes towards information and information technology. I will also critically evaluate the claim that the Internet will enable a new global ethic that provides a unified moral framework for all cultures.

Intercultural Information Ethics

The notion of an *intercultural information ethics* (IIE) was first introduced by Rafael Capurro (2005, 2007), who defined it as a field of research in which moral questions regarding information technology and the use of information are reflected on in a comparative manner on the basis of different cultural traditions. I will adopt Capurro's definition, but differ with him on what the central tasks of an IIE should be. Capurro defines the tasks of IIE very broadly. For him, they do not only involve the comparative study of value systems in different cultures in relation to their use of information and information technology, but also studies of the effect of information technology on customs, languages and everyday problems, the changes produced by the Internet on traditional media, and the economic impact of the Internet to the extent that it can become an instrument of cultural oppression and colonialism.

I hold, in contrast, that studies of the effects of information technology in non-Western cultures are more appropriately delegated to the social sciences (including communication studies, cultural studies, anthropology and science and technology studies). An intercultural information ethics should primarily focus on the comparative study of moral systems. Its overall aim would be to interpret, compare and critically evaluate moral systems in different cultures regarding their moral attitudes towards and behavior towards information and information technology.

This task for IIE can be broken down into four subtasks, the first two of which are exercises in descriptive ethics and the latter two of which belong to normative ethics. First, IIE should engage in *interpretive studies* of moral systems in particular cultures, including the systems of value contained in the religious and political ideologies that are dominant in these cultures. The primary

focus in such interpretive studies within the context of IIE should be on resulting moral attitudes towards the use and implications of information technology and on the moral problems generated by uses of information technology within the context of the prevailing moral system. Second, IIE should engage in *comparative studies* of moral systems from different cultures, and arrive at analyses of both similarities and differences in the way that these moral systems are organized and operate, with a specific focus on the way in which they have different moral attitudes towards implications of information technology and on differences in moral problems generated by the use of information technology.

Third, IIE should engage in *critical studies* in which the moral systems of particular cultures are criticized based on the insights gained through the interpretive and comparative studies alluded to above, particularly in their dealings with information technology. Critical studies may be directed towards criticizing moral values and beliefs in cultures other than one's own, and proposing modifications in the culture's moral system and ways in which it should solve moral problems, but may also involve self-criticism, in which one's own moral values and the moral system of one's own culture is criticized based on insights gained from the study of alternative moral systems. Fourth, IIE should engage in *interrelational studies* that focus on the construction of normative models for interaction between cultures in their dealings with information and information technology that respect their different moral systems. Interrelational studies hence investigate what moral compromises cultures can make and ought to make in their interactions and what shared moral principles can be constructed to govern their interactions.

Global Ethics and the Information Revolution

Some authors have argued that globalization and the emergence of the Internet have created a global community, and that this community requires its own moral system that transcends and unifies the moral systems of all cultures and nations that participate in this global community. The ethics needed for the construction of such a moral system has been called *global ethics*. The idea of a global ethics or ethic was first introduced by German theologian Hans Küng in 1990 and later elaborated by him in a book (Küng, 2001). His aim was to work towards a shared moral framework for humanity that would contain a minimal consensus concerning binding values and moral principles that could be invoked by members of a global community in order to overcome differences and avoid conflict.

Krystyna Górniak-Kocikowska (1996) has argued that the computer revolution that has taken place has made it clear that a future global ethic will have to be a computer ethic or information ethic. As she explains, actions in cyberspace are not local, and therefore the ethical rules governing such actions cannot be rooted in a particular local culture. Therefore, unifying ethical rules have to be constructed in cyberspace that can serve as a new global ethic. Similar arguments have been presented by Bao and Xiang (2006) and De George (2006).

No one would deny that a global ethic, as proposed by Küng, would be desirable. The construction of an explicit, shared moral framework that would bind all nations and cultures would evidently be immensely valuable. It should be obvious, however, that such a framework could only develop as an addition to existing local moral systems, not as a replacement of them. It would be a framework designed to help solve global problems, and would exist next to the local moral systems that people use to solve their local problems. In addition, it remains to be seen if cross-cultural interactions over the Internet yield more than a mere set of rules for conduct online, a global netiquette, and will result in a global ethic that can serve as a common moral framework for intercultural dialogue and joint action. Hongladarom (2001) has concluded, based on empirical studies, that the Internet does not create a worldwide monolithic culture but rather reduplicates existing cultural boundaries. It does create an umbrella cosmopolitan culture to some extent, but only for those Internet users who engage in cross-cultural dialogue, which is a minority, and this umbrella culture is rather superficial. Claims that the Internet will enable a new global ethic may therefore be somewhat premature. In any case, such intercultural dialogue online will have to be supplemented with serious academic work in intercultural information ethics, as well as intercultural ethics at large.

CONCLUSION

It was found in this essay that very different moral attitudes exist in Western and nonwestern countries regarding three key issues in information ethics: privacy, intellectual property, and freedom of information. In nonwestern countries like China, Japan and Thailand, there is no strong recognition of individual rights in relation to these three issues. These differences were analyzed in the context of a difference, proposed by philosopher David Wong, between rights-centered moralities that dominate in the West and virtue-centered moralities that prevail in traditional cultures, including those in South and East Asia. It was then argued that cross-cultural normative ethics cannot be practiced without a thorough understanding of the prevailing moral system in the culture that is being addressed. When such an understanding has been attained, scholars can proceed to engage in moral criticism of practices in the culture and propose standards and solutions to moral problems. It was argued, following Rafael Capurro, that we need an intercultural information ethics that engages in interpretive, comparative and normative studies of moral problems and issues in information ethics in different cultures. It is to be hoped that researchers in both Western and nonwestern countries will take up this challenge and engage in collaborative studies and dialogue on an issue that may be of key importance to future international relations.

REFERENCES

Bao, X., & Xiang, Y. (2006). Digitalization and global ethics. *Ethics and Information Technology 8,* 41–47.

Capurro, R. (2005). Privacy: An intercultural perspective. *Ethics and Information Technology 7(1)*, 37-47.

Capurro, R. (2007). Intercultural information ethics. In R. Capurro, J. Frühbaure and T. Hausmanningers (Eds.), *Localizing the Internet. Ethical issues in intercultural perspective.* Munich: Fink Verlag.

De George, R. (2006). Information technology, Globalization and ethics. *Ethics and Information Technology 8,* 29–40.

Ess, C. (2002). Computer-mediated colonization, the renaissance, And educational imperatives for an intercultural global village. *Ethics and Information Technology 4(1)*, 11–22.

Gorniak-Kocikowska, K. (1996). The computer revolution and the problem of global ethics. *Science and Engineering Ethics 2,* 177–190.

Harman, G. (1996). Moral Relativism. In G. Harman and J.J. Thompson (Eds.), *Moral relativism and moral objectivity* (pp. 3-64). Cambridge MA: Blackwell Publishers

Harman, G. (2000). Is There a Single True Morality? In G. Harman, *Explaining value: And other essays in moral philosophy* (pp. 77-99), Oxford: Clarendon Press, (Orig. 1984)

Hofstede, G. (2001). *Culture's consequences.* Beverly Hills CA: Sage.

Hongladarom, S. (2001). Global Culture, Local Cultures and the Internet: The Thai Example. In C. Ess (Ed.), *Culture, technology, communication: Towards an intercultural global village* (pp. 307–324). Albany NY: State University of New York Press.

Human Rights Watch (2006). Race to the bottom. Corporate complicity in Chinese Internet censorship. *Human Rights Watch report 18(8).* Retrieved March 13, 2008, from http://www.hrw.org/reports/2006/china0806/

Johnson, D. (2000). *Computer ethics,* 3rd ed, Upper Sadle River: Prentice Hall.

Jingchun, C. (2005). Protecting the right to privacy in China. *Victoria University of Wellington Law Review 38(3).* Retrieved March 13, 2008, from http://www.austlii.edu.au/nz/journals/VUWLRev/2005/25.html.

Kitiyadisai, K. (2005). Privacy rights and protection: Foreign values in modern Thai context. *Ethics and Information Technology 7,* 17–26.

Küng, H. (2001). *A global ethic for global politics and economics.* Hong Kong: Logos and Pneuma Press.

Lü, Yao-Huai (2005). Privacy and data privacy issues in contemporary China. *Ethics and Information Technology 7,* 7–15.

McDougall, B., & Hansson, A. (eds.) (2002). *Chinese concepts of privacy.* Leiden: Brill Academic Publishers.

Mizutani, M., Dorsey, J., & Moor, J. (2004). The Internet and Japanese conception of privacy. *Ethics and Information Technology 6*(2), 121-128.

Nakada, M., & Tamura, T. (2005). Japanese conceptions of privacy: An intercultural perspective. *Ethics and Information Technology 7,* 27–36.

Wong, D. (1984). *Moral relativity.* Berkeley, CA: University of California Press.

Wong, D. (1993). Relativism. In P. Singer (ed.), *A companion to ethics* (pp. 442-450). Cambridge MA: Blackwell.

Wong, D. (2006). *Natural moralities: A defense of pluralistic relativism.* Oxford: Oxford University Press.

KEY TERMS

Cultural Values: Values shared by the members of a culture

Freedom of Information: The freedom, without interference by others, to communicate or have access to, information

Information Ethics: The study of ethical issues in the use of information and information technology

Intellectual Property Rights: Rights regarding the use and commercial exploitation of creations of the mind, such as literary and artistic works, symbols, names, images, and inventions

Moral Relativism: This names either the position that as a matter of empirical fact, there is extensive diversity between the values and moral principles of societies, groups, cultures, historical periods or individuals *(descriptive moral relativism)* or that the truth or justification of moral judgments is not absolute or objective, but relative to societies, groups, cultures, historical periods or individuals *(metaethical moral relativism)*

Privacy: The extent to which individuals are able to determine themselves whether personal information about them is divulged or whether they can maintain a personal space free from interference by others

ENDNOTES

[1] By information ethics I mean the study of ethical issues in the use of information and information technology. Contemporary information ethics is a result of the digital revolution (or information revolution) and focuses mainly on ethical issues in the production, use and dissemination of digital information and information technologies. It encloses the field of computer ethics (Johnson, 2000) as well as concerns that belong to classical information ethics (which was a branch of library and information science), media ethics and journalism ethics.

[2] This doctrine is called metaethical rather than normative because it does not make any normative claims, but rather makes claims about the nature of moral judgments. *Normative moral relativism* would be the thesis that it is morally wrong to judge or interfere with the moral practices of societies, groups, cultures or individuals who have moral values different from one's own. This is a normative thesis because it makes prescriptions for behavior.

[3] Worthen, B. (2006). Intellectual Property: China's Three Realities. *CIO Blogs.* Retrieved October, 2006, from http://blogs.cio.com/intellectual_property_chinas_three_realities.

Chapter II
Protection of Privacy
on the Web

Thomas M. Chen
Swansea University, UK

Zhi (Judy) Fu
Motorola Labs, USA

ABSTRACT

Most people are concerned about online privacy but may not be aware of the various ways that their personal information is collected during routine Web browsing. We review the types of personal information that may be collected voluntarily or involuntarily through the Web browser or disclosed by a Web server. We present a taxonomy of regulatory and technological approaches to protect privacy. All approaches to date have only been partial solutions. By its nature, the Web was designed to be an open system to facilitate data sharing, and hence Web privacy continues to be a challenging problem.

INTRODUCTION

The main appeal of the World Wide Web is convenient and instant access to a wealth of information and services. Many people will start research on a topic with a Google search. The number of Web sites has grown exponentially and reached more than 149 million in November 2007 according to Netcraft (http://news.netcraft.com/archives/web_server_survey.html).

In their search for services, users may not keep in mind that the Web is capable of collecting data as well as displaying data. The most obvious means of data collection are Web forms for registrations, logins, and messaging. These forms are voluntary disclosures of personal information that most people understand to be necessary for shopping, online banking, and other personalized services. However, users may not fully appreciate that Web sites collect information about them routinely without their consent or even notification. Web sites keep track of clients' IP (Internet protocol) addresses at a minimum and often additional information such as browser version, operating system, viewed resources, and clicked links. Moreover, this collected information may be shared among organizations in the background without the public's knowledge.

Some users may have unrealistic expectations about online privacy because they ignore the fact that the Web is an open system. By design, just about anyone can easily put up a Web site and make its contents globally accessible. This means that sites should not be assumed to be trustworthy. Contrary to natural inclinations, it would be more reasonable to assume sites are untrustworthy, until a trust relationship is established (e.g., through prior experience, reputation, or third-party validation).

Web privacy is certainly not a new issue. However, if anything, concerns have escalated rather than decreased due to increasing prevalence of phishing and malware (malicious software) attacks. In phishing attacks, innocent users are lured to malicious sites designed to deceive them into revealing valuable personal information. Common types of malware include spyware, bots, and keyloggers, which can steal personal data. They can be downloaded in various ways, often without a user's awareness.

The consequences of privacy loss will be growing distrust of the Web and diminishing usage of online services. Thus, protection of privacy is an important practical problem with economic ramifications. This chapter examines regulatory and technological approaches to protect privacy on the Web. First, we survey the various threats to online privacy. Then we offer a taxonomy of approaches to provide and protect privacy.

TYPES OF PRIVATE INFORMATION

Clearly there are different types of personal information, with varying degrees of sensitivity. As shown in Figure 1, personal information on the Web might be classified into three types (Rezgui, Bouguettaya, and Eltoweissy, 2003):

- personal data such as name, address, and history;
- surfing behavior consisting of visited sites, online transactions, and searches;
- communications such as bulletin boards, messages, and feedback forms.

Personal data can be classified further into anonymous information (which can not be traceable to a specific person); personally identifiable information; or private information (Garfinkel, 2002). Information can be anonymized by "scrubbing" any identifying aspects or by aggregating multiple records into a single record. Personally identifiable information can be traced to an individual, such as name, address, e-mail address, or phone number. Although this information is personal, it is often published and can be found with effort. Disclosure of personal information may be undesirable but generally not harmful. On the other hand, disclosure of private information (such as bank records or passwords) may be considered harmful or at least embarrassing. Private information has an obvious value to criminals. Phishing and malware attacks usually have the goal to steal private information to make profits by identity theft or selling the information to other criminals.

Surfing behavior has a value primarily for advertisers who wish to understand the interests of users in order to target advertisements. Advertisements are far more effective if the audience is likely to be interested.

Another concern has been government monitoring of surfing behavior. The U.S. government has argued that Web monitoring is useful in anti-terrorism programs, which has been a federal priority since 9/11. The argument essentially seeks to barter a loss of privacy for increased security.

Figure 1. Types of personal information on the Web

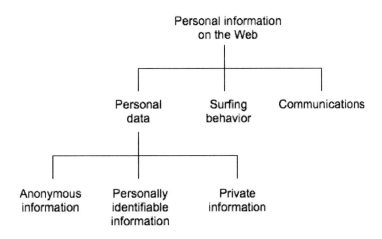

THREATS TO WEB PRIVACY

Threats to privacy can arise at the Web client or server side. Naturally, privacy might also be lost within the network but network security is not addressed here as it is not specifically related to the Web. Eavesdropping in the network is a broad problem involving all IP-based communications. IP packets are normally not protected cryptographically against eavesdropping. Web transactions can be protected by SSL (secure sockets layer) or TLS (transport layer security). TLS is the successor standardized by the Internet Engineering Task Force (IETF) to SSL version 3.0 but they are essentially similar (Dierks and Rescorla, 2006). SSL/TLS uses encryption to protect Web transactions from eavesdropping. In addition, SSL/TLS uses cryptography to authenticate the identities of clients and servers to each other, and to protect messages from tampering in transit in the network.

Information Collected at Clients

Information can be collected at the client side either voluntarily, automatically, or involuntarily.

Voluntary disclosure: In many routine cases, users voluntarily submit many types of information in order to access online services such as banking, shopping, downloads, and searches. Common examples of voluntarily disclosed information include names, addresses, e-mail addresses, telephone numbers, credit card numbers, login IDs, passwords, and search queries. Voluntarily disclosed information is typically sent to a Web site and stored in a database.

Unfortunately, it can be difficult to determine if a site is legitimate, particularly if a criminal has carefully created a malicious site to masquerade as a legitimate site. Phishing attacks depend on social engineering techniques to trick users into believing that a phishing site is legitimate and submitting their personal information voluntarily. For example, a user may receive an e-mail appearing to come from a bank requesting the customer to update his/her account information. Following a link in the e-mail, the user is directed to a phishing Web site, looking exactly like the real bank Web site. When the user enters his/her login information, it is sent to the malicious site's owner.

For the year from October 2006 to September 2007, the Anti-Phishing Working Group counted an average of 31,987 new phishing sites per month (http://www.antiphishing.org). It has been estimated that millions of U.S. consumers are victimized annually by phishing.

Automatic disclosure: Most users may not realize that information about their computer is automatically disclosed in the normal HTTP (hypertext transfer protocol) messages used in Web communications. HTTP is an application layer protocol working over TCP (transmission control protocol) and IP. IP packets reveal the client's IP address to the server. Moreover, HTTP request messages contain a so-called user agent string that identifies the browser name, version, client operating system, and language. An example user agent string might be: "Mozilla/5.0 (Macintosh; U; Intel Mac OS X; en; rv:1.8.1.11) Gecko/20071128 Camino/1.5.4" which reveals that the client is running Mac OS X on an Intel-based Mac computer, and the browser is Camino version 1.5.4 in English (containing the Mozilla-based Gecko engine). The client's IP address and user agent string may be stored in a Web server's logs, which usually records all transactions.

HTTP requests also contain a "referer URL" which is the URL for the page viewed by the user before making the HTTP request. That is, it identifies the URL where the user is coming from. An example of unintentional information disclosure is the referer link: "http://www.google.com/search?hl=en&q=privacy." Unfortunately, it reveals that the user just viewed a Google search for "privacy." The problem is that the search query terms are encoded in the URL itself. The URL probably reveals more than the user expects.

Cookies are another means of automatic information disclosure (Kristol, 2001). Cookies were first developed and implemented by Netscape Communications as a way to keep "state" in Web transactions, particularly online shopping. HTTP is a stateless protocol meaning that a server does not remember a client's previous visits. This makes it difficult to keep track of items in an online shopping cart. Cookies solve the problem by caching text-based information in the client browser, in the form of "name=value" strings. A cookie can also include an expiration time, domain name, path, and whether SSL/TLS should be used. A server first passes a cookie to the browser, and the browser returns the cookie upon revisiting the same site.

Third-party cookies have been controversial. An HTML document often contains images or elements provided by other sites. When these elements are requested, the other sites may set a third-party cookie (called third party because the other sites may be outside the domain of the requested page). A controversial practice is Web banners or advertisements setting third-party cookies to track users across different sites. Once a cookie is set, the cookie is returned whenever the user visits a site with the same ads. A well known example is DoubleClick which serves ads on many different sites. An example cookie for the domain "doubleclick.net" might be: "id=800009fb4447d5a; expires Oct. 14, 2009; secure=no." The cookie contains an identifier that is unique for each user, which allows DoubleClick to track individuals across multiple sites. Browser such as Mozilla and Opera can be configured to block third-party cookies. However, DoubleClick can also track the same client IP address across sites which serve DoubleClick ads.

Involuntary disclosure: Clients can disclose information involuntarily by means of malware. On the Web, malware can be downloaded to a client through social engineering (human deception) or exploiting a vulnerability in the client. A so-called drive-by download is triggered by a client visiting a malicious site which contains, for instance, a zero-dimension iframe (inline frame). The iframe would not be displayed but its HTML contents would be interpreted by the browser. The contents might include exploit code to compromise the client through a vulnerability and download malware without the user's knowledge.

Many forms of malware are known, including:

- viruses: self-replicating pieces of code attached to normal programs or files;
- worms: self-replicating standalone programs that spread to vulnerable hosts through the network;
- downloaders: small programs for downloading other malware;
- Trojan horses: programs hiding their malicious functions by appearing to be useful;
- bots: programs to remotely control a compromised client as a member of a bot net following instructions from a bot herder;
- spyware: programs to covertly steal client data.

In the context of the Web privacy, spyware has become a particularly worrisome problem affecting a significant fraction of PC users (Shukla and Nah, 2005). Thousands of spyware variants have been found, creating a new commercial market for anti-spyware programs. Common types of spyware include: adware tracking browsing behavior to target ads more effectively; browser changers that modify start pages and other browser settings; browser plug-ins adding functions to browsers; bundleware installed with other software; keyloggers recording keyboard inputs; and dialers changing dial-up connection settings.

The Web is known to be a common avenue for spyware, installed knowingly by consent (perhaps bundled with useful software) or unknowingly by drive-by downloads. Studies have found that spyware can be encountered on a wide variety of sites, even well known popular sites and sites rated as trustworthy.

Information Collected at Servers

As already mentioned, Web servers collect data in logs and databases. Concerns about server side privacy are related to how servers collect data, control access to data, share data, and make use of data (Rezgui, Bouguettaya, and Eltoweissy, 2003).

Web bugs: One of the covert means for tracking users is Web bugs, also called Web beacons or clear gifs. One study found that 58% of popular sites and 36% of randomly chosen sites had Web bugs close to their home pages (Martin, Wu, and Alsaid, 2003). A Web bug is a transparent GIF image with dimensions of one pixel by one pixel hosted on a third party server. When the Web bug is requested as an element in a Web page, the client's IP address is recorded by the hosting server. By matching IP addresses, a specific user might be tracked across multiple Web sites. Tracking could be done with any HTML element but a small transparent GIF image will not be perceptible to users.

Search queries: Many users may not realize that their search queries are logged and could be used for profiling. Google has been the main focus of privacy concerns due to the enormous amount of data it sees as the predominant search engine, and the common belief that Google retains permanent records of every search query (although Google claims that its data is not personally identifiable).

Concerns about Google were heightened by its acquisition of DoubleClick in April 2007. Google has extensive data about searching behavior, while DoubleClick specializes in monitoring the viewing of ads across many different sites. Their combination places an unprecedented amount of personal data in one organization.

Server vulnerabilities: Various attacks on servers are possible. Like other computers, servers control access mainly through passwords which are subject to cracking attacks. Hence, the security of server data depends mainly on password security. In addition, servers can have vulnerabilities like other computers. The vast majority of Web servers use Apache or Microsoft IIS (Internet Information Server), and both have records of vulnerabilities (easily found on various Web sites).

Database vulnerabilities: Web servers often have a SQL (structured query language) database backend. SQL is an ANSI/ISO standard language for querying and manipulating databases. SQL injection attacks take advantage of user data input through Web forms. If a SQL injection vulnerability exists, the input data is passed to the SQL database without proper filtering for string literal escape characters, such as quotes. These characters in the input data will cause the database to interpret the data as SQL statements. By carefully crafting the input data, an attacker could learn data or manipulate data stored in the database.

Cross-site user tracking: In November 2007, it was discovered that Facebook's Beacon system tracks the activities of Facebook users on more than 40 affiliate Beacon sites, which report those activities to the user's Facebook friends. The reporting is done even when users are logged out of Facebook or deactivated their Facebook account. Furthermore, the reporting is done by affiliate Beacon sites without explicit notification to users.

ASSURANCES OF PRIVACY

An individual's legal right to privacy was argued by Samuel Warren and Louis Brandeis in 1890 (Warren and Brandeis, 1890). The right protects anyone from having to unwillingly disclose information that is not of "legitimate" public concern. Furthermore, the right is violated if a person's information is disclosed against their will, regardless of whether the information is accurate or not, and regardless of the motive. The notion of an inherent right to privacy against involuntary disclosure was reaffirmed in the United Nations' 1948 Universal Declaration of Human Rights.

More recently, Alan Westin described "informational privacy" as the right of people to "determine for themselves when, how, and to what extent information about them is communicated to others" (Westin, 1967). Thus, privacy involves an individual's control over how personal information is shared. The issue of control matters, for example, when a user submits personal information to a trusted Web site. The user may be trusting the site to keep the information internal from other organizations. However, the user does not have much control in reality over how the site uses the submitted information.

Approaches to protect privacy can be classified as regulatory or technological (Rezgui, Bouguettaya, and Eltoweissy, 2003). A taxonomy is shown in Figure 2.

Regulatory Protection of Privacy

As we discussed before, Web sites may collect consumers' personal data and share the data with third parties without the consumers' consent. Regulations provide some governance on how businesses should collect and process consumers personal data. Regulatory protection of privacy includes voluntary and mandatory approaches, and both approaches are being used today (Rezgui, Bouguettaya, and Eltoweissy, 2003).

Voluntary self-regulations: The U.S. government has historically preferred not to use an overarching federal law to protect consumers' online privacy but instead recommended self-regulation for industries to implement. In general, technology industries have also preferred self-regulation over the alternative of government regulation.

In 1998, the Online Privacy Alliance (OPA) was formed as a group of global companies and associations to "lead and support self-regulatory initiatives to promote business-wide actions that create an environment of trust and that foster the protection of individuals' privacy online and in electronic commerce" (http://www.privacyalliance.org). The OPA advocates online businesses to post privacy policies following at least five principles:

- adoption of a privacy policy;
- identification of what information is being collected and how it is shared and used;

Figre 2. Approaches to privacy assurance

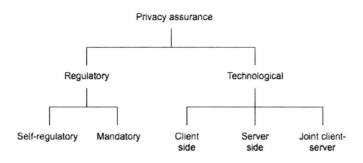

- a choice for individuals to give consent to (or opt out of) other uses of their data;
- adequate protection of personal data from misuse, loss, or tampering;
- assurance that data is kept accurate, complete, and up to date.

Additionally OPA offers guidelines effective self regulation and principles for protecting the privacy of children's online activities. These guidelines are recognized as the industry standard for online privacy.

Privacy seal programs are one of the means for effective self regulation. The major privacy seal programs are TRUSTe, CPA WebTrust, and BBBOnline. TRUSTe was founded by the Electronic Frontier Foundation (EFF) and the CommerceNet Consortium to act as an independent, nonprofit organization dedicated to building consumers' trust and confidence on the Internet (Benassi, 1999). Web sites conforming to TRUSTe's privacy standard can display the TRUSTe "trustmark" shown in Figure 3.

A displayed TRUSTe trustmark gives assurance to users that the visited site has agreed to disclose their information collection and dissemination practices, and that their disclosure and practice have been verified by a credible third party. Specifically, the site has met at least five requirements:

- a posted privacy statement disclosing its personal data collection and dissemination practices;
- a choice for users to opt out of having their personal information used for non-primary purposes;
- a means for users to correct inaccurate information;
- reasonable procedures to protect personal information from loss, misuse, or tampering;
- verification of compliance by TRUSTe.

It should be noted that a privacy seal does not mean that data will be kept private. A privacy seal only implies that policy statements have been made and verified, but policies are not required to protect privacy. The adequacy of a site's policies must be judged by each user. Although privacy seals are intended to ultimately encourage more e-commerce, studies suggest that most users are unaware of the requirements for a site to obtain a privacy seal, and can not differentiate between a genuine or fake privacy seal (Moores, 2005).

Mandatory regulations: In the 1960s and 1970s, the U.S. government investigated the implications of computers on consumer credit reporting and privacy. One of the important outcomes was a 1973 commission report that created the Code of Fair Information Practices. This report would

Figure 3. TRUSTe privacy seal

have a later impact on European regulations on data protection. The Code of Fair Information Practices prescribed five principles:

- systems for recording personal data should not be kept secret;
- individuals are entitled to discover what personal data about them is recorded and how it is used;
- personal data about a person obtained for one purpose must have the person's consent to be used for another purpose;
- individuals are entitled to dispute and correct a personal record;
- organizations involved in keeping personal records must ensure that data is used only as intended.

Regulations for data protection in the U.S. have been piecemeal, covered by various laws over the years, such as the Fair Credit Reporting Act, Privacy Act of 1974, Freedom of Information Act, and the Children's Online Privacy Protection Act (COPPA).

For health care industries, the U.S. Congress recognized the need to protect the privacy of patients' personal data and enacted the Health Insurance Portability and Accountability Act of 1996 (HIPAA), also known as Public Law 104-191 (Anton, Earp, Vail, Jain, Gheen, and Frink, 2007). It included administrative simplification to make healthcare services more efficient, portability of medical coverage for pre-existing conditions,

and standards for electronic billing and claims transmission. The privacy part of HIPAA requires that access to patient information be limited to only authorized individuals and only the information necessary to perform the assigned tasks. All personal health information must be protected and kept confidential. The final version of the HIPAA privacy regulations were issued in December 2000 and went into effect in April 2001 with a two-year grace period for compliance.

Recently, the collection and sharing of consumers' personal information by financial institutions was addressed at the federal level by the Gramm-Leach-Bliley Act, also known as the Financial Modernization Act of 1999. There are three parts of the legislation related to data privacy:

The Financial Privacy Rule addresses the collection and disclosure of customers' personal financial information by financial institutions. Provisions require financial institutions to give consumers privacy notices that clearly explain the organizations' information-sharing practices. In turn, consumers have the right to opt out of sharing their information with third parties. However, opting out is not allowed in certain circumstances, such as when data sharing is required by law.

The Safeguards Rule requires all financial institutions, including credit reporting agencies, to implement safeguards to protect customer information.

The Pretexting provision protects consumers from individuals and companies that obtain their personal financial information under false pretenses (pretexting).

The federal law allows states to pass stronger privacy laws. For example, California passed the Online Privacy Protection Act of 2003 (OPPA) which requires all commercial sites or online services that collect personal information from California residents to:

- post their privacy policies and dates on their Web sites and comply with those posted policies;
- describe the types of personal data collected and how the data is shared with third parties;
- describe the process for notifying users of policy changes;
- describe the process for consumers to request changes to any of their information (if allowed).

Violators are given 30 days to comply after notification, under threat of civil suit for unfair business practices.

While the U.S. has traditionally preferred an approach combining self-regulation and local legislation, the European Union (EU) has been more consistent in broadly recognizing privacy rights. A recognition of the fundamental right to privacy was included in the 1950 European Convention on Human Rights (Article 8) and the Council of Europe's 1981 Convention for the Protection of Individuals with regard to Automatic Processing of Personal Data. Concerned with maintaining uniformity, the EU issued an overarching Directive on Protection of Personal Data in 1995, formally known as Directive 95/46/EC, to regulate the collection and processing of consumers' personal information within the EU member countries. Based on the Code of Fair Information Practices from the U.S. and 1980 recommendations issued by the Organization for Economic Cooperation and Development (OECD), the directive aims for a balance "between a high level of protection for the privacy of individuals and the free movement of personal data within the EU." The directive sets certain limits on the collection and use of personal data and requires each EU member to set up an independent national body (supervisory authority) responsible for the protection of personal data. The directive sets conditions related to three categories: transparency, legitimate purpose and proportionality.

Transparency means that personal data may be processed when that person has given his consent or when the data processing is necessary (e.g., for compliance with law or for contracted services). In addition, the person has the right to access his/her personal data and correct or delete inaccurate data.

Legitimate purpose means that personal data can be processed only for specified and legitimate purposes.

Proportionality means that personal data may be processed only as it is adequate, relevant and not excessive in relation to the purposes for which they are collected. Personal data must be accurate and kept up to date.

The directive also regulates the transfer of personal data to countries that do not belong to the EU and may not have adequate privacy protection. The U.S. has an arrangement with the EU called the Safe Harbor Program to streamline the process for US companies to comply with Directive 95/46/EC. US companies can opt into the program if they adhere to the seven basic principles outlined in the directive:

- individuals should be informed that their data is being collected and about how it will be used;
- individuals must be given the choice to opt out of data collection or data sharing.
- data may be transferred only to third parties with adequate data protection;
- reasonable efforts must be made to protect collected information from loss;
- data must be relevant and reliable for the purpose it was collected for;

- individuals must be able to access their personal information, and correct or delete inaccurate data.
- there must be effective means of enforcing these rules.

U.S. companies can demonstrate compliance by self-assessment or third-party assessment.

Technological Protection of Privacy

While regulations are obviously important in establishing trust between online businesses and consumers, they are not likely to be sufficient by themselves. Fortunately, a variety of technological solutions exist (Linn, 2005; Rezgui, Bouguettaya, and Eltoweissy, 2003). Technological approaches to privacy protection might be divided into client side, server side, or joint client-server (again, network-based protection such as IPSEC is not addressed here because it is not specific to the Web). Protection done at the client includes encryption, anonymizers, personal firewalls, cookie disabling, ad blocking, anti-spyware, and anti-phishing. On the server side, data protection consists of preventing unauthorized intrusions by means of strong passwords, firewalls, vulnerability testing, and intrusion detection systems. Joint client-server approaches involve cooperation between clients and servers, and the main example today is the Platform for Privacy Preferences Project (P3P).

Encryption: Encryption uses mathematical algorithms to change plaintext (the original data) before transmission into ciphertext (encrypted data) that would be not understandable to an eavesdropper. Many encryption algorithms, such as RSA (Rivest-Shamir-Adleman) and the U.S. standardized AES (advanced encryption standard), are known and used in practical applications. Typically, the encryption algorithm used for communications is known, but not the encryption key. In symmetric or secret key encryption, the key is known only by the sender and receiver. The key at the receiver allows decryption of the ciphertext into plaintext, exactly reversing the encryption process, as shown in Figure 4.

Protection against eavesdropping can be accomplished similarly by asymmetric or public key cryptography, where the sender uses a public key for encryption and the receiver uses the corresponding private key for decryption as shown in Figure 5. The public key is known to everyone while the private key is known only to its owner. Although the public and private keys are mathematically related to each other, it should be very difficult to deduce the private key from the public key. Compared to secret key encryption, public key encryption offers the great advantage that the sender and receiver do not have to share a secret before they can start communicating with each other.

A Web server can present its public key to clients in a verifiable public key certificate. To obtain a certificate, the site owner registers with a trusted third-party certificate authority. A public-private key pair is arranged by the certificate authority. The public key is recorded with the key owner's identity and expiration time in a certificate, along

Figure 4. Secret key cryptography

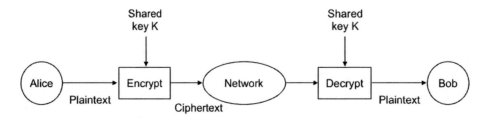

Figure 5. Public key cryptography

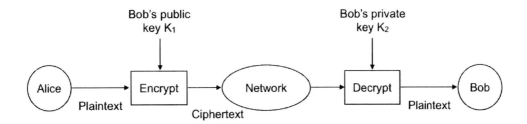

with the certificate authority's digital signature. The digital signature is cryptographic evidence that the certificate was created by the certificate authority and has not been altered. The certificate authority essentially vouches for the public key owned by the server. With the certificate presented by the server, a client can send data encrypted with the public key; presumably the server is the only one who owns the private key and can decrypt the encrypted data.

TLS/SSL is the protocol used in practice for ensuring private communications between a Web client and server. First, the server presents its public key certificate to the client. The client may present a certificate to the server but usually this is not done. Web browsers are pre-programmed with a set of certificate authorities that it will recognize. Then the client and server perform a TLS/SSL handshaking procedure to negotiate a secret key encryption algorithm, parameters, and a "master secret" to use for the duration of the session. Two encryption keys, one for each direction between the client and server, are derived from the master secret. The actual data exchanged between the client and server will use secret key encryption with the derived keys. The secret key encryption protects the transmitted data from eavesdropping.

It should be noted that encryption provides confidentiality in messages but does not hide the messages themselves. In particular, it is impossible to encrypt the source and destination IP addresses in IP packets because routers must be able to read the addresses to forward the packets. Hence, encryption does not prevent the source and destination IP addresses from being observed by eavesdroppers. An eavesdropper would be able to see that a client has contacted a server, but not see the contents of the request or reply.

Anonymizing agents: The purpose of anonymizing agents is to prevent Web requests from being traceable to the original IP address. Anonymizing agents can be single point agents such as Anonymizer or networked agents such as onion routers.

The basic idea of Anonymizer is to submit Web requests on behalf of its users through secure servers. The original version in 1996 was simply a proxy server sitting between clients and servers. A user submitted a URL into the "www.anonymizer.com" site, which fetched and forwarded the requested Web page. The server then deleted all history of the transaction.

A popular example of a Web proxy is Privoxy (privacy enhancing proxy) based on an earlier commercial program called Internet Junkbuster (http://www.privoxy.org). Sitting between the client and server, Privoxy works by filtering ads, banners, Web bugs, animated GIFs, Javascript annoyances, and other unwanted contents from fetched Web pages. Ads are recognized by examining the image's size and URL reference.

The original Anonymizer service was vulnerable to eavesdropping because URL requests were sent without protection. The next version of Anonymizer added SSL encryption between the client and the anonymizer proxy. Additional features include cookie caching, filtering out viruses and spyware, cleaning up malicious Javascript or other scripts, and blocking the client from reaching known malicious Web sites.

LPWA (Lucent Personalized Web Assistant) was a research project adding a pseudonym agent ("persona generator") to a Web proxy (Gabber, Gibbons, Kristol, Matias, and Mayer, 1999). The purpose of the persona generator is to maintain a persistent session with an alias on behalf of a user. The user connects to the Web proxy. For each requested Web site, the persona generator creates an alias consisting of an alias username, alias password, and alias e-mail address. A Web site sees the alias instead of the user's real information, and can even send e-mail to the user (through the alias e-mail address). The main advantage of LPWA over an anonymizing service such as Anonymizer is the capability of LPWA to maintain personalized services for a user.

Numerous Web sites are available to act as proxies for anonymous Web surfing and searching. Proxies offering anonymous search often use Google for searching but will block Google from setting their cookie (an unique identifier to track a user's searches).

A disadvantage of single anonymizing agents is a requirement that the agent is trusted. The agent is an attractive target for attacks. It is also tempting for attackers to observe the inputs and outputs, and attempt to analyze traffic by correlating the inputs and outputs. Logically, a network of anonymizing agents might offer more resilience against attacks and reveal less to traffic analysis.

A widely influential idea for a network of anonymizing agents was David Chaum's "cascade of mixes" (Chaum, 1981). A mix is a computer that sits between a set of senders and receivers, as shown simplified in Figure 6. The goal is to confuse any observer from analyzing the traffic to learn both the source and destination of a message. Here

K_m is the public key of the mix; K_b is the public key of receiver Bob; and M is the message. First, the message M is encrypted with Bob's public key K_b. Alice attaches Bob's address to the encrypted message, and encrypts the entire thing with the mix's public key K_m. One can view the message as double layers of encryption. Only the mix can decrypt the outer layer and read Bob's address as the recipient. The mix will forward (output) messages in a different order than it receives (inputs) messages. The mix does not have to be entirely trusted. If the mix delivers Bob's message to a different receiver, only Bob can decrypt the message with his private key.

The process is slightly complicated by cascading or placing multiple mixes in series, but the idea is the same. The message must be encrypted with an additional layer of encryption for each mix in the cascade. Each mix successively removes a layer of encryption until the innermost encrypted message is delivered to the recipient. The advantage of a cascade is that any single mix can provide the secrecy of the correspondence between the senders and receivers.

Onion routing is conceptually similar to cascades of mixes. Onion routing works by forwarding encrypted HTTP requests through a series of onion routers (Goldschlag, Reed, and Syverson, 1999). Each onion router successively removes a "layer" of encryption until the HTTP request is ultimately delivered to the Web server with the IP address of the last onion router, making it impossible to trace back to the original requester. Each onion router knows its predecessor and successor in a message's route but not the entire route. A proof of concept was demonstrated, but a practical system was not built.

TOR (The Onion Router) is a second-generation onion router (Dingledine, Mathewson, and Syverson, 2004). It adds numerous improvements to the original onion routing design, including low latency and better anonymity. Perhaps most importantly, TOR has been released as free software and deployed with several hundred nodes with

Figure 6. Simplified operation of a mix

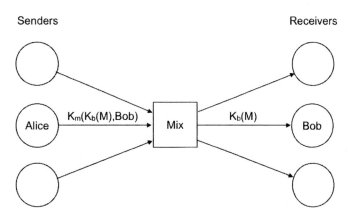

support from the Electronic Frontier Foundation. Consequently, various other software projects are being designed to work with TOR. For instance, XeroBank Browser, formerly called Torpark, is a variant of Firefox with built-in TOR access through secure and encrypted connections. Opera-TOR is a bundle combining the Opera browser, TOR, and Privoxy.

As the name suggests, Crowds works by blending individuals into a big group of Crowds users (Reiter and Rubin, 1999). Each Crowds user runs a local "jondo" process that serves as a Web proxy and an HTTP request forwarding agent. When the user wants to visit a Web site, the HTTP request is handled by his/her local jondo. The jondo will randomly choose to forward the request to another jondo (Crowds member) with probability P or to the requested Web site with probability 1-P. If forwarded to another jondo, the next jondo will make another random choice to forward the request to another jondo with probability P or the requested Web site with probability 1-P. The system-wide parameter P is configurable and affects the method's effectiveness. HTTP requests are thus forwarded along a random path through the Crowds. None of the group knows the identity of the original requester. Each jondo remembers its predecessor and successor, because replies from the server are returned along the same path in the backward direction. For additional privacy, all links are encrypted using a private key shared by the nodes on each end of the link.

Another variation of Chaum's cascade of mixes can be found in Freenet (Clarke, Miller, Wong, Sandberg, and Wiley, 2002). Freenet is a self-organizing peer-to-peer network designed to pool unused disk space on member PCs into a vast collaborative virtual file system. Privacy is enforced by forwarding messages from node to node, re-encrypted on each link. Each node is aware of its predecessor and successor, but not the original sender or ultimate recipient. Tarzan is another peer-to-peer network realization of mixes (Freedman and Morris, 2002).

Firewalls: Organizations typically deploy firewalls at the perimeters of their enterprise network to filter out unwanted traffic from the Internet. Firewalls are an essential component for protecting servers from attackers. However, the effectiveness of firewalls depends greatly on its filtering rules. Effective firewall rules generally require a high level of technical expertise. Also, although other ports can be closed, port 80 (default for HTTP) and perhaps port 443 (for secure HTTP) must be kept open for a Web server. Attacks can still be carried out over these ports.

PCs typically contain personal firewalls which can block incoming malicious traffic. Again, their effectiveness depends on proper configuration of filtering rules.

Cookie disabling: Fortunately, modern browsers offer users a good degree of control of cookies. Browsers can be set to reject cookies, selectively accept cookies, or ask every time before accepting each cookie. Cookies can be deleted manually, or automatically after each session or a specific expiration time.

Ad blocking: Modern browsers can be configured to block images, although this is mostly to improve rendering speed. It would be desirable to selectively block images of zero or one pixel dimensions that are probably Web bugs, but this is complicated by the practice of some sites to use small images for composing the site's appearance. Hence, blocking these small images could change the appearance of a site.

Anti-spyware: Spyware has become a considerable threat for identity theft. Many anti-virus programs will look for spyware, and numerous specialized anti-spyware software is available as well. The main function of anti-spyware is recognition of spyware, which is more difficult than might be expected because spyware authors are constantly developing new spyware and trying new tactics to evade detection. The most accurate approach to detection is signatures (unique characteristics) developed from careful examination of spyware samples. Unfortunately, signatures can take considerable time to develop, test, and distribute. Also, anti-spyware must be continually updated with the latest signatures. If signatures are inaccurate, anti-spyware might miss detection of spyware (a false negative) or mistake a legitimate program as spyware (a false positive). A zero rate of false negatives and false positives would obviously be ideal, but the complexity and stealthiness of spyware make false negatives and positives unavoidable. If detection is possible,

anti-spyware should ideally be able to disinfect a computer (remove the spyware) and protect it from future infections. Unfortunately, these tasks may also be complicated by the damage done by spyware. In many cases, the best approach may be erasing a computer completely and installing a clean operating system.

Anti-phishing tools: Phishing has become a widespread threat due to the ease of spam, ease of setting up phishing sites, and mostly, the ease of deceiving enough consumers into disclosing their valuable personal information to make phishing profitable. A variety of anti-phishing methods exist today. The main non-technical method is user education. If users are alert to phishing attempts, the response rate might be reduced sufficiently to make it unprofitable for criminals to continue. Technical methods include spam filtering to block phishing lures; phishing site detection (by various methods) and blacklisting or take down; and browser aids such as toolbar add-ons. Browser toolbars usually work by checking URLs against blacklists of known phishing sites and whitelists of legitimate sites, combined with heuristic tests of a site's HTML contents.

Strong passwords: Web servers are typically protected by passwords. Most computers today enforce policies for choosing strong passwords. Unfortunately, passwords are still vulnerable to a multitude of password cracking tools. Also, system administrators sometimes neglect to change the default accounts and passwords shipped with many computers.

Vulnerability testing and patching: Like all complex software programs, browsers and servers are susceptible to having vulnerabilities - security weaknesses that may be targeted by exploits, pieces of software written specifically to take advantage of a security weakness. Historically, common exploits have been buffer overflow exploits which attempt to compromise a target by running arbitrary malicious code.

The computer industry publishes known vulnerabilities to enable system administrators to patch their computers with the latest software updates. In addition, numerous vulnerability scanners are available for testing systems to identify their vulnerabilities. Vulnerabilities should be eliminated by patching, or if patches are not available (because patches take time to create and distribute), by other means such as firewalls.

Intrusion detection: Host-based intrusion detection systems run on computers and monitor their activities for signs of malicious intent, while network-based intrusion detection systems monitor network traffic for malicious signs. Both host-based and network-based intrusion detection systems are widely deployed in combination with firewalls and other security measures.

Similar to anti-spyware, intrusion detection systems depend mostly on attack signatures, called misuse detection. Signatures allow accurate identification of attacks, but signature-based detection is limited to known attacks. It is possible for new unknown attacks to evade detection if they are significantly different from signatures. A new signature can be developed after a new attack is detected.

A different approach is anomaly detection, which characterizes normal activities or traffic. Anything different from the normal profile is detected as an anomaly. Anomaly detection has the advantage of possibly catching new unknown attacks, under the assumption that attacks will be different from the normal profile. However, there are significant drawbacks to anomaly detection that continue to challenge researchers. First, normal behavior or traffic is complex and always changing. The normal profile must be continually updated. Second, anomaly detection is imprecise. Anomalies are unusual activities or traffic but not necessarily malicious. By itself, anomaly detection does not identify the exact nature of the anomaly, only that it is not normal. Indeed, only a small fraction of anomalies may be malicious, but all of them will require investigation, possibly wasting a great amount of effort.

P3P: The World Wide Web Consortium's Platform for Privacy Preferences Project (P3P) aims to provide a standardized method for Web sites to communicate their policies for data collection and use. Descriptions of these policies are sent from a P3P-enabled server to a P3P-enabled browser in machine-readable XML (extensible markup language) format. The site's policies are automatically compared to the user's preferences, saving the user from having to read and understand the site's entire policy. The browser can warn the user about differences or disable certain functionalities. However, P3P does not specify what policies should be, nor does it ensure that a site will actually follow its stated policy. It simply describes an XML-based vocabulary for representing privacy policies.

The number of commercial sites with privacy policies satisfying customers with strict P3P privacy preferences is an issue. The concern is that the lack of acceptable sites will cause users to lower their privacy requirements, defeating the purpose of P3P. Hence, the future of P3P is in doubt.

Few sites appear to be motivated to use P3P due to the time and money required to prepare their privacy policy statements in support of P3P. In fact, the total number of P3P-enabled Web sites appears to be small. A survey done in 2003 found only 9.4% sites adopting P3P, and a later survey completed in late 2005 found about the same unchanged adoption level (Reay, Beatty, Dick, and Miller, 2007). Deployment of P3P appears to be stagnant.

To summarize, many technological solutions have been deployed to address different aspects of Web privacy issues:

- Encryption and SSL/TLS are used to protect message transmission across Internet from eavesdropping and alteration.
- While encryption only protects message content but not source and destination addresses, anonymizing agent methods are

used to protect from tracking of users' surfing behaviors, for example, using Web bug or search query tracking etc.

- For cookie abuse in attacks like cross site request forgery, Web servers can use cryptographic method in addition to cookie to identify a session, while Web clients provide options to disable cookies.
- For privacy policy enforcement, P3P standardizes communication protocol for P3P enabled browser to help users to ensure that Web sites implemented adequate privacy protection of users.
- For annoying adware, ad blocking can be enabled.
- For social engineering and phishing attacks, users can use anti-phishing tools like spoofstick and phishing filters. In addition, choosing strong password, being aware of social engineering techniques and not directly clicking on links in suspicious emails all provide protection to their online accounts.
- Many drive-by-downloads of malware and spyware are based on exploits of browser vulnerabilities. To protect against exploits, existing solutions include a combination of firewall and intrusion detection at both network and hosts, as well as vulnerability testing and patching and up-to-date antivirus and antispyware programs.

The above protections can be deployed at client side, server side or within the network infrastructure. As it is often said, security equals to the weakest link. Both client side and server side need to be fortified to defend against various Web attacks. In addition, to build strong and layered defenses, specialized security boxes, e.g. anonymizing agent and intrusion detection/prevention systems, can be deployed within network infrastructure to provide scalable and effective defense for Web privacy.

FUTURE TRENDS

The real problem is to keep the convenience of personalized online services while protecting privacy at the same time (Kobsa, 2007). By privacy protection, we mean that individuals have control over the collection, sharing, and use of their personal data. As seen in this chapter, privacy protection can be approached through regulations or technology.

Nations have a number of regulations related to privacy protection, but mandatory regulations are not uniform or very far reaching. The U.S. has been reluctant to attempt comprehensive mandatory regulations. Most likely the U.S. will continue to rely on voluntary regulations. Today self regulations consist mainly of privacy seal programs. However, they are probably not well understood by most consumers, nor do privacy seals actually ensure the privacy of data. Hence, one could argue that the regulatory approach to privacy protection will continue to be largely ineffectual.

It could be argued that technological approach are more promising. In the past few years, significant progress has been seen in the deployment of TLS/SSL, anonymizing agents (such as TOR), and privacy options in major browsers (such as ad blocking). It is relative easy today to do Web surfing or searches with anonymity. In a way, these have been the easy problems.

Identity thefts by phishing or spyware continue to be open problems. Although various methods are used to fight phishing, identity theft is a growing problem because phishers invent new techniques. The same is true for spyware. These problems are more difficult because they are adversarial and continually changing.

CONCLUSION

By just about every measure, the Web has been phenomenally successful. Obviously the Web has become pervasive in social, business, and industrial contexts. Its ubiquity is evidence of its success but also the reason for public concern. As our dependence on the Web grows, more pieces of personal information become exposed. Not only are pieces collected, but it is possible that isolated pieces of personal information may be correlated together and mined into more threatening invasions of privacy.

As seen in this chapter, a variety of non-technical and technical approaches exist to protect online privacy. Yet all approaches to date have only been partial solutions. By its nature, the Web was designed as an open system to facilitate data sharing. There are many ways to collect personal information through the Web, and there are companies and even governments that are interested in collecting this information. Also, most people tend to be willing to lose a certain amount of privacy to gain access to online services. A universal solution does not seem likely, but even if a solution was available, it is not clear where the balance between privacy and convenience should be drawn.

REFERENCES

Anton, A., Earp, J., Vail, M., Jain, N., Gheen, C., & Frink, J. (2007). HIPAA's effect on Web site privacy policies. *IEEE Security and Privacy, 5*(1), 45-52.

Benassi, P. (1999). TRUSTe: An online privacy seal program. *Communications of the ACM, 42*(2), 56-59.

Chaum, D. (1981). Untraceable electronic mail, return addresses, and digital pseudonyms. *Communications of the ACM, 24*(2), 84-88.

Clarke, I., Miller, S., Wong, T., Sandberg, O., & Wiley, B. (2002). Protecting free expression online with Freenet. *IEEE Internet Computing, 6*(1), 40-49.

Dierks, T., & Rescorla, E. (2006). *The Transport Layer Security (TLS) protocol version 1.1.* Internet Engineering Task Force RFC 4346.

Dingledine, R., Mathewson, N., & Syverson, P. (2004). Tor: The second-generation onion router. *Presented at 13th USENIX Security Symposium,* San Diego, CA.

Freedman, M., & Morris, R. (2002). Tarzan: A peer-to-peer anonymizing network layer. *Proceedings of the 9th Conference on Computer and Communications Security,* ACM Press, 193-206.

Gabber, E., Gibbons, P., Kristol, D., Matias, Y., & Mayer, A. (1999). Consistent, yet anonymous, Web access with LPWA. *Communications of the ACM, 42*(2), 42-47.

Garfinkel, S. (2002). *Web Security, Privacy, and Commerce,* 2nd ed. Sebastopol, CA: O'Reilly and Associates.

Goldschlag, D., Reed, M., & Syverson, P. (1999). Onion routing. *Communications of the ACM, 42*(2), 39-41.

Kobsa, A. (2007). Privacy-enhanced personalization. *Communications of the ACM, 50*(8), 24-33.

Kristol, D. (2001). HTTP cookies: standards, privacy, and politics. *ACM Transactions on Internet Technology, 1*(2), 151-198.

Linn, J. (2005). Technology and Web user data privacy. *IEEE Security and Privacy, 3*(1), 52-58.

Martin, D., Wu, H., & Alsaid, A. (2003). Hidden surveillance by Web sites: Web bugs in contemporary use. *Communications of the ACM, 46*(12), 258-264.

Moores, T. (2005). Do consumers understand the role of privacy seals in E-Commerce? *Communications of the ACM, 48*(3), 86-91.

Reay, I., Beatty, P., Dick, S., & Miller, J. (2007). A survey and analysis of the P3P protocol's agents, adoption, maintenance, and future. *IEEE Transactions on Dependable and Secure Computing, 4*(2), 151-164.

Reiter, M., & Rubin, A. (1999). Anonymous Web transactions with Crowds. *Communications of the ACM, 42*(2), 32-48.

Rezgui, A., Bougeuettaya, A., & Eltoweissy, M. (2003). Privacy on the Web: Facts, challenges, and solutions. *IEEE Security & Privacy, 1*(6), 40-49.

Shukla, S., & Nah, F. (2005). Web browsing and spyware intrusion. *Communications of the ACM, 48*(8), 85-90.

Warren, S., & Brandeis, L. (1890). *The right to privacy. Harvard Law Review, 4*(5), 193-220.

Westin, A. (1967). *The Right to Privacy.* Boston, MA: Atheneum Press.

KEY TERMS

Anonymizing Agent: A program acting as an intermediary between client and server to make Web requests untraceable to the original client.

Client: An application such as a Web browser running on a user's computer that sends a request to a server as necessary.

Cookie: A text string stored in a browser to keep state across multiple Web transactions.

Cryptography: The use of mathematical algorithms to protect transmitted data from eavesdropping.

Phishing: The use of malicious Web sites masquerading as legitimate sites to deceive users into disclosing personal information.

Privacy: Protection of personal information from disclosure.

Server: An application running on a computer for responding to a client's request.

Spyware: A type of malicious software designed to covertly steal a computer user's personal information.

Web Bug: A small, usually invisible image embedded in a Web page used to detect the IP addresses of users viewing the page.

Chapter III
Metaphors and Models for Data Mining Ethics

Peter Danielson
University of British Columbia, Canada

ABSTRACT

Our regulatory institutions, broadly taken, include our moral norms and models and have not fully adapted to significant changes in data mining technology. For example, we suggest that the metaphors — Big Brother and "data mining" itself — commonly used to describe and assess this new technology are deficient, overemphasizing social discipline by the state and the passivity of the so-called data subject. We move from metaphors to a set of models more adequate for building an ethics of data mining, using a framework of informal game theory. We sketch three models of interaction: pure conflict, pure coordination, and a mixed motive cooperation game, with special application to security, health, and commerce, respectively. We recommend these three models as heuristics within a simple account of an ethics of data mining regulated by informed consent.

INTRODUCTION

Many problems in the ethics of technology arise because our regulatory institutions, including our moral norms and mental models, take time to adapt to technological change. Data mining is a good example of this institutional inertia. Twenty years ago, (Clarke, 1988) set out a policy framework for the emerging information technologies that he called 'dataveillance' that now includes data mining (see Key Terms). As Clarke predicted, the growth of information technology in general, and the Internet in particular, has exacerbated the problems he catalogued. Nonetheless, neither the weak regulatory framework nor individual ignorance of common data mining practice has changed in the U.S. We will focus on the U.S. as the extreme case of a democratic society where data mining technology is highly developed and widely used but weakly regulated and poorly understood. (We will discuss the (Turow, Feldman, & Meltzer, 2005) survey data below, as well as a survey of U.K. physicians attitudes towards privacy, to ground our discussion in what may be local cultural attitudes towards privacy.) Where early U.S. database matching focused on target subjects in government databases – welfare recipients and government employees – today almost everyone in the U.S. economy is a data subject in multiple data bases. For example, "Acxiom gathers and sorts information about 196 million Americans …'Metromail…has a detailed data base on more than 90 per cent of American households'" (Whitaker, 1999, pp. 132 -13 3).

Discussing a related topic, (Danielson, 2005) argued that inappropriate informal models hampered our understanding of surveillance and impeded construction of an adequate ethics for the subject. In that case, metaphors such as Jeremy Bentham's Panopticon supported static and one-sided thinking about surveillance, displacing the more nuanced models needed for ethics. In this chapter we extend this argument from surveillance to data mining, where metaphors and models are even more central to understanding the more abstract technology involved. We begin with the deficiencies in two common metaphors that guide thinking about data mining, beginning with "Big Brother" and moving to "data mining" itself. We suggest moving from metaphors to more precise models, sketching three broad types of interaction in which data mining plays a role: pure conflict, pure coordination, and a mixed motive cooperation game. This chapter deploys a framework of informal game theory to elucidate some of the ethical issues raised by data mining technology. We do not use "games" to diminish the importance of the issues we discuss, but rather to highlight their interactive, strategic, and dynamic aspects. Indeed, a game theoretic approach is particularly suited to the topic of data mining, for two reasons. First, descriptively, the point of

morally significant data mining is strategic. In both main uses of the technology, security and commerce, one mines personal data to know more about one's opponent, aiming to change the terms of interaction in one's favor. Therefore, taking a game theory approach does not import or overemphasize strategic considerations. A second and more normative reason to use a game theory approach is to emphasize people as active agents in contrast to the passive data subjects assumed by some data mining practice. This agent-centered approach provides us with a critical perspective, focusing on how choices and alternatives might be better structured by data mining technologies, regulations, and norms, and thus yielding new opportunities for ethics to guide us.

BACKGROUND: MORALS, METAPHORS, & MODELS

Moral Scope

The basic technologies used in data mining—machine learning and automated statistical analysis applied to large data bases—are not themselves morally problematic. They only become so when used on morally significant data, typically information about persons gathered without their full consent (Wahlstrom & Roddick, 2001, p. 23). Contrast the case of bioinformatics – data mining applied to genomic and other biological data – applied to a typical species used in research, such as the c. elegans worm and applied to humans. In the worm case, with no morally significant personal data, the use of data mining tools raises no new ethical issues unlike the latter case of human bioinformatics. Data mining can be used for other morally problematic activities, where the victims are firms, or states, or perhaps animals, but personal data and consent are the core moral problem and the focus of the models introduced in this chapter.

However, the powerful techniques used in data mining can find new meaning by linking otherwise trivial transaction data, putting great pressure on pre-existing categories of personal data and consented uses. Ideally, valid consent should be informed by the knowledge of the uses that available technology allows, but this is seldom the case. For example, few in the U.S. are aware that commercial data mining community considers use of a toll free telephone information number as granting consent to link a profile to the telephone number the toll free services reveals.

Delimiting the scope of the technologies to discuss here is more difficult. The obvious focus is data bases assembled for the purpose of data mining of personal information. But this may be too restrictive: "[t]he World Wide Web can be seen as the largest database in the world. This huge, and ever-growing amount of data is a fertile area for data mining research " (van Wel & Royakkers, 2004, p. 129). Similarly, much cell-phone data may be mined by cell-phone service providers (Sylvers, 2008). The objection to limiting the scope of the problem is that the typical Web or cell phone user does not realize that they are contributing data that may be mined for distant purposes. Aside from material explicitly published on the Web, which raises distinct issues, we will take this penumbra of searchable personal data on the Web to be part of the data mining problem.

Third, the contrast with publication sharpens our focus on personal information and consent as our ethical foci. Personal information is information that ought not to be used without the relevant person's consent to that use. Publication stands at the limit of broad consent, since published information may legitimately even be used to undermine or refute the purpose for which it was published, according to the critical mechanisms of a free press and scientific peer review. This reminds us that while it is important to protect personal information from non-consented uses, it is also important to be able to release it for con-

sented uses. Ethics needs to address and inform these choices at the core of data mining.

Metaphors

Metaphors are important for the ethics of technology. An apt metaphor can simplify a complex technology, providing a set of roles and heuristics for thinking about interaction with other people and organizations mediated by the technology. All of us need to distill complex technologies down to the workable abstractions: my computer, the Internet, my cell-phone. So the question for the ethics of technology is not whether we should tolerate simplifying metaphors, but which metaphors provide better guidance.

Turing to our first example, if we think of data mining through (Orwell, 1949)'s Big Brother metaphor, we will likely focus our concerns on government surveillance supporting tyranny, ignoring the way multiple private databases impact the ethical landscape. Following (Solove, 2001), we contend that the Big Brother metaphor is misleading for many issues raised by data mining. The Big Brother metaphor focuses our attention on a central government as the data agent, surveillance as the key technology, and social discipline as the goal. Data mining often differs in each respect.

First, there has been a shift away from governments as the main data gatherers. Now massive multiple databases are compiled by private firms in credit, merchandizing, medical, and marketing fields. This trend may be misleading. Governments still collect and use massive amounts of data and in they may use non-governmental data to extend these collections. Also, one reason for the shift from government to non-governmental collections has been increased regulation of government data collection and use. None the less, the Big Brother metaphor misleads us on this point; government tyranny is not the sole threat posed by data mining in an advanced economy.

This change has led some to modify the metaphor to a plurality of Little Brothers (Whitaker, 1999). This case indicates a general problem with metaphors: they can be very crude models, in this case with one "size" slot filled by variants of 'big.' But in the shift from government to non-governmental data collection the crucial parameter is not the number of players; within "the government" there are likely many data collecting agencies. The more important feature of the shift is the difference in strategic purpose, from "security" or social discipline, to changing the terms of trade between market players. Moreover, the Little Brothers metaphor is not well focused, as some commentators use it to refer to ordinary people using cell phone cameras (Weeks, 2007). However, cell phone camera users are not usefully considered in the same category as either government surveillance or business intelligence. The proliferation of cameras does mean that crudely, there is a greater chance that more data about one will be collected, but the parallel proliferation of collectors of this data make it very difficult to predict its effect on our lives. Here extending a familiar metaphor gives us a false sense of comprehending a new technology in familiar categories. We suggest it is better to see the rise of ubiquitous private networked cameras and associated social networking sites, as quite new with unexplored potential rather than as a extension of Big Brother (Danielson, 2002). For example, cell phone based "photo-journalism" has tended to be anti-authoritarian.

Second, the technology used in data mining is more abstract than the technology for Big Brother's direct surveillance, which makes the former harder to understand, assess, and monitor. In the extreme case, direct surveillance merely mediates viewer and viewed with video cameras and monitors. In a very early and influential example in Chaplin's Modern Times (1936) a two-way screen allows the factory boss to reprimand the hero during a cigarette break in the men's room. Contrast data mining's abstract "sensors" that record myriad transactions at point of sale terminals, telephone calls, web surfing, and the like. No one needs to watch these events in real time; they are filed away in databases.

Physical and even communications surveillance are labor-intensive activities, which have so far proved difficult to automate. Dataveillance is essentially computer based, with the "watch and report" responsibility delegated to a reliable, ever-wakeful servant. It is increasingly cost-effective for organizations to place people under surveillance via their records and transactions, and traditional methods are being relegated to the role of complementary techniques. Further-more, because dataveillance is cheaper than traditional methods, there is a tendency for more organizations to monitor more people: Both personal and mass surveillance are becoming routinized (Clarke, 1988, p. 501).

The economic effect of this difference is crucial. Since CPU cycles and computer storage are cheap and getting cheaper, while human labor tends to increase in cost, data mining can afford to be ubiquitous. Even in regions subject to intense surveillance like the U.K., most locations remain off camera. In contrast, no credit card purchase or telephone call or airline flight goes unrecorded. There is also obviously a difference in the time scale of the two, with surveillance operating on hours and days and data mining on years of data. Finally, as (Solove, 2001, pp. 1417-1418) emphasizes, the role of human judgment in surveillance makes a crucial psychological difference: "Being observed by an insect on the wall is not invasive for privacy; rather privacy is threatened by being subject to human observation, which involves judgments that can affect one's life and reputation." Aggregation of data and manipulation by algorithms distances most data mining in this respect. As a user of Gmail, where algorithms mine mail messages in order to place advertisements,

I can report that I do not feel as if someone were reading my mail, because no one is.

This leads to the third difference: many data miners, unlike Big Brother, do not aim at social discipline, but typically to influence market transactions. "The goal of much data collection by marketers aims not at suppressing individuality but at studying it and exploiting it" (Solove, 2001, p. 1147). This is a key point in our analysis. The Big Brother metaphor overemphasizes the role of social discipline, and thus pure conflict over coordination and cooperation, models of which we will develop below.

Finally, while we intend to replace misleading metaphors with more informative models, we do not want to lose the pragmatic value of metaphors. We need models of technologies – especially new and abstract technologies like data mining – which people can use to sort cases into appropriate categories; good models and metaphors are essential to a democratic ethics of technology. For this reason we stress that our use of game theory below will be quite informal, relying on simple versions of familiar games to sketch three ideal types of interaction.

Data Mining as Metaphor

'Data mining' is itself a metaphor that influences our thinking about digital dossiers.

The mining metaphor is helpful in highlighting how sparsely located value needs to be aggregated. It also reminds us that much of the data mined is historical, and thus "uses data collected for one purpose for another purpose" (Wahlstrom & Roddick, 2001, p. 12). Nonetheless the mining metaphor is misleading in two respects.

First, while extracting ore from the earth is concrete, data mining is doubly abstract. A model – the digital dossier – is extracted from bigger social models – various databases. This first difference develops the contrast of data mining with surveillance. Where direct surveillance connects the observer and the subject, data min-

ing constructs a model of the data subject from his or her records in other models, not the social world directly. These intermediating models are rich contexts that make data mining intrinsically more complex than surveillance as any data-based model is based on a set of assumptions about which data is relevant and constraints on which data is available and accurate.

Second, the data mining metaphor fits cases such as the worm bioinformatics example mentioned above, which assembles models of static genomic data; similarly there is good fit for real geological data mining, where various geophysical data sources are combined in a model. In contrast, morally significant data mining typically creates a model of people, their actions and relations. The model needs to be dynamic if it is to reflect social relations between people accurately and therefore it will need ongoing input from those data subjects to correct inevitable errors. However, the mining metaphor targets only extraction to the exclusion of these complementary value-building processes. It is one sided to focus on the extraction of value from databases, assuming this model is somehow exogenously built and verified. Physical mining is quite different; we need not worry about how the valued ore came to be deposited long ago. Nor will the c. elegans worm behave differently due to our data collection. In contrast, people will like behave differently were they informed that their activity was being collected as data and used to model them for others' purposes. Accurate personal data is a fragile and renewable resource; we must manage or renegotiate its re-creation constantly. Talk of extraction ignores the need to provide incentives for agents to provide or correct valuable data about themselves. "These various schemes [identifying individuals by name] may be of a reasonable level of integrity where data subjects have an interest in their accuracy, but are otherwise of, at best, only moderate integrity" (Clarke, 1988, p. 501). The data-mining metaphor ignores the strategic relationships upon which the practice depends, supporting unethical and otherwise unsustainable interactions. Indeed, an agricultural metaphor – say 'data husbandry' – would better capture this feature and remind us of the attending risk of exploitation.

Summing up, both problems with the data-mining metaphor exacerbate the tendency, noted with the Big Brother metaphor, to assume exploitation of a passive data subject by extracting data. On the contrary, we will stress the need to elicit fair cooperation from people—active agents in the data collection and model building, which, of course, makes ethics relevant.

MODELS

The ethics of data mining requires thinking about models, for three reasons. First, as we have already noted, data mining works on models of human behavior – the data subject and the data base(s) – not directly on the world. Typically there are many data subjects in the world model for each real person and sometimes more than one person for each data subject, intentionally in the case of identity theft. (Whitaker, 1999) uses the interesting image of the data subject as "ghost". To keep the models up to date and accurate—to eliminate ghosts—requires input on the part of the data subjects.

Second, this raises questions whether the subject understands that the particular model exists, how it will be used, and consents to his role in it. That is to say, the data subject needs a model of data mining: "Your conceptual model of a product or service—and the feedback that you receive—is essential in establishing and maintaining trust" (Norman, 2005, p. 142).

A third reason we need models in the ethics of data mining is the wide range of applications involved. Data mining refers to a set of techniques used in a wide variety of contexts ranging from policing, marketing and customer relations, bio-banking and bioinformatics. Obviously, the ethics of gathering personal data into actionable

"intelligence" will vary in such a wide range of contexts. We will need some simplifying models to allow us to address this broad topic in a single chapter. On our approach to ethics, the central role of models is entirely appropriate: ethics is based on the models agents use to structure their interactions. As we have seen, our thinking about issues like data mining and privacy can be influenced by very casual metaphors - like Big Brother and mining - that structure description and evaluation of the technology. Having begun with these more or less familiar metaphors, we now move to more precise models that distinguish three paradigm cases of conflicting, coordinative, and cooperative uses of data mining.

Pure Conflict: Too Bleak for Ethics

The Big Brother metaphor suggests a model of pure conflict, where the observer and the data subject have no common interest, such as counter-terrorism, credit card fraud detection, and welfare fraud (Marx & Reichman, 1984). Figure 1 models these extreme applications of data mining as a simplified two person two strategy evasion/detection game of hide and seek. The four pairs of numbers represent Seeker's and Hider's preferences respectively for the four possible outcomes. The Hider's strategies are to use false "identities" or personae of two types. The Seeker has two counter-strategies that work particularly well for each type of false identity. Hider wins by choosing B to Seeker's Counter-A (the -1, 1 outcome in the upper right quadrant) and A to Seeker's Counter-B. Seeker wins in the other two cases, where his counter strategies match Hider's deceptions. Their preferences are strictly opposed, hence the label: zero-sum game as a model of pure conflicting preferences.

We argue in (Danielson, 2005) that Big Brother and the panopticon metaphors mislead even in cases like this for which they are most suited, by suggesting that Seeker holds a monopoly on power. The prevalence of credit-card fraud and

Figure 1. Pure conflict

		Hider	
		Identity A	Identity B
Seeker	Strategy Counter-A	1,-1	-1,1
	Strategy Counter-B	-1,1	1,-1

identity theft make it obvious that this is not so in the data mining arena. Hiders have options and help determine the outcome; this is what makes the situation strategic. While it may look as if the data-gathering seeker has all the power, this is misleading. The Hider party has the power to create a situation where resources need to be devoted to this search, plus imposing the inconvenience of these procedures and the burden of false positives on innocent third parties (omitted from this simple model). The obvious lesson from game theory is for both Hiders and Seekers to mix strategies: unpredictably choose identities and counter-strategies, respectively. Each player will "win" (value = 1) some of the time (half the time in our simple model) and neither can improve on the resulting outcome, which makes it an equilibrium. It follows from this account that both parties will restrict information and use deception. For example, in conflict situations, there are strategic reasons to refuse even to identify who is a data subject; U.S. Homeland Security Secretary Michael Chertoff recently wrote. "As a matter of policy, the United States generally does not discuss whether an individual is, or is not, on a U.S. border control 'watch list'" (Rennie, 2008).

There are three important conclusions from our first model. First, there are good reasons for hiding and deception in this type of situation.

Hider need not be a criminal; we should all be hiding our passwords and credentials from the illicit Seekers on the Internet: phishers and social engineers. Therefore, in any situation with an element of pure conflict, we should not expect data to be trustworthy. Second, ethics has very little traction on these situations of extreme conflict. Secretary Chernoff's refusing to indentify who is a data subject is obviously contrary to principles of fair information use, but fairness and consent are not moral categories applied to suspected foreign terrorists. While welfare applicants and credit-card users have more rights that constrain the authoritative Seeker in the conflict modeled, we should not expect the criminals sought to exhibit much moral constraint in their interaction with the institutions and individuals that they attempt to defraud. These zero-sum situations define a landscape too bleak for most ethical improvement. On many accounts, ethics only has a place where all parties can gain (Danielson, 1992; Rawls, 1971), or at least where there are multiple equilibria (Binmore, 2004). This is our model's second lesson for the ethics of data mining: we should avoid conflating the quite distinct uses of the technology for security and more cooperative commercial purposes. This is not to ignore the real – and increasing – use of the technology for security and social discipline, but rather to stress that overemphasizing power and conflict to the exclusion of the possibility of coordination and cooperation reduces the arena for ethical appraisal and action. For this we need to move to models that have more room for mutual advantage in the sections below.

Pure Coordination

At the opposite extreme from conflict is pure co-ordination: situations where two parties' interests are the same. The relevant cases for the ethics of data mining involve important personal data collected by highly trusted agents, who legally and ethically are required to act in the data subject's interest. One's physician and other clinicians collecting personal health records and agents of one's bank collecting personal financial data are central and common examples. In these cases we want our agents to have full and accurate information so they can serve our interests. We want them to mine this data so that we benefit from non-obvious connections, for example, via pharmacy networks that can catch potential drug interactions between pharmaceuticals prescribed by different physicians. Figure 2 is a model of pure coordination. As in Figure 1 the preferences for the four outcomes are to row and column chooser (now labeled Agent and Patient) respectively. The column chooser can display one of two health or financial record sets, A or B. But now both Patient and her Agent literally want to be "on the same page" (to use a phrase common among coordinat-

ing team-members). So Agent and Patient both win (1,1) when they successfully coordinate on the same record set in the upper left and lower right quadrants and both lose (0,0) when they fail to coordinate on the other two diagonals. As (Priest, 2008) reported in a story about the enthusiasm among both patients and care-givers for on line medical records in Canada, one wants one's medical records to be just "a mouse click away" from those that want to help you.

While it is easy to become cynical about trusting these agents, especially in the financial case, we need to be reminded of the importance of the pure coordination case for two reasons. First, it reminds us why limiting information use to the purposes for which it was collected is so crucial. Since there are situations in which we have very good reasons to divulge highly sensitive data, without barriers we would suffer seriously harmful consequences from the spread of this information. In addition, fears of misuse of information would lead those at risk to revealing less or even misleading information. (See (Brandt, 1987) for the history of underreporting of syphilis in the U.S.) None the less, the fear is of misuse of the information; this makes the cooperative case quite different from the conflict model "Big Brother" brings to mind. Consider the recent controversy over the U.K.'s National Health System's proposal to move fifty million patient's records to a single national database ('the spine'). The Guardian had a poll of more than 1,000 doctors taken, which

Figure 2. Pure coordination

		Patient	
		Record Set A	Record Set B
Agent	Record Set A	1,1	0,0
	Record Set B	0,0	1,1

"found 59% of GPs in England are unwilling to upload any record without the patient's specific consent. …Three-quarters of family doctors said medical records would become less secure when they are put on a database that will eventually be used by NHS and social services staff throughout England. Half thought the records would be vulnerable to hackers and unauthorised access by officials outside the NHS. A quarter feared bribery or blackmail of people with access to the records and 21% suspected that social services staff would not adhere to the confidentiality rules" (Carvel, 2007).

The risks are misuse and unauthorized access. These are problems of mis-coordination; Patient and Agent want to share a record but some third party uses the information instead. While such security risks are serious, notice how different this situation is from using medical clinical information for social discipline. To enforce pro-natalist policy in the Romanian communist dictatorship, "in 1984 … compulsory monthly medical examinations for all women of childbearing age were introduced to prevent abortions" (Judt, 2005). These were not unauthorized uses of clinical information; physicians were instruments of social discipline.

Second, pure coordination is rare but our motivation in pure coordination cases may explain our tendency to over-cooperate in other situations. Indeed, pure coordination with trusted agents is rare in part because of the large burden of legal and ethical regulation needed to align our trusted agents' interests with ours (Buchanen, 1996). There are projects that attract us to give up information where it is difficult to limit the spread of information from trusted agents to others. For example, a recent controversial project, 23andme.com, involves sharing genetic information via a social networking site (Goetz, 2007). "We will analyze your genetic and other voluntarily contributed personal information as part of our scientific research with the purpose of advancing the field of genetics and human health" (23andme.

com, 2008). "'I think people really want to help other people', [co-founder Linda] Avey said" of 23andme.com (Abraham, 2008). But as the holder of newly aggregated genetic, health, and lifestyle information, this company ceases to be the simple helping agent modeled above. We need a more complex model for the most prevalent cases of data mining.

Mixed Motives: Cooperation

Fortunately most of us are not criminals; we prefer to engage cooperatively with almost all of the organizations we encounter. On the other hand, most of these organizations are not our agents in the strict sense: they have other interests besides ours that align with our interests to varying degrees. Our next model attempts to capture this more standard situation where conflict and coordination are mixed. Figure 3 depicts a stylized two-player game between the roles of Buyer and Seller. Seller controls the monitoring (data mining) technology. Seller can reveal the technique (profile) or conceal it. Buyer is a data subject exposed to the data mining technology. He can simply reveal his actions or take measures to conceal his personal data. In the more trusting and transparent situation on the upper two cells Buyer prefers to be candid (value = 3 > 2), for the sake of the benefits of low transaction costs. In the less trusting situation on the bottom, Buyer prefers to conceal his data (value = 1 > 0).

Buyer prefers the transparent situation (value = 3) to the secretive one (value = 1). Since the technology is asymmetrical, Seller is in a different position and has different preferences. Seller does best in the lower left quadrant where Buyer reveals his data but Seller does not reveal that he uses the technology (value = 3 > 2). Concretely Seller gets to greet Buyer by name, manipulating his emotions, or can refer to previous purchases and financial data, shaping the bargaining situation to Seller's advantage. In terms of informal game theory, Seller and Buyer are playing different

Figure 3. Mixed motive cooperation game

		Buyer	
		Reveal Data	Conceal data
Seller	Reveal monitoring	2,3	0,2
	Conceal monitoring	3,0	1,1

games. Buyer's preferences are those of a fair or cautiously reciprocal cooperative strategy, which the literature finds generally successful under selection in a wide variety of situations (Danielson, 2002). For this agent, the Conceal/Conceal outcome ranks lower (value = 1) than the Reveal/Reveal (value = 3) outcome, reflecting the costs of mutual countermeasures. Buyer's preferences lead him to play an Assurance Game or Stag Hunt, which has recently attracted attention in the literature on game theory and ethics (Kollock, 1998; Skyrms, 2003). This game has two equilibria, meaning that well-informed players would reveal in transparent situations and conceal otherwise. Unfortunately, Seller's preferences lead him to play a different game: a Prisoner's Dilemma, where the non-cooperative strategy, Conceal, is always preferred (3 > 2 and 1 > 0). This game has only one equilibrium outcome: concealment is Seller's best move whatever Buyer does. The joint game has only one equilibrium: Seller will Conceal and Buyer will also Conceal.

However, this will be the real outcome only on the assumption that the situation is common knowledge. (Our informal approach allows us to relax this assumption.) If Buyer is unaware of Seller's technological options, he may well mistake the situation, and cooperate by revealing information when it is not in his interests. And since Concealing data mining technology is the

preferred strategy for Seller, we can expect that that too little will be known about this technology inducing Buyers naively to reveal more information.

The first two lessons from this model are that Buyers will over-expose their data – they will mistakenly over cooperate – and sellers will conceal their data mining technology. The emerging Personal Health Record (PHR) data mining systems discussed in the section above exemplify these conclusions. As we noted, companies like 23andme.com use the language of health care; "We will analyze your genetic and other voluntarily contributed personal information." But according to the applicable U.S. regulation, the Health Insurance Portability and Accountability Act, health information transferred to these services not longer counts as a protected health record:

Because of the structure of HIPAA, its privacy protections do not generally follow a health record. The applicability of HIPAA's privacy protections depends on the kind of entity that processes a health care record. The basic idea is that if a health care provider (hospital, physician, pharmacist, etc.) or a health plan maintains a health care record, the record is protected under HIPAA. However, if a person or business that is not a covered entity under HIPAA holds the records, then HIPAA does not apply (Gellman, 2008, pp. 3-4).

This counter-intuitive regulatory structure makes it too easy for patients to lose control of their personal health information. They may think that they are sharing with an additional restricted health care provider when in fact they are unintentionally publishing personal information. On the opposite side, our third model predicts that the PHR providers have an interest in underplaying their non-regulated status, in effect concealing the monitoring that their unregulated status permits. "The term HIPAA-compliant is sometimes used by PHR companies that are not covered by HIPAA. This term can be confusing to consumers who do not clearly understand the difference between HIPAA-covered and HIPAA compliant" (Gellman, 2008, p. 15). Our model also reveals the exploitative possibilities in this situation. While the patient may see the interaction with the Personal Health Record system as one with a trusted agent, it really amounts to a purchase of valuable information by the PHR system, even it the service offered is free or paid for by the individual. Our model makes strategies of Revealing or Concealing information explicit which is helpful in the new PHR case. As in the case of private health insurance, where sophisticated Buyers now seek anonymous tests for conditions that might disqualify them for insurance, our model suggests that sophisticated PHR users might do better using the system under a pseudonym.

A third lesson looks to the dynamics of the situation. Our model predicts that most Buyers will reveal data for the sake of being distinguished from those fraudulent "Buyers" who drastically raise transaction costs. But data mining allows Sellers to move the line between desirable and undesirable customers: "[S]tores have been trying to find ways to discourage shopping from what some retailers call 'bottom feeders' – customers who visit them mostly for bargains and return products too often" (Turow, Feldman, & Meltzer, 2005, p. 10). While most of us will draw a categorical line, permitting the exclusion of shoplifters,

we would likely not support shifting it in this way. "Price discrimination based on profiling, [consumer advocates] say, invariably means using information about individuals in ways that do not involves their permission" (Turow, Feldman, & Meltzer, 2005, p. 11). This is clearly true of those Buyers discriminated against, and, if our model applies, may even by true of those Buyers who benefit by price discrimination but would not knowingly consent to contribute data to this form of market manipulation.

RECOMMENDATIONS AND FUTURE TRENDS

We have already recommended that we need models more suited to the diversity of data mining than the standard metaphors. In this section we sketch the role of these new models in the standard account of information ethics: industry and government data collectors regulated to respect informed consent by data subjects to information use.

Unfortunately, there are barriers to each of these elements: regulation, consent, and informed subjects.

First, the regulation of data mining is extremely uneven. We have already discussed the example of the U.S. Health Insurance Portability and Accountability Act that regulates designated health record holders, instead of protecting an individual's health records themselves. Another outstanding example is the special protection given videotape rental records in the U.S. while most similar commercial records have no protection. This makes little sense, aside from the particular historical path that led to the passage of the Video Privacy Protection Act, after the nomination scandal turning on Judge Robert Bork's video rental records. A patchwork of laws is difficult for ordinary citizens to use; I got the videotape question wrong on the (Turow, Feldman, & Meltzer, 2005) survey; only 29% of the respondents answered it correctly. Isolated patchwork regulatory protection may mislead in other ways. For example, "We found that 75% of internet-using adults do not know the correct response – false – to the statement, 'When a website has a privacy policy, it means the site will not share my information with other websites and companies.' For many people, then, the label is deceptive; they assume it indicates protection for them" (Turow, Feldman, & Meltzer, 2005, p. 30). Turow appropriately recommends that this link read "Using Your Information".

The second pillar in our ethical model is consent. The simple problem with consent is the lack of agreement about what actions constitute consent to data use in various contexts. Toll-free access numbers provide a clear example of this confusion in the U.S. "Like others in the industry, [major U.S. data mining firm] Acxiom believes consumers grant permission to gather and use information about them when they make toll-free calls and engage company agents, regardless of the fact that almost no one knows that he or she has made such a bargain, or what it might entail" (O'Harrow, 2006, p. 51). This problem is relatively simple as regulations could be crafted to require toll-free services to make their data policy explicit when connecting, as many services reveal quality assurance monitoring of customer telephone calls.

Consent to data mining faces a deeper problem revealed by 'knowledge discovery', an alternative name for data mining. 'Knowledge Discovery' reminds us that "the specific purpose of a [Knowledge Discovery] application is largely unknown until it has successfully revealed some previously unknown information" (Wahlstrom & Roddick, 2001, p. 12). So consent to using personal data for data mining can lead to the discovery of knowledge the consenting party did not envision. In the extreme case of publication that we mentioned at the start, this is a fair outcome. The reputation effect of publication depends on the risk of exposure and even ridicule. But to the majority who do not

realize that an "innocent" toll-free call has linked their telephone number to a personal profile, revealing their telephone in other transactions may have unfair unintended effects.

Third, our three models reveal deep problems with the model of informed consent, since only pure coordination provides incentives for both parties to be transparent and thus provide the information that is the basis for informed consent. In the mixed case, our model predicts that Sellers will avoid a transparent information policy or providing any clarity on this matter. Here is a suggestion that suppressing the information needed for informed consent is widespread in some industries:

Wang Jianzhou, the chief executive of China Mobile, the world's largest mobile phone company ranked by the number subscribers, ... told a room full of politicians and business leaders what everybody knows, but generally do not say in a sort of code of silence by the phone companies: 'We know who you are, but also where you are,' Wang was quoted as saying about location-based advertising. In doing so, he broke an unwritten rule of operators in Western markets not to discuss openly how much information they collect (Sylvers, 2008).

(Whitaker, 1999, p. 136f.) makes the important point that corporate data base operators have no incentive to discover or correct errors about individuals: "The result is a kind of social triage."

Generally there is the problem that a cheap and efficient technology like data mining transforms social relations very quickly, making it difficult to update even our conceptual models, not to say regulations. Data mining does not just effect existing marketing practices, but allows whole new activities to be converted into marketing. For example, "enrollment management" enabled by data mining technology increasingly structures recruiting to many U.S. colleges and universities.

[A]dvanced financial-aid leveraging goes beyond general categories to forecast how much each student is willing to pay, and guarantee the best class at the lowest price. Schools and consultants combine test scores, grades, and class rankings from the testing services and students' high schools with demographic and financial data purchased from a credit-reporting agency such as Equifax. All this information is eventually reduced to the seven or eight variables that best predict a student's responsiveness to price" (Quirk, 2005).

CONCLUSION

Our main ethical recommendation can be summarized: so-called "data subjects" should become agents in the process of data mining personal information. Agents make their own choices, based on their mental models and shared norms classifying the situations they encounter. This is a turn away from models of technology as determining that people be treated as data subjects or focused on the data users as the sole or main agents. Agents need to be aware of the salient features of the main types of situation they encounter, as each calls for a distinct ethical response. We offer our three model situations as serviceable heuristic guides to a complex landscape.

Our models have some advantages compared to the metaphors we hope they will replace. First, compared to "Big Brother" they remind us of the range of interactions, players, and problems, decoupling the growth of information technology and the growth of social discipline by the political state. Second, in place of rigid metaphors, our models provide a toolkit of templates that can be combined to account for more complex situations. For example, while attempting to cooperate by sharing information with one's physician, one needs to be aware that hackers have opposed interest, and are in conflict with both of you. Similarly, the rapid growth of markets for minable personal information places new moral hazards on the path to cooperation, as commercial firms sell

one's transaction information to distant "partners" who allow them to use it to one's disadvantage in trade.

Second, our models can be translated into rough heuristics to help agents make better choices. Reviewing our results in terms of information restriction we recommend to agents:

One should default to extreme caution, assuming a situation of conflicting interests, where revealing personal information risks harmful outcomes, until and unless one has good reasons to expect a more cooperative situation. This is not a council of paranoia; one should treat the Internet, for example, with the same caution one would bring to a strange city as a tourist. Conflict situations are not all out war, but they remind us to lower our expectations of ethical behavior from random others.

Even where cooperation is an option, one should demand transparency as a condition of explicitly consenting to limited release of personal information. This follows from the incentives to conceal data extraction that the model of cooperation reveals. Knowing that these incentives exist, and how easily one can reveal too much information, which cannot be easily corrected or retracted, caution is advised.

Release of personal information to trusted agents should be explicitly limited by the terms of the trusted relation. Trust is a valuable but limited social good; one should not expect trust to extend beyond concrete relations. Thus skepticism about entrusting health records to new systems is warranted in both the case of the U.K.'s "NHS spine", for technical reasons, and with Personal Health Record systems that shift from regulated to un-regulated record holders.

If we act and regulate around rules like this, we give incentives to move data mining to a more cooperative, consented, and thus ethical and sustainable basis.

ACKNOWLEDGMENT

This research is supported in part by a grant from the Social Science and Humanities Research Council of Canada on Modeling Ethical Mechanisms. The analysis in this chapter was first developed in (Danielson, 2005) from which some material is taken. Thanks to the anonymous referee whose comments improved this chapter.

REFERENCES

23andme.com. Consent and legal agreement. Retrieved Feb 18, 2008, from https://www.23andme.com/about/consent/

Abraham, C. (2008). Click here to unlock your DNA code. *The Globe and Mail.*

Binmore, K. (2004). *Natural Justice.* Cambridge, Mass.: MIT Press.

Brandt, A. M. (1987). *No magic bullet: A social history of venereal disease in the United States since 1880* (Expanded ed.). New York: Oxford University Press.

Buchanen, A. (1996). Toward a Theory of the Ethics of Bureaucratic Organizations. Business Ethics Quarterly, 6(4), 419 - 440.

Carvel, J. (2007). Family doctors to shun national database of patients' records. *The Guardian*, Nov. 20 2007.

Chaplin, C., Goddard, P., Bergman, H., Sandford, S., Conklin, C., Mann, H. et al. (1992). *Modern times* ([Version with additional material] ed.). United States: CBS-Fox Video.

Clarke, R. (1988). Information Technology and Dataveillance. *Communications of the Association for Computing Machinery, 31*(5), 498-512.

Danielson, P. (1992). *Artificial morality: Virtuous robots for virtual games.* London: Routledge.

Danielson, P. (2002). Video Surveillance for the Rest of Us: Proliferation, Privacy, and Ethics Education. *Paper presented at the 2002 International Symposium on Technology and Society (ISTAS'02).*

Danielson, P. (2005). Ethics of Workplace Surveillance Games. In J. Weckert (Ed.), *Electronic Monitoring in the Workplace: Controversies and Solutions.* (pp. 19 - 34). Hershey PA: Idea Group Publishing.

Gellman, R. (2008). Personal Health Records: Why Many PHRs Threaten Privacy. Retrieved 23 Feb, 2008, from http://www.worldprivacyforum.org/pdf/WPF_PHR_02_20_2008fs.pdf

Goetz, T. (2007). 23AndMe Will Decode Your DNA for $1,000. Welcome to the Age of Genomics. *WIRED, 15*(12).

Judt, T. (2005). *Postwar: A History of Europe since 1945.* New York: Penguin Press.

Kollock, P. (1998). Transforming Social Dilemmas: Group Identity and Co-operation. In P. Danielson (Ed.), *Modeling Rationality, Morality, and Evolution 7.* New York: Oxford University Press.

Marx, G. T., & Reichman, N. (1984). Routinizing the Discovery of Secrets: Computers as Informants. *American Behavioral Scientist, 27,* 423 - 452.

Norman, D. A. (2005). *Emotional Design: Why We Love (or Hate) Everyday Things.* Basic Books.

O'Harrow, R. (2006). *No Place to Hide.* Free Press.

Orwell, G. (1949). *Nineteen eighty-four, a novel.* New York: Harcourt Brace.

Priest, L. (2008). Your medical chart, just a mouse click away. *The Globe and Mail*, p. 6.

Quirk, M. (2005). The Best Class Money Can Buy. *The Atlantic, 17.*

Rawls, J. (1971). *A Theory of Justice.* Cambridge Mass: Harvard University Press.

Rennie, S. (2008). Day tried four times to get Arar off U.S. no-fly list. *The Globe and Mail*, p. A8.

Skyrms, B. (2003). *The Stag Hunt and the Evolution of Social Structure.* Cambridge ; New York: Cambridge University Press.

Solove, D. J. (2001, July). Privacy and Power: Computer Databases and Metaphors for Information Privacy. *Stanford Law Review, 53*, 1393-1462.

Sylvers, E. (2008). Privacy on hold in cellphone business. *International Herald Tribune.*

Turow, J., Feldman, L., & Meltzer, K. (2005). Open to Exploitation: American Shoppers Online and Offline. Retrieved Jan 30, 2008, from http://www.annenbergpublicpolicycenter.org/04_info_society/Turow_APPC_Report_WEB_FINAL.pdf

van Wel, L., & Royakkers, L. (2004). Ethical issues in Web data mining. *Ethics and Information Technology, 6*(2), 129 - 140.

Wahlstrom, K., & Roddick, J. F. (2001). *On the Impact of Knowledge Discovery and Data Mining.* Canberra.

Weeks, C. (2007, September 24). *Army of little brothers as bad as Big Brother: Privacy czar Technology turning citizens into unintended spies, federal commissioner warns ahead of conference.* Edmonton Journal.

Whitaker, R. (1999). *The end of privacy: How total surveillance is becoming a reality.* New York: New Press.

KEY TERMS

Data Mining: "The non-trivial extraction of implicit, previously unknown and potentially useful information from data. These tools use knowledge-based machine learning and statistics over very large databases to reveal interesting nuggets of information." (Wahlstrom & Roddick, 2001) ("In KDD jargon, data mining is just one step in the entire process. The term, 'data mining,' however is often used to refer to the whole process" (van Wel & Royakkers, 2004, p. 129).

Data Subject: The model of a person created out of data extracted from data bases.

Dataveillance: "The systematic use of personal data systems in the investigation or monitoring of the actions or communications of one or more persons." (Clarke, 1988)'s term for the broad area that includes data mining.

Digital Dossier: Another term for the data subject.

Identity Theft: Using another person's credentials for fraudulent purposes.

Knowledge Discovery in Databases (KDD): "The process of extracting previously unknown information from (usually large quantities of) data, which can, in the right context, lead to knowledge" (van Wel & Royakkers, 2004, p. 129).

Phishing: Attempting to fraudulently obtain personal information by communication masquerading as a trusted institution.

Chapter IV
Information Privacy and Security for e–CRM

Jerry Fjermestad
New Jersey Institute of Technology, USA

Nicholas C. Romano, Jr.
Oklahoma State University, USA

ABSTRACT

This chapter presents a value exchange model of privacy and security for electronic customer relationship management within an electronic commerce environment. Enterprises and customers must carefully manage these new virtual relationships in order to ensure that they both derive value from them and minimize unintended consequences that result from the concomitant exchange of personal information that occurs in e-commerce. Based upon a customer's requirements of privacy and an enterprise requirement to establish markets and sell goods and services, there is a value exchange relationship. The model is an integration of the customer sphere of privacy, sphere of security and privacy/security sphere of implementation.

INTRODUCTION

New technologies have fostered a shift from a transaction-based economy through an Electronic Data Interchange (EDI) informational-exchange economy to relationship-based Electronic Commerce (EC) one (Keen 1999.) We have moved from "*first order*" *transactional* value exchanges through "*second-order*" *informational* value exchanges to "*third-order*" *relational* value exchanges (Widmeyer 2004.) Three important types of EC relationships have been identified: between enterprises and customers (B2C); between enterprises (B2B); and between customers (C2C) (Kalakota 1996.). Additional relationships between Governments (G2G), enterprises (G2B) and customers (G2C) have become more important as EC and e-government have matured and legislation, regulation and oversight have increased (Friel 2004; Reddick 2004); however these are not the focus of this paper. Relational value exchanges have become central to success and competitive advantage in B2C EC and it here that we focus on privacy and security in the age of virtual relationships.

Both enterprises and customers must carefully manage these new virtual relationships to ensure that they derive value from them and to minimize the possible unintended negative consequences that result from the concomitant exchange of personal information that occurs when goods are services are purchased through EC. The need to manage these relationships has resulted in the development of Electronic Customer Relationship Management (eCRM) systems and processes (Romano and Fjermestad 2001-2002). eCRM is used for different reasons by enterprises and customers. It is important to understand how and why both of the players participate in *relational value exchanges*" that accompany the economic transaction and informational value exchanges of EC.

Enterprises use eCRM to establish and maintain *intimate virtual relationships* with their *economically valuable* customers to derive additional value beyond that which results from economic value exchanges to improve return-on-investment from customer relationships.

Customers obtain goods, services and information (economic value) through EC for purposes such as convenience, increased selection and reduced costs. EC requires customers to reveal personal information to organizations in order for transactions to be completed. The exchange of information between customers and organizations leads to the possibility of privacy violations perpetrated against the customer and the responsibility for organizations to provide privacy policies and security measures that will engender customer trust.

In this paper we present a series of models *"sphere of privacy model," "sphere of security*

model," "privacy/security sphere of implementation model,"* and then integrate them into the *"relational value exchange model*" to explain privacy and security in the context of eCRM from the perspective of both customers and enterprises to provide guidance for future research and practice in this important area. It is important for both customers and firms to understand each others' vested interests in terms of privacy and security and to establish and maintain policies and measures that ensure both are satisfactorily implemented to minimize damage in terms of unintended consequences associated with security breaches that violate privacy and lead to relationship breakdowns.

The reminder of this paper is structured as follows: First, we explain why privacy and security are critically important issues for companies and customers that engage in EC and the consequences that can result from failure to recognize their importance or poor implementation of measures to ensure both for the organization and its customers. Second, we define privacy and security and their interrelationship in the context of CRM. Third, we present our relational value exchange model for privacy and security in eCRM; next, we discuss

Customer Relationship Management Privacy and Security: Who Cares?

"The data contained within a CRM application is often a company's most critical asset, yet because of the pivotal role this information plays in day-to-day business activities, it is also often the most vulnerable to security breaches and disruptions." (Seitz 2006)

Before we explain and define privacy and security in detail and our models and the relational value exchange model we will describe the costs associated with failure to understand these concepts and failure to effectively ensure that both are protected in terms that firms and customers can understand: dollars and lost customers.

Economic Cost of Customer Security Breaches

The economic cost of security breaches, that is the release or loss of customers personal information, has been studied in a number of surveys over the past decade and while some studies show declines in the total and average losses over time the costs are still staggering for many firms and new threats and vulnerabilities have arisen in the recent past and these lower costs are most likely offset by increased expenditures to implement security measures and training.

The Computer Security Institute (CSI) and the Federal Bureau of Investigation (FBI) have conducted eleven annual surveys of computer crime and security since 1995. Some of the results of the last seven are presented (Power 2002; Richardson 2003; Gordon, et al. 2004; Gordon, et al. 2005; Gordon, et al. 2006). The Ponemon Institute also conducted two surveys on the costs and effects of data security breaches (Ponemon 2005a; Ponemon 2005b) and we will also present a portion of their results as well.

The CSI/FBI surveys have tracked the costs (losses) associated with security breaches for thirteen years; we focus on summary data from the last seven years to illustrate trends and changes in the economic costs of security breaches for organizations that responded with loss data. Table 1 reveals some interesting aspects about security breach costs over the past seven years. Several types of costs have been reported across all the years of the survey, these include: theft of proprietary information, sabotage of data or networks, system penetration, insider abuse of network access, financial fraud, denial of service, viruses, unauthorized insider access, telecom fraud, and laptop theft.

Other types of losses were reported in early years of the period but not in later periods or were

reported in only the last three or even only the final survey in 2006; indicating that some threats have been better managed and new ones have arisen or been identified and quantified. Specifically, losses from telecom eavesdropping were reported to be on average from a high of $1.2M in 2002 to a low on $15K in 2003; however there were no reported losses in 2004, 2005 or 2006. Active wiretapping is another loss that was reported as an average of $5M in 2000 and 4325K in 2003, but not reported in any of the other years. Theft of proprietary information was reported as the highest loss for the four years from 200 to 2003; then viruses took over the top spot in 2004 and remained the highest loss IN 2005 and 2006. The results also show that between 2002 and 2003 that there is a 62% reduction in the reported losses and between 2003 and 2004 there is a 90% reduction in the losses. Thus, the enterprises are responding to the need for privacy and security. In 2004 three new loss types were reported: website defacement, misuse of a public web application, and abuse of wireless networks. All three of these losses were also reported in 2005 and 2006. Six new losses were reported in 2006: Bots (zombies) within the organization; Phishing in which your organization was fraudulently represented as sender; instant messaging misuse; password sniffing; DNS server exploitation; and a general category of other.

The time-series results reveal the dynamic nature of the security environment and the threats and costs over time as companies identify them and take actions t try to minimize or eliminate losses. Figure 1 reveals that losses from security breaches appear to be going down over time, which is a positive finding; however they do not tell the whole story because the same surveys from which the data in Table 1 are taken also found that budgets in terms of operating expenses and capitol investment for security and training and also rose at the same time.

Figure 2 shows the reported average expenditure per employee for operations, capitol investment and awareness training from 2004 to

Table 1. Average loss per year per loss type

	2000	2001	2002	2003	2004	2005	2006
Theft of proprietary info.	$ 3,032,818	$ 4,447,900	$ 6,571,000	$ 2,699,842	$ 42,602	$ 48,408	$ 19,278
Sabotage of data or networks	$ 969,577	$ 199,350	$ 541,000	$ 214,521	$ 3,238	$ 533	$ 831
Telecom eavesdropping	$ 66,080	$ 55,375	$ 1,205,000	$ 15,200			
System penetration by outsider	$ 244,965	$ 453,967	$ 226,000	$ 56,212	$ 3,351	$ 1,317	$ 2,422
Insider abuse of Net access	$ 307,524	$ 357,160	$ 536,000	$ 135,255	$ 39,409	$ 10,730	$ 5,910
Financial fraud	$ 1,646,941	$ 4,420,738	$ 4,632,000	$ 328,594	$ 28,515	$ 4,014	$ 8,169
Denial of service	$ 108,717	$ 122,389	$ 297,000	$ 1,427,028	$ 96,892	$ 11,441	$ 9,335
Virus	$ 180,092	$ 243,835	$ 283,000	$ 199,871	$ 204,661	$ 66,961	$ 50,132
Unauthorized insider access	$ 1,124,725	$ 275,636	$ 300,000	$ 31,254	$ 15,904	$ 48,878	$ 33,920
Telecom fraud	$ 212,000	$ 502,278	$ 22,000	$ 50,107	$ 14,861	$ 379	$ 4,033
Active wiretapping	$ 5,000,000	$ -	$ -	$ 352,500			
Laptop theft	$ 58,794	$ 61,881	$ 89,000	$ 47,107	$ 25,035	$ 6,428	$ 21,223
Web site defacement					$ 3,562	$ 180	$ 519
Misuse of public web application					$ 10,212	$ 3,486	$ 861
Abuse of wireless network					$ 37,767	$ 852	$ 1,498
Bots (zombies) within the organization							$ 2,951
Phishing in which your organization was fraudulently represented as sender							$ 2,069
instant messaging misuse							$ 931
password sniffing							$ 515
DNS server exploitation							$ 288
Other							$ 2,827
Totals	$12,886,153	$10,688,458	$14,702,000	$5,557,491	$438,809	$203,661	$167712

(Data from (Power 2002; Richardson 2003; Gordon, et al. 2004; Gordon, et al. 2005; Gordon, et al. 2006)

Figure 1. Total reported losses per year across 7 CSI/FBI surveys

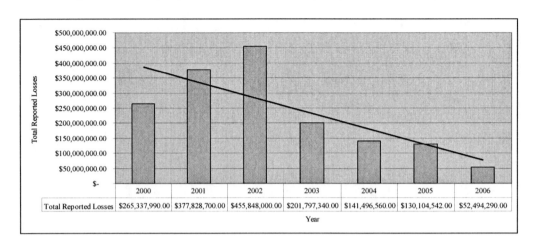

(Data from (Power 2002; Richardson 2003; Gordon, et al. 2004; Gordon, et al. 2005; Gordon, et al. 2006))

2006 for four different sized companies based on reported revenues. It is important to keep in mind that these are *average* expenditures *per employee* and so for any given company the total outlay would be calculated by multiplying the number of employees in the organization by their actual expenditures, which could be higher or lower than the average.

This time series of expenditures for security reveals interesting trends as well. One is that there appear to be economies of scale for security measures, that is organizations with higher revenue seem to have smaller expenditures per employee (Gordon et al., 2006), but that may not translate into smaller overall expenditures. A second similar trend is that lower revenue firms seem to have had increases in security expenditures while higher revenue firms have seen decreases. Regardless of these trends the reduction in losses due to security breaches and attacks have been accompanied by increased investment in security software, hardware and training; therefore it is logical to conclude that either through losses or through increased defense expenditures security continues to have a large economic impact on

firms. Finally it also reveals that in 2006 firms began to spend funds for security awareness training that were not reported in the previous years of the CSI/FBI surveys.

In November 2005 The Ponemon Institute (Ponemon 2005a) surveyed the costs incurred by 14 firms in 11 different industries that experienced security breaches. The size of the breaches in terms of customer records ranged from 900,000 to 1,500 for a total of 1,395,340 records and an average of 99,667 per breach.

Table 2 summarizes total average cost (including direct, indirect, and opportunity costs) for all 14 firms. The average total cost per company was $13,795,000 or $138 per lost customer record. These 14 firms had total losses of $193,103,545.

The economic cost of security breaches is still a staggering amount of money. Many enterprises have been able to reduce the losses by expending large amounts of resources. However, as shown in Table 1, new threats and vulnerabilities are being unleashed on enterprises every year. The lower costs are most likely offset by increased expenditures to implement new security measures and training. These economic costs are only

Figure 2. Reported average expenditure per employee

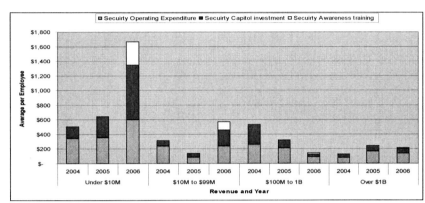

(Data from (Power 2002; Richardson 2003; Gordon, et al. 2004; Gordon, et al. 2005; Gordon, et al. 2006)

Table 2. Costs of security breaches for 14 firms in 2005

	Direct Costs	**Indirect Costs**	**Lost Customer costs**	**Total Costs**
Total Cost for all companies	$49,840,593	$123,262,952	(factored into indirect costs)	$193,103,545
Average Cost Per Company	$4,990,000	$1,347,000	$7,458,000	$13,795,000
Average Cost Per Lost Record	$50	$14	$75	$138

(Data from (Ponemon 2005a))

part of the story; because there are also costs associated with lost customers and opportunity costs associated with potential customers going elsewhere due the security breach publicity. The next section discusses losses in these less tangible, but critically important areas.

Cost of Security Breaches in Terms of Lost Customers

The Ponemon (2005a) survey found that security breaches have potentially severe costs to organizations in terms of lost customers and decreased customer trust in the organizations' ability to secure data and maintain the levels of privacy and confidentiality that customers expect. Ponemon also found that roughly 86% of security breaches involved loss or theft of customer information.

Ponemon (2005b) in "The National Survey on Data Security Breach Notification" polled 9,154 adult-aged respondents in all major US regions and found that "*Damage to corporate reputation, corporate brand, and customer retention was very high among affected individuals*":

- 1,109 (11.6%) reported that an organization had communicated to them a loss or theft of their personal information.
- Upon receipt of a notification of a breach nearly 20% of respondents reported that they had terminated their relationship with the firm.
- 40% of those that received notification reported they might terminate the relationship due to the breach.
- 58% reported that they believed that the breach had lowered their confidence and trust in the organization that reported it.
- 92% of respondents blamed the company that notified them for the breach.
- Only 14% of respondents that were notified of a breach were not concerned.
- Greater than 85% of all respondents reported they were concerned or very concerned about the effect a data breach would have on them.

Furthermore, the National Survey on Data Security Breach Notification (Ponemon 2005b) reported that the majority of respondents were not satisfied with the quality of the notification and communication processes. This is where CRM becomes important and how enterprises communicate security breaches to their customers has an impact. The survey highlighted the following communication experiences:

- Companies that reported breaches to consumers were more than four times (417%) as likely to experience customer churn if they **failed** to communicate to the victim in a clear, consistent and timely fashion.
- Companies that sent e-mails or form letters to communicate a breach of consumer data were more than three times (326%) as likely to experience customer churn than companies that used telephone or personalized letters (or a combination of both).

- Over 82% of respondents believed that it is always necessary for an organization to report a breach even if the lost or stolen data was encrypted, or there was no criminal intent. The type of information involved in the breach was also not a factor.
- About 59% of respondents do not have confidence in U.S. state or federal regulations to protect the public from data security breaches by organizations.

The high cost of security breaches comes from efforts to prevent them and the cost of the aftermath of a breach. Customers appear to be more likely to terminate their relationship with an enterprise after a security breach. In addition, the timeliness and manner in which a breach notification is delivered is important. It appears that telephone calls immediately after (or at least before a public discloser) followed up with a personal letter is best to maintain trust and manage the relationship with the customer. Customers are concerned about protecting their privacy and identity and they expect companies to be vigilant in securing any data they share. In the next two sections we discuss and define both privacy and security within the context of EC and eCRM.

PRIVACY DEFINED

The concept of privacy dates back into antiquity: for example Aristotle (384–327 BCE) made explicit distinctions between a public sphere and political life 'πολιχ' (*polis, city*) and one's private sphere or family life 'οικοχ' (*oikos, home) that refers to a separate private domain (Roy 1999; Rykwert 2001; DeCew 2002).*

DeCew (2002) explains that privacy does not have a single shared definition:

"The term 'privacy' is used frequently in ordinary language as well as in philosophical, political and

legal discussions, yet there is no single definition or analysis or meaning of the term. The concept of privacy has broad historical roots in sociological and anthropological discussions about how extensively it is valued and preserved in various cultures. Moreover, the concept has historical origins in well known philosophical discussions, most notably Aristotle's distinction between the public sphere of political activity and the private sphere associated with family and domestic life. Yet historical use of the term is not uniform, and there remains confusion over the meaning, value and scope of the concept of privacy."

DeCew (2002) further explains that there are several specific types or meanings of privacy that include control of information, Human dignity (individual dignity and integrity, personal autonomy and independence), degrees of intimacy, social relationships, and unwanted access by others. Each of these conceptualizations of privacy is important and meaningful; however within the scope of this paper, and information systems (IS) research and practice in general and EC specifically we adopt the concept of '*informational privacy*' (DeCew 2002). Privacy is an important issue for EC because new technologies have enabled personal information to be communicated in ways that were not possible in earlier time periods. Next we discuss the historical background of informational privacy and define privacy within the scope of this chapter.

Informational Privacy

Warren and Brandeis (*later Supreme Court Justice Brandeis*) (Warren and Brandeis) in their well known essay *"The Right to Privacy"* cited *"political, social, and economic changes"* and recognized *"the right to be let alone"* to argue that extent law at the time did afford for protection of individual privacy. In 1890 technologies such as newspapers, photography and others had led to privacy invasions through dissemination

of details of peoples' private lives (Warren and Brandeis 1890). They argued that the right to privacy is based on the general principle of *"the right to one's personality"* and the more specific principle of *"inviolate personality"* (Warren and Brandeis 1890).

They asserted that the privacy principle was a part of the common law and the protection of a *"man's house as his castle;"* however they also argued that new technologies had changed how private information was disseminated and thus required recognition of a separate and explicit protection of individual privacy (Warren and Brandeis 1890). Their essay laid the foundation for what would become the idea of privacy as a person's control over information about themselves.

Two theories of privacy have stood the test of time and also have figured prominently in major privacy reviews in the 1970s, 1980's and 1990s (Margulis 2003): Westin's (1967) four states and four functions of privacy and Altman's five properties of privacy. We focus here on Westin's theory.

Westin (1967) defined four states of privacy; that is how privacy is achieved (Margulis 2003):

1. **Solitude:** An individual separated from the group and freed from the observation of other persons.
2. **Intimacy:** An individual as part of a small unit.
3. **Anonymity:** An individual in public but still seeks and finds freedom from identification and surveillance.
4. **Reserve:** Based on a desire to limit disclosures to others; it requires others to recognize and respect that desire.

and four functions (purposes) privacy; that is why one seeks privacy (Margulis 2003):

1. **Personal autonomy:** desire to avoid being manipulated, dominated, or exposed by

others or Control over when information is made public

2. **Emotional release** release from the tensions of social life such as role demands, emotional states, minor deviances, and the management of losses and of bodily functions. Privacy, whether alone or with supportive others, provides the "time out" from social demands, hence opportunities for emotional release.

3. **Self-evaluation:** integrating experience into meaningful patterns and exerting individuality on events. It includes processing information, supporting the planning process (e.g., the timing of disclosures), integrating experiences, and allowing moral and religious contemplation.

4. **Limited and protected communication:** Limited communication sets interpersonal boundaries; protected communication provides for sharing personal information with trusted others.

Westin's (1967)definition is the one that we adopt for this paper and we think is the one that should be adopted by IS researchers and practitioners as well as EC customers:

"Privacy is the claim of individuals, groups or institutions to determine for themselves when, how, and to what extent information about them is communicated to others."

Westin (1967) also pointed out that privacy is not an absolute but that:

"Each individual is continually engaged in a personal adjustment process in which he balances the desire for privacy with the desire for disclosure and communication...."

With this definition in mind we again turn to recent surveys of consumers and businesses to gain an understanding of how security breaches that violate privacy are perceived and handled. Ackerman et al. (1999) surveyed consumers to learn how comfortable they were with providing different types on personal information with businesses; while Ponemon (2005b) gathered data on actual breaches. Table 3 illustrates that data from the Ackerman, et al. (1999) survey of consumer concerns and the Ponemon (2005b) survey of actual data breaches reveals that there may be a mismatch in terms of what information consumers would prefer not to have revealed and what has actually been lost or stolen. Ponemon (2005b) surprisingly found that some of the more sensitive information that consumers are most reticent to reveal and that could result in the most damage are the ones that are most often released.

Only 1% of consumers surveyed were comfortable always or usually providing information their Social security numbers (Ackerman, et al. 1999), yet 38% of all breaches reported in another survey involved SSNs (Ponemon 2005b). Similar types of mismatches can be seen for several other data types in Table 3. These results illustrate that companies may not secure the types of personal information that consumers are most concerned about well enough (SSNs, credit Card Numbers and Home Telephone) and may place to much emphasis on the security of information that consumers are more willing to share (i.e. email addresses and mailing addresses.) This leads us to question whether firms take into consideration the privacy expectations of consumers when they decide how to protect different types of data. We think that firms should take consumer expectations and willingness to reveal information into account when establishing security measures to protect different types of information as this would focus resources in such a way as to engender trust from the consumer and also to minimize potential losses due to breaches.

Figure 3 presents our model of the Personal "Sphere of privacy" based on Ackerman's findings that illustrates how firms might establish levels of security that are consonant with both consumer

Table 3. Comparison of actual data types released and consumer concern

Data Type	Data released	Consumer Comfort Level
Name	54%	54%
SSN	38%	1%
Credit Card Number	37%	3%
Home Telephone	36%	11%
Mailing address	23%	44%
E-mail Addresses	10%	76%

Data from (Ackerman, et al 1999) and (Ponemon 2005b)

willingness (comfort) to reveal information and also with the potential amount of damage that could occur from a breach of specific types of customer information.

We argue that firms should be most vigilant in securing information that consumers would most like to protect and should establish levels or zones of security of different strengths. Later in the paper we will tie this model to security strategies and technology implications.

Based on Ackerman et al (1999) and Ponemon's (2005b) data (see Table 3) it is clear the consumers want their SSNs, credit card numbers and telephone numbers kept private. In other words consumers place maximum value on these data items in contrast to their mailing address and their email address. Enterprises need to be sure and recognize what information is critical so as to protect it and ensure business continuity (Gordon and Loeb, 2002).

This leads us to the next section on security. Security is the technology and policies that an enterprise and consumer have to keep their valuable information secure.

SECURITY

Security breaches affect most enterprises and government agencies. A recent survey reports

that 84% of all enterprises will be affected by a security breach, which is a 17% increase over the last three years (2004-2006) (Ferguson 2006). Those enterprises and government agencies in the survey reported that when a security breach happened 54 percent lost productivity, 20 percent reported lost revenue and 25 percent claimed to have suffered some sort of public backlash with either damage to their reputation or loss of customer trust. Thirty-eight percent of these organizations reported that the breach was internal. Furthermore, according to the survey many of them did not take the issue seriously enough. Only one percent of those surveyed thought IT security spending was too high, while 38 percent said it was much too low (Ferguson, 2006). The results suggest that even though organizations are investing in security technologies, they still aren't achieving the results they seek.

Security Defined

The term security can be used in reference to crime and accidents of all kinds. Security is a vast topic including security of countries against terrorist attack, security of computers against hackers, home security against burglars and other intruders, financial security against economic collapse and many other related situations.

Figure 3. Model of the customer "Sphere of Privacy"

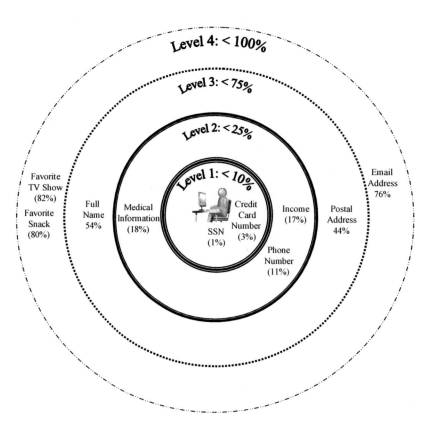

(Data from (Ackerman, et al. 1999))

Following are four definitions that provide a narrower focus:

1. **Security:** A very general term covering everything.

2. **Computer Security:** The discipline that helps free us from worrying about our computers."(Landwehr 2001) Computer security is the effort to create a secure computing platform, designed so that agents (users or programs) can only perform actions that have been allowed. This involves specifying and implementing a security policy. The actions in question can be re-

duced to operations of access, modification and deletion. Computer security can be seen as a subfield of security engineering, which looks at broader security issues in addition to computer security.

3. **Information Security:** Is the protection of information systems against unauthorized access to or modification of information whether in storage, processing, or transit, and against denial of service to authorized users, including those measures necessary to detect, document, and counter such threats. (**NSTISSC** 1999) IS Security has previously concentrated on confidentiality

of information stored electronically. The rapid growth in the volume of such information and the uptake of E-commerce within organizations have heightened the need for increased security to protect the privacy of this information and prevent fraudulent activities (Spinellis, et al. 1999)

4. **Data Security:** The most important part of security- securing the data from unauthorized use.

From the point of view of eCRM the above definitions do not help us much. In the section on privacy information such as SSN and credit card numbers were more critical to consumers than an email address. Thus, we need to look at the security components.

Security Components

A recent meta-analysis of critical themes in electronic commerce research by Wareham et al.(Wareham, et al. 2005) identified security as an underserved area in IS Research. They suggest and support Gordon and Loeb's (2002) assertion that information is an asset of value to an organization and consequently needs to be suitably protected in order to ensure business continuity, minimize business damage, maximize ROIs, and business opportunities (BSI 1999). The purpose of information security could be characterized as the preservation of confidentiality, integrity and availability for information asset to keep business value (BSI 1999; Sheth, et al. 2000; Gordon and Loeb 2002) Then, in general, IS security is the effective implementation of policies to ensure the confidentiality, availability, and integrity of information and assets to protect from theft, tampering, manipulation, or corruption. (Smith and Jamieson 2006) This also follows from the ISO 1799 Information Security Standard (ISO/IEC 2005).

The ISO 17799 standard is an internationally recognized information security management guidance standard (ISO/IEC 2005), ISO 17799 is high level, broad in scope, and conceptual in nature. This approach allows it to be applied across multiple types of enterprises and applications. It has also made the standard controversial among those who believe standards should be more precise. In spite of this controversy, ISO 17799 is the only "standard" devoted to Information Security Management in a field generally governed by "Guidelines" and "Best Practices." (ISO/IEC 2005)

ISO 17799 defines information as an asset that may exist in many forms and has value to an organization. Thus, the goal of information security is to suitably protect this asset in order to ensure business continuity, minimize business damage, and maximize return on investments. The objective of the standard is to safe guard:

- **Confidentiality:** ensuring that information is accessible only to those authorized to have access.
- **Integrity:** safeguarding the accuracy and completeness of information and processing methods.
- **Availability:** ensuring that authorized users have access to information and associated assets when required.

Thus, our basic definition of security in the e-commerce environment is the necessary hardware, software, network controls, data encryption, policies and procedures in place for an enterprise to ensure that a consumer's information is confidential, has integrity and is available for use, e-commerce use.

Enterprise and Consumer Views of Security

Enterprises ands the consumers will view the security components some what differently. Table 4 shows the enterprise and the consumer view. For confidentiality, both the enterprise and consumer expect the security features to prevent unauthorized access to the data. For integrity the enterprise must use the data supplied by the consumer only for business purposes and must not sell or release the personal data to other enterprises without authorization from the consumer. It us the consumers obligation to assure that the data is correct. For availability it is the enterprises responsibility to assure that the data is available for the consumer and for e-commerce. From the consumers point of view the data need to be available for modification (i.e. change of address, change of preferences).

IS Security has previously concentrated on confidentiality of information stored electronically. The rapid growth in the volume of such information and the uptake of E-commerce within organizations have heightened the need for increased security to protect the privacy of this information and prevent fraudulent activities (Spinellis, et al. 1999)

Computer security is the effort to create a secure computing platform, designed so that agents (users or programs) can only perform actions that have been allowed. This involves specifying and implementing a security policy. The actions in question can be reduced to operations of access, modification and deletion. Computer security can be seen as a subfield of security engineering, which looks at broader security issues in addition to computer security.

Security Threats and Vulnerabilities

Table 5 highlights the major threats and vulnerabilities of enterprise networks and consumer use. Threats are any type of unwanted or unauthorized intrusions, attach , or exploit on to the system (Volonino and Robinson 2004). Vulnerabilities are two fold: from the consumer point of view - human error- using poor passwords, participating in chat rooms; from the enterprise side- is the complexity of the software which results in misconfigurations, programming errors, or other flaws. The major internet security breaches are (Volonino and Robinson 2004):

In a recent trade press chapter (August 29, 2006), AT&T revealed (Preimesberger 2006) that an undisclosed number of unauthorized persons had illegally hacked into one of its computer systems and accessed the personal data, including credit card information, of about 19,000 customers who had purchased DSL equipment through the company's online store. The unauthorized electronic access took place over the weekend of Aug. 26-27, 2006 and was discovered within hours, according to a company spokesperson. The electronic store was shut down immediately and remained offline as we write this paper. The cost of this security breach has not been disclosed, however, the company is also working with law enforcement to investigate the incident and pursue the perpetrators. The

Table 4. Security components

Security Components	Enterprise/Organization	Consumers
Confidentiality	Prevent unauthorized access Secure all personal information	Prevent unauthorized access How my data is being protected
Integrity	Data used for only business purposes Data not sold without authorization	Data is correct
Availability	Data available for customer Data available for e-commerce	Data available for modification

Table 5. Security threats and vulnerabilities

Internal Threats		External Threats	
Organizations	Consumers	Organizations	Consumers
• Illness of personnel • Temporary staff • Loss of key personnel • Loss of network service • Disgruntled employees • Disgruntled consultants • Labor dispute • Malware • Software bugs	• User misuse • Malware • Software bugs • Poor passwords • Chat room participation	• Severe storms • Utility outage • Natural disasters • Theft of hardware • Software compromise • Hackers • Adversaries	• Severe storms • Utility outage • Natural disasters • Unauthorized access • Unauthorized sale • Theft of computer • Hackers • Denial of service

19,000 customers are being notified by e-mail, phone calls and letters. Furthermore, AT&T intends to pay for credit monitoring services for customers whose accounts have been impacted. Clearly breaches are still occurring, even to the largest companies that we would expect would have adequate security in place.

Security: No More than Managing Risk

Gordon and Loeb (2002) suggest that the optimal amount to spend on information security is an increasing function of the level of vulnerability of the information. However, the optimal amount to spend on information security does not always increase with the level of vulnerability of such information. They further suggest that managers should budget for security on information that is in a midrange of vulnerability to security breaches. Furthermore, managers may want to consider partitioning information sets into low, middle, and high levels of security breach vulnerability. Some information may be difficult to protect at a high security level and thus is best defended at a more moderate level. Their findings suggest that the optimal amount to spend on information security never exceeds 37% of the expected loss

resulting from a security breach.

Smith and Spafford (2004) also suggest that security is managing risk. In addition, they suggest that the major security challenges are:

1. Stop epidemic-style attacks
2. Build trustworthy large-scale systems
3. Make quantitative information systems risk management as good as quantitative financial risk management
4. Give end users security they can understand and privacy they can control

Kuper (2005) suggests that the sole reason that information technology exists is to leverage the critical asset of data. Thus, security is data and network integrity, the protection of and access to the data. Also, (Kuper 2005) from 2000 to 2005 enterprises have spent $15 billion on perimeter level security (antivirus, firewalls, and approximately $1.5 billion on encryption software, one of the more obvious technologies for protecting the data. This supports Gordon and Loeb (2002) assertion that the amount spent does not always match the required level of vulnerability.

Kuper (2005) suggests several new approaches to data security:

1. Data and network integrity- protecting access to data
2. Inclusion/exclusion security- trusted, known users are handled differently than unknown users (nodes)
3. Embedded security- more security into all aspects of IT components (hardware, software, or service)
4. Improved approaches- dynamic XML and web service architectures.

In this regard, enterprises need to work at the data level (using encryption) to secure the most critical data. The second element is that of trust, trusted consumers should be treated differently than unknown consumers. This is one of the objectives of CRM. Next, embedded security for the enterprise at the hardware/software and server level can help to minimize security breaches. Last, new dynamic approaches can be used.

Table 6 illustrates how privacy and security are interrelated in terms of the levels of data, security strategy and technologies required to achieve appropriate vigilance. Our model of the sphere of privacy suggests that some information is not as critical to secure (i.e. email address) while other information, consumer's SSN, is critical to secure. Kuper (2005) suggests that initially enterprises focused security at the perimeter, but as they learned from persistent attacks they moved from the edge down deeper, layer by layer, to secure the very data itself through encryption. We rename this as the Enterprise "Sphere of Security" model (See figure 4.) Different technologies are required at the different levels and the most crucial level data requires encryption to ensure that it is not released (Volonino and Robinson, 2004). At the perimeter (level 4) firewalls and malware prevention software may offer enough protection for data that is no as sensitive.

Enterprise Privacy/Security Sphere of Implementation

There is an adage that you cannot ensure privacy if you don't first have security. Thus enterprises and consumers need to be prepared for an increasingly hostile public network. Both must provide the right (and updateable) hardware control, data and software controls, and encryption controls to ensure optimal security. Both must also consider the risks, costs and possible consequences of releasing private information.

A complete solution to either the security or the privacy problem requires the following three steps which become our privacy/security sphere of implementation model:

Policy: The first step is to develop a security or privacy policy. The policy precisely defines the requirements that are to be implemented within the hardware and software of the computing system and those that are external to the computing system, including physical, personnel, and procedural controls. The policy lays down broad goals without specifying how to achieve them.

Mechanism: The security or privacy policy is made more concrete with the mechanism necessary to implement the requirements of the policy. It is important that the mechanism perform the intended functions.

Assurance: The last step deals with the assurance issue. It provides guidelines for ensuring that the mechanism meets the policy requirements with a high degree of assurance. Assurance is directly related to the effort required to subvert the mechanism. Low-assurance mechanisms are easy to implement, but also relatively easy to subvert; on the other hand, high-assurance mechanisms are notoriously difficult to implement.

Table 6. Complementarity of privacy, security, and technology

Sphere of Privacy (Ackerman , 1999)	Sphere of Security (derived from Kuper, 2005)	Technology (Volonino & Robinson, 2004)
Level 4: Email	Perimeter	Hardware/Software
Level 3: Full name	Network	Network Security
Level 2: Phone #	Application	Process & Procedures
Level 1: SSN	Data	Encryption

Figure 4. Model of the enterprise "Sphere of Security"

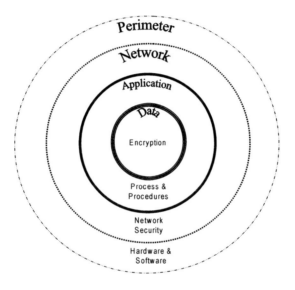

CONDITIONAL RELATIONAL "VALUE EXCHANGE" MODEL

Figure 5 illustrates customer data flow and some privacy and security issues related to eCRM. The figure shows that each customer has their own personal identity as well as personal and confidential information they may choose to share or unknowingly (unwittingly) share with online businesses with which they interact or with others that obtain the information through some other mechanism than a known direct transfer. The fig-ure illustrates both intentional and unintentional information transfer from customers to other entities. Three representative customers interact with one or more of three online businesses, as well as other players. Several different scenarios that can affect privacy and security are depicted in the figure.

Scenarios for Customer John Doe. Mr. Doe interacts with online businesses ABC.COM and PDQ.COM and reveals 'some' personally iden-tifiable information to both; but not necessarily the same information. Once this data is revealed

Figure 5. Customer dataflow and privacy and security issues

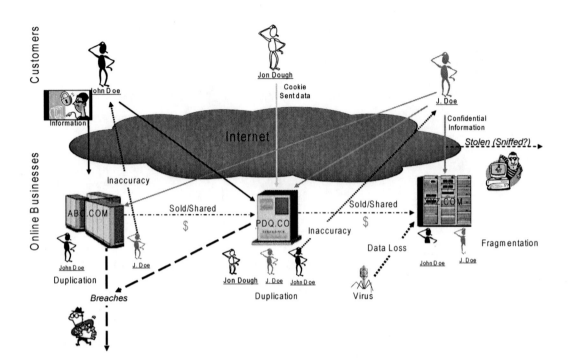

ABC.COM and PDQ.COM have a responsibility to keep it secure and accurate; however both may fail in these responsibilities. If they share or sell the information to other companies there will then be duplicate copies of the information in multiple systems, each of which has different levels of security and protection and the risk that John Doe's information may be used for purposes other than he intended increases. Additionally, duplicate copies may not be updated if Mr. Doe changes his address, email or phone number and thus inaccuracies due to redundant data that is not synchronized can and do multiply. Another possible security and privacy issue is that data from other customers with similar names to John Doe may be inaccurately associated with him;

or he may be inaccurately associated with their data. This can result in unwanted offers being sent, invalid information being released or even inaccurate information that changes the customers status and affects their credit score, ability to purchase or reputation. The complex data exchange environment and the increase in the number and types of attacks and threats makes it very hard for customers to be confident that their data will be secured and their privacy not violated.

Figures 6 and 7 present our conditional relational "value exchange" model. The basic value exchange model (Figure 6) integrates our customer sphere of privacy with our sphere of security model and the enterprise privacy/security sphere of implementation. If an enterprise is to succeed in

Figure 6. Conditional relational "Value Exchange" model

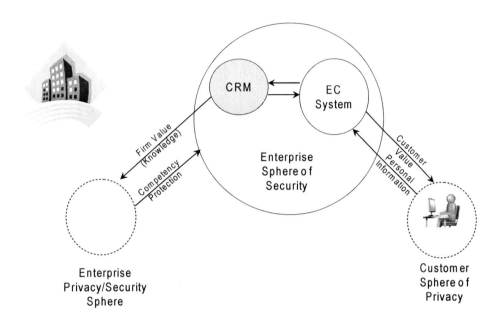

the EC environment, it must provide the necessary security to attract and retain customers. Surveys have shown that (Ackerman, et al., 1999; Ponemon, 2005a) customers will churn if they feel that there privacy has been or may be violated.

The value exchange model works through the EC system. The customer interested in obtaining information, evaluating a product or service, or even buying a product or service connects with the EC system and then provides the information that is required from their sphere of privacy. Simultaneous with the customer's inquiry or purchase (the customer's value exchange) the eCRM system is updated. This in turn becomes the enterprise's value exchange. Then based upon detailed internal and external analysis the enterprise's privacy/security policies, assurances and mechanisms should be modified.

Clearly this is a value exchange model. Prabhaker (2000) suggests that business can add

value to their EC offerings by leveraging Internet technology (the sphere of security) in coordination with proactive measures (Privacy/Security Sphere of implementation) to preserve consumer privacy (the customer sphere of privacy). This is further supported by Schoder and Madeja (2004) who suggest that eCRM built upon knowledge about their customers and their ability to serve their customers based on that knowledge has proven to be a key success factor in EC. They also suggest that the most effective way to collect customer data online is through an interactive, feature-rich environment that matches the customers' expectations of an enterprise. In other words, there should be a match between the enterprise's sphere of security and the customer's sphere of privacy.

Figure 7 is the extended value exchange model. This model adds in the interrelationships between the customers, the enterprise, the government, standards organizations, industry and society and watchdogs agencies (i.e. the Better Business Bureau BBB). This is a very complex open model. Fletcher (2003) suggests consumer backlash to perceived invasions of privacy is causing government agencies, standards organizations, industry and other watchdogs to be more proactive in developing guidelines and policies. Most major EC companies have a detailed privacy statement on their home page. For example, Amazon.com has 11 major items from "What personal information about customers does Amazon.com gather?" to "Examples of information collected. Their objective is to assure that the information that they collects from customers helps them personalize and continually improve the customer's shopping experience at Amazon.com (http:\\www.amazon.com Accessed 8/31/2006).

IMPLICATIONS FOR ENTERPRISES AND CUSTOMERS

Enterprises continue to collect more and more personal information from online transactions and are using this data to improve sales and service effectiveness (Fletcher, 2003; Romano and Fjermestad, 2003) this is eCRM in the e-commerce environment. This has become one of the most significant issues confronting enterprises in the electronic age. The issues are securing privacy and security of consumer data while using advanced information systems technology (i.e. eCRM, business intelligence, data warehousing, and data mining) to sell more goods and services to the consumer.

Consumers on the other hand want to get benefits (i.e. reduced time and reduced costs) from e-commerce, however, they are not willing to

Figure 7. Extended model with watchdogs, government, society, and standards organizations

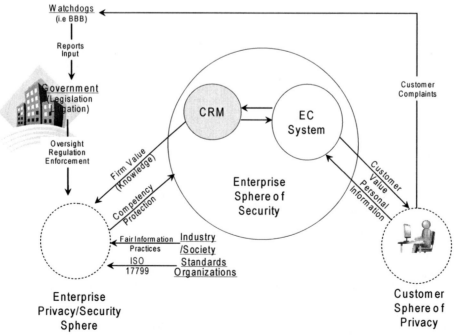

sacrifice data items such as SSN and credit card number to achieve these benefits. Consumers require the enterprises safeguard their data.

CONCLUSION AND DIRECTIONS FOR FUTURE RESEARCH

The objective of this paper was to develop an integrated value exchange model for enterprises and consumers in an e-commerce environment. Enterprises want to attract and retain economically valuable customers (Romano and Fjermestad, 2001-2002). Typically this is through eCRM. However, the prime ingredient is customer data. Thus, an enterprise must employ the right levels of privacy, security, and policy spheres to enable the continued collection and use of consumer data. Gordon and Lobe (2002) suggest that information is an asset of value to an organization and consequently needs to be suitably protected in order to ensure business continuity, minimize business damage, maximize ROIs, and business opportunities. Information security is then characterized as the preservation of confidentiality, integrity and availability of this information asset to maintain business value (BSI 1999; Sheth, et al. 2000; Gordon and Loeb 2002.) IS security is the effective implementation of policies to ensure the confidentiality, availability, and integrity of information and assets to protect it from theft, tampering, manipulation, or corruption (Smith and Jamieson 2006).

Enterprises can lose customers if they do not respond quickly enough and through the right communication channel after a security breach. Research suggests that this is best handled with personal telephone calls and follow-up personal letters (Ponemon 2005b). The use of spam e-mail will not be effective and can in fact make customers more upset due to feeling disrespected on top of their personal information being lost.

Our contributions are four-fold. First is our model of the customer sphere of privacy adapted

from Ackerman, et al.'s (1999) survey findings. This model presents the idea of levels of privacy for a consumer in terms of how willing they are to reveal personal information of different types. The highest level, level 1, corresponds to any personal information that consumers are almost never comfortable revealing, such as their Social Security Number or Credit card numbers. Consumers will not revel such information unless they fully trust the recipient. The lowest level, level 4, corresponds to personal information that many consumers are very comfortable revealing, such as their email address. These levels also correspond with the potential seriousness of consequences from the consumers' information getting into the wrong hands. Release of an SSN or Credit card number can result in identity theft or monetary losses; while release of an email address may only result in additional spam email. Both are negative consequences; but clearly the former is much more serious than the latter.

The second contribution is our enterprise sphere of security derived from Kuper's (2005) levels of security. This model represents the level of security required to support customer privacy ranging from the deepest internal data level to the externally focused perimeter level. Accompanying this model is the technology required to support it. At the perimeter level hardware and software (i.e. routers and firewalls) provide a modest level of protection; while at the data level more secure technologies such as encryption or perturbation are required to more vigilantly ensure protection of consumer privacy. The third contribution is the enterprise privacy/security sphere of implementation. These are the policies, mechanisms, and assurances to support privacy and security. Many enterprises provide such a policy statement on their website.

Our fourth contribution is the integrated value exchange model and the extended model. This model is built upon the interrelationships among the three spheres. The model proposes that both the enterprise and customer exchange information when they transact via EC. The customer exchanges personal information in order to obtain customer value (reduced time and cost, as well as the goods, services or information purchased). The enterprise gains customers and via aggregation and data mining competitive advantage from the knowledge about their customers. In order to keep their customers the enterprise must provide competent protection for the customers' information. The extended model shows that there is substantial input from industry, standards organizations, the government and other watchdog organizations.

In many case the major asset of an enterprise is its customers and data about them. There is a delicate balance (as the value exchange model illustrates) that must be maintained. The customers are only a mouse click away from an enterprise's competitors. Customers also have responsibilities to be careful and vigilant when that they must give up personal information in order to receive the benefits of EC. They must provide accurate and reliable information and also verify that a firm is trustworthy and employing adequate levels of security before revealing personal information. They should also think carefully about what information is required for a given transaction and not provide additional information that is not necessary. This can assist customers to make more informed queries and purchases and at the same time helps the enterprise market to them and to other customers more effectively through new mechanisms such a recommender systems, cross selling and preference discounts.

In the Age of ECRM Enterprises and Customers have vast new opportunities to exchange value more quickly and effectively than ever before; however along with these come new vulnerabilities and responsibilities to secure and protect privacy. Enterprises that fail to protect the privacy of their customers may find that many leave for the competition that will do so. ECRM is about establishing and maintaining intimate relationships with customers to generate additional value

and long term loyalty; enterprises cannot do this if they do not provide the security required to protect their customers' privacy at the level of vigilance they expect. It may be necessary to provide personalized levels of security for the very best customers if they demand it. Just as investors can choose the level of risk they are willing to take for a potential return on investment, consumers will also choose which firms to do business with via EC based on the level of perceived risk they associate with them. Future research and practice in Information Assurance (Security and Privacy) will have to take the consumer's perspective more into account than at present.

REFERENCES

Ackerman, M. S., Cranor, L. F., & Reagle, J. (1999). *Beyond Concern: Understanding Net Users' Attitudes About Online Privacy,* AT&T Labs. 2006, online at: http://citeseer.ist.psu.edu/cranor99beyond.html (accessed 8-31-2006).

BSI. (1999). Information Security Management – Part 1, Code of Practice for Information Security Management, BS 7799-1, BSI Group, London, UK.

DeCew, J. (2002). Privacy. The Stanford Encyclopedia of Philosophy. E. N. Zalta online at: http://plato.stanford.edu/archives/sum2002/entries/privacy/ (accessed 8-31-2006).

Ferguson, S. (2006). Study: Security Breaches Afflict Most Enterprises, Governments. *eWeek,* July 7, 2006. http://www.eweek.com/chapter2/0,1895,1986066,00.asp (accessed 8-31-2006).

Fletcher, K. (2003). Consumer power and privacy: the changing nature of CRM. *International Journal of Advertising, 22,* 249-272.

Friel, A. L. (2004). Privacy Patchwork. *Marketing Management 13*(6), 48-51.

Gordon, A. A., & Loeb, M. P. (2002). The economics of information security investment. *ACM Transactions on Information and System Security* 5(4), 438-457.

Gordon, L. A., Loeb, M. P, Lucyshyn, W., & Richardson, R. (2004). *Ninth Annual CSI/FBI Computer Crime And Security Survey.* Computer Security Institute: Online at.

Gordon, L. A., Loeb, M. P., Lucyshyn, W., & Richardson, R. (2005). *Tenth Annual CSI/FBI Computer Crime And Security Survey.* Computer Security Institute: Online at.

Gordon, L. A., Loeb, M. P., Lucyshyn, W., & Richardson, R. (2006). *Eleventh Annual CSI/FBI Computer Crime And Security Survey.* Computer Security Institute: Online at.

ISO/IEC, Ed. (2005). ISO/IEC 17799:2005 *Information technology - Security techniques - Code of practice for information security management.* International Organization for Standardization.

Kalakota, R., & Whinston, A. B. (1996). *Frontiers of Electronic Commerce*, 1st edition. New York, NY: Addison Wesley Publishing Co.

Keen, P. G. W. (1999). C*ompeting in chapter 2 of internet business: Navigating in a new world.* Delft, The Netherlands: Eburon Publishers

Kuper, P. (2005). The state of security. *IEEE Security and Privacy, 3*(5), 51-53.

Landwehr, C. E. (2001). Computer security. *International Journal of Information Security 1*(1), 3-13.

Margulis, S. T. (2003). On the Status and Contribution of Westin's and Altman's Theories of Privacy. *Journal of Social Issues, 59*(2), 411-429.

NSTISSC (1999). National Information Systems security (INFOSEC) Glossary. *National security Telecommunications and Information Systems security Committee (NSTISSC), 4.*

Ponemon, L. (2005a). Lost Customer Information: What Does a Data Breach Cost Companies? Tucson, Arizona, USA: Ponemon Institue (online at: http://www.securitymanagement.com/library/Ponemon_DataStudy0106.pdf) (accessed 8-31-2006)

Ponemon, L. (2005b). The National Survey on Data Security Breach Notification. Tucson, Arizona, USA: Ponemon Institute (online at: http://www.whitecase.com/files/Publication/bdf5cd75-ecd2-41f2-a54d-a087ea9c0029/Presentation/PublicationAttachment/2f92d91b-a565-4a07-bf68-aa21118006bb/Security_Breach_Survey%5B1%5D.pdf) (accessed 8-31-2006)

Power, R. (2002). CSI/FBI computer crime and security survey. *Computer Security Issues & Trends VIH,* (1), 1-22.

Preimesberger, C. (2006). Hackers Hit AT&T System, Get Credit Card Info. *eWeek*, August 29, 2006, http://www.eweek.com/chapter2/0,1895,2010001,00.asp?kc=EWNAVEMNL083006EOA (accessed 8-31-2006).

Reddick, C. G. (2004). A two-stage model of e-government growth: Theories and empirical evidence for U.S. cities. *Government Information Quarterly 21*(1), 51-64.

Richardson, R. (2003). Eighth Annual CSI/FBI Computer Crime And Security Survey, Computer Security Institute: Online at. http://www.reddshell.com/docs/csi_fbi_2003.pdf#search=%22Eighth%20Annual%20CSI%2FFBI%20COMPUTER%20CRIME%20AND%20SECURITY%20SURVEY%22 (accessed 8-31-2006)

Romano Jr., N. C., & Fjermestad, J. (2001-2002). Customer Relationship Management Research: An Assessment of Research. *International Journal of Electronic Commerce 6*(3 Winter)), 61-114.

Romano Jr., N. C., & Fjermestad, J. (2003). Electronic Commerce Customer Relationship

Management: A Research Agenda. *Information Technology and Management, 4*, 233-258.

Roy, J. (1999). Polis and oikos in classical Athens. *Greece & Rome, 46*(1), 1-18.

Rykwert, J. (2001). Privacy in Antiquity. *Social Research, 68*(1), 29-40.

Schoder, D., & Madeja, N. (2004). Is customer relationship management a success factor in electronic commerce? *Journal of Electronic Commerce Research, 5*(1), 38-53.

Seitz, K. (2006). Taking Steps To Ensure CRM Data Security. *Customer Inter@ction Solutions 24*(11), 62-64,66.

Sheth, J. N., Sisodia, R. S., & Sharma, S. (2000). The antecedents and consequences of customer-centric marketing. *Journal of the Academy of Marketing Science, 28*(1 Winter), 55-66.

Smith, S., & Jamieson, R. (2006). Determining Key Factors In E-Government Information System Security. *Information Systems Management, 23*(2), 23-33.

Smith, S. W., & Spafford, E. H. (2004). Grand challenges in information security: process and output. *IEEE Security and Privacy 2*(1), 69-71.

Spinellis, D., Kokolakis, D., & Gritzalis, S. (1999). Security requirements, risks and recommendations for small enterprise and home-office environments. *Information Management & Computer security, 7*(3), 121-128.

Volonino, L., & Robinson, S. R. (2004). Principles and Practice of Information Security. Upper Saddle River, NJ, USA: Pearson Prentice Hall.

Wareham, J., Zheng, J. G., & Straub, D. (2005). Critical themes in electronic commerce research: a meta-analysis. *Journal of Information Technology 20*(1), 1-19.

Warren, S., & Brandeis, L. (1890). The Right to Privacy. *Harvard Law Review, 4*(5 December), 193-220.

Westin, A. (1967). *Privacy and Freedom.* New York, NY, USA: Atheneum.

Widmeyer, G. R. (2004). The Trichotomy Of Processes: A Philosophical Basis For Information Systems. *The Australian Journal of Information Systems, 11*(1), 3-11.

KEY TERMS

e-CRM: An information system used to establish and maintain *intimate virtual relationships* with their *economically valuable* customers to derive additional value beyond that which results from economic value exchanges to improve return-on-investment from customer relationships

Information: Data items that reveal characteristics and parameters of an individual

Privacy: The right to keep certain information inaccessible to others.

Security: The protection of information systems against unauthorized access to or modification of information whether in storage, processing, or transit, and against denial of service to authorized users, including those measures necessary to detect, document, and counter such threats.

Security Breaches: Security violations with the intent to do harm.

Security Threats: Various forms of interference, capture and collections of information which can cause potential economic or personal loss.

Value Exchange: The relationship between a customer and a business where t each customer has their own personal identity as well as personal and confidential information they may choose to share or unknowingly (unwittingly) share with online businesses with which they interact or with others that obtain the information through some other mechanism than a known direct transfer.

Chapter V
Networking Serendipitous Social Encounters in Urban Neighbourhoods

Marcus Foth
Queensland University of Technology, Australia

ABSTRACT

In Australian urban residential environments and other developed countries, Internet access is on the verge of becoming a ubiquitous utility, like water or electricity. From an urban informatics perspective, this chapter discusses emerging qualities of social formations of urban residents that are based on networked individualism and the potential of Internet-based systems to support them. It proposes that appropriate opportunities and instruments that are needed to encourage and support local interaction in urban neighbourhoods. The chapter challenges the view that a mere re-appropriation of applications used to support dispersed online communities is adequate to meet the place and proximity-based design requirements that community networks in urban neighbourhoods pose. It argues that the key factors influencing the successful design and uptake of interactive systems to support social networks in urban neighbourhoods include the swarming social behaviour of urban dwellers, the dynamics of their existing communicative ecology, and the serendipitous, voluntary and place-based nature of interaction between residents on the basis of choice, like-mindedness, mutual interest, and support needs. Drawing on an analysis of these factors, the conceptual design framework of an "urban tribe incubator" is presented.

INTRODUCTION

The area of technology and human computer interaction is cross-disciplinary and requires many different academic fields and design practices to work together effectively to generate a better understanding of the social context and human factors in technology design, development and usage. This chapter focuses on the social communication aspects of this field and hopes to establish a greater awareness for the contribution community media and communication studies can make to the field of human computer interaction. It seeks to build a theoretical foundation for an analysis of two interrelated issues which are discussed in turn.

First, the importance of place and the continued purpose and relevance of urban neighbourhoods is established. New media and networked information and communication technologies have not led to the diminishment of local place and proximity. However, they have given rise to new types of social interaction and to new emerging social formations. Understanding the nature and quality of interaction in these new social formations can inform the successful animation of neighbourhood community and sociality in them.

Second, appropriate opportunities and instruments to encourage and support local interaction in urban neighbourhood networks are not limited to technology, but technology can be a key facilitator. Thus, system designers and engineers are crucial allies to social scientists in the search for hybrid methodologies that integrate community development approaches with technology design. This chapter questions whether it is sufficient to appropriate tools originally designed for dispersed online (that is, virtual) communities in the context of 'community networks' (Schuler, 1996) for urban neighbourhoods. Purpose-built tools and instruments are required that afford (a) interactive linkages between the resident's communicative ecologies of cyberspace and lo-

cal place; and (b) personalised social networking between proximate neighbours *of choice*. Such an approach would allow the non-virtual and place-based assets in a resident's portfolio of sociability to become more attractive. It would establish an opportunity to create and maintain local social ties, and ultimately to find out who is living next door and who is socially compatible.

From the discussion of these issues, some of the key factors influencing the successful design and uptake of interactive systems to support social networks in urban neighbourhoods are derived. Drawing on an analysis of these factors, the conceptual framework of an 'urban tribe incubator' is presented.

This chapter seeks to set up the interdisciplinary conceptual foundation necessary to drive a thorough theoretical and empirical investigation into the interaction of people, place and technology and the way they function together to facilitate access to the social and cultural life of cities. The purpose of this chapter is not only to introduce and illustrate the issues at stake and to present a design framework but also to stimulate transfer and exchange of knowledge across academic disciplines and especially to invite discussion and comment from a broader interdisciplinary audience. Supporting efforts to build bridges between the social and the engineering sciences is paramount to the field of technology and human interaction, and this chapter contributes to the development of a dialogue between these disciplines. An interdisciplinary approach that brings together views and expertise from sociology, urban studies, interaction design and related disciplines will assist with efforts to facilitate urban neighbourhood community building, social inclusion, public consultation and debate, fair access to local information and services, urban sustainability and stronger local economies.

TECHNICAL AFFORDANCES AND NEW SOCIAL FORMATIONS IN THE CONTEXT OF NETWORKED INDIVIDUALISM

The Internet has found its way into many households of urban dwellers in Australia and other developed countries, to the extent that Internet access is on the verge of becoming a ubiquitous utility like water, gas and electricity. The Internet has advanced to become a communication tool that co-exists with other established communication devices such as the telephone, short message service (SMS), new media and face-to-face interaction. E-mail, instant messaging, online chats and other online applications are now instrumental in establishing and maintaining social ties with family, friends, co-workers and other peers, thus creating a private 'portfolio of sociability' (Castells, 2001, p. 132).

The Internet has entered people's everyday life and plays a significant role in the communication pattern of urban residents. The Internet has not substituted but supplemented offline interaction with online interaction (Fallows, 2004; Wellman & Haythornthwaite, 2002). People still chat on the phone and meet face-to-face. However, the Internet as well as mobile communication devices such as mobile phones, laptops and personal digital assistants (PDA) allow people to maintain social ties in different ways by taking advantage of new features. The mobile phone introduced place-independent communication, and the emerging third and next generation mobile telephony adds audiovisual tele-presence. Email and SMS afford asynchronous communication and notification mechanisms. Online chats offer broadcast-style many-to-many communication, whereas private chat rooms enable users to engage in multiple peer-to-peer dialogues. Instant messaging tools combine the features of online chat rooms with ambient awareness by adding availability or other status information to a user's nickname (e.g. 'Elija | busy', 'Tim | out to lunch').

However, these tools are used more often to connect with family, friends, co-workers and peers and less with neighbours. The telephone has long evolved into a ubiquitous communication device, but it per se has not contributed to overcome 'urban alienation'. Sociologists such as Wellman (2001; 2002; Wellman *et al.*, 2003) describe how people construct their social networks with the help of the telephone and other devices. Wellman argues that while people become more accustomed with the features these tools offer, the nature of the social ties people establish and maintain changes from door-to-door and place-to-place to person-to-person and role-to-role relationships. He creates a holistic theoretical framework that builds on the dual nature in the interplay between 'community' and 'the individual'. He describes the emerging qualities of this behaviour as 'networked individualism'.

Residential areas such as apartment buildings, townhouse complexes, master-planned developments and the residents and tenants of these units form the focal point in this chapter to examine the interplay between people, place and technology. The results and findings of this theoretical analysis will help to shed light onto some aspects of the community question, especially the continued purpose and relevance of neighbourhoods in urban habitation, by investigating the ironic relationship between endemic urban alienation and the widespread use of mobile and ubiquitous communications technology by urban dwellers that allows them to interact with each other (Walmsley, 2000).

Before this technology became ubiquitous and entered the everyday life of city dwellers, predecessors and variations had been designed for (or have first become popular in) workplace-based environments to support communication and collaboration among professionals. This was later followed by their diffusion into everyday life and their re-appropriation for social use. The act of re-appropriation, e.g., from the professional use of a Pager to the social use of SMS, implies that there are opportunities to design and develop purpose-built systems from the ground up that – instead of merely trying to make ends meet – take the unique requirements into account of the social and place-based context they are used in. Tools to animate and network urban neighbourhoods require a consideration and treatment of notions of sociability, place, privacy and proximity in order to take full advantage of the communicative opportunities that this environment offers its inhabitants and the wider society.

PLACE MATTERS: COMMUNICATION AND INTERACTION IN URBAN NEIGHBOURHOODS

Tönnies' (1887) idea of community as *Gemeinschaft* implies a well-connected, place-based, collective, village-like community. However, this notion of community represents an overly romanticised image of community and ignores more contemporary forms of community which have been explored by recent sociological studies (e.g., Amin, 2007; DeFilippis, Fisher, & Shragge, 2006; Delanty, 2000; Shaw, 2008; Wellman, 2001, 2002; Willson, 2006). *Gemeinschaft* might resemble 'Hobbiton' in 'The Shire' described by Tolkien (1966). This communitarian notion (de Tocqueville, 2000; Etzioni, 1995) is still frequently referred to in the community development literature, although the homogeneous, egalitarian and all encompassing nature of *Gemeinschaft* is a utopian ideal which is less and less compatible with contemporary characteristics of community as social networks in today's network society.

Before the advent of modern information and communication technology, human interaction was limited by the reach of the physical presence of self or the representations of self (e.g., letters and photographs) and available means of transportation. The need to socialise and to communicate was commonly satisfied with family members in the same household, with friends and peers nearby, at work or within the vicinity of the neighbourhood people lived in. Human relations were door-to-door or place-to-place (Wellman, 2001). The fact that people residing in the immediate surroundings were known also established a feeling of security, community identity and a sense of belonging – a feeling that clashes with the experience of living in today's high density, compact urban environments.

The invention and introduction of new information and communication technologies into society has usually been accompanied by foresights which predict that people will be less dependent on place and location. To an extent, this is true. The phone was the first major invention to introduce personal tele-presence and to allow everybody to communicate in real time with others outside their own physical locality. Instead of being restricted to people within proximity of oneself, the phone enables long-distance communication to maintain work and social relationships. However, it is unlikely that anyone lifts the telephone handset to introduce themselves to a neighbour nearby they have not met before.

The Internet affords both synchronous and asynchronous applications which enable communication between one or multiple users, one-to-many or many-to-many broadcasts to a closed group, and public announcements to an open audience. The abstract nature of internet-mediated communication gave rise to the widespread use of the metaphor 'cyberspace' which visualises the emergence of a new spatial dimension.

However, people's bodies cannot be atomised in the same way their audiovisual representations can be digitised, mediated and sent across the world. Thus, people depend and will remain to depend on place and locality and on collocated face-to-face interaction. Bits and bytes travel in the virtual space of flows spanned by the Internet, but humans prefer to travel in the physical space of flows that modern transportation affords.

Place and proximity continue to matter in every socio-economic context, because there are no Internet applications that can completely substitute real-time collocated face-to-face interaction. This is evident by rising car and air travel sales (Wellman, 2001, p. 247), by people commuting to work instead of working from home, by the formation of economic clusters, precincts and hotspots where industries based along the same value chain collocate to take advantage of synergy effects. Florida rightly argues that "the economy itself increasingly takes form around real concentrations of people in real places" (Florida, 2003, p. 4). In the light of new urbanism (De Villiers, 1997) and master-planned residential developments (Gleeson, 2004; Minnery & Bajracharya, 1999), his statement holds true not just for the economy but for society in general.

Attempts to bridge distance for the purpose of 'more than just communication' have seen initiatives such as telework and distance education, yet they remain at the edge of mainstream usage and have not replaced face-to-face interaction (Dhanarajan, 2001; Gillespie & Richardson, 2004). To enable economic efficiencies, the goal of Computer Supported Co-operative Work (CSCW) and groupware applications is to supplement, not substitute, place-based work practices.

Wellman (2002) points out that the dichotomies of 'physical place' and 'cyberspace'; or of 'online' and 'offline', are misleading. Even as the Internet grows exponentially, place-based units such as 'home', 'work' and 'school' remain at the core of our understanding of everyday life. The Internet and other information and communication technology add new qualities to the portfolio of communication tools available to us, enriching our communicative ecology (Foth & Hearn, 2007; Hearn & Foth, 2007), and adding on to the variety of media channels at our disposal. We do not rely on the central location of traditional meeting places anymore such as the market place or town square in order to meet with friends and peers. Instead, we use mobile communications technology which

we can carry around (e.g., mobile phone, SMS), or ubiquitous communications technology which we can access anywhere (e.g., wireless networks) not to avoid but to negotiate on-the-fly meeting places and venues anywhere and anytime. Teenagers for example use their mobile phones to arrange meeting places on the spot, this could be the local café, the shopping mall or someone's home (Satchell, 2003). This emerging behaviour introduces challenges to conventional understandings of 'place' and 'public places' and opens up opportunities for residential architecture, town planning and urban design (Dave, 2007; Foth, 2008; Foth & Sanders, 2008; Graham, 2004).

In a lively online discussion about the continued purpose and relevance of neighbourhood communities, one participant (eric_brissette, 2004) illustrates the point that having less exposure to neighbours (as opposed to co-workers or friends) does not mean that it is less likely that there are in fact prospective friends living in the neighbourhood:

I guess it all depends on where you live. I live in a rural town of about 10,000. Most people say "hello" or "good morning" to you as you pass them on the sidewalk. I can't say I've known all of my neighbors well, but I have at least spoken with them enough to know a bit about who they are. Visiting larger cities like Boston or New York makes me feel weird. Nobody looks you in the eye, and everyone seems constantly pissed off, almost like everyone is scared of everyone else... yet this all seems perfectly normal to them. [...] Chances are good that there are people in your neighborhood that share your [interests] or are at least [compatible] at the personality level who you wouldn't normally interact with on a daily basis.

In today's networked society, it is questionable to project the image of the rural village and use it as a best practice 'urban village' model for a city, because of inherent differences between both places and their inhabitants. Yet, the specific characteristics of a city can give rise to a different model of 'urban village' that acknowledge the potential opportunities that this particular environment offers its residents. For example, the simple fact that a city accommodates a larger number of residents could offer the individual greater choice and thus a chance to find the right social interaction partners.

However, the motivation for and process of the search itself remains to be examined. Getting to know someone in their role as a 'neighbour' is less likely than getting to know them in their role as a 'co-worker' or being the friend of a friend. Neighbours may still be part of a resident's social portfolio, but the communication devices used to maintain these ties are inherently place-independent and ephemeral: A phone call or an email does not distinguish between close or distant friends. Proximity does matter when it comes to physical encounters and face-to-face meetings. Most frequent social ties, including online interaction, are maintained with people who can easily be reached physically, that is, they usually reside within the same city, the surrounding suburbs, or the same neighbourhood (Horrigan, 2001; Horrigan, Rainie, & Fox, 2001). The majority of phone calls, SMS and emails help the parties involved to co-ordinate meetings or social gatherings, e.g. to 'catch up' over coffee in a café nearby.

These ties are primarily based on common friendship, workplace, or interest, and not shared locality. We may be introduced and subsequently get along well with the friend of a co-worker who happens to live in the same street, but it is unlikely that we would have found out about them without the co-worker introducing us first.

Many urban neighbourhoods are the result of what town planners and developers call 'master-planned communities'. Traditional conceptual models of community development limit action to tangible places of public interaction such as kindergartens, public schools, parks, libraries, etc. (Gleeson, 2004). This 'build it, they will come' approach lacks engagement with the findings of recent community development research (Gilchrist, 2004; Pinkett, 2003). It ignores both the human factors involved in urban renewal and sociocultural neighbourhood animation as well as the potential that information and communication technology can offer urban residents such as online community networks and location-based new media (Day & Schuler, 2004; Rheingold, 2002).

Gilchrist points out that "community development involves human horticulture rather than social engineering" (Gilchrist, 2000, p. 269). Social encounters in urban neighbourhoods cannot be master-planned. They are based on coincidence and serendipity. Neighbours meet through friends of friends who happen to live close by; they meet when walking the dogs, or in some cases when a local problem affects multiple residents (Hampton, 2003). However, more often than not, they do not meet at all, and even if they wanted to, there is usually little opportunity beyond serendipity. Our preliminary results indicate that the majority of residents surveyed believe, just like Eric above, that chances are good that there *are* people in their neighbourhood who share their interests or are at least compatible at the personality level with whom they do not normally interact on a daily basis. For those who would like to find out about them and who still believe in good neighbourhood relations, the question remains: What can be done to avoid relying on good fortune and fate? How can those who want to, coax luck?

A step towards a more strategic approach to develop urban neighbourhoods encompass online community networks (Schuler, 1996). Community networks are integrated online systems designed for residential communities that have so far usually comprised of communication tools such as mailing lists, discussion boards and newsletters. Ideally, community networks allow residents to communicate and interact with other users and take advantage of the proximity to other residents in the neighbourhood. Thus, these systems have the potential to build a bridge between virtual public spaces and physical public places and foster network social capital and neighbourhood identity.

COMMUNITY NETWORKS IN URBAN NEIGHBOURHOODS

Arnold states that "for the ordinary citizen, social interaction is the 'killer application' of the Internet" (2003, p. 83). This development has sparked an increased interest amongst researchers from a range of disciplines to investigate online communication and online communities (Preece, 2000). Yet, the majority of the work undertaken so far in this research field focuses on globally dispersed online (virtual) communities and not on the use of information and communication technology for communities of place (Papadakis, 2004).

There is a small but growing body of literature that reports on the use of information and communication technology for community development in place-based contexts – mostly within the emerging discipline that Gurstein terms 'community informatics' (2001; 2000). However, most of these accounts investigate communities that are in one way or another deprived (e.g., tele-centres or community access centres in rural and remote locations; and ICT for development and poverty reduction in developing countries). The transferability of these studies to urban settings is questionable. Urban dwellers may think of themselves as being quite 'well-off' and may lack common disadvantages such as low income or unemployment. Such instances of deprivation could contribute to shared agony which may ultimately help to establish a collective need for change (Foth, 2004b) and thus a reason to make use of technology for action and change. In its absence however, alternative motivations to form neighbourhood community need to be found.

Today, the value of door-to-door and place-to-place relationships in urban neighbourhoods seems to be on the decline. Researchers and practitioners endeavour to counter this trend through 'community networking', that is, the application of Internet- and web-based tools in residential environments to introduce and sustain local communication and interaction among neighbours (Day, 2002). Although the term is sometimes used broadly in other contexts of community development and community informatics, the focus in this paper is on urban neighbourhoods and on urban informatics (Ellison, Burrows, & Parker, 2007; Foth, 2008).

A residential community comprises people who live or stay in a geographically demarcated area. Such communities are sometimes also referred to as local communities, physically or geographically based communities, or communities of place. Apart from the fact that members of a residential community share the same location or address, they are not necessarily bound by any other common characteristic such as interest, age group, or occupation. As such, residential communities are not 'communities' or 'neighbourhoods' a priori. An apartment complex might consist of residents who do not know each other.

A range of research projects have been undertaken to examine whether online community networks can facilitate the process of establishing neighbourhood identity. These projects set out to design and implement online community networks for both large and small residential sites with various aims and with varying degrees of success (Arnold, Gibbs, & Wright, 2003; Carroll & Rosson, 2003; Cohill & Kavanaugh, 2000; De Cindio, Gentile, Grew, & Redolfi, 2003; Hampton & Wellman, 2003; Meredyth, Ewing, & Thomas, 2004; Pinkett, 2003).

Reaching a critical mass of users is considered to be one of the key criteria of success (Arnold et al., 2003; Butler, 2001; Patterson & Kavanaugh, 2001) and has been reported as one of the most common stumbling blocks: "If you build it, they will not necessarily come" (Maloney-Krichmar, Abras, & Preece, 2002, p. 19). This statement seems to be common sense; nonetheless it provides the opportunity for a deeper analysis of the reasons and motivations for urban residents to communicate, interact and get together with other residents and to actively participate in an urban neighbourhood network.

Dunbar (1996) suggests that the size of human social networks is limited for biological and sociological reasons to a value of around 150 nodes. Barabási (2003) and Watts (2003) provide a more far-reaching overview of recent advances in network theory and their impact on business, science and everyday life. Some ideas are crucial in understanding community networks: They usually increase or decrease in size, that is, social network research and systems design need to find ways to capture their dynamics. Their structure is not random or chaotic, but follow preferential attachment ('rich get richer') and fitness ('fit get richer'). In the context of communities of place, Jankowski and his colleagues support this thesis with empirical research by pointing out that "those geographic communities already rich in social capital may become richer thanks to community networks, and those communities poor in social capital may remain poor" (Jankowski, Van Selm, & Hollander, 2001, p. 113). Hampton & Wellman support this notion by stating that, "connectivity seems to go to the connected: greater social benefit from the Internet accrues to those already well situated socially" (2003, p. 283). Then the next questions are, what constitutes 'richness' and 'fitness' in urban social settings, how do residents get 'rich' (and become a 'hub' in their social network) and how can community networks facilitate 'enrichment' in a fair and ethical manner?

The reasons and motivations for participation in dispersed online (virtual) communities provide further insight into the answers to these questions. A person suffering from cancer might prefer the expertise, empathy and perhaps anonymity available in an international online community of cancer patients. Philatelists will find more like-minded people in an appropriate virtual community of interest such as a newsgroup or discussion board which is open to any Internet user, and which is not restricted to the residents of just one apartment complex or one suburb. The impossibility or impracticability of a face-to-face exchange in a dispersed online community does usually not impact negatively upon the value participants derive from such online interactions. The large number of active online communities tells its own tale.

The core characteristic of such dispersed online communities is their collective nature, that is, they accumulate participants who share a common interest, profession or support need into an entity which acts as a collective group with a shared purpose. The tools that are used to support online communities, including mailing lists, newsletters, discussion boards, etc., are closer designed towards a many-to-many broadcast approach instead of a peer-to-peer networking approach. They assume a pre-existing motivation to participate in and use the virtual space. In the case of shared interest, profession or support need, that may be the case. However, in the case of residents of urban neighbourhoods the only shared attribute is place and collocation. Apart from occasions where an item of discussion or a topic of interest directly relates to the shared place that residents co-inhabit, most interaction is located *within* place but not necessarily *about* place. Thus, place and proximity are insufficient attributes to attract residents to a community network and to sustain it. Furthermore, a re-appropriation of the tools used to support online (virtual) communities in the context of urban neighbourhood networks opens up further issues, because a community of place is inherently different from a dispersed community of interest. As well, connectivity per se does not ensure community – and proximity does not ensure neighbourliness.

The unique selling proposition that could give online community networks for urban neighbourhoods a competitive advantage over dispersed online communities is proximity. Community networks allow residents to interact online and to take and continue online interaction offline, in real life and face-to-face with other residents who live in the same location. As such, they can be an effective tool for local community engagement and activism if the community faces a shared problem or a common 'enemy' that provides the required motivation for residents to come together. Hampton (2003) describes the experience with residents in Netville who faced the prospect of losing broadband Internet access which had previously been provided to them free of charge. The issue and the presence of a common 'enemy', that is, the Internet Service Provider, unified residents in community activism to advocate for a continuation of the service, and the traffic in the online community network (in the form of an electronic mailing list) increased significantly. The unifying vigour of a common problem or issue can (temporarily) transform a certain number of residents into a residential collective and thus sustain an online community network (cf. Foth & Brereton, 2004).

In the absence of a common enemy, a shared purpose or a pre-existing village-like atmosphere, are there other reasons and motivations for social encounters to occur and for the formation of residential networks in urban neighbourhoods? Examining existing urban communities may help to answer this question. Watters (2003) describes the emergence of clusters of under 35 year old urban dwellers mostly in America but also in other parts of the word as 'urban tribes'. They represent a social network, a swarming group of friends who live in the same city and who are all connected with each other through strong and weak ties. The interaction between members of urban tribes is facilitated through the use of mobile phones, email and face-to-face gatherings. Watters does not mention the use of neighbourhood or similar ICT-supported networks, but his

account of the behaviour of urban tribes allows to imagine a new generation of purpose-built interactive community networks for residents in urban neighbourhoods.

THE URBAN TRIBE INCUBATOR

The previous section discussed the conditions under which residents might ultimately engage in neighbourhood community networks and thus talk to people within their vicinity. For these conditions to emerge, competitive tools need to be designed that allow residents to find out who is living around them and that facilitate local communication and interaction that so far relied on coincidence and serendipity. However, conventional community networks do not necessarily address these needs. They are very delicate, organic entities. They thrive only in favourable circumstances (e.g., similar demographic and professional orientation), with special nurturing (e.g., free Internet access) (Hampton & Wellman, 2003; Kavanaugh, Reese, Carroll, & Rosson, 2003), and chances are high that else, they may fail (Arnold et al., 2003).

The findings of these sociological studies provide essential insights for a new design that can guide the successful development of interactive systems and devices to stimulate local interaction and animate urban neighbourhoods. A prototype system of an 'urban tribe incubator' is currently being developed and tested in three urban residential sites in Australia (Foth, 2004a). Action research (Hearn & Foth, 2005; Hearn, Tacchi, Foth, & Lennie, 2008, forthcoming) and participatory design (Foth & Axup, 2006; Greenwood, 2002) play crucial roles in iteratively constructing and testing a successful prototype. The participation of residents in the design and development is essential to integrate the range of communication channels they use and to allow residents to take social ownership of the system.

The previous discussion of the factors influencing systems that support social networks in urban neighbourhoods gives rise to a set of design considerations which are being integrated into the design of the urban tribe incubator prototype. These are now discussed in turn.

Size, Growth, and Critical Mass

Popular services and functions in conventional community networking systems include electronic newsletters, mailing lists and discussion boards. In order to keep these systems interesting and appealing, content needs to be generated by either a systems administrator or delegate but ideally by the community of users itself. Thus a critical mass of users is required to maintain an ongoing supply of discussion board postings and reponses, mailing submissions and newsletter contributions. It requires residents to invest a reasonable amount of time and effort to collectively sustain the system's viability.

The urban tribe incubator may include such collective, broadcast-style, many-to-many functions, but the core will be a residents directory which does not require maintenance on a regular basis unless details have changed and need to be updated. A resident's personal profile may comprise information about skills, trade, interests, hobbies and contact details. The profile becomes the virtual representation of a potential node that invites other residents to link to and from. The system does not require users to use the directory on a regular basis to interact with all other users. Rather, the system allows users to opt-in and opt-out as they please and as a need arises by facilitating personalised networking, that is, to voluntarily initiate contact and build social ties with people of their choice. Thus, the directory becomes the catalyst for personalised 'peer-to-peer' social networks to form.

The size and growth of the directory itself is in no linear relation to the size and growth of an individual resident's social network. The system acknowledges different levels of social 'richness' and 'fitness' and thus the point of saturation remains a personal preference. If an individual's personal limit of social saturation is reached, they can opt-out. In conventional community networks for example, users can usually not control how many people will respond to their posting on a discussion board: It may be none, or it may set off an avalanche of responses. In an instant messenger application however, users remain in control of the social network they engage with, their private 'buddy list'.

Diversity, Individualism, and Choice

The urban tribe incubator is not designed to host an online community of a particular interest or support need, but rather allows for the diversity of individual residents with different interests and support needs to find each other and to form smaller social clusters. The system presents residents with choice in relation to the number and characteristics of communication partners and modes of interaction. It provides easy and convenient ways for residents to identify birds of a feather, that is, to find like-minded people with common interests or support needs.

The system raises awareness amongst residents of who is living around them in order to facilitate peer-to-peer connections. The resident directory that links to individual profiles allows residents to choose what personal information they publish online or whether to keep certain information private or only available upon request. The goal of a resident directory is not to facilitate residents initiating virtual contact first (although it can be used in this way), but rather to simplify the process of strengthening serendipitous social encounters that happen while 'walking the dog'. Without an urban tribe incubator, such informal contacts that have the potential to develop into rich interaction, may remain superficial and transitory.

The system does not require residents to keep communication within the system, but allows them to move it to other sycnhronous or asynchronous communication platforms and devices. Having access to an online directory, a resident is able to maintain contact with a new acquaintance and to integrate this contact into their usage of existing personal peer-to-peer communication devices that they use already such as instant messengers, email, SMS, and online chat.

Privacy and Social Control

To safeguard privacy, residents have control over their personal information and the scope of their online engagement. Enhanced local sociability is welcomed by most residents but must not come at the cost of losing security and control of the voluntary and selective nature of one's social networks. Our preliminary results are encouraging insofar as residents seem to be trusting their (yet personally mostly unknown) neighbours with personal details such as name, phone numbers, email addresses, photo, occupation, interests, hobbies, etc. In our survey, the majority of residents has indicated that they are willing to share this kind of personal information online with other residents in the building.

Nevertheless, issues of privacy and social control have to be translated into appropriate terms and conditions that govern the usage of the system and the interaction among residents of the building. It is imperative to ensure that residents have the chance to opt-in and opt-out at any time without missing out on any essential information. Hence, it is worthwhile to consider supplementing official online communication channels with public announcements on digital public screens in prominent places within the building (e.g., carpark entry, reception or entrance area, manager's office door, elevators) to provide alternative ways of accessing community information.

Network of Networks, Identity, and Sense of Belonging

The urban tribe incubator may resemble more the *networked* nature of, for example, an online dating

site than the *collective* nature of, for example, an online discussion board. What may emerge from this process of personalised networking (or 'online dating') is a complex web of social networks that span the anonymous void of the building complex, a web of 'urban tribes' (Watters, 2003). Social 'hubs' will continue to play a crucial role as their bridging links (Kavanaugh *et al.*, 2003) connect different social networks and establish connectivity in the sense of community and solidarity. Drawing on viral marketing strategies (Godin, 2001; Goldsmith, 2002), the incubator allows individuals to cross-invite and introduce peers to the other networks they participate in – both inside and outside the neighbourhood. The feeling of a neighbourhood identity and a sense of belonging can only emerge if bridging social links between members of different urban tribes contribute to the formation of a 'mesh-work' of urban tribes that is "networked to the 'edge of chaos'" (Gilchrist, 2000, 2004). In this context, identity and a sense of belonging are not derived from the collective feeling of being collocated in the same place but from the feeling of being connected to a group of friends who are part of a greater group of peers living close by.

CONCLUSION AND OUTLOOK

The design considerations presented here will guide the development of the core prototype system. We then envision to extend this core with more sophisticated features that for example, allow users to produce and exchange creative content (photos, audio, video, digital storytelling) (Klaebe, Foth, Burgess, & Bilandzic, 2007) and simplify the tasks of organising and managing social gatherings such as calendaring, inviting, RSVPs, synchronising with SMS and email, etc. As well, in this environment, the social aspects of the urban tribe incubator can be combined with managerial features that allow apartment owners to interact with the body corporate and tenants with the on-site management. In this role, the system can manage rates and rent payments, entry notices, mailings and notifications, personalised information on contractors and house rules, thus adding further value to the system and encouraging uptake and usage. Cross-platform compatibility is key. As such, the urban tribe incubator is anticipated to be a technical framework that can be accessed not only on the home or office computer, but also on mobile and other devices.

The future holds interesting outlooks for platform developments. New urbanism, urban renewal and the move towards more and more compact cities create opportunities to re-think the communicative paradigm of apartment complexes and vertical real estate as well as the sociological qualities of the office environment most social software is accessed in. The kitchen is associated with the preparation of food which is an essential part of one's social life, as opposed to the office that is the centre of professional life. Hence, modern residential architecture often links the kitchen area with the living room to form one seamless space that can be re-purposed for entertainment and leisure. In this context, the much scorned Internet fridge might see a revival as an integrated local communication hub that combines the functionality of a simple touchscreen display interface, a ubiquitous instant messenger and a synchronised resident buddy list with location-aware services and groupware functionality. The rationale for choosing the fridge is not based on the inherent cooling functionality of the fridge itself, but its position and prominence within the environment of many urban homes.

This chapter hopes to contribute towards substantiating a new *Zeitgeist* of designing residential community networks for urban neighbourhoods which is characterised by combining current understandings of social networks inherent in Wellman's theory of networked individualism with the affordances of ubiquitous communication devices and applications for personalised place-based networking such as the Internet, instant messengers, and mobile phones. Putnam argues that, "the Internet will not *automatically* offset the decline in more conventional forms of social capital, but that it has that potential. In fact, it is hard to imagine solving our contemporary civic dilemmas without computer-mediated communication" (Putnam, 2000, p. 180). If online community networks for residential communities are designed to include features that cater for both collective as well as network interaction, they have the potential to contribute to the creation of neighbourhood identity and to increase network capital and social capital in urban environments (cf. Florida, 2003; Huysman & Wulf, 2004; Quan-Haase, Wellman, Witte, & Hampton, 2002). Thus, they may prove to be a milestone in the quest to animate urban neighbourhoods, to revive forms of civic engagement in society, and to enact global connectivity for local action in order to move from the vision of the 'global village' to a new understanding of the 'urban village'.

ACKNOWLEDGMENT

An earlier version of this chapter has been published as Foth, M. (2006). Analyzing the Factors Influencing the Successful Design and Uptake of Interactive Systems to Support Social Networks in Urban Neighborhoods. *International Journal of Technology and Human Interaction*, 2(2), 65-79.

This research is supported under the Australian Research Council's Discovery Projects funding scheme (project number DP0663854) and Dr Marcus Foth is the recipient of an Australian Postdoctoral Fellowship. The author thanks Greg Hearn, Lucy Montgomery, Jean Burgess, Joshua Green, Robbie Spence, Barbara Adkins, Nick Jankowski, Mark Gaved, Bernd Carsten Stahl, Peter Day, Wal Taylor and the anonymous reviewers for valuable comments on earlier versions of this chapter.

REFERENCES

Amin, A. (2007). Re-thinking the urban social. *City, 11*(1), 100-114.

Arnold, M. (2003). Intranets, Community, and Social Capital: The Case of Williams Bay. *Bulletin of Science, Technology & Society, 23*(2), 78-87.

Arnold, M., Gibbs, M. R., & Wright, P. (2003). Intranets and Local Community: 'Yes, an intranet is all very well, but do we still get free beer and a barbeque?' In M. Huysman, E. Wenger & V. Wulf (Eds.), *Proceedings of the First International Conference on Communities and Technologies* (pp. 185-204). Amsterdam, NL: Kluwer Academic Publishers.

Barabási, A.-L. (2003). *Linked: How Everything Is Connected to Everything Else and What It Means for Business, Science, and Everyday Life.* New York: Plume.

Butler, B. S. (2001). Membership Size, Communication Activity, and Sustainability. *Information System Research, 12*(4), 346-362.

Carroll, J. M., & Rosson, M. B. (2003). A Trajectory for Community Networks. *The Information Society, 19*(5), 381-394.

Castells, M. (2001). Virtual Communities or Network Society? In *The Internet Galaxy: Reflections on the Internet, Business, and Society* (pp. 116-136). Oxford: Oxford University Press.

Cohill, A. M., & Kavanaugh, A. L. (Eds.). (2000). *Community Networks: Lessons from Blacksburg, Virginia* (2nd ed.). Norwood: Artech House.

Dave, B. (2007). Space, sociality, and pervasive computing. *Environment and Planning B: Planning and Design, 34*(3), 381-382.

Day, P. (2002). Designing Democratic Community Networks: Involving Communities through Civil Participation. In M. Tanabe, P. van den Besselaar & T. Ishida (Eds.), *Digital Cities II: Second Kyoto Workshop on Digital Cities* (Vol. LNCS 2362, pp. 86-100). Heidelberg, Germany: Springer.

Day, P., & Schuler, D. (Eds.). (2004). *Community Practice in the Network Society: Local Action / Global Interaction.* London: Routledge.

De Cindio, F., Gentile, O., Grew, P., & Redolfi, D. (2003). Community Networks: Rules of Behavior and Social Structure. *The Information Society, 19*(5), 395-406.

de Tocqueville, A. (2000). *Democracy in America* (H. C. Mansfield & D. Winthrop, Trans.). Chicago: University of Chicago Press.

De Villiers, P. (1997). New Urbanism: A critical review. *Australian Planner, 34*(1), 30-34.

DeFilippis, J., Fisher, R., & Shragge, E. (2006). Neither Romance Nor Regulation: Re-evaluating Community. *International Journal of Urban and Regional Research, 30*(3), 673-689.

Delanty, G. (2000). Postmodernism and the Possibility of Community. In *Modernity and Postmodernity: Knowledge, Power and the Self* (pp. 114-130). London: Sage.

Dhanarajan, G. (2001). Distance Education: Promise, Performance and Potential. *Open Learning, 16*(1), 61-68.

Dunbar, R. I. M. (1996). *Grooming, Gossip, and the Evolution of Language.* Cambridge, MA: Harvard University Press.

e_brissette (2004, Sep 3). Personal comment. Retrieved Nov 11, 2004, from http://slashdot.org/comments.pl?cid=10147964&sid=120406

Ellison, N., Burrows, R., & Parker, S. (Eds.). (2007). *Urban Informatics: Software, Cities and the New Cartographies of Knowing Capitalism. Guest editors of a special issue of Information, Communication & Society, 10(6).* London: Routledge.

Etzioni, A. (1995). *The Spirit of Community: Rights, Responsibilities, and the Communitarian Agenda*. London: Fontana Press.

Fallows, D. (2004). *The Internet and Daily Life*. Washington, DC: Pew Internet & American Life Project.

Florida, R. L. (2003). Cities and the Creative Class. *City and Community, 2*(1), 3-19.

Foth, M. (2004a). Animating personalised networking in a student apartment complex through participatory design. In A. Bond, A. Clement, F. de Cindio, D. Schuler & P. van den Besselaar (Eds.), *Proceedings of the Participatory Design Conference, Toronto, Canada, July 27-31* (Vol. 2, pp. 175-178). Palo Alto, CA: CPSR.

Foth, M. (2004b). Designing networks for sustainable neighbourhoods: A case study of a student apartment complex. In G. Johanson & L. Stillman (Eds.), *Community Informatics Research Network (CIRN) 2004 Colloquium and Conference Proceedings. 29 Sep - 1 Oct 2004* (Vol. 1, pp. 161-172). Prato, Italy.

Foth, M. (Ed.). (2008). *Handbook of research on urban informatics: The practice and promise of real-time city*. Hershey, PA: Information Science Reference.

Foth, M., & Axup, J. (2006, Jul 31 - Aug 5). *Participatory Design and Action Research: Identical Twins or Synergetic Pair?* Paper presented at the Participatory Design Conference (PDC), Trento, Italy.

Foth, M., & Brereton, M. (2004). Enabling local interaction and personalised networking in residential communities through action research and participatory design. In P. Hyland & L. Vrazalic (Eds.), *Proceedings of OZCHI 2004: Supporting Community Interaction. 20-24 Nov 2004*. Wollongong, NSW: University of Wollongong.

Foth, M., & Hearn, G. (2007). Networked Individualism of Urban Residents: Discovering the communicative ecology in inner-city apartment buildings. *Information, Communication & Society, 10*(5), 749-772.

Foth, M., & Sanders, P. (2008). Impacts of Social Interaction on the Architecture of Urban Spaces. In A. Aurigi & F. De Cindio (Eds.), *Augmented Urban Spaces: Articulating the Physical and Electronic City*. Aldershot, UK: Ashgate.

Gilchrist, A. (2000). The well-connected community: networking to the 'edge of chaos'. *Community Development Journal, 35*(3), 264-275.

Gilchrist, A. (2004). *The Well-Connected Community: A Networking Approach to Community Development*. Bristol, UK: The Policy Press.

Gillespie, A., & Richardson, R. (2004). Teleworking and the City: Myths of Workplace Transcendence and Travel Reduction. In S. Graham (Ed.), *The Cybercities Reader* (pp. 212-218). London: Routledge.

Gleeson, B. (2004). Deprogramming Planning: Collaboration and Inclusion in New Urban Development. *Urban Policy and Research, 22*(3), 315-322.

Godin, S. (2001). *Unleashing the Ideavirus*. New York: Hyperion.

Goldsmith, R. (2002). *Viral Marketing*. London: Pearson Education.

Graham, S. (Ed.). (2004). *The Cybercities Reader*. London: Routledge.

Greenwood, D. J. (2002). Action research: Unfulfilled promises and unmet challenges. *Concepts and Transformation, 7*(2), 117-139.

Gurstein, M. (2001). Community informatics, community networks and strategies for flexible networking. In L. Keeble & B. D. Loader (Eds.), *Community Informatics: Shaping Computer-Mediated Social Relations* (pp. 263-283). New York: Routledge.

Gurstein, M. (Ed.). (2000). *Community Informatics: Enabling Communities with Information and Communication Technologies.* Hershey, PA: Idea Group.

Hampton, K. N. (2003). Grieving For a Lost Network: Collective Action in a Wired Suburb. *The Information Society, 19*(5), 417-428.

Hampton, K. N., & Wellman, B. (2003). Neighboring in Netville: How the Internet Supports Community and Social Capital in a Wired Suburb. *City and Community, 2*(4), 277-311.

Hearn, G., & Foth, M. (2005). Action Research in the Design of New Media and ICT Systems. In K. Kwansah-Aidoo (Ed.), *Topical Issues in Communications and Media Research* (pp. 79-94). New York, NY: Nova Science.

Hearn, G., & Foth, M. (Eds.). (2007). *Communicative Ecologies. Special issue of the Electronic Journal of Communication, 17(1-2)*. New York: Communication Institute for Online Scholarship.

Hearn, G., Tacchi, J., Foth, M., & Lennie, J. (2008, forthcoming). *Action Research and New Media: Concepts, Methods and Cases.* Cresskill, NJ: Hampton Press.

Horrigan, J. B. (2001). *Cities Online: Urban Development and the Internet.* Washington, DC: Pew Internet & American Life Project.

Horrigan, J. B., Rainie, L., & Fox, S. (2001). *Online Communities: Networks that nurture long-distance relationships and local ties.* Washington, DC: Pew Internet & American Life Project.

Huysman, M., & Wulf, V. (Eds.). (2004). *Social Capital and Information Technology.* Cambridge, MA: MIT Press.

Jankowski, N. W., Van Selm, M., & Hollander, E. (2001). On crafting a study of digital community networks: Theoretical and methodological considerations. In L. Keeble & B. D. Loader (Eds.),

Community Informatics: Shaping Computer-Mediated Social Relations (pp. 101-117). New York: Routledge.

Kavanaugh, A. L., Reese, D. D., Carroll, J. M., & Rosson, M. B. (2003). Weak Ties in Networked Communities. In M. Huysman, E. Wenger & V. Wulf (Eds.), *Proceedings of the First International Conference on Communities and Technologies* (pp. 265-286). Amsterdam, NL: Kluwer Academic Publishers.

Klaebe, H., Foth, M., Burgess, J., & Bilandzic, M. (2007, Sep 23-26). *Digital Storytelling and History Lines: Community Engagement in a Master-Planned Development.* Paper presented at the 13th International Conference on Virtual Systems and Multimedia (VSMM'07), Brisbane, QLD.

Maloney-Krichmar, D., Abras, C., & Preece, J. (2002, Jun 6-8). *Revitalizing an Online Community.* Paper presented at the International Symposium on Technology and Society (ISTAS) – Social Implications of Information and Communication Technology, Raleigh, NC.

Meredyth, D., Ewing, S., & Thomas, J. (2004). Neighbourhood Renewal and Government by Community. *International Journal of Cultural Policy, 10*(1), 85-101.

Minnery, J., & Bajracharya, B. (1999). Visions, planning processes and outcomes: Master planned communities in South East Queensland. *Australian Planner, 36*(1), 33-41.

Papadakis, M. C. (2004). *Computer-Mediated Communities: A Bibliography on Information, Communication, and Computational Technologies and Communities of Place* (SRI Project Report No. P10446.004). Arlington, VA: SRI International.

Patterson, S. J., & Kavanaugh, A. L. (2001). Building a sustainable community network: An application of critical mass theory. *The Electronic Journal of Communication, 11*(2).

Pinkett, R. D. (2003). Community Technology and Community Building: Early Results from the Creating Community Connections Project. *The Information Society, 19*(5), 365-379.

Polanyi, M. (1966). *The tacit dimension.* Gloucester, MA: Peter Smith.

Preece, J. (2000). *Online communities: designing usability, supporting sociability.* Chichester: John Wiley.

Putnam, R. D. (2000). *Bowling Alone: The Collapse and Revival of American Community.* New York: Simon & Schuster.

Quan-Haase, A., Wellman, B., Witte, J. C., & Hampton, K. N. (2002). Capitalizing on the Net: Social Contact, Civic Engagement, and Sense of Community. In B. Wellman & C. A. Haythornthwaite (Eds.), *The Internet in everyday life* (pp. 291-324). Oxford: Blackwell.

Rheingold, H. (2002). *Smart Mobs: The Next Social Revolution.* Cambridge, MA: Perseus.

Satchell, C. (2003). The Swarm: Facilitating Fluidity and Control in Young People's Use of Mobile Phones. In S. Viller & P. Wyeth (Eds.), *Proceedings of OZCHI 2003: New directions in interaction, information environments, media and technology. 26-28 Nov 2003.* Brisbane, QLD: Information Environments Program, University of Queensland.

Schuler, D. (1996). *New Community Networks: Wired for Change.* New York: ACM Press.

Shaw, M. (2008). Community development and the politics of community. *Community Development Journal, 43*(1), 24-36.

Tolkien, J. R. R. (1966). *The Lord of the Rings* (2nd ed.). London: Allen & Unwin.

Tönnies, F. (1887). *Gemeinschaft und Gesellschaft* (3rd ed.). Darmstadt, Germany: Wissenschaftliche Buchgesellschaft.

Walmsley, D. J. (2000). Community, Place and Cyberspace. *Australian Geographer, 31*(1), 5-19.

Watters, E. (2003). *Urban Tribes: Are Friends the New Family?* London: Bloomsbury.

Watts, D. J. (2003). *Six Degrees: The Science of a Connected Age.* New York: Norton.

Wellman, B. (2001). Physical Place and Cyberplace: The Rise of Personalized Networking. *International Journal of Urban and Regional Research, 25*(2), 227-252.

Wellman, B. (2002). Little Boxes, Glocalization, and Networked Individualism. In M. Tanabe, P. van den Besselaar & T. Ishida (Eds.), *Digital Cities II: Second Kyoto Workshop on Digital Cities* (Vol. LNCS 2362, pp. 10-25). Heidelberg, Germany: Springer.

Wellman, B., & Haythornthwaite, C. A. (Eds.). (2002). *The Internet in Everyday Life.* Oxford, UK: Blackwell.

Wellman, B., Quan-Haase, A., Boase, J., Chen, W., Hampton, K. N., Díaz de Isla Gómez, I., et al. (2003). The Social Affordances of the Internet for Networked Individualism. *Journal of Computer-Mediated Communication, 8*(3).

Willson, M. A. (2006). *Technically Together: Rethinking Community within Techno-Society.* New York: Peter Lang.

KEY TERMS

Action Research: A research approach which is operationalised by constant cycles of planning, acting, observing and reflecting, which encourages the participation of local people as active agents in the research process, and which works hand in hand with people-centred research methodologies.

Collective Interaction: Characterised by a shared goal or common purpose, a focus on the community rather than the individual. The interaction is more public and formal than private and informal, and resembles many-to-many broadcasts. The mode of interaction is often asynchronous, permanent and hierarchically structured. Technology that supports collective interaction includes online discussion boards and mailing list.

Communicative Ecology (as defined by Hearn & Foth, 2007): Comprises a technological layer which consists of the devices and connecting media that enable communication and interaction. A social layer which consists of people and social modes of organising those people – which might include, for example, everything from friendship groups to more formal community organisations, as well as companies or legal entities. And a discursive layer which is the content of communication – that is, the ideas or themes that constitute the known social universe that the ecology operates in.

Digital Storytelling: Refers to a specific tradition based around the production of digital stories in intensive collaborative workshops. The outcome is a short autobiographical narrative recorded as a voiceover, combined with photographic images (often sourced from the participants' own photo albums) and sometimes music (or other sonic ambience). These textual elements are combined to produce a 2-3 minute video. This form of digital storytelling originated in the late 1990s at the University of California at Berkeley's Centre for Digital Storytelling (www.storycenter.org), headed by Dana Atchley and Joe Lambert.

Local Knowledge: Knowledge, or even knowing, is the justified belief that something is true. Knowledge is thus different from opinion. Local knowledge refers to facts and information acquired by a person which are relevant to a specific locale or have been elicited from a place-based context. It can also include specific skills or experiences made in a particular location. In this regard, local knowledge can be tacitly held, that is, knowledge we draw upon to perform and act but we may not be able to easily and explicitly articulate it: "We can know things, and important things, that we cannot tell" (Polanyi, 1966).

Master-Planned Communities: Urban developments guided by a central planning document which outlines strategic design principles and specifications pertaining to road infrastructure, building design, zoning, technology and social and community facilities. They are usually built on vacant land and thus in contrast with the type of ad-hoc organic growth of existing city settlements.

Networked Interaction: Characterised by an interest in personal social networking and a focus on individual relationships. The interaction is more private and informal than public and formal, and resembles a peer-to-peer switchboard. The mode of interaction is often synchronous, transitory and appears chaotic from the outside. Technology that supports networked interaction includes instant messengers, email and SMS.

Chapter VI
Information Security Effectiveness:
Conceptualization and Validation of a Theory

Kenneth J. Knapp
U.S. Air Force Academy, USA

Thomas E. Marshall
Auburn University, USA

R. Kelly Rainer, Jr.
Auburn University, USA

F. Nelson Ford
Auburn University, USA

ABSTRACT

Taking a sequential qualitative-quantitative methodological approach, we propose and test a theoretical model that includes four variables through which top management can positively influence security effectiveness: user training, security culture, policy relevance, and policy enforcement. During the qualitative phase of the study, we generated the model based on textual responses to a series of questions given to a sample of 220 information security practitioners. During the quantitative phase, we analyzed survey data collected from a sample of 740 information security practitioners. After data collection, we analyzed the survey responses using structural equation modeling and found evidence to support the hypothesized model. We also tested an alternative, higher-order factor version of the original model that demonstrated an improved overall fit and general applicability across the various demographics of the sampled data. We then linked the finding of this study to existing top management support literature, general deterrence theory research, and the theoretical notion of the dilemma of the supervisor.

INTRODUCTION

With modern national economies dependent upon information technology for survival, the need to protect information and mitigate risk has become paramount. One can find evidence of poor information security in the frequency of media reports about security breaches and from published survey data. As of this writing, media headlines about security incidents have become a regular occurrence, with one of the more embarrassing breaches occurring when a laptop went missing that contained sensitive information of millions of U.S. veterans and military personnel (Files, 2006). Multiple national surveys confirm a high number of attacks against organizational information resources (Bagchi & Udo, 2003; Computer Emergency Response Team (CERT), 2004; Gordon, Loeb, Lucyshyn, & Richardson, 2005). Between 1998 and 2003, the number of reported incidents to the U.S. Computer Emergency Response Team (CERT) has nearly doubled each year with 137,529 reported incidents in 2003 alone.[1] An Ernst and Young analysis found that security incidents can cost companies between $17 and $28 million each occurrence (Garg, Curtis, & Halper, 2003). Because incidents are frequent and costly, management must take security seriously to protect organizational information.

Noting the disappointing state of information systems (IS) security in organizations, Dhillon & Backhouse (2001) called for more empirical research to develop key principles that will help in the management of IS security. Despite the call, few studies have developed and empirically tested theoretical models of IS security (Kotulic & Clark, 2004). In some studies, the sensitive nature of the security topic (Straub & Welke, 1998) impeded the collection of a sufficient sample willing to participate in the research (Kotulic & Clark, 2004). The few empirical studies that contained information security effectiveness as a dependent variable used general deterrence theory as a research foundation (Kankanhalli,

Hock-Hai, Bernard, & Kwok-Kee, 2003; Straub, 1990). Sensing that other variables in addition to those related to deterrence theory might significantly predict information security effectiveness, we engaged in a study to develop and empirically test a model of effectiveness that is not based on predetermined independent variables.

Using a sequential quantitative-qualitative methodological approach, we developed and tested a theoretical model that illustrates four practices through which top management can positively influence security effectiveness. The role of management support has been identified as a critical success factor in a wide area of information system implementations and IT projects (Jasperson et al., 2002; Sharma & Yetton, 2003). Management support has been called the variable most frequently hypothesized as contributing to IS success, but empirical analysis has limited modeling "success" as a simple linear function of management support (Sharma & Yetton, 2003, p. 535). Our model offers a more comprehensive view by including four critical mediator variables through which management can improve security effectiveness: user training, security culture, policy relevance, and policy enforcement. By doing so, the theoretical model proposed in this study provides practical help to professionals and researchers who seek to advance the managerial effectiveness of information security programs.

The following methodology section describes our qualitative approach used to conceptualize the theoretical model and the survey instrument to test the model. Using survey data, we then quantitatively test the model using structural equation modeling (SEM). We also proposed and analyzed an alternate structural model. To add credibility to the results of this study, the discussion section links our findings to related theory including previous IS studies based on general deterrence theory. We close our paper with limitations, implications and a conclusion.

RESEARCH METHODOLOGY

Rather than developing a theoretical model based on existing theory in the literature, we used a qualitative strategy that closely followed grounded theory to develop a theoretical model. For this reason, we are going straight into the methodology section. Later in the discussion section, we will appropriately link our findings to theory in the literature. This format is consistent with the grounded theory approach, which aims to discover theory directly from a corpus of data rather than from theory generated by logical deduction based on *a priori* assumptions (Glaser & Strauss, 1967). Using a coding process consistent with developing grounded theory, question responses provided by a sample of information security practitioners are analyzed to identify key issues in IS security. A theoretical model emerges based on the categorical relationships among the key managerial issues identified in the responses. After developing and giving the survey to a sample of information security practitioners, we test the model using structural equation modeling. We then explore an alternative model where the four mediator variables are represented by a higher order factor.

Our study combines qualitative and quantitative techniques over a six step methodological process. Figure 1 illustrates the methodological steps of the study. The following subsections describe each of these steps.

Step One: Qualitative Data Collection

An announcement was placed on the International Information Systems Security Certification Consortium [(ISC)²] Web site (www.isc2.org) calling for Certified Information System Security Professionals (CISSPs) to volunteer for this research project. (ISC)² is a non-profit organization that manages the CISSP program. Among the requirements to earn a CISSP designation, candidates must pass a rigorous exam, consent to an ethical code, and possess a minimum of four years of professional experience in the field or three years experience plus a college degree. To maintain certification, a CISSP must earn continuing professional education credits.

Two hundred and twenty CISSPs responded to the first question: What are the top five information security issues facing organizations today? Respondents gave a short title and rationale for each issue. By asking respondents to identify and describe their top issues, we took as our starting point the concerns of the participants, which is a practical approach for grounded theory studies (Galal, 2001). In the process of gathering and analyzing the responses, we asked several follow-on questions, both to the entire sample (N=220) and to specific individuals for the purpose of obtaining clarifications, getting additional details, or receiving feedback on researcher analysis. After this series of interactions with the participants, we accumulated a database containing over 146,000 words of question responses suitable for the purposes of our study.

Step Two: Qualitative Analysis

The grounded theory approach entails a series of highly structured steps involving the systematic comparison of units of data and the gradual construction of a system of categories describing the observed phenomena. This approach involves the discovery of emergent theory from qualitative, empirical data. The grounded theory methodology we used was introduced by Glaser & Strauss (1967) and further refined as a series of structured steps by Strauss & Corbin (1998). Using these steps, we coded respondent statements into logical categories where each category represented a critical information security issue. Through a process of continuous interplay between the researchers and the data (Strauss & Corbin, 1998, p. 13), a list of 58 logical categories emerged. A committee of two university faculty members and one (ISC)²

Figure 1. Methodology steps

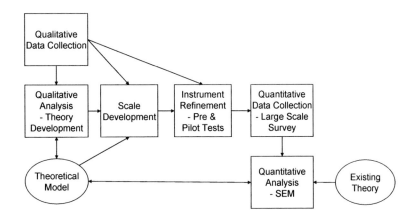

board member reviewed the categories for clarity and accuracy resulting in minor improvements.

Next, we iteratively integrated and refined the categories to discover patterns in the data that suggested theoretical relationships among the categories (Strauss & Corbin, 1998, p. 143). This process led to a model with top management support as the independent variable, security effectiveness as a dependent variable, and four variables mediating the relationship. A mediator is defined as a variable or mechanism through which an independent or predictor variable influences an outcome (Frazier, Barron, & Tix, 2004). Our data suggested that top management could influence security effectiveness through various security programs and policies. Yet, some responses stated that management could also directly influence security effectiveness, suggesting that the four mediator variables are partial mediators since they do not fully explain the relationship between the independent and dependent variables. Practically interpreted, top management can influence effectiveness directly, such as through the employee perception that management has taken ownership of an organization's security program, or indirectly, such as by supporting security training goals.

Figure 2 illustrates the hypothesized model and Table 1 contains formal statements of hypotheses. Table 2 provides ten examples of respondent statements supporting the six hypotheses. Underlined words refer to the predictor variables of the hypothesized model. These statements are representative of the larger body of responses.

Step Three: Scale Development

We developed measurement items through a process of extracting words and phrases from the participant responses to build a pool of candidate items. Extracting items directly from the responses assured that both the content and the language of the questionnaire items would be familiar to the likely sample and thus reduce possible construct bias (Karahanna, Evaristo, & Srite, 2004). Psychometricians emphasize that the validity of a measurement scale is built in from the outset. Careful construction of the initial scale items helps to ensure that they will representatively cover the specified domain of interest, and thus possess content validity (Nunnally, 1978).

We extended the technique of theoretical saturation (Strauss & Corbin, 1998) as a guide to help determine the number of items appropriate for the item pool (DeVellis, 2003). Theoretical

Figure 2. Hypothesized model

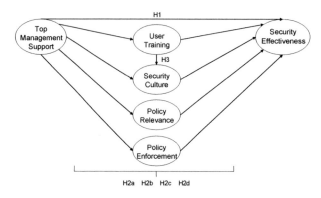

Table 1. Formal hypotheses

H1	Top management support is positively associated with security effectiveness.
H2a	Top management support and security effectiveness is partially mediated by user training.
H2b	Top management support and security effectiveness is partially mediated by security culture.
H2c	Top management support and security effectiveness is partially mediated by policy relevance.
H2d	Top management support and security effectiveness is partially mediated by policy enforcement.
H3	User training is positively associated with security culture.

saturation implies that when adding items to the pool contributes little marginal value to the scale or seems counterproductive, the item pool may be theoretically saturated. This approach links the size of the candidate item pool to the assessed content domain. Applying this method, we generated candidate items until the addition of new items contributed little to the scale, indicating that a construct is theoretically saturated. Testing for instrument construct validity began once the quality and quantity of the item pool seemed satisfactory with the concept of theoretical saturation.

Step Four: Instrument Refinement

This step had two major objectives. The first concerned the construct validity of the candidate survey items. The second concerned the perceived sensitive nature of the questions asked. An expert panel of twelve CISSPs evaluated every candidate item from the two perspectives (construct validity and intrusiveness). We invited the twelve CISSPs to be members of this panel based on their high quality and critical answers to the earlier questions while also trying to preserve the demographic diversity of the CISSP population. Combined, the twelve expert panelists earned forty professional IT certifications, fourteen bachelor degrees, and five graduate degrees, while representing four countries and five industries.

For construct validity, expert panelists matched each item in the item pool to one of seven constructs in two separate evaluation rounds. The seven constructs in the scale included the independent and mediating variables from the study

Table 2. Participant responses supporting the hypothesized model

Representative responses from the qualitative data	H1	H2a	H2b	H2c	H2d	H3
"It is imperative to have top management support all security programs…If there's no management support, real or perceived, all INFOSEC programs will fail."	✓					
"The importance of information security by the company's leadership permeates throughout the organization resulting in either successful or poor information security programs."	✓					
"Without support and understanding of both management and employee, an effective security program is impossible."	✓	✓				
"Obviously, without top management support and involvement, the creation, training and enforcement of the organization's security policies…would not be taken seriously by the employees. Top management support must happen first if the other issues are to be handled effectively."		✓			✓	
"Management direction will set the expectations of employees and form a security-aware organization culture."			✓			
"Without top down support for security, the enterprise culture cannot reflect a security conscious business practice and security cannot gain a significant foothold in a business."			✓			
"Frequent security policy updates need to happen in a timely manner…we see policy updates as an important task."				✓		
"Management must not only communicate the 'contents' of the policy, but also the need for it. Management should reinforce the need and importance with consistent enforcement as well as a clearly defined process for updates and reviews."				✓	✓	
"Enforcement (and) policy violations may also be an excellent indicator for security staffs on the effectiveness of their policies…and the general security state of the organization."					✓	
"Without an established and widespread awareness and education effort it is difficult if not impossible to integrate security into the corporate culture."						✓

Table 3. Willingness-to-answer scale

Scale		Definition
1.	Unacceptably Intrusive	Many respondents may be unwilling to answer; a problem question.
2.	Moderately Intrusive	Some respondents may be unwilling to answer.
3.	Slightly Intrusive	A small number of respondents may be unwilling to answer.
4.	Not Intrusive	Respondents should be willing to answer; the question is OK

Table 4. Intrusiveness scores of dropped items

Proposed Survey Question (Item)	Slightly or Not Intrusive	Mean Score (4.0 max)
Dropped Policy Enforcement Items		
Security policies have no teeth. [Reverse Code (RC)]	50%	2.75
There is conflict between security staff and employees regarding policy enforcement. (RC)	67%	3.00
Policies are selectively enforced. (RC)	67%	3.00
Computer security abuses often go unpunished. (RC)	67%	2.75
Dropped Security Effectiveness Items		
Sensitive information is sufficiently protected.	45%	2.42
Valuable information is effectively secured.	64%	2.58
Our organization has adequate computer security.	64%	2.67

plus two decoy variables (policy development and organizational governance). Items that obtained at least a 75% agreement rate among the panelists were retained for the survey (Hinkin, 1998). If the agreement rate was less than 75%, then the item was dropped or modified and reevaluated. Although this item-to-construct matching process does not guarantee construct validity, this refinement effort produced a list of 70 questionnaire items that exhibited preliminary evidence of construct validity for the constructs of this study. This important step helped minimize potential problems, such as cross loading of items across constructs.

The second objective concerned the issue of the perceived sensitive nature of security-related questions. Some consider information security research an extremely sensitive research topic (Straub &

Welke, 1998) and recommend a cautious research approach because of a general mistrust by practitioners of attempts to gain data about the behaviors of security professionals (Kotulic & Clark, 2004). To minimize the problem of unacceptably high levels of perceived intrusiveness, the same expert panel evaluated each item using a willingness-to-answer scale specifically developed for this study and provided in *Table 3*. While a certain level of perceived intrusiveness is unavoidable, we removed items with the higher intrusive scores. This step is critical in the domain of security because items perceived to be unacceptably intrusive might discourage or influence survey completion.

In addition to scoring every item on the willingness-to-answer scale, some of the feedback from the expert panel addressed the more intrusive items in the pool. For instance, one panelist commented about an item, "(I) find it hard to believe you would get an honest or accurate answer" and subsequently rated the item as *unacceptably intrusive*. Based on this and other feedback, the item was dropped. We compared both the quantitative intrusiveness scores of each item with the qualitative feedback when evaluating problematic items. Through this analysis, we established the following guidelines to help us judge the perceived intrusiveness of each item. We judged an acceptable item to:

- be rated as either slightly (3) or not intrusive (4) by at least 70% of the panelists and
- have a mean score from all the panelists of at least a 2.75 on a 4.0 scale.

Based on the expert panel results, perceived intrusiveness problems did not surface with four of the six constructs in the theoretical model. All of the items intending to measure the top management support, security culture, user training, and policy relevance constructs met the two intrusiveness guidelines. However, 22% of the initial policy enforcement and 33% of the security effectiveness items did not meet the two guidelines. Table 4 contains the panelists' intrusiveness scores for

the dropped policy enforcement and effectiveness questions from the initial item pool.

The willingness-to-answer scale was not the only consideration for reducing perceived intrusiveness. Other factors may influence a potential respondent's participation more than simply perceived intrusiveness of the questionnaire's items. Some of these possible factors include the visible sponsorship of a research project by a reputable organization such as (ISC)², clearly written survey instructions, approval of a university human subjects office, implementation of secure sockets layer encryption at the survey Web site, a posted privacy policy, and a general impression of professionalism. This study addressed all of these factors in an effort to minimize the perception of intrusiveness.

The expert panel process produced a survey instrument containing 63 candidate items. We then pilot tested the instrument with a convenience sample of 68 CISSPs who did not participate in previous steps of the project. Based on a confirmatory factor analysis of each construct modeled in isolation, we removed 28 of the 63 items because of high cross loads and poor fit. The pilot test resulted in a 35-item instrument exhibiting six dimensions that was ready for a larger scale test. The Appendix lists all 35 items.

Figure 3. Three-phased approach to data collection

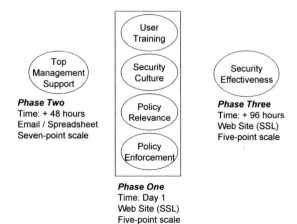

Step Five: Quantitative Data Collection

For the large-scale survey, we collected data in three phases to help control for the potential validity threat of common method variance. Common method variance is a type of method bias where variable correlations are vulnerable to artificial inflation (or deflation) due to the method used during data collection. Common method variance is one of the main sources of measurement error that can threaten the validity of empirical research conclusions (Campbell & Fiske, 1959; Podsakoff, MacKenzie, Lee, & Podsakoff, 2003). It is a particular concern with self-report surveys where predictor and criterion variables come from the same source. Fortunately, investigators can strengthen their research studies by taking steps to control and even eliminate this validity threat. The key to controlling method variance is to identify what the measures of the predictor and criterion variables have in common and to minimize this commonality through the design of the study. For example, time gaps in data collection is a remedy that helps ensure that respondents are in different cognitive mood states when providing answers to predictor and criterion variables. Gaps can also reduce the chance of respondents engaging in hypothesis guessing (Straub, Limayem, & Karahanna-Evaristo, 1995) and minimize the tendency to answer in a socially desirable manner (Podsakoff et al., 2003). While it is impossible to eliminate all forms of bias in a study, our goal is to reduce the plausibility of method bias as an explanation of the relationships between the constructs.

We used two design remedies to reduce common method variance (Podsakoff et al., 2003). First, at least a 48-hour hiatus separated the collection of the independent, mediator, and dependent variables. Second, we designed a different response format and Likert scale for collection of the independent variable, top management

support. Figure 3 illustrates the phased data collection approach used in this study.

Step Six: Quantitative Data Analysis

The results section presents an analysis of the data collected in step five. We used structural equation modeling (SEM) software to test our proposed model.

RESULTS

This section is divided into three parts. First, we describe our sample demographics. Second, we provide a statistical analysis of each construct modeled in isolation. Third, we evaluate the hypothesized model as well as an alternative, second-order factor model. We also provide a sub-sample analysis using the two models.

Demographics

A single e-mail notification (no reminders) was sent to approximately 30,000 constituents of $(ISC)^2$, inviting them to participate in a three-phased research survey. The message was an official "e-blast" containing one other unrelated item of $(ISC)^2$ business. Table 5 lists the survey response rates by phase and the actual average time that respondents took to complete each of the phases. Tables 6 and 7 provide sample demographics (N = 740).

Statistical Analysis of Each Construct

We used the Amos 5.0.1 program to test the theoretical model. We modeled each of the measured factors in isolation, then in pairs, and then as a collective network (Segars & Grover, 1998). To support convergent validity, all item loadings should be statistically significant and above .707

Table 5. Sample size and response rates by phase

	Phase 1	Phase 2	Phase 3	Usable
N	936	760	743	740
Response Rate	3% of 30,000	81% of Phase 1	79% of Phase 1	79% of Phase 1
Actual Mean of Temporal Separation	Day 1	84 hours after Phase 1	192 hours after Phase 1	---

Table 6. Country demographics

Country	Count	Percent	Country	Count	Percent
United States	402	54.3%	Malaysia	6	0.8%
Canada	60	8.1%	Sweden	6	0.8%
United Kingdom	36	4.9%	Italy	5	0.7%
Hong Kong	20	2.7%	New Zealand	5	0.7%
Australia	18	2.4%	Saudi Arabia	5	0.7%
India	17	2.3%	Belgium	4	0.5%
Netherlands	16	2.2%	Denmark	4	0.5%
Finland	12	1.6%	France	4	0.5%
Singapore	12	1.6%	Germany	4	0.5%
China	9	1.2%	Ireland	4	0.5%
South Africa	8	1.1%	Mexico	4	0.5%
Russian Federation	7	0.9%	Nigeria	4	0.5%
Brazil	6	0.8%	Others	53	7.2%
Korea, South	6	0.8%	Not provided	3	0.4%
			Total	740	100%

indicating that over half the variance is captured by the latent construct. Supporting both convergent and discriminant validity, GFI, NFI, AGFI, CFI and RMSEA should be within acceptable ranges (Straub, Boudreau, & Gefen, 2004). Table 8 presents a list of acceptable cut-off values.

During this process, we dropped six items from the 35-item instrument due to low item reliability and high cross loads resulting in a more parsimonious 29-item instrument. The Appendix provides the 35-item instrument and identifies the six dropped items. *Table 9* presents the measurement properties of the final six constructs, each modeled in isolation. The results indicate acceptable scale reliability and construct validity (convergent and discriminant). We conducted an additional test for discriminant validity between each pair of constructs by comparing the chi-square statistic of a constrained and an unconstrained two-construct model based on procedures provided in Segars & Grover (1998, p. 153). The chi-square differences between each construct showed significant differences ($p < .001$) suggesting the six constructs are distinct conceptual entities.

Table 7. Industry demographic

Industry	Count	Percent
Info Tech, Security, Telecommunications	201	27.2%
Finance, Banking, Insurance	187	25.3%
Government	184	24.9%
Consulting	166	22.4%
Manufacturing	69	9.3%
Healthcare	63	8.5%
Other	50	6.8%
Consumer Products, Retail, Wholesale	47	6.4%
Education, Training	47	6.4%
Professional Services (legal, marketing, etc.)	30	4.1%
Utilities	29	3.9%
Energy	24	3.2%
Transportation, Warehousing	15	2.0%
Industrial Technology	14	1.9%
Non-Profit	13	1.8%
Travel & Hospitality	11	1.5%
Entertainment	6	0.8%
Publishing	5	0.7%
Real Estate, Rental, Leasing	4	0.5%

Note: Respondents were free to indicate multiple industries

Theoretical Models

Next, we tested the original hypothesized model as a collective network. *Table 10* provides the measurement model: standardized factor loadings, critical value (z-statistic), and squared multiple correlations (SMC) for each of the 29 indicators of the final instrument. Figure 4 presents the path model: the standardized causal path findings, selected fit indices, and SMC values.[2] All hypothesized paths are significant with indices indicating the data is consistent with the hypothesized model. Based on this analysis, each of the hypotheses from Table 1 is supported.

In the survey, respondents provided demographic information that aided in sub-sample analysis. We used this information to detect dif-

ferences among demographics based on geography, organizational size, and industry. *Table 11* provides results of testing the hypothesized model using key demographic sub-samples. Because of the smaller size of some of the sub-samples (e.g., n < 200), interpretations should be made with caution.

In addition to the original model, we tested an alternative model that posits a second-order factor governing the correlations among *user training, security culture, policy relevance,* and *policy enforcement.* Illustrated in Figure 5, this model provides an additional perspective on the factor analytic structure of the original model. The motivation for proposing and testing the alternative model is the recognition that a more general latent construct may determine the first-order latent

Table 8. Summary of acceptable cut-off values of reliability and fit

Measure	Cut-Off Value
Cronbach's alpha	$\geq .70$
Item loadings	Significant and $\geq .707$
Adjusted chi-square	≤ 3.0
GFI	$\geq .90$
AGFI	$\geq .80$
CFI	$\geq .90$
NFI	$\geq .90$
RMSEA	$\leq .08$

Table 9. Measurement properties of constructs (29-item instrument)

Construct	Phase	Items	Alpha	χ^2/df	GFI	AGFI	CFI	NFI	RMSEA
Top Mgt Support	2	6	.93	4.98	.98	.95	.99	.99	.073
User Training	1	5	.93	3.95	.99	.97	1.00	.99	.063
Security Culture	1	5	.90	2.33	.99	.98	1.00	1.00	.042
Pol. Relevance	1	4	.90	.379	1.00	1.00	1.00	1.00	.000
Pol. Enforcement	1	4	.87	1.55	.99	.99	.99	1.00	.027
Sec. Effectiveness	3	5	.91	1.32	1.00	.99	1.00	1.00	.020

constructs. The four mediator variables may be influenced by a second-order factor that does not have direct effects on the observed variables of the study (Bollen, 1989). This alternative model is an exploratory investigation of the original. Unlike the original, it was not conceptualized from reading the qualitative responses. Yet, it is valuable because it offers a different way of thinking about the relationships among the constructs. Our interpretation of the second-order factor is *managerial practice* in information security. In the model, managerial practice represents the repeated actions and instructions of management to promote information security effectiveness in their organization. Table 12 illustrates the results of analyzing the alternative model using the same demographic sub-samples from Table 11.

Empirical support for both the original and alternative models are found in the magnitude and significance of the estimated parameters as well as the amount of variance explained by the structural equations (Segars & Grover, 1998). The alternative model is a more parsimonious representation of the observed covariance (six paths versus ten paths in the original model). Unlike the original model, all paths in the alternative model are significant at p < .001. The amount of explained variance measured by SMC is higher in each variable in the alternative model. Additionally, every model fit index improved in the alternative model including those measures that account for degrees of freedom (e.g., AGFI). In the demographic analysis using the alternate model, every path is significant at p < .001 including the

Table 10. Measurement model

Constructs	Indicators	Loadings	Critical Value	SMC
Top Management Support alpha = .93	TM1	.84	31.33	0.71
	TM2	.79	27.53	0.62
	TM3	.78	27.34	0.62
	TM4	.87	33.83	0.77
	TM5	.88	---	0.78
	TM6	.83	30.13	0.68
Employee Training alpha = .93	UT1	.81	31.39	0.66
	UT2	.88	37.56	0.78
	UT4	.92	---	0.85
	UT5	.85	34.77	0.72
	UT6	.81	31.20	0.66
Security Culture alpha = .90	SC1	.75	23.54	0.57
	SC3	.77	24.52	0.59
	SC4	.83	27.12	0.69
	SC5	.85	---	0.72
	SC6	.84	28.35	0.70
Policy Relevance alpha = .90	PR1	.90	34.98	0.81
	PR2	.73	24.01	0.53
	PR4	.80	27.98	0.64
	PR5	.90	---	0.81
Policy Enforcement alpha = .87	PE1	.85	---	0.72
	PE2	.78	23.78	0.60
	PE3	.83	26.32	0.70
	PE4	.72	21.29	0.51
Security Effectiveness alpha = .91	EF1	.85	31.36	0.72
	EF2	.83	30.69	0.70
	EF3	.75	25.31	0.56
	EF4	.89	---	0.79
	EF5	.77	26.84	0.60

Note: All loadings significant at p < .001

Figure 4. Path diagram of hypothesized model

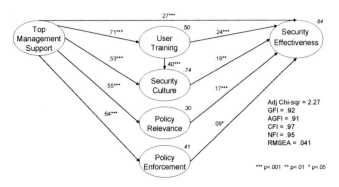

Note: Each endogenous variables' SMC estimate is to the upper-right of the construct

Table 11. Demographic tests of the hypothesized model

| Sample | n | Top Mgt Support | | | | | UT | UT | SC | PR | PE | Fit |
		EF	UT	SC	PR	PE	SC	Security Effectiveness				GFI CFI RMSEA
U.S. & Canada	462	***	***	***	***	***	***	***	**	**	NS	.91 .97 .042
Europe	121	*	***	***	***	***	***	NS	*	**	NS	.79 .96 .051
Asia-Pacific	104	*	***	***	***	***	**	NS	NS	NS	NS	.76 .93 .065
Government Sector	184	NS	***	***	***	***	***	***	*	*	NS	.84 .97 .046
Finance, Banking Sector	187	**	***	***	***	***	***	NS	NS	*	**	.84 .96 .050
Info Tech (IT) Sector	201	*	***	***	***	***	***	**	NS	*	NS	.84 .96 .052
Small (< 500 employees)	193	NS	***	***	***	***	***	**	*	**	**	.84 .96 .049
Med. (500-15,000 employees)	302	***	***	***	***	***	***	NS	NS	***	NS	.88 .97 .048
Large (>15,000 employees)	245	*	***	***	***	***	***	***	NS	NS	NS	.85 .95 .054
No top officer in organization[#]	267	***	***	***	***	***	***	NS	*	**	*	.87 .96 .044
Yes, top officer in organization	460	**	***	***	***	***	***	***	*	***	NS	.91 .97 .041

Notes:

***p<.001; **p<.01; *p<.05; NS Not Significant

EF: security effectiveness; UT: user training; SC: sec. culture; PR: policy relevance; PE: policy enforcement

[#] *Does the organization have a top security officer (e.g., Chief Security Officer, Director of Information Security)?*

Figure 5. Alternative, second-order factor model

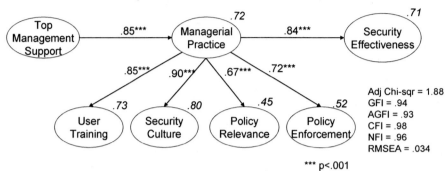

Table 12. Demographic tests of second-order factor model

Sample	n	Top Mgt Support	Managerial Practice				Mgt Practice	Fit
		Mgt Practice	UT	SC	PR	PE	Sec Effect	GFI CFI RMSEA
U.S. & Canada	462	***	***	***	***	***	***	.92 .98 .035
Europe	121	***	***	***	***	***	***	.80 .96 .045
Asia-Pacific	104	***	***	***	***	***	***	.77 .94 .062
Government sector	184	***	***	***	***	***	***	.84 .97 .045
Finance, Banking, sector	187	***	***	***	***	***	***	.84 .96 .050
Info Tech (IT) sector	201	***	***	***	***	***	***	.85 .97 .045
Small (<500 employees)	193	***	***	***	***	***	***	.84 .97 .045
Medium (500-15,000 employees)	302	***	***	***	***	***	***	.89 .97 .041
Large (>15,000 employees)	245	***	***	***	***	***	***	.87 .96 .049
No top officer in organization	267	***	***	***	***	***	***	.88 .97 .039
Yes, top officer in organization	460	***	***	***	***	***	***	.92 .98 .035

ManagementranefEfft

Figure 6. General forms of the theoretical models of this study

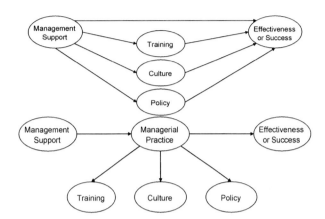

smaller sub-samples such as from Asia-Pacific respondents (n=104). Moreover, the model-fit generally improved from the original model for each sub-sample. Thus, results suggest that the alternative model has general applicability across the demographic categories of the sampled data of this study.

The improved fit in the alternative model does not necessarily mean it is the better of the two models. The original model, for instance, had the advantage of measuring the magnitude of the direct effect of each mediator variable on the dependent variable. This advantage was lost in the alternative model due to the inclusion of the more general second-order factor. This advantage of the original model was instrumental in bringing about one of the findings of the study pertaining to policy enforcement that we will discuss in the next section of this paper.

Tests were conducted to estimate the amount of common method variance in the collected data (N=740) using confirmatory procedures provided in the literature (Facteau, Dobbins, Russell, Ladd, & Kudisch, 1995; Williams, Cote, & Buckley, 1989). Confirmatory factor analysis shows that a single latent factor representing common variance did not fit the data well (χ^2/df = 14.1). For

comparison, the alternative model (*Figure 5*) provides a better fit (χ^2/df = 1.9). The chi-square difference between the single latent factor and alternative models is significant at *p <.001* [$\Delta\chi^2$ (6 df) = 4598.4]. Since there was a significant improvement in model fit between the single latent factor model and the alternative model, we have evidence that common method variance is not problematic in the sampled data. This finding is not surprising since the procedural remedies used during data collection aimed to minimize the effect of undesirable method variance among the constructs of the study. Researchers considering using this instrument can take further steps to minimize common method variance by obtaining measures of the dependent variable from a different source. For example, data for security effectiveness can come from employees other than full-time security professionals.

Based on the empirical results presented, we found support for both the original and alternative theoretical models. The next section discusses the findings of the study.

LINKS TO EXISTING THEORY

In their seminal text, Glaser & Strauss (1967) stated that it is desirable to link grounded models to existing theory to enhance internal validity and generalizability [see also Orlikowski (1993)]. In this section, we link aspects of this study to three existing theories and make suggestions for future research. These aspects include top management support, general deterrence theory, and the "dilemma of the supervisor" notion.

Existing Notions of Management Support

Top management support refers to the degree that senior management understands the importance of the security function and the extent to which management is perceived supporting security goals and priorities. By virtue of their position, top management can significantly influence resource allocation and act as a champion of change in creating an organizational environment conducive to security goals. Support from top management has been recognized for at least four decades as necessary for computer security management. For example, Joseph Wasserman discussed the importance of executive support stating, "Computer security thus involves a review of every possible source of control breakdown…one factor that has made the job more difficult is lack of awareness by many executives of new control concepts required for computer systems" (1969, p. 120).

The qualitative data from this study suggests that obtaining top management support is important for an effective information security program. As one CISSP stated, "Management buy-in and increasing the security awareness of employees is key. Technology is great, but without…management's backing, all the bits in the world won't help." The quantitative results of this study also suggest that management support is especially important to information security effectiveness. Among the results from the SEM portion of this study, the positive association between *top management support* and *security effectiveness* was significantly demonstrated in a wide-range of demographic data (see Figures 4, 5 and Tables 11, 12).

A substantial IS literature stream exists about the management support construct. With few exceptions, much of the empirical analysis has limited the effect of management support on a dependent "success" variable to a simple linear function (Jarvenpaa & Ives, 1991; Sharma & Yetton, 2003). Consequently, the current study contributes to the IS literature by offering a model that substantially mediates the relationships between management support and a dependent variable. This finding is valuable because the mediator variables of the study help show the complex relationship between management support and an appropriate dependent variable.

Both the original and alternative models of this study may be structured in a general form, which we illustrate in *Figure 6*. Future research can apply these forms to areas outside the realm of IS security, especially in organizational environments where top management support is critical to success. For instance, based on a meta-analysis of research published in 82 articles, Jasperson et al. (2002) offered several metaconjectures about environments where top management support may be especially critical. One such environment is characterized by resource conflict of IT projects. Research that studies organizational environments with considerable resource conflict may be able to benefit from the general models by applying them in their research setting.

We do not suggest that the general models are all-comprehensive depictions of mediators between top management support and information security effectiveness. Depending on the study, researchers can add different mediator variables to the model. For example, an added mediator variable could represent financial resource support. For this study, we considered adding such a variable during the qualitative steps of the study since many respondents indicated that obtaining financial resources for security programs is a critical organizational issue. However, we felt that asking financially related survey questions could have an adverse effect on the perceived intrusiveness of the survey instrument. Other studies where perceived intrusiveness is less of a concern could consider adding a financial resource type of variable to the model.

Deterrence Theory

The criminology theory of general deterrence emphasizes policing as a means of warding off potential abusive acts primarily through the fear of sanctions and unpleasant consequences (Parker, 1981; Straub, 1990). In the IS realm, deterrents are passive, administrative controls that can include security training sessions and policy statements that specify the proper use of an information system (Straub & Nance, 1990). Administrative deterrent efforts have been empirically demonstrated to result in fewer IS abuses (Straub, 1990). In the IS literature, the application of deterrence theory has been widely applied in related security studies to include software piracy (Gopal & Sanders, 1997; Peace, Galletta, & Thong, 2002), ethics (Harrington, 1996), risk management (Straub & Welke, 1998), abuse detection (Straub & Nance, 1990), social control theory (Lee, Lee, & Yoo, 2004), and security effectiveness (Kankanhalli et al., 2003; Straub, 1990).

Our study has parallels with the Kankanhalli et al. (2003) and Straub (1990) studies that are worth discussing. First, the Kankanhalli et al. study included top management support in a model of IS security effectiveness that was based on both deterrence and preventive efforts. Although their results of the hypothesized model were mixed, the top management support variable demonstrated a significant relationship on effectiveness through a mediating variable identified as *preventive efforts*. Second, while discussing the practical implications from his empirical study, Straub (1990, p.

272) suggests four actions to improve security effectiveness. First, managers who desire security improvements should establish policies as the precondition to effective deterrence efforts. Second, once polices are established, management needs to ensure users are educated and informed about proper IS use. Security officers should stress that policy violations will be accordingly punished. Third, with policy in place, managers can ensure that appropriate monitoring and surveillance programs of employee activities are utilized to enforce policy. Security officers should then follow up on all identified violations to help deter potential abusers. Finally, management should ensure the implementation of preventive mechanisms with security software that proactively helps to minimize security incidents. When comparing Straub's action plan to our study, four of the five predictor variables in our model are implied in Straub's suggested actions. The variable in our model not in Straub's suggestions is security culture. Yet, the literature supports culture as an important part of successful security programs (Leach, 2003; von Solms & von Solms, 2004). The culture construct has also been suggested for inclusion in future deterrence based security studies (Kankanhalli et al., 2003). Hence, while we did not base our study *a priori* on deterrence, the variables in our model may be interpreted through the lens of general deterrence theory.

The Dilemma of the Supervisor

The *policy enforcement* construct, while demonstrating acceptable scale reliability ($\alpha = .87$) and fit (e.g., GFI = .99; CFI = .99), had the weakest effect on the dependent variable compared to the other variables of the study. This weaker relationship is apparent in two areas. First, in the original theoretical model, the relationship between policy enforcement and the dependent variable had the lowest level of statistical significance compared to the other variables in the study. Second, as

Table 11 shows, eight of the eleven sub-samples had non-significant *policy enforcement – security effectiveness* paths.

We propose that the "dilemma of the supervisor" notion may help explain the weaker relationship between *policy enforcement* and *security effectiveness*. This dilemma is described by Strickland (1958) as occurring when the excessive use of surveillance, monitoring, and authority leads to management's distrust of employees and the perception of an increased need for more surveillance and control. Because managers see employees as motivated by the controls in place, managers develop a jaundiced view of their people (Ghoshal, 2005, p. 85). Too much surveillance and monitoring of employee activities to enforce policy compliance is then perceived by employees as overly controlling, which may damage employee self-perception, deteriorate trust, and decrease intrinsic motivation (Ghoshal, 2005). Applying this notion to our study, the relationship between *policy enforcement* and *security effectiveness* may be non-linear. If organizations want to encourage employees to intrinsically behave in a security-minded fashion, then an optimum level of policy enforcement may exist. Either too much or too little enforcement may have negative consequence on effectiveness.

A careful review of the qualitative data did not reveal participants identifying potential problems associated with excessive monitoring. However, this notion has been identified in the IS literature. While monitoring can help enforce important security policies, some employees may regard this as negatively affecting their work habits and privacy (Ariss, 2002). Managers have a key role to play in designing monitoring and enforcement systems that are effective, yet not viewed as too onerous or invasive. In this way, employees not only tolerate the monitoring system, but understand and approve of it (George, 1996). Based on this discussion, future research can further study the potential non-linear relationship between policy enforcement and security effectiveness.

LIMITATIONS

This study developed and empirically tested a theory of information security effectiveness in organizations; however the findings are limited in that the sample was homogeneous to the $(ISC)^2$ constituency. Participant concerns from this population may have biased the models in favor of organizational environments that typically hire certified security professionals. Before generalizing the results to other populations, researchers should apply these theoretical models to samples from different national cultures, specific industries, organization contexts, or in case studies. Research has shown that certain management practices can be compatible and others incompatible depending on the culture of a society (Hofstede, 1993). We recommend that any application of the models in culture-specific settings (i.e., consulting or case studies) should take national culture into account (McCoy, Galletta, & King, 2005). In our study, the CISSP certification requirements and the global nature of modern Internet security threats may have acted to minimize many cultural differences (Yang, 1986). The proliferation of IT certification bodies with rigorous entrance requirements like $(ISC)^2$ and their role in minimizing cross-cultural differences is a potential question for future research.

Another limitation of this study is the use of self-report, perception-based variables versus objective measures. The literature contains arguments both for and against the use of subjective measures (Podsakoff & Organ, 1986; Spector, 1994; Straub et al., 2004). Some evidence suggests that perceived and objective measures are positively associated (Venkatraman & Ramanujam, 1987), while others suggest they are not positively associated (Srinivasan, 1985). The use of objective data can be especially problematic in the area of security. Many companies are hesitant to provide hard data regarding computer abuse or security ineffectiveness because they may not want to risk embarrassing media reports. In addition, it is difficult to know if hard data (e.g., number of incidents, financial loss) is accurate and complete considering that security incidents often are underreported or undiscovered (Gordon et al., 2005; Straub & Nance, 1990). An alternative to hard data is to measure security effectiveness using a professional subjective judgment as accomplished in this study. One can even argue that a qualified judgment about an organization's overall security program is more sensitive than the sharing of hard, objective data since a professional judgment can take a holistic view of an organization's security program while taking into account aspects that are difficult to measure objectively. Despite the limitation of using perception-based variables, subjective measures can be an appropriate research tool for exploratory studies into a phenomenon of interest (Spector, 1994). Taken as a whole, it would be prudent for organizations attempting to measure security effectiveness to take a multifaceted approach by collecting both hard, objective data as well as soft, subjective perceptions. This type of combined approach is most likely to lead to an accurate view of the state of an organization's information security program.

IMPLICATIONS AND CONCLUSION

The models proposed in this study emerged from an analysis of qualitative data. Grounded models are especially relevant to practitioners because the practitioner community provided the data from which the models emerged. This is important considering that IS researchers continue to struggle to make research relevant to practitioners (Baskerville & Myers, 2004) despite the frequent calls for IS researchers to do so (Benbasat & Zmud, 1999). Since the constructs of this study embody relevant issues of IS security, managers can improve security effectiveness by thinking about and applying the theoretical model of this study in their organizations. While the scales and

the model do not include every aspect that should be important to managers, the model does focus on some of the most critical areas that managers can influence to bring about an effective information security program. We believe a key implication of this research is the development of a theoretical model that is useful and relevant to information security practitioners.

Considering that many IT executives now consider security among their top issues, the findings of this study should be highly relevant to IT management. While no organization can have perfect security, there are specific practices that management can do to maximize the protection of their critical information resources. Results of this study suggest that sufficient levels of top management support, user training, security culture, policy relevance and appropriate policy enforcement are significant predictors of the effectiveness of an information security program. Because many computer and information security problems today require managerial solutions, the model proposed in this study can help management focus their efforts in the areas where they can make the most difference.

We summarize our findings by suggesting the following proposition: An organization's overall security health can be accurately predicted by asking a single question: Does top management visibly and actively support the organization's information security program? The answer to this question is a strong indicator and predictor into the overall health and effectiveness of the organization's information security program. If answered in the affirmative, it is likely that an organization's information security program is achieving its goals. If answered in the negative, it is less likely the program is accomplishing its goals. We argue that the findings of this study support this proposition.

REFERENCES

Ariss, S.S. (2002). Computer monitoring: Benefits and pitfalls facing management. *Information & Management, 39*(7), 553-558.

Bagchi, K., & Udo, G. (2003). An analysis of the growth of computer and internet security breaches. *Communications of the AIS, 12*(46), 684-700.

Baskerville, R.L., & Myers, M.D. (2004). Special issue on action research in information systems: Making IS research relevant to practice. Forward. *MIS Quarterly, 28*(3), 329-335.

Benbasat, I., & Zmud, R.W. (1999). Empirical research in information systems: The practice of relevance. *MIS Quarterly, 23*(1), 3-16.

Bollen, K.A. (1989). *Structural equations with latent variables.* New York: John Wiley & Sons.

Campbell, D.T., & Fiske, D.W. (1959). Convergent and discriminant validation by the multi-trait-multimethod matrix. *Psychological Bulletin, 56*(2), 81-105.

Computer Emergency Response Team (CERT). (2004). *CERT statistics.* Retrieved May 2004, from http://www.cert.org/stats/cert_stats.html#incidents.

DeVellis, R.F. (2003). *Scale development. Theory and applications* (2nd ed.) (Vol. 26). Thousand Oaks, CA: Sage Publications.

Dhillon, G., & Backhouse, J. (2001). Current directions in IS security research: Towards socio-organizational perspectives. *Information Systems Journal, 11*(2), 127-153.

Facteau, J.D., Dobbins, G.H., Russell, J.E.A., Ladd, R.T., & Kudisch, J.D. (1995). The influence of general perceptions of training environment on pretraining motivation and perceived training transfer. *Journal of Management, 21*(1), 1-25.

Files, J. (2006, June 29). Missing laptop with veterans' data is found. *New York Times.*

Frazier, P.A., Barron, K.E., & Tix, A.P. (2004). Testing moderator and mediator effects in counseling psychology. *Journal of Counseling Psychology, 51*(1), 115-134.

Galal, G.H. (2001). From contexts to constructs: The use of grounded theory in operationalising contingent process models. *European Journal of Information Systems, 10*, 2-14.

Garg, A., Curtis, J., & Halper, H. (2003). The financial impact of IT security breaches: What do investors think? *Information Systems Security, 12*(1), 22-34.

Gefen, D. (2003). Assessing unidimensionality through LISREL: An explanation and example. *Communications of the AIS, 12*, 23-46.

George, J.F. (1996). Computer-based monitoring: Common perceptions and empirical results. *MIS Quarterly, 20*(4), 459-480.

Ghoshal, S. (2005). Bad management theories are destroying good management practices. *Academy of Management Learning & Education, 4*(1), 75-91.

Glaser, B.G., & Strauss, A.L. (1967). *The discovery of grounded theory: Strategies for qualitative research.* New York: Aldine Publishing Company.

Gopal, R.D., & Sanders, G.L. (1997). Preventive and deterrent controls for software piracy. *Journal of Management Information Systems, 13*(4), 29-47.

Gordon, L.A., Loeb, M.P., Lucyshyn, W., & Richardson, R. (2005). *10th annual CSI/FBI computer crime and security survey.* San Francisco, CA: Computer Security Institute.

Harrington, S.J. (1996). The effect of codes of ethics and personal denial of responsibility on computer abuse judgments and intentions. *MIS Quarterly, 20*(3), 257-278.

Hinkin, T.R. (1998). A brief tutorial on the development of measures for use in survey questionnaires. *Organizational Research Methods, 1*(1), 104-121.

Hofstede, G. (1993). Cultural constraints in management theories. *Academy of Management Journal, 7*(1), 81-94.

Jarvenpaa, S.L., & Ives, B. (1991). Executive involvement and participation in the management of information technology. *MIS Quarterly, 15*(2), 205-221.

Jasperson, J.S., Carte, T.A., Saunders, C.S., Butler, B.S., Croes, H.J.P., & Zheng, W. (2002). Power and information technology research: A metatriangulation review. *MIS Quarterly, 26*(4), 397-459.

Kankanhalli, A., Hock-Hai, T., Bernard, C.Y.T., & Kwok-Kee, W. (2003). An integrative study of information systems security effectiveness. *International Journal of Information Management, 23*(2), 139-154.

Karahanna, E., Evaristo, R., & Srite, M. (2004). Methodological issues in MIS cross-cultural research. In M.E. Whitman & A.B. Woszczynski (Eds.), *The handbook of information systems research* (pp. 166-177). Hershey, PA: Idea Group Publishing.

Kotulic, A.G., & Clark, J.G. (2004). Why there aren't more information security research studies. *Information & Management, 41*(5), 597-607.

Leach, J. (2003). Improving user security behavior. *Computers & Security, 22*(8), 685-692.

Lee, S.M., Lee, S.G., & Yoo, S. (2004). An integrative model of computer abuse based on social control and general deterrence theories. *Information & Management, 41*(6), 707-718.

MacKinnon, D.P., Krull, J.L., & Lockwood, C. (2000). Mediation, confounding, and suppression: Different names for the same effect. *Prevention Science, 2*, 15-27.

McCoy, S., Galletta, D.F., & King, W.R. (2005). Integrating national culture into IS research: The need for current individual-level measures. *Communications of the Association for Information Systems, 15*, 211-224.

Nunnally, J. (1978). *Psychometric theory.* New York: McGraw-Hill.

Orlikowski, W. (1993). CASE tools as organizational change: Investigating incremental and radical changes in systems development. *MIS Quarterly, 17*(3), 309-340.

Parker, D.B. (1981). *Computer security management.* Reston, VA: Reston Publishing Company.

Peace, A.G., Galletta, D.F., & Thong, J.Y.L. (2002). Software piracy in the workplace: A model and empirical test. *Journal of Management Information Systems, 20*(1), 153-177.

Podsakoff, P.M., MacKenzie, S.B., Lee, J.Y., & Podsakoff, N.P. (2003). Common method bias in behavioral research: A critical review of the literature and recommended remedies. *Journal of Applied Psychology, 88*(5), 879-903.

Podsakoff, P.M., & Organ, D.W. (1986). Self-reports in organizational research: Problems and prospects. *Journal of Management, 12*(4), 531-544.

Segars, A.H., & Grover, V. (1998). Strategic information systems planning success: An investigation of the construct and its measurement. *MIS Quarterly, 22*(2), 139-163.

Sharma, R., & Yetton, P. (2003). The contingent effects of management support and task interdependence on successful information systems implementation. *MIS Quarterly, 27*(4), 533-555.

Spector, P.E. (1994). Using self-report questionnaires in OB research: A comment on the use of a controversial method. *Journal of Organizational Behavior, 15*, 385-392.

Srinivasan, A. (1985). Alternative measures of system effectiveness: Associations and implications. *MIS Quarterly, 9*(3), 243-253.

Straub, D.W. (1990). Effective IS security: An empirical study. *Information Systems Research, 1*(3), 255-276.

Straub, D.W., Boudreau, M.C., & Gefen, D. (2004). Validating guidelines for IS positivist research. *Communications of the AIS, 13*(24), 380-427.

Straub, D.W., Limayem, M., & Karahanna-Evaristo, E. (1995). Measuring system usage: Implications for IS theory testing. *MIS Quarterly, 41*(8), 1328-1342.

Straub, D.W., & Nance, W.D. (1990). Discovering and disciplining computer abuse in organizations: A field study. *MIS Quarterly, 14*(1), 45-60.

Straub, D.W., & Welke, R.J. (1998). Coping with systems risk: Security planning models for management decision making. *MIS Quarterly, 22*(4), 441-469.

Strauss, A., & Corbin, J. (1998). *Basics of qualitative research. Techniques and procedures for developing grounded theory* (2nd ed.). Thousand Oaks, CA: Sage.

Strickland, L.H. (1958). Surveillance and trust. *Journal of Personality, 26*, 200-215.

Venkatraman, N., & Ramanujam, V. (1987). Measurement of business economic performance: An examination of method convergency. *Journal of Management, 13*(1), 109-122.

von Solms, R., & von Solms, B. (2004). From policies to culture. *Computers & Security, 23*, 275-279.

Wasserman, J.J. (1969). Plugging the leaks in computer security. *Harvard Business Review, 47*(5), 119-129.

Williams, L.J., Cote, J.A., & Buckley, M.R. (1989). Lack of method variance in self-reported affect and perceptions at work: Reality or artifact? *Journal of Applied Psychology, 74*, 462-468.

Yang, K.S. (1986). Will societal modernization eventually eliminate cross-cultural psychological differences. In M.H. Bond (Ed.), *The cross-cultural challenge to social psychology.* Newbury Park, CA: Sage.

ENDNOTES

[*] Opinions, conclusions and recommendations expressed or implied within are solely those of the authors and do not necessarily represent the views of USAF Academy, USAF, the DoD or any other government agency.

[1] In part because attacks against Internet-connected systems have become so commonplace, the CERT no longer publishes incident numbers. See http://www.cert.org/stats.

[2] We also conducted various mediation tests described in the literature (MacKinnon, Krull, & Lockwood, 2000). In our model, the total percent mediated by the four mediator variables on the dependent variable was 61%. The percent mediated of each variable: user training 25%, security culture 15%, policy relevance 13%, and policy enforcement 8%.

APPENDIX A. SURVEY INSTRUMENT

The pilot test supported a 35-item instrument. During the large-scale survey, we dropped six items resulting in a 29-item instrument. We coded reasons for dropping each item as follows:

X = high cross loading with other constructs.
R = low reliability.
U = high residual covariance with other items (Gefen, 2003)

Constructs:

TM = top management support;
UT = user training;
SC = security culture;
PR = policy relevance;
PE = policy enforcement;
EF = security effectiveness

Code	Item. Each begins with, "In the organization,"
TM1	Top management considers information security an important organizational priority.
TM2	Top executives are interested in security issues.
TM3	Top management takes security issues into account when planning corporate strategies.
TM4	Senior leadership's words and actions demonstrate that security is a priority.
TM5	Visible support for security goals by senior management is obvious.
TM6	Senior management gives strong and consistent support to the security program.
UT1	Necessary efforts are made to educate employees about *new* security polices.
UT2	Information security awareness is communicated well.
UT3 R	A variety of business communications (notices, posters, newsletters, etc.) are used to promote security awareness.
UT4	An effective security awareness program exists.
UT5	A continuous, ongoing security awareness program exists.
UT6	Users receive adequate security refresher training appropriate for their job function.
SC1	Employees value the importance of security.
SC2 X	A culture exists that promotes good security practices.
SC3	Security has traditionally been considered an important organizational value.
SC4	Practicing good security is the accepted way of doing business.
SC5	The overall environment fosters security-minded thinking.
SC6	Information security is a key norm shared by organizational members.
PR1	Information security policy is consistently updated on a periodic basis.
PR2	Information security policy is updated when technology changes require it.
PR3 X R U	Policy is updated when legal & regulatory changes require it.
PR4	An established information security policy review and update process exists.
PR5	Security policy is properly updated on a regular basis.
PR6 X	Information security policies are aligned with business goals.
PR7 X	Information security policies reflect the objectives of the organization.
PR8 X	Risk assessments are conducted prior to writing new security polices.
PE1	Employees caught violating important security policies are appropriately corrected.
PE2	Information security rules are enforced by sanctioning the employees who break them.
PE3	Repeat security offenders are appropriately disciplined.
PE4	Termination is a consideration for employees who repeatedly break security rules.
EF1	The information security program achieves most of its goals.

EF2 The information security program accomplishes its most important objectives.
EF3 Generally speaking, information is sufficiently protected.
EF4 Overall, the information security program is effective.
EF5 The information security program has kept risks to a minimum.

This work was previously published in International Journal of Information Security and Privacy, Vol. 1, Issue 2, edited by H. Nemati, pp. 37-60, copyright 2007 by IGI Publishing, formerly known as Idea Group Publishing (an imprint of IGI Global).

Chapter VII
Business Collaboration by Privacy-Preserving Clustering

Stanley R. M. Oliveira
Embrapa Informática Agropecuária, Brazil

Osmar R. Zaïane
University of Alberta, Canada

ABSTRACT

The sharing of data is beneficial in data mining applications and widely acknowledged as advantageous in business. However, information sharing can become controversial and thwarted by privacy regulations and other privacy concerns. Rather than simply hindering data owners from sharing information for data analysis, a solution could be designed to meet privacy requirements and guarantee valid data clustering results. To achieve this dual goal, this chapter introduces a method for privacy-preserving clustering, called Dimensionality Reduction-Based Transformation (DRBT). This method relies on the intuition behind random projection to protect the underlying attribute values subjected to cluster analysis. It is shown analytically and empirically that transforming a dataset using DRBT, a data owner can achieve privacy preservation and get accurate clustering with little overhead of communication cost. The advantages of such a method are: it is independent of distance-based clustering algorithms; it has

INTRODUCTION

Data clustering is of capital importance in business and it fosters business collaboration as sharing data for clustering improves the prospects of identifying optimal customer targets, market more effectively and understand customer behaviour. Data Clustering maximizes return on investment supporting business collaboration (Lo, 2002; Berry & Linoff, 1997). Often combining different data sources provides better clustering analysis opportunities. Limiting the clustering on only some attributes of the data confines the correctness of the grouping, while benefiting from additional attributes could yield more accurate and actionable clusters. For example, it does not suffice to cluster customers based on their purchasing history, but combining purchasing history, vital statistics and other demographic and financial information for clustering purposes can lead to better and more accurate customer behaviour analysis. More often than not, needed data sources are distributed, partitioned and owned by different parties insinuating a requirement for sharing data, often sensitive, between parties. Despite its benefits to support both modern business and social goals, clustering can also, in the absence of adequate safeguards, jeopardize individuals' privacy. The fundamental question addressed in this chapter is: how can data owners protect personal data shared for cluster analysis and meet their needs to support decision making or to promote social benefits? To address this problem, data owners must not only meet privacy requirements but also guarantee valid clustering results.

Achieving privacy preservation, when sharing data for clustering, poses challenges for novel uses of data mining technology. Each application poses a new set of challenges. Let us consider two real-life examples in which the sharing of data poses different constraints:

- Two organizations, an Internet marketing company and an on-line retail company, have datasets with different attributes for a common set of individuals. These organizations decide to share their data for clustering to find the optimal customer targets so as to maximize return on investments. How can these organizations learn about their clusters using each other's data without learning anything about the attribute values of each other?
- Suppose that a hospital shares some data for research purposes (e.g., to group patients who have a similar disease). The hospital's security administrator may suppress some identifiers (e.g., name, address, phone number, etc) from patient records to meet privacy requirements. However, the released data

may not be fully protected. A patient record may contain other information that can be linked with other datasets to re-identify individuals or entities (Sweeney, 2002). How can we identify groups of patients with a similar pathology or characteristics without revealing the values of the attributes associated with them?

The above scenarios describe two different problems of privacy-preserving clustering (PPC). We refer to the former as PPC over centralized data and the latter as PPC over vertically partitioned data. To address these scenarios, we introduce a new PPC method called Dimensionality_Reduction-Based Transformation (DRBT). This method allows data owners to find a trade-off between privacy, accuracy, and communication cost. Communication cost is the cost (typically in size) of the data exchanged between parties in order to achieve secure clustering.

This chapter focuses on random projection, a powerful method for dimensionality reduction. The accuracy obtained after the dimensionality has been reduced, using random projection, is almost as good as the original accuracy (Kaski, 1999; Achlioptas, 2001; Bingham & Mannila, 2001). More formally, when a vector in d-dimensional space is projected onto a random k dimensional subspace, the distances between any pair of points are not distorted by more than a factor of $(1 \pm \varepsilon)$, for any $0 < \varepsilon < 1$, with probability $O(1/n^2)$, where n is the number of objects under analysis (Johnson & Lindenstrauss, 1984).

The motivation for exploring random projection is based on the following aspects. First, it is a general data reduction technique. In contrast to the other methods, such as PCA, random projection does not use any defined interestingness criterion to optimize the projection. Second, random projection has shown to have promising theoretical properties for high dimensional data clustering (Fern & Brodley, 2003; Bingham & Mannila, 2001). Third, despite its computational simplicity, random projection does not introduce a significant distortion in the data. Finally, the dimensions found by random projection are not a subset of the original dimensions but rather a transformation, which is relevant for privacy preservation.

In this chapter, random projection is used to mask the underlying attribute values subjected to clustering, protecting them from being revealed. In tandem with the benefit of privacy preservation, the method DRBT benefits from the fact that random projection preserves the distances (or similarities) between data objects quite nicely, which is desirable in cluster analysis. We show analytically and experimentally that using DRBT, a data owner can meet privacy requirements without losing the benefit of clustering. The major features of our method DRBT are: a) it is independent of distance-based clustering algorithms; b) it has a sound mathematical foundation; and c) it does not require CPU intensive operations.

This chapter is organized as follows. In the next section, we provide the basic concepts that are necessary to understand the issues addressed in this paper. We then describe the research problem employed in our study. We then introduce our method DRBT to address PPC over centralized data and over vertically partitioned data, and an overview of the existing PPC solutions. Subsequently, the experimental results are presented followed by our conclusions.

BACKGROUND

In this section, we briefly review the basics of clustering, notably the concepts of data matrix and dissimilarity matrix. Subsequently, we review the basics of dimensionality reduction. In particular, we focus on the background of random projection.

Data Matrix

Objects (e.g., individuals, observations, events) are usually represented as points (vectors) in a multi-dimensional space. Each dimension represents a distinct attribute describing the object. Thus, objects are represented as an $m \times n$ matrix D, where there are m rows, one for each object, and n columns, one for each attribute. This matrix may contain binary, categorical, or numerical attributes. It is referred to as a data matrix, represented as follows:

$$D = \begin{bmatrix} a_{11} & \cdots & a_{1k} & \cdots & a_{1n} \\ a_{21} & \cdots & a_{2k} & \cdots & a_{2n} \\ \vdots & & \vdots & \ddots & \vdots \\ a_{m1} & \cdots & a_{mk} & \cdots & a_{mn} \end{bmatrix} \qquad (1)$$

The attributes in a data matrix are sometimes transformed before being used. The main reason is that different attributes may be measured on different scales (e.g., centimeters and kilograms). When the range of values differs widely from attribute to attribute, attributes with large range can influence the results of the cluster analysis. For this reason, it is common to standardize the data so that all attributes are on the same scale. There are many methods for data normalization (Han & Kamber, 2006). We review only two of them in this section: *min-max normalization* and *z-score normalization*.

Min-max normalization performs a linear transformation on the original data. Each attribute is normalized by scaling its values so that they fall within a small specific range, such as 0.0 and 1.0. Min-max normalization maps a value v of an attribute A to v' as follows:

$$v' = \frac{v - min_A}{max_A - min_A} \times \left(new\_max_A - new\_min_A\right) + new\_min_A$$

$$(2)$$

where min_A and max_A represent the minimum and maximum values of an attribute A, respectively, while new_min_A and new_max_A are the new range in which the normalized data will fall. When the actual minimum and maximum of an attribute are unknown, or when there are outliers that dominate the min-max normalization, z-score normalization (also called zero-mean normalization) should be used. In z-score normalization, the values for an attribute A are normalized based on the mean and the standard deviation of A. A value v is mapped to v' as follows:

$$v' = \frac{v - \overline{A}}{\sigma_A} \qquad (3)$$

where $\overline{A}$ and σ_A are the mean and the standard deviation of the attribute A, respectively.

Dissimilarity Matrix

A dissimilarity matrix stores a collection of proximities that are available for all pairs of objects. This matrix is often represented by an $m \times m$ table such as:

$$DM = \begin{bmatrix} 0 & & & & \\ d(2,1) & 0 & & & \\ d(3,1) & d(3,2) & 0 & & \\ \cdots & \cdots & \cdots & & \\ d(m,1) & d(m,2) & \cdots & \cdots & 0 \end{bmatrix} \qquad (4)$$

We can see the dissimilarity matrix DM corresponding to the data matrix D in *(1)*, where each element $d(i, j)$ represents the difference or dissimilarity between objects i and j. In general, $d(i, j)$ is a non-negative number that is close to zero when the objects i and j are very similar to each other, and becomes larger the more they differ. Several distance measures could be used to calculate the dissimilarity matrix of a set of points in d-dimensional space (Han & Kamber, 2006). The Euclidean distance is the most popular distance measure. If $i = (x_{i1}, x_{i2}, ..., x_{in})$ and $j = (x_{j1}, x_{j2}, ..., x_{jn})$ are n-dimensional data objects, the Euclidean distance between i and j is given by:

$$d(i,j) = \sqrt{\sum_{k=1}^{n} \left| x_{ik} - x_{jk} \right|^2} \qquad (5)$$

The Euclidean distance satisfies the following constraints:

- $d(i, j) \geq 0$: distance is a non-negative number.
- $d(i, i) = 0$: the distance of an object to itself.
- $d(i, j) = d(j, i)$: distance is a symmetric function.
- $d(i, j) \leq d(i, k) + d(k, j)$: distance satisfies the triangular inequality.

Dimensionality Reduction

In many applications of data mining, the high dimensionality of the data restricts the choice of data processing methods. Examples of such applications include market basket data, text classification, and clustering. In these cases, the dimensionality is large due to either a wealth of alternative products, a large vocabulary, or an expressive number of attributes to be analyzed in Euclidean space, respectively.

When data vectors are defined in a high-dimensional space, it is computationally intractable to use data analysis or pattern recognition algorithms which repeatedly compute similarities or distances in the original data space. It is therefore necessary to reduce the dimensionality before, for instance, clustering the data (Fern & Brodley, 2003).

The goal of the methods designed for dimensionality reduction is to map d-dimensional objects into k-dimensional objects, where $k \ll d$ (Kaski, 1999). These methods map each object to a point in a k-dimensional space minimizing the stress function:

$$stress^2 = \frac{\sum_{i,j}\left(\hat{d}_{ij} - d_{ij}\right)^2}{\sum_{i,j}d_{ij}^{\;2}} \qquad (6)$$

where d_{ij} is the dissimilarity measure between objects i and j in a d-dimensional space, and $\hat{d}_{ij}$ is the dissimilarity measure between objects i and j in a k-dimensional space. The function *stress* gives the relative error that the distances in k-d space suffer from, on the average.

There are numerous methods for reducing the dimensionality of data, ranging from different feature extraction methods (Kaski, 1999) to multidimensional scaling (Young, 1987). Another alternative for dimensionality reduction is to project the data onto a lower-dimensional orthogonal subspace that captures as much of the variation of the data as possible. The best and most widely way to do so is Principal Component Analysis (Fukunaga, 1990).

Random projection has recently emerged as a powerful method for dimensionality reduction.

The accuracy obtained after the dimensionality has been reduced, using random projection, is almost as good as the original accuracy (Kaski, 1999; Achlioptas, 2001; Bingham & Mannila, 2001). The key idea of random projection arises from the Johnson-Lindenstrauss lemma (Johnson & Lindenstrauss, 1984): "if points in a vector space are projected onto a randomly selected subspace of suitably high dimension, then the distances between the points are approximately preserved."

Lemma 1 (Johnson & Lindenstrauss, 1984). *Given $\varepsilon > 0$ and an integer n, let k be a positive integer such that $k \geq k_0 = O(\varepsilon^{-2}\log n)$. For every set P of n points in $\mathfrak{R}^d$ there exists f: $\mathfrak{R}^d \rightarrow \mathfrak{R}^k$ such that for all $u, v \in P$:*

$$\left(1-\varepsilon\right)\|u - v\|^2 \leq \|f(u) - f(v)\|^2 \leq (1+\varepsilon)\|u - v\|^2$$

The classic result of Johnson and Lindenstrauss (Johnson & Lindenstrauss, 1984) asserts that any set of n points in d-dimensional Euclidean space can be embedded into k-dimensional space, where k is logarithmic in n and independent of d. We provide the background of random projection in the next section.

Random Projection

A random projection from d dimensions to k dimensions is a linear transformation represented by a $d \times k$ matrix R, which is generated by first setting each entry of the matrix to a value drawn from an i.i.d. $\sim N(0,1)$ distribution (i.e., zero mean and unit variance) and then normalizing the columns to unit length. Given a d-dimensional dataset represented as an $n \times d$ matrix D, the mapping $D \times R$ results in a reduced-dimension dataset D', i.e.,

$$D'_{n\times k} = D_{n\times d}R_{d\times k} \qquad (7)$$

Random projection is computationally very simple. Given the random matrix R and projecting the $n \times d$ matrix D into k dimensions is of the order $O(ndk)$, and if the matrix D is sparse with about c nonzero entries per column, the complexity is of the order $O(cnk)$ (Bingham & Mannila, 2001).

After applying random projection to a dataset, the distance between two d-dimensional vectors i and j is approximated by the scaled Euclidean distance of these vectors in the reduced space as follows:

$$\sqrt{\frac{d}{k}}\left\|R_i - R_j\right\| \qquad (8)$$

where d is the original and k the reduced dimensionality of the dataset. The scaling term $\sqrt{d/k}$ takes into account the decrease in the dimensionality of the data.

To satisfy Lemma 1, the random matrix R must hold the follow constraints:

- The columns of the random matrix R are composed of orthonormal vectors, i.e, they have unit length and are orthogonal.
- The elements r_{ij} of R have zero mean and unit variance.

Clearly, the choice of the random matrix R is one of the key points of interest. The elements r_{ij} of R are often Gaussian distributed, but this need not to be the case. Achlioptas (Achlioptas, 2001) showed that the Gaussian distribution can be replaced by a much simpler distribution, as follows:

$$r_j = \sqrt{3} \times \begin{cases} +1 & with \quad probability \quad 1/6 \\ 0 & with \quad probability \quad 2/3 \\ -1 & with \quad probability \quad 1/6 \end{cases}$$

$$(9)$$

In fact, practically all zero mean, unit variance distributions of r_{ij} would give a mapping that still satisfies the Johnson-Lindenstrauss lemma. Achlioptas' result means further computational savings in database applications since the computations can be performed using integer arithmetic.

PROBLEM DEFINITION

The goal of privacy-preserving clustering is to protect the underlying attribute values of objects subjected to clustering analysis. In doing so, the privacy of individuals would be protected.

The problem of privacy preservation in clustering can be stated as follows: Let D be a relational database and C a set of clusters generated from D. The goal is to transform D into D' so that the following restrictions hold:

- A transformation T when applied to D must preserve the privacy of individual records,

so that the released database D' conceals the values of confidential attributes, such as salary, disease diagnosis, credit rating, and others.

- The similarity between objects in D' must be the same as that one in D, or just slightly altered by the transformation process. Although the transformed database D' looks very different from D, the clusters in D and D' should be as close as possible since the distances between objects are preserved or marginally changed.

We will approach the problem of PPC by first dividing it into two sub-problems: PPC over centralized data and PPC over vertically partitioned data. In the centralized data approach, different entities are described with the same schema in a unique centralized data repository, while in a vertical partition, the attributes of the same entities are split across the partitions. We do not address the case of horizontally partitioned data.

PPC over Centralized Data

In this scenario, two parties, **A** and **B**, are involved, party **A** owning a dataset D and party **B** wanting to mine it for clustering. In this context, the data are assumed to be a matrix $D_{m \times n}$, where each of the m rows represents an object, and each object contains values for each of the n attributes.

We assume that the matrix $D_{m \times n}$ contains numerical attributes only, and the attribute values associated with an object are private and must be protected. After transformation, the attribute values of an object in D would look very different from the original. Therefore, miners would rely on the transformed data to build valid results, i.e., clusters.

Before sharing the dataset D with party **B**, party **A** must transform D to preserve the privacy of individual data records. However, the transformation applied to D must not jeopardize the similarity between objects. Our second real-life motivating example, in the Introduction of this article, is a particular case of PPC over centralized data.

PPC over Vertically Partitioned Data

Consider a scenario wherein k parties, such that $k \geq 2$, have different attributes for a common set of objects, as mentioned in the first real-life example, in Section *Introduction*. Here, the goal is to do a join over the k parties and cluster the common objects. The data matrix for this case is given as follows:

$$
\begin{bmatrix}
Party_1 & & & Party_2 & & & \cdots & & Party_k & & \\
a_1 & \cdots & a_{1i} & a_{1i+1} & \cdots & a_{1j} & & a_{1p+1} & \cdots & a_{1n} \\
& \vdots & & & \vdots & & \cdots & & \vdots & \\
a_{m1} & \cdots & a_{mi} & a_{mi+1} & \cdots & a_{mj} & & a_{mp+1} & \cdots & a_{mn}
\end{bmatrix} \quad (10)
$$

Note that, after doing a join over the k parties, the problem of PPC over vertically partitioned data becomes a problem of PPC over centralized data. For simplicity, we do not consider communication cost here since this issue is addressed later.

In our model for PPC over vertically partitioned data, one of the parties is the central one which is in charge of merging the data and finding the clusters in the merged data. After finding the clusters, the central party would share the clustering results with the other parties. The challenge here is how to move the data from each party to a central party concealing the values of the attributes of each party. However, before moving the data to a central party, each party must transform its data to protect the privacy of the attribute values. We assume that the existence of an object (ID) should be revealed for the purpose of the join operation, but the values of the associated attributes are private.

The Communication Protocol

To address the problem of PPC over vertically partitioned data, we need to design a communication protocol. This protocol is used between two parties: the first party is the central one and the other represents any of the $k - 1$ parties, assuming that we have k parties. We refer to the central party as *party(c)* and any of the other parties as *party(k)*. There are two threads on the *party(k)* side, one for selecting the attributes to be shared, as can be seen in Table 1, and the other for selecting the objects before the sharing data, as can be seen in Table 2.

THE DIMENSIONALITY REDUCTION-BASED TRANSFORMATION

In this section, we show that the triple-goal of achieving privacy preservation and valid clustering results at a reduced communication cost in PPC can be accomplished by dimensionality reduction. By reducing the dimensionality of a dataset to a sufficiently small value, one can find a trade-off between privacy, accuracy, and communication cost. In particular, random project can fulfill this triple-goal. We refer to this solution as the Dimensionality Reduction-Based Transformation (DRBT).

General Assumptions

The solution to the problem of PPC based on random projection draws the following assumptions:

- The data matrix D subjected to clustering contains only numerical attributes that must be transformed to protect individuals' data values before the data sharing for clustering occurs.
- In PPC over centralized data, the existence of an object (ID) should be replaced by a fictitious identifier. In PPC over vertically partitioned data, the IDs of the objects are used for the join purposes between the parties involved in the solution, and the existence of an object at a site is not considered private.

Table 1. Thread of selecting the attributes on the party(k) side

Steps to select the attributes for clustering on the *party(k)* side:
1. Negotiate the attributes for clustering before the sharing of data. 2. Wait for the list of attributes available in *party(c)*. 3. Upon receiving the list of attributes from *party(c)*:   Select the attributes of the objects to be shared.

Table 2. Thread of selecting the objects on the party(k) side

Steps to select the list of objects on the *party(k)* side:

1. Negotiate the list of *m* objects before the sharing of data.
2. Wait for the list of *m* object IDs.
3. Upon receiving the list of *m* object IDs from *party(c)*:
    a) Select the *m* objects to be shared;
    b) Transform the attribute values of the *m* objects;
    c) Send the transformed *m* objects to *party(c)*.

- The transformation (random projection) applied to the original data might slightly modify the distance between data points. Such a transformation justifies the trade-off between privacy, accuracy, and communication cost.

One interesting characteristic of the solution based on random projection is that, once the dimensionality of a database is reduced, the attribute names in the released database are irrelevant. In other words, the released database preserves, in general, the similarity between the objects, but the underlying data values are completely different from the original ones. We refer to the released database as a *disguised database*, which is shared for clustering.

PPC over Centralized Data

To address PPC over centralized data, the DRBT performs three major steps before sharing the data for clustering:

- **Step 1—Suppressing identifiers:** Attributes that are not subjected to clustering (e.g., address, phone number, etc.) are suppressed.
- **Step 2—Reducing the dimension of the original dataset:** After pre-processing the data according to *Step 1*, an original dataset *D* is then transformed into the disguised dataset *D'* using random projection.
- **Step 3—Computing the stress function:** This function is used to determine whether the accuracy of the transformed dataset is marginally modified, which guarantees the usefulness of the data for clustering. A data owner can compute the stress function using Equation (6).

To illustrate how this solution works, let us consider the sample relational database in Table 3.

This sample contains real data from the Cardiac Arrhythmia Database available at the UCI Reposi-

Table 3. A cardiac arrhythmia database.

ID	age	weight	H_rate	Int_def	QRS	PR_int
123	75	80	63	32	91	193
342	56	64	53	24	81	174
254	40	52	70	24	77	129
446	28	58	76	40	83	251
286	44	90	68	44	109	128

tory of Machine Learning Databases (Blake & Merz, 1998). The attributes for this example are: *age*, *weight*, *h rate* (number of heart beats per minute), *int def* (number of intrinsic deflections), *QRS* (average of QRS duration in msec.), and *PR int* (average duration between onset of P and Q waves in msec.).

We are going to reduce the dimension of this dataset from 6 to 3, one at a time, and compute the error (stress function). To reduce the dimension of this dataset, we apply Equation (7). In set corresponds to the matrix D. We compute a random matrix R_1 by setting each entry of the matrix to a value drawn from an independent and identically distributed (i.i.d.) $N(0,1)$ distribution and then normalizing the columns to unit length. We also compute a random matrix R_2 where each element r_{ij} is computed using Equation (9). We transform D into D' using both R_1 and R_2. The random transformation RP_1 refers to the random projection using R_1, and RP_2 refers to the random projection using R_2.

The relative error that the distances in 6-3 space suffer from, on the average, is computed using Equation (6). Table 4 shows the values of the error using RP_1 and RP_2. In this Table, k represents the number of dimensions in the disguised database D'.

In this case, we have reduced the dimension of D from 6 to 3, i.e, the transformed dataset has only 50% of the dimensions in the original dataset. Note that the error is relatively small for both RP_1 and RP_2, especially for RP_2. However, this error is minimized when the **random projection** is applied to high dimensional datasets, as can be seen in Figure 1, in Section *Measuring the effectiveness of the DRBT Over Centralized Data*.

After applying random projection to a dataset, the attribute values of the transformed dataset are completely disguised to preserve the privacy of individuals. Table 5 shows the attribute values of the transformed database with 3 dimensions, using both RP_1 and RP_2. In this table, we have the attributes labeled *Att1*, *Att2*, and *Att3* since we

Table 4. The relative error that the distances in 6-3 space suffer from, on the average.

Transformations	k=6	k=5	k=4	K=3
RP_1	0.0000	0.0223	0.0490	0.2425
RP_2	0.0000	0.0281	0.0375	0.1120

Table 5. Disguised dataset D_ using RP1 and RP2

ID	D' using RP$_1$			D' using RP$_2$		
	Att1	Att2	Att3	Att1	Att2	Att3
123	-50.40	17.33	12.31	-55.50	-95.26	-107.96
342	-37.08	6.27	12.22	-51.00	-84.29	-83.13
254	-55.86	20.69	-0.66	-65.50	-70.43	-66.97
446	-37.61	-31.66	-17.58	-85.50	-140.87	-72.74
286	-62.72	37.64	18.16	-88.50	-50.22	-102.76

do not know the labels for the disguised dataset. Using random projection, one cannot select the attributes to be reduced beforehand. The attributes are reduced randomly. More formally, $\forall i$ if $Attr_i \in D'$, then $Attr_i \notin D$.

As can be seen in Table 5, the attribute values are entirely different from those in Table 3.

PPC over Vertically Partitioned Data

The solution for PPC over vertically partitioned data is a generalization of the solution for PPC over centralized data. In particular, if we have k parties involved in this case, each party must apply the random projection over its dataset and then send the reduced data matrix to a central party. Note that any of the k parties can be the central one. When k parties ($k \geq 2$) share some data for PPC over vertically partitioned data, these parties must satisfy the following constraints:

- **Agreement:** The k parties must follow the communication protocol described in Section *The communication protocol.*
- **Mutual exclusivity:** We assume that the attribute split across the k parties are mutually exclusive. More formally, if $A(D1)$, $A(D2)...,A(Dk)$ are a set of attributes of the k parties, $\forall i \neq j\ A(Di) \cap A(Dj) = \varphi$. The only

exception is that IDs are shared for the join purpose.

The solution based on random projection for PPC over vertically partitioned data is performed as follows:

- **Step 1—Individual transformation:** If k parties, $k \geq 2$, share their data in a collaborative project for clustering, each party k_i must transform its data according to the steps in Section *PPC Over Centralized Data.*
- **Step 2—Data exchanging or sharing:** Once the data are disguised by using random projection, the k parties are able to exchange the data among themselves. However, one party could be the central one to aggregate and cluster the data.
- **Step 3—Sharing clustering results:** After the data have been aggregated and mined in a central party k_i, the results could be shared with the other parties.

How Secure is the DRBT?

In the previous sections, we showed that transforming a database using random projection is a promising solution for PPC over centralized data and consequently for PPC over vertically partitioned data since the similarities between objects are marginally changed. Now we show that random projection also has promising theoretical properties for privacy preservation. In particular, we demonstrate that a random projection from d dimensions to k, where $k \ll d$, is a non-invertible transformation.

Lemma 2. *A random projection from d dimensions to k dimensions, where k ≪ d, is a noninvertible linear transformation.*

Proof: A classic result from Linear Algebra asserts that there is no invertible linear transformation between Euclidean spaces of different dimensions (Auer, 1991). Thus, if there is an invertible linear transformations from $\Re^m$ to $\Re^n$, then the constraint $m = n$ must hold. A random projection is a linear transformation from $\Re^d$ to $\Re^k$, where $k \ll d$. Hence, a random projection from d dimensions to k dimensions is a non-invertible linear transformation.

Even when sufficient care is taken, a solution that adheres to DRBT can be still vulnerable to disclosure. For instance, if an adversary knows the positions of $d + 1$ points (where d is the number of dimensions), and the distances between these points, then one can make some estimates of the coordinates of all points. However, it is important to note that the violation of the solution that adheres to DRBT becomes progressively harder as the number of attributes (dimensions) in a database increases since an adversary would need to know $d + 1$ points to disclose the original data. On the other hand, when the number of dimensions grows, the accuracy regarding the distances between points is improved.

The Accuracy of the DRBT

When using random projection, a perfect reproduction of the Euclidean distances may not be the best possible result. The clusters in the transformed datasets should be equal to those in the original database. However, this is not always the case, and we have some potential problems after dimensionality reduction: a) a noise data point ends up clustered; b) a point from a cluster becomes a noise point; and c) a point from a cluster migrates to a different cluster. In this research, we focus primarily on partitioning methods. In particular, we use K-means (Macqueen, 1967), one of the most used clustering algorithms. Since K-means is sensitive to noise points and clusters all the points in a dataset, we have to deal with the third problem mentioned above (a point from a cluster migrates to a different cluster).

Our evaluation approach focuses on the overall quality of generated clusters after dimensionality reduction. We compare how closely each cluster in the transformed data matches its corresponding cluster in the original dataset. To do so, we first identify the matching of clusters by computing the matrix of frequencies showed in Table 6. We refer to such a matrix as the clustering membership matrix (CMM), where the rows represent the clusters in the original dataset, the columns represent the clusters in the transformed dataset, and $freq_{i,j}$ is the number of points in cluster c_i that falls in cluster c'_j in the transformed dataset.

After computing the frequencies $freq_{i,j}$, we scan the clustering membership matrix calculating precision, recall, and F-measure for each cluster c'_j with respect to c_i in the original dataset (Larsen & Aone, 1999). These formulas are given by the following equations:

$$\mathrm{Pr}\,ecision(P) = \frac{freq_{i,j}}{\left|c'_i\right|} \tag{11}$$

$$\mathrm{Re}\,call(R) = \frac{freq_{i,j}}{\left|c_i\right|} \tag{12}$$

$$F - measure(F) = \frac{2 \times P \times R}{(P + R)} \tag{13}$$

Table 6. The number of points in cluster c_i that falls in cluster c'_j in the transformed dataset

	c'_1	c'_2	...	s'_k
c_1	$freq_{1,1}$	$freq_{1,2}$	...	$freq_{1,k}$
c_2	$freq_{2,1}$	$freq_{2,2}$	...	$freq_{2,k}$
...	...	...	...	...
c_k	$freq_{k,1}$	$freq_{k,2}$	...	$freq_{k,k}$

where $|X|$ is the number of points in the cluster X.

For each cluster c_i, we first find a cluster c'_j that has the highest F-measure among all the c'_l, $1 \leq l \leq k$. Let $F(c_i)$ be the highest F-measure for cluster c_i, we denote the overall F-measure (OF) as the weighted average of $F(c_i)$, $1 \leq i \leq k$, as follows:

$$OF = \frac{\sum_{i=1}^{k} |c_i| \times F(c_i)}{\sum_{i=1}^{k} |c_i|} \qquad (14)$$

In the section *Experimental Results*, we present our performance evaluation results for clustering based on Equation (14).

The Complexity of the DRBT

One of the major benefits of a solution that adheres to the DRBT is the communication cost to send a disguised dataset from one party to a central one. In general, a disguised data matrix is of size $m \times k$, where m is the number of objects and k is the number of attributes (dimensions).

The complexity of DRBT is of the order $O(m \times k)$, however $k \ll m$.

To quantify the communication cost of one solution, we consider the number of bits or words required to transmit a dataset from one party to a central or third party. Using DRBT, the bit communication cost to transmit a dataset from one party to another is $O(mlk)$, where l represents the size (in bits) of one element of the $m \times k$ disguised data matrix.

OTHER PRIVACY-PRESERVING CLUSTERING SOLUTIONS

Some effort has been made to address the problem of PPC. In this section, we present an overview of the existing solutions over distributed data.

Solutions for PPC Over Distributed Data

Regarding PPC over distributed data, we classify the existing solutions in two groups: *PPC over vertically partitioned data* and *PPC over horizontally partitioned data*.

Vertically Partitioned Data: In a vertical partition approach, the attributes of the same objects are split across the partitions. The idea behind this solution is that two or more parties want to conduct a computation based on their private inputs. The issue here is how to conduct such a computation so that no party knows anything except its own input and the results. This problem is referred to as the secure multi-party computation problem (Pinkas, 2002). The existing solution that falls in this category was introduced in (Vaidya & Clifton, 2003). Specifically, a method for k-means was proposed when different sites contain different attributes for a common set of entities. In this solution, each site learns the global clusters, but learns nothing about the attributes at other sites. This work ensures reasonable privacy while limiting communication cost.

Horizontally Partitioned Data: In a horizontal partition approach, different objects are described with the same schema in all partitions. A solution for PPC over horizontally partitioned data was proposed in (Meregu & Ghosh, 2003). This solution is based on generative models. In this approach, rather than sharing parts of the original data or perturbed data, the parameters of suitable generative models are built at each local site. Then such parameters are transmitted to a central location. The best representative of all data is a certain "mean" model. It was empirically shown that such a model can be approximated by generating artificial samples from the underlying distributions using Markov Chain Monte Carlo techniques. This approach achieves high quality distributed clustering with acceptable privacy loss and low communication cost.

Attribute Reduction: This is the approach presented in this paper: the attributes of a database are reduced to a smaller number. The small number of attributes is not a subset of the original attributes since the transformation disguises the original attribute values by projecting them onto a random space. Our data transformation that lies in this category is called Dimensionality Reduction-Based Transformation (DRBT) (Oliveira & Zaïane, 2007). This data transformation can be applied to both PPC over centralized data and PPC over vertically partitioned data. The idea behind this data transformation is that by reducing the dimensionality of a database to a sufficiently small value, one can find a trade-off between privacy and accuracy. Once the dimensionality of a database is reduced, the released database preserves (or slightly modifies) the distances between data points. In tandem with the benefit

of preserving the similarity between points, this solution protects individuals' privacy since the underlying data values of the objects

subjected to clustering are completely different from the original ones.

EXPERIMENTAL RESULTS

In this section, we empirically validate our method DRBT. We start by describing the real datasets used in our experiments. We then describe the methodology used to validate our method. Subsequently, we study the effectiveness of our method to address PPC over centralized data and PPC over vertically partitioned data. We conclude this section discussing the main lessons learned from our experiments.

Datasets

We validated our method DRBT for privacy-preserving clustering using five real datasets. These datasets are described as follows:

1. **Accidents:** This dataset concerning traffic accidents was obtained from the National Institute of Statistics (NIS) for the region of Flanders in Belgium. The transactions are traffic accident forms filled out by police officers for each traffic accident that occurred involving injuries or deaths on a public road in Belgium. There are 340,183 traffic accident records included in the dataset. We used 18 columns of this dataset after removing missing values.
2. **Mushroom:** This dataset is available at the UCI Repository of Machine Learning Databases (Blake & Merz, 1998). Mushroom contains records drawn from The Audubon Society Field Guide to North American Mushrooms. There are 8,124 records and 23 numerical attributes.

The chess endgame. The first 36 attributes describe the board. The last (37th) attribute is the classification: "win" or "nowin". Chess is available at the UCI Repository of Machine Learning Databases (Blake & Merz, 1998) and contains 3,196 records. There is no missing value in this dataset.

4. **Connect:** This database contains all legal 8-ply positions in the game of connect-4 in which neither player has won yet, and in which the next move is not forced. Connect is composed of 67,557 records and 43 attributes without missing values. This dataset is also available at the UCI Repository of Machine Learning Databases (Blake & Merz, 1998).

5. **Pumsb:** The Pumsb dataset contains census data for population and housing. This dataset is available at http://www.almaden.ibm.com/software/quest. There are 49,046 records and 74 attribute values without missing values.

Table 7 shows the summary of the datasets used in our experiments. The columns represent, respectively, the database name, the total number of records, and the number of attributes in each dataset.

Methodology

We performed two series of experiments to evaluate the effectiveness of DRBT when addressing PPC over centralized data and PPC over vertically partitioned data. Our evaluation approach focused on the overall quality of generated clusters after dimensionality reduction. One question that we wanted to answer was: *What is the quality of the clustering results mined from the transformed data when the data are both sparse and dense?*

Our performance evaluation was carried out through the following steps:

Step 1: we normalized the attribute values of the five real datasets used in our experiments. To do so, we used the z-score normalization given in Equation (3). The results presented in the next sections were obtained after normalization.

Step 2: we considered random projection based on two different approaches. First, the traditional way to compute random projection, by setting each entry of the random matrix R_1 to a value drawn from an i.i.d. $N(0,1)$ distribution and then normalizing the columns to unit length. Second, we used the random matrix R_2 where each element r_{ij} is computed using Equation (9). We refer to the former random projection as RP_1 and the latter as RP_2. We repeated each experiment (for random projection) 5 times. In the next section, we present results by showing only the average value.

Table 7. A summary of the datasets used in our experiments

Dataset	# Records	# Attributes
Accidents	340,183	18
Mushroom	8,124	23
Chess	3,196	37
Connect	67,557	43
Pumsb	49,046	74

126

Step 3: we computed the relative error that the distances in *d-k* space suffer from, on the average, by using the stress function given in Equation (6). The stress function was computed for each dataset.

Step 4: we selected K-means to find the clusters in our performance evaluation. Our selection was influenced by the following aspects: (a) K-means is one of the best known clustering algorithm and is scalable; (b) When using random projection, a perfect reproduction of the Euclidean distances may not be the best possible result. However, the rank order of the distances between the vectors is meaningful. Thus, when running K-means over the transformed data, one can find the clusters that would be mined from the original datasets with a reasonable accuracy.

Step 5: we compared how closely each cluster in the transformed dataset matches its corresponding cluster in the original dataset. We expressed the quality of the generated clusters by computing the F-measure given in Equation (14). Considering that K-means is not deterministic (due to its use of random seed selection), we repeated each experiment 10 times. We then computed the minimum, average, maximum, and standard deviation for each measured value of the F-measure. We present the results by showing only the average value.

We should point out that the steps described above were performed to evaluate the effectiveness of the DRBT when addressing PPC over centralized and vertically partitioned data.

Measuring the Effectiveness of the DRBT over Centralized Data

To measure the effectiveness of DRBT in PPC over centralized data, we started by computing the relative error that the distances in *d-k* space suffer from, on the average. To do so, we used the

two random projection approaches (RP_1 and RP_2) mentioned in Step 3 of Section *Methodology*.

A word of notation: hereafter we denote the original dimension of a dataset as d_o and reduced dimension of the transformed dataset as d_r. This notation is to avoid confusion between the reduced dimension of a dataset (k) and the number of clusters used as input of the algorithm K-means.

An important feature of the DRBT is its versatility to trade privacy, accuracy, and communication cost. The privacy preservation is assured because random projection is a non-invertible transformation, as discussed in Section *How Secure is the DRBT?* We here study the trade-off between accuracy and communication cost. The accuracy is represented by the error that the distances in d_o-d_r space suffer from, while the communication cost is represented by the number of dimensions that we reduce in the datasets. We selected two datasets: Pumsb and Chess with 74 and 37 dimensions, respectively. We reduced the dimensions of these datasets and computed the error. Figure 1(a) shows the error produced by RP_1 and RP_2 on the dataset Pumsb and Figure 1(b) shows the error produced by RP_1 and RP_2 on the dataset Chess. These results represent the average value of five trials. The error produced by RP_1 and RP_2 on the other datasets can be found in (Oliveira & Zaïane, 2007).

We observed that, in general, RP_2 yielded the best results in terms of the error produced on the datasets (the lower the better). In the dataset Chess the difference between RP_2 and RP_1 was not significant. These results confirm the same findings in (Bingham & Mannila, 2001) and backup the theory of random projection (the choice of the random matrix) proposed in (Achlioptas, 2001). We noticed from the figures that the DRBT trades well accuracy (error) and communication cost (number of reduced dimensions) when the data are reduced up to 50% of the dimensions. In this case, the trade-off between the error and the communication cost is linear. However, reducing more than 50% of the dimensions, the communication cost is improved but the accuracy is compromised since the error produced on the datasets grows faster. Therefore, a data owner should consider carefully this trade-off before releasing some data for clustering.

After evaluating the error produced on the datasets, we used the algorithm K-means to find the clusters in the original and transformed datasets. We varied the number of clusters from 2 to 5 in the five datasets. Subsequently, we compared how closely each cluster in the transformed dataset matches its corresponding cluster in the original dataset by computing the F-measure given in Equation (14).

Table 8 shows the results of the F-measure for the Accidents dataset. We reduced the original 18 dimensions to 12. We repeated each experiment 10 times and computed the minimum, average, maximum, and standard deviation for each measured value of the F-measure. We simplify the results by showing only one dataset (Accidents). The values of the F-measure for the other datasets can be found in (Oliveira & Zaïane, 2007). Note that we computed the values of the F-measure only for

the random projection RP_2 since its results were slightly better than those yielded by RP_1.

We noticed that the values of the F-measure for the Chess and Connect datasets were relatively low when compared with the results of the F-measure for the other datasets. Details can be found in (Oliveira & Zaïane, 2007). The main reason is that the data points in these datasets are densely distributed. Thus, applying a partitioning clustering algorithm (e.g., K-means) to datasets of this nature increases the number of misclassified data points. On the other hand, when the attribute values of the objects are sparsely distributed, the clustering results are much better. Consider, for example, the Iris dataset available at the UCI Repository of Machine Learning Databases. Iris is perhaps the best known database to be found in the pattern recognition literature. This dataset has two clusters well defined and the data are sparsely distributed. We reduced the original 5 dimensions to 3. Then we applied random projection RP_2 to the Iris dataset and computed the minimum, average, maximum, and standard deviation for each measured value of the F-measure. We repeated

Figure 1. (a) The error produced on the dataset Pumsb (do = 74); (b) the error produced on the dataset Chess (do = 37)

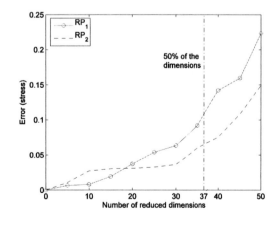

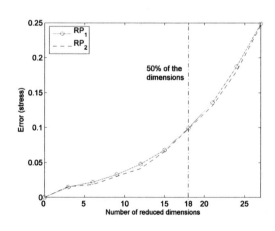

(a)

(b)

Table 8. Average of the F-measure (10 trials) for the Accidents dataset (do = 18, dr = 12)

Data Transformation	k=2				k=3			
	Min	Max	Avg	Std	Min	Max	Avg	Std
RP_2	0.931	0.952	0.941	0.014	0.903	0.921	0.912	0.009
Data Transformation	k=4				k=5			
	Min	Max	Avg	Std	Min	Max	Avg	Std
RP_2	0.870	0.891	0.881	0.010	0.878	0.898	0.885	0.006

Table 9. Average of the F-measure (10 trials) for the Iris dataset (d_o = 5, d_r = 3)

Data Transformation	k=2				k=3			
	Min	Max	Avg	Std	Min	Max	Avg	Std
RP_2	1.000	1.000	1.000	0.000	0.094	0.096	0.948	0.010
Data Transformation	k=4				k=5			
	Min	Max	Avg	Std	Min	Max	Avg	Std
RP_2	0.773	0.973	0.858	0.089	0.711	0.960	0.833	0.072

each experiment 10 times. Table 9 shows that the standard deviation for two clusters ($k=2$) was zero and the average of the F-measure was one.

Measuring the Effectiveness of the DRBT over Vertically Partitioned Data

Now we move on to measure the effectiveness of DRBT to address PPC over vertically partitioned data. To do so, we split the Pumsb dataset (74 dimensions) from 1 up to 4 parties (partitions) and fixed the number of dimensions to be reduced (38 dimensions). Table 10 shows the number of parties, the number of attributes per party, and the number of attributes in the merged dataset which is subjected to clustering. Recall that in a vertically partitioned data approach, one of the parties will centralize the data before mining.

In this example, each partition with 37, 25,

24, 19, and 18 attributes was reduced to 19, 13, 12, 10, and 9 attributes, respectively. We applied the random projections RP_1 and RP_2 to each partition and then merged the partitions in one central repository. Subsequently, we computed the stress error on the merged dataset and compared the error with that one produced on the original dataset (without partitioning). Figure 2 shows the error produced on the Pumsb dataset in the vertically partitioned data approach. As we can see, the results yielded by RP_2 were again slightly better than those yielded by RP_1. Note that we reduced approximately 50% of the dimensions of the dataset Pumsb and the trade-off between accuracy and communication cost is still efficient for PPC over vertically partitioned data.

We also evaluated the quality of clusters generated by mining the merged dataset and comparing the clustering results with those mined from the original dataset. To do so, we computed the F-

Table 10. An example of partitioning for the Pumsb dataset

No. of parties	No. of attributes per party	No. of attributes in the merged dataset
1	1 partition with 74 attributes	38
2	2 partitions with 37 attributes	38
3	2 partitions with 25 and 1 with 24 attributes	38
4	2 partitions with 18 and 2 with 19 attributes	38

Figure 2. The error produced on the dataset Pumsb over vertically partitioned data

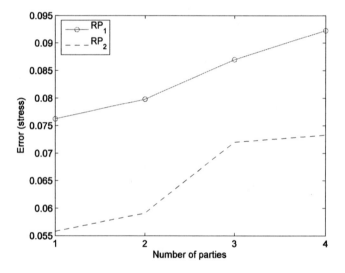

measure for the merged dataset in each scenario, i.e., from 1 up to 4 parties. We varied the number of clusters from 2 to 5. Table 11 shows values of the F-measure (average and standard deviation) for the Pumsb dataset over vertically partitioned data. These values represent the average of 10 trials considering the random projection RP_2.

We notice from Table 11 that the results of the F-measure slightly decrease when we increase the number of parties in the scenario of PPC over vertically partitioned data. Despite this fact, the DRBT is still effective to address PPC

over vertically partitioned data in preserving the quality of the clustering results as measured by F-measure.

Discussion on the DRBT When Addressing PPC

The evaluation of the DRBT involves three important issues: security, communication cost, and quality of the clustering results. We previously discussed the issues of security based on Lemma 2, and the issues of communication cost and space

Table 11. Average of the F-measure (10 trials) for the Pumsb dataset over vertically partitioned data

No. of parties	k=2		k=3		k=4		k=5	
	Avg	Std	Avg	Std	Avg	Std	Avg	Std
1	0.909	0.140	0.965	0.081	0.891	0.028	0.838	0.041
2	0.904	0.117	0.931	0.101	0.894	0.059	0.840	0.047
3	0.874	0.168	0.887	0.095	0.873	0.081	0.801	0.073
4	0.802	0.155	0.812	0.117	0.866	0.088	0.831	0.078

requirements in Section *The Complexity of the DRBT*. In this Section, we have focused on the quality of the clustering results.

We have evaluated our proposed data transformation method(DRBT) to address PPC. We have learned some lessons from this evaluation, as follows:

- **The application domain of the DRBT:** we observed that the DRBT does not present acceptable clustering results in terms of accuracy when the data subjected to clustering are dense. Slightly changing the distances between data points by random projection results in misclassification, i.e., points will migrate from one cluster to another in the transformed dataset. This problem is somehow understandable since partitioning clustering methods are not effective to find clusters in dense data. The Connect dataset is one example which confirms this finding. On the other hand, our experiments demonstrated that the quality of the clustering results obtained from sparse data is promising.

- **The versatility of the DRBT:** using the DRBT, a data owner can tune the number of dimensions to be reduced in a dataset trading privacy, accuracy, and communication costs before sharing the dataset for clustering.

Most importantly, the DRBT can be used to address PPC over centralized and vertically partitioned data.

- **The choice of the random matrix:** from the performance evaluation of the DRBT we noticed that the random projection RP_2 yielded the best results for the error produced on the datasets and the values of F-measure, in general. The random projection RP_2 is based on the random matrix proposed in Equation (9).

CONCLUSION

In this chapter, we introduced a new method to address Privacy-Preserving Clustering (PPC) over centralized data and over vertically partitioned data, called the Dimensionality Reduction-Based Transformation (DRBT) and showed analytically and experimentally that PPC is possible. This method was designed to support business collaboration considering privacy regulations, without losing the benefit of data analysis.

The privacy-preserving clustering method, DRBT, relies on the idea behind random projection to protect the underlying attribute values subjected to clustering.

We evaluated the DRBT taking into account three important issues: security, communication cost, and accuracy (quality of the clustering results). Our experiments revealed that using DRBT, a data owner can meet privacy requirements without losing the benefit of clustering since the similarity between data points is preserved or marginally changed. From the performance evaluation, we suggested guidance on which scenario a data owner can achieve the best quality of the clustering when using the DRBT. In addition, we suggested guidance on the choice of the random matrix to obtain the best results in terms of the error produced on the datasets and the values of F-measure.

The advantages of the DRBT are that the method is independent of distance-based clustering algorithms. We used k-means for our experiments but other clustering algorithms are also possible; DRBT has a sound mathematical foundation; the method does not require CPU-intensive operations; and it can be applied to address PPC over centralized data a well as PPC over vertically partitioned data.

REFERENCES

Achlioptas, D. (2001). Database-Friendly Random projections. In *Proc. of the 20th ACM Symposium on Principles of Database Systems* (p. 274-281). Santa Barbara, CA, USA.

Auer, J. W. (1991). *Linear Algebra With Applications*. Scarborough, Ontario, Canada: Prentice-Hall Canada Inc.,

Berry, M., & Linoff, G. (1997). Data Mining Techniques - For Marketing, Sales, and Customer Support. New York, USA: John Wiley and Sons.

Bingham, E., & Mannila, H. (2001). Random projection in Dimensionality Reduction: Applications to Image and Text Data. In *Proc. of the 7th ACM SIGKDD International Conference on Knowledge Discovery and Data Mining* (p. 245-250). San Francisco, CA, USA.

Blake, C., & Merz, C. (1998). *UCI Repository of Machine Learning Databases*. University of California, Irvine: Dept. of Information and Computer Sciences.

Fern, X. Z., & Brodley, C. E. (2003). Random projection for High Dimensional Data Clustering: A Cluster Ensemble Approach. In *Proc. of the 20th International Conference on Machine Learning (ICML 2003)*. Washington DC, USA.

Fukunaga, K. (1990). *Introduction to Statistical Pattern Recognition*. 2nd. Edition. Academic Press.

Han, J., & Kamber, M. (2006). *Data Mining: Concepts and Techniques*. San Francisco, CA: Morgan Kaufmann Publishers

Johnson, W. B., & Lindenstrauss, J. (1984). Extensions of Lipshitz Mapping Into Hilbert Space. In *Proc. of the Conference in Modern Analysis and Probability* (p. 189-206), volume 26 of Contemporary Mathematics.

Kaski, S. (1999). Dimensionality Reduction by Random Mapping. In *Proc. of the International Joint Conference on Neural Networks* (p. 413-418). Anchorage, Alaska.

Larsen, B., & Aone, C. (1999). Fast and Effective Text Mining Using Linear-Time Document Clustering. In *Proceedings of the 5th ACM SIGKDD International Conference on Knowledge Discovery and Data Mining* (p. 16-22). San Diego, CA, USA.

Lo, V. S. Y. (2002). The True Lift Model - A Novel Data Mining Approach to Response Modeling in Database Marketing. *SIGKDD Explorations, 4*(2), 78-86.

Macqueen, J. (1967). Some Methods for Classification and Analysis of Multivariate Observations. In *Proc. of the 5th Berkeley Symposium on Mathematical Statistics and Probability, 1*, 281-297). Berkeley: University of California Press.

Meregu, S., & Ghosh, J. (2003). Privacy-Preserving Distributed Clustering Using Generative Models. In *Proc. of the 3rd IEEE International Conference on Data Mining (ICDM'03)* (p. 211-218). Melbourne, Florida, USA.

Oliveira, S. R. M., & Zaïane, O. R. (2007). Privacy-Preserving Clustering to Uphold Business Collaboration: A Dimensionality Reduction-Based Transformation Approach. *International Journal of Information Security and Privacy (IJISP), 1*(2), 13-36.

Oliveira, S. R. M. (2005, June). *Data Transformation For Privacy-Preserving Data Mining.* PhD thesis, Department of Computing Science, University of Alberta, Edmonton, AB, Canada.

Pinkas, B (2002, December). Cryptographic Techniques For Privacy-Preserving Data Mining. *SIGKDD Explorations, 4*(2), 12–19.

Sweeney, L. (2002). K-Anonymity: A Model for Protecting Privacy. *International Journal on Uncertainty, Fuzziness and Knowledge-Based Systems, 10*(5), 557-570.

Vaidya, J., & Clifton, C. (2003). Privacy-Preserving K-Means Clustering Over Vertically Partitioned Data. In Proc. *of the 9th ACM SIGKDD Intl. Conf. on Knowledge Discovery and Data Mining* (p. 206-215). Washington, DC, USA.

Young, F. W. (1987). *Multidimensional Scaling.* Lawrence Erlbaum Associates, Hillsdale, New Jersey.

KEY TERMS

Dimensionality Reduction-Based Transformation (DRBT): A method to address Privacy-Preserving Clustering (PPC) over centralized data and over vertically partitioned data. This method relies on the intuition behind random projection to protect the underlying attribute values subjected to cluster analysis.

Privacy-Preserving Clustering (PPC): Is a privacy preservation approach in which data owners share information for data analysis in a collaborative project. Such a solution is designed to meet privacy requirements and guarantee valid data clustering results.

Privacy-Preserving Data Mining: Encompasses the dual goal of meeting privacy requirements and providing valid data mining results.

PPC Over Centralized Data: In this approach, different entities are described with the same schema in a unique centralized data repository.

PPC Over Horizontally Partitioned Data: Different objects are described with the same schema in all partitions.

PPC Over Vertically Partitioned Data: The attributes of the same entities are split across the partitions.

Random Projection: A linear transformation asserting that any set of n points in d-dimensional Euclidean space can be embedded into k-dimensional space, where k is logarithmic in n and independent of d (and $k \ll d$).

Chapter VIII
Classification of Web Pages Using Machine Learning Techniques

K. Selvakuberan
Innovation Labs (Web 2.0), TATA Consultancy Services, India

M. Indra Devi
Thiagarajar College of Engineering, Madurai, India

R. Rajaram
Thiagarajar College of Engineering, Madurai, India

ABSTRACT

The explosive growth of the Web makes it a very useful information resource to all types of users. Today, everyone accesses the Internet for various purposes and retrieving the required information within the stipulated time is the major demand from users. Also, the Internet provides millions of Web pages for each and every search term. Getting interesting and required results from the Web becomes very difficult and turning the classification of Web pages into relevant categories is the current research topic. Web page classification is the current research problem that focuses on classifying the documents into different categories, which are used by search engines for producing the result. In this chapter we focus on different machine learning techniques and how Web pages can be classified using these machine learning techniques. The automatic classification of Web pages using machine learning techniques is the most efficient way used by search engines to provide accurate results to the users. Machine learning classifiers may also be trained to preserve the personal details from unauthenticated users and for privacy preserving data mining.

INTRODUCTION

Over the past decade we have witnessed an explosive growth on the Internet, with millions of web pages on every topic easily accessible through the Web. The Internet is a powerful medium for communication between computers and for accessing online documents all over the world but it is not a tool for locating or organizing the mass of information. Tools like search engines assist users in locating information on the Internet. They perform excellently in locating but provide limited ability in organizing the web pages. Internet users are now confronted with thousands of web pages returned by a search engine using simple keyword search. Searching through those web pages is in itself becoming impossible for users. Thus it has been of more interest in tools that can help make a relevant and quick selection of information that we are seeking. There is also estimation that 15 to 30 billion pages are accessible on the World Wide Web with millions of pages being added daily. Describing and organizing this vast amount of content is essential for realizing the web's full potential as an information resource. Accomplishing this in a meaningful way will require consistent use of metadata and other descriptive data structures such as semantic linking. We find that HTML meta tags are a good source of text features, but are not in wide use despite their role in search engine rankings. But most of the pages will not contain meta data. (John Pierre, M., 2001, Tom Mitchell, M., 1999, Sebastiani, F.,2002)

Automatic Web-page classification by using hypertext is a major approach to categorizing large quantities of Web pages. Two major kinds of approaches have been studied for Web-page classification: content-based and context-based approaches. Typical content-based classification methods utilize words or phrases of a target document to train the classifier. Context based approaches take into account the structure of the HTML pages to train the classifier. This is because sometimes a Web page contains no obvious clues

textually for its category. For example, some pages contain only images and little text information. By exploiting the hyper textual information, context-based approaches additionally exploit the relationships between the Web pages to build a classifier. Web page classifiers trained both using content and contextual features classify the web pages more accurately even though following any one approach produces the desirable result. The main objective of this chapter is to focus on the web page classification issues and the machine learning techniques practiced by researchers to solve the web page classification problem.

LITERATURE SURVEY

Susan Dumais and Hao Chen (2000) explore the use of hierarchical structure for classifying web Pages using Support Vector Machine Classifiers. The hierarchical structure is initially used to train different second-level classifiers. In the hierarchical case, a model is learned to distinguish a second-level category from other categories within the same top level.

In the past, classification of the news has been done manually. Chee-Hong Chan, Aixin Sun, & Ee-Peng Lim (2001) experiment an automated approach to classify news based on SVM classifier which results in good classification accuracy. In personalized classification users define their own categories using specific keywords. By constructing search queries using these keywords, categorizer obtains positive and negative examples and performs classification. Online news represents a type of web information that is frequently referenced. The categorizer adopts SVM to classify the web pages into pre-defined categories (general categories) or user-defined categories (special categories). With personalized categories users are allowed to search their related article with the minimum effort.

Gautam Pant and Padmini Srinivasan (2006) proposed a method for classifying web pages using link contexts. Context of a hyperlink can be defined as the terms that are present in the text around a hyperlink within a web page. This link context is very much useful in Web Information retrieval and categorization tasks. This methodology can be very much used in web crawling purposes. The crawlers automatically navigate the hyperlinked structure using link contexts to predict the benefit of the corresponding hyperlinks with the necessary theme and it is used for fast retrieval. They used SVM for classification purposes. They used Open Directory Project (ODP) for their experimental purposes. They defined a performance metric called harvest rate (number of crawled web pages that are relevant to the topic). Their experimental results proved that the performance rate is better. They have also made a comparison with the link contexts to the contents of the web page.

Aixin Sun, EePeng Lim and WeeKeong Ng (2002) propose the use of Support Vector Machine (SVM) classifiers to classify web pages using both their text and context feature sets. Web page classification is entirely different from other text classification because of the presence of HTML tags and hyperlinks. They took Webkb data set for their experimental purposes. The main objective is to study the impact of different web page features on the performance of web classification. They have experimented text features alone as the baseline features and try out different combinations of text, title and hyperlink features. They have proved that by considering the text, title and anchor words as features then the best classification accuracy can be obtained.

Offer Drori (2005) developed a software tool (Text Analysis tool) which locates the subject of a document. The output of the tool is a set of significant words from the document, which effectively constitute the subject of the document by presenting in topics. The software tool uses statistical analysis to determine the most frequent words in the document. The text is analyzed after words that are meaningless for the subject are

eliminated using a Stop List, and after limited processing of linguistic elements. His research focuses on the displaying the subject of a document that the user wants the documents that meets his interests. The subject of a document can be the category from the pre defined list of categories or some words found in the texts of a document or list of keywords. His research results are addition of keywords to the information displayed on the list of search results will minimize users searching time, increase users satisfaction and ease.

Arul Prakash Asirvatham and Kiranthi Kumar Ravi (2001) implemented a structure based categorization system to categorize the web page into three broad categories.

(i) Information pages (ii) Research pages (iii) Personal Home pages. They have taken into account the images and the structure of the page for the automatic classification of web pages into these three categories. They proposed a method called Structure approach which exploits many other features apart from the text contents. Usually human mind categorizes pages into a few broad categories at first sight without knowing the exact contents of the web page. It uses other features like the structure of the web pages, images, links contained in the web page and their placement for classification. Web pages belonging to a particular category have some similarity in their structure. The structure of the web pages can be deduced from placement of links, text and images. Web pages belonging to a particular category are having some similarity in the structure. They observed some features like link text to normal text ratio which are present in all categories of documents but at varying degrees and there are some features which are particular to some kind of documents. They have identified the following as the characteristics of each and every category. A typical information page has a logo on the top followed by a navigation bar linking the page to other important pages. The link text to normal text ratio is relatively high in these pages. Research pages usually contain large amounts of text, equations and graphs in the form of images. The images can be described using histograms. Personal home pages follow a standard layout. The name, address and photo of the person are prominently present in the top of the page. In the bottom of the page useful links about the person such as publications of the particular person is listed. The categorization is carried out in two phases- feature selection phase and classification phase.

Ismail Sengör Altingövde and Özgür Ulusoy (2004) propose a crawler which employs canonical topic taxonomy to train a naïve-Bayesian classifier, which then helps determine the relevancy of crawled pages. The crawler also relies on the assumption of topical locality to decide which URLs to visit next. Building on this crawler, they developed a rule-based crawler, which uses simple rules derived from interclass (topic) linkage patterns to decide its next move. This rule-based crawler also enhances the baseline crawler by supporting tunneling.

Jiu-Zhen Lung deals (2004) with support vector machine (SVM) for multi-classification problem and its application to web page document classification. They focus on direct design of multiclassifier of SVM and its application to web page classification. For special application problems, most of a multi-class classifier of a system is limited to a certain class. They chose SVM for their classification because of its advantage on non-effective of feature dimension scale.

Ali Selamat, Hidekazu Yanagimoto and Sigeru Omatu (2002) propose a news web page classification method (WPCM). The WPCM uses a neural network with inputs obtained by both the principal components and class profile-based features (CPBF). The fixed number of regular words from each class will be used as a feature vectors with the reduced features from the PCA. These feature vectors are then used as the input to the neural networks for classification.

Oh-Woog Kwon and Jong-Hyeok Lee (2000) propose a Web page classifier based on an adaptation of k-NN approach. The k-NN approach is characterized as follows: a feature selection method to reduce noise terms in training samples, a term weighting scheme using HTML tags, and a document-document similarity measure with matching factor proposed in this paper. They represented the documents using vector space model. They experimented with Korean commercial directory and found out that K-NN approach for web page classification improved the classification accuracy. The k-NN approach can be broken down into two steps: The first step is to find the k-nearest samples by document similarity approach. The second step is to determine the likelihood by summing the weights of the category of k nearest documents.

PROBLEM DEFINITION

The main objective of this article is to classify the web pages based on the category or categories based on the features found on the web pages. In this section we focus on the definition of web page classification, web page structure and various forms of representing the web page.

Web Page Classification Definition

Web page classification, also known as web page categorization, may be defined as the task of determining whether a web page belongs to a category or categories. Formally, let $C = \{c_1, ..., c_k\}$ be a set of predefined categories, $D = \{d_1, ..., d_n\}$ be a set of Web pages to be classified, and $A = D \times C$ be a decision matrix: where, each entry a_{ij} (1=i to N, 1=j to K) represents whether web page d_i belongs to category c_j or not. Each $a_{ij}=\{0, 1\}$, where 1 indicates web page d_i belongs to category c_j and 0 for not belonging. A web page can belong to more than one category. The task of web page classification is to approximate the unknown assignment function f: D X C $\rightarrow$ {0,1} by means of a learned function f': D X C $\rightarrow$ {0,1}, called a classifier, a model, or a hypothesis, such that f' coincides to f as much as possible. The function f' is usually obtained by machine learning over a set of training examples of web pages. Each training example is tagged with a category label. The function f' is induced during the training phase and is then used during the classification phase to assign web pages to categories.

Need for Web Page Classification

Automatic classification of web pages is needed for the following reasons. (a) Large amount of information available in the internet makes it difficult for the human experts to classify them manually (b) The amount of Expertise needed is high (c) Web pages are dynamic in nature and more effort is needed for updating the classification regularly (d) Web pages are volatile in nature (e) More time and effort are required for classification. (f) Same type of classification scheme may not be applied to all pages (g) More experts needed for classification. Web page classification techniques use concepts from many fields like information filtering and retrieval, Artificial Intelligence, Text mining, and machine learning. Within the machine learning paradigm, a general inductive process (called the learner) automatically builds a classifier (also called the rule, or the hypothesis) by "learning", from a set of previously classified documents, the characteristics of one or more categories. The advantages of this approach are a very good effectiveness, a considerable savings in terms of expert manpower, and domain independence.

Issues in Web Page Classification

Feature Selection is the first issue to be considered for Web Page Classification. The web pages may contain many irrelevant words for classification (like stop words, HTML tags, infrequent words,

punctuation symbols), which decreases the classification accuracy and requires more storage and time for classification. So these less useful words may be removed from the web pages. The terms more useful for classification are called as features. Feature Extraction techniques are used to extract the more relevant words useful for the classification of web pages. Some other techniques remove the stop words, infrequent words, punctuation symbols, HTML tags, e-Classification from the web page and prepare the page for the classification process. Feature Selection techniques selects the useful features from the web pages. There are so many feature selection techniques given in the literature. Most of the research papers discuss the Weighted Feature Selection algorithm as the best algorithm for Web Page Classification. In this algorithm, all the features relevant for classification are extracted and are assigned weights according to their relevance. For example features found in the URL are given more weight followed by features found in the META and TITLE tags and less weight is assigned to the features found in the body text. The total weight for each feature is considered for selection of the feature.

Another issue in the Web Page Classification is high dimension of Web Pages. The Web pages may be represented using Bag-Of-Words representation or Vector space representation and preprocessing techniques are applied for dimensionality reduction. Finding best features for Web Page Classification – Content features or Context features is another issue. Even though most of the text mining methods applied for classification consider the web page as plain text, the HTML structure of Web page plays a major role in Web Page Classification. The URL information, HTML META and TITLE tags, Tables, Frames, Visual layout are more useful features for classification than the body text in the web page. Combining both content and context features serves as the best features for classification.

MACHINE LEARNING

In the 1980s, the most popular approach for the creation of automatic document classifiers consisted in manually building, by means of knowledge engineering (KE) techniques, an expert system capable of taking Text Categorization decisions. Such an expert system would typically consist of a set of manually defined logical rules and clauses. The document is classified under the particular category if it satisfies the logical rules, or at least one of the clauses. The drawback of this approach is the knowledge acquisition bottleneck well known from the expert systems literature. That is, the rules must be manually defined by a knowledge engineer with the aid of a domain expert (in this case, an expert in the membership of documents in the chosen set of categories. In the late 1990s by state-of-the-art Machine Learning techniques come into existence. Since the early 1990s, the Machine Learning approach to Classification has gained popularity and has eventually become the dominant one, at least in the research community. Within the machine learning paradigm, a general inductive process automatically builds an automatic text classifier by "learning", from a set of previously classified web documents, the characteristics of the categories of interest. The advantages of this approach are accuracy comparable to human performance and a considerable savings in terms of expert manpower, since no intervention from either knowledge engineers or domain experts is needed. Currently web page categorization may be seen as the meeting point of machine learning and information retrieval. As Machine Learning aims to address larger, more complex tasks, the problem of focusing on the most relevant information in a potentially overwhelming quantity of data has become increasingly important. For instance, data mining of corporate or scientific records often involves dealing with both many features and many examples, and the internet and World Wide Web have put a huge volume of low-quality information at the easy access of a learning system. Similar issues arise in the personalization of filtering systems for information retrieval, electronic mail, net news.

Machine learning methods gain more importance in the classification of web pages. They are also used for feature selection, preprocessing.

Why Machine Learning Techniques?

The advantages of the Machine Learning approach over the Knowledge Engineering approach are evident. The engineering effort goes toward the construction not of a classifier, but of an automatic builder of classifiers (the learner). This means that if a learner is available off-the-shelf, all that is needed is the inductive, automatic construction of a classifier from a set of manually classified documents. The same happens if a classifier already exists and the original set of categories is updated, or if the classifier is ported to a completely different domain. In the Machine Learning approach, the pre classified documents are then the key resource.(John Pierre, M., 2001 Tom Mitchell, M., 1999, Anagnostopoulos I., Kouzas G. Anagnostopoulos C., Vergados D., Papaleonidopoulos I., Generalis A., Loumos V. and Kayafas E., 2002)

The machine learning approach is more convenient than the Knowledge Engineering approach also in this latter case. In fact, it is easier to manually classify a set of documents than to build and tune a set of rules, since it is easier to characterize a concept extensionally (i.e., to select instances of it) than intentionally. Classifiers built by means of Machine Learning techniques nowadays achieve impressive levels of effectiveness making automatic classification a qualitatively (and not only economically) viable alternative to manual classification.

WEB PAGE STRUCTURE

Web pages are heterogeneous in nature. They may be unstructured documents like text document, semi structured documents like HTML files or fully structured documents like XML file. Web pages may also contain image files, audio files etc. There may not be any uniform structure or content in the related web pages or web pages under a same website. Some web pages may not contain a single word even in the home page itself. META tags are very useful for the classification of web pages but they are not properly defined in all the web pages. Most of the web pages do not contain this META tags and some provide TITLE and DESCRIPTION tags to aid classification of the web page. The web pages may vary in length and contain stop words, HTML tags, infrequent words, punctuation symbols, etc which decreases the classification accuracy and requires more storage and time for classification. So these less useful words may be removed while the web page is considered for classification. The terms more useful for classification are extracted from the web pages and these are called as features. There are so many well-defined feature extraction algorithms to extract relevant features from the page and these features are used for training the classifiers into categories. The web pages can be represented in various ways. It is the simplest form to represent a web page is to extract a text found in the BODY element. This representation does not exploit the peculiarities of web pages that is HTML structure and hyper textual nature of web pages.

HTML Structure

For improving web page representation, exploiting HTML structure will help us identify where the more representative terms can be found. For example, we can consider that a term enclosed within the <title> and </title> tags is generally more representative for the topic of a web page than a term enclosed within the <body> and </body> tags.

For instance, several sources (elements) for web page representation are:

- BODY, the body part of a web page;
- TITLE, the title of a web page;
- H1~H6, section headings;
- EM, emphasized content;
- URL, hyperlinks that may contain descriptor for the linked web pages. If keywords can be extracted from an URL, these keywords are relatively important
- META describes the meta-description of a web page. It is invisible to users of web browsing, but it may provide description, keywords, and date for a web page.(Daniele Riboni 2002)

WEB PAGE REPRESENTATION

There are various representations of the web page. Some of them are given below which are commonly used by researchers.

Vector Space Model

To denote the dimension of a vector (or the number of features in the training corpus) the vector space model is used. A web page is usually represented by a vector $d_i = \{w_1, w_2 ..., w_M\}$, where each w_i is the weight of a feature of the web page and M is the size of feature space. Predefined categories are denoted by a set $C=\{c_1, c_2 ..., c_K\}$, where each c_i is a category label and there are K categories.

Bag of Terms (Bag of Words)

In the simplest way, a web page is represented by a vector of M weighted index words. This is often referred to as bag-of-words representation. The basic hypothesis behind the bag-of-words representation is that each word in a document

Figure 1. Vector space representation of a web page

The explosive growth of the web makes it a very useful information resource to all types of users a nd t oday e veryone accesses the Internet for various purposes and retrieving the required information within the stipulated time is the major demand f rom users. Also, the Internet provides m illions of web p ages f or e ach and every search term, getting interesting and required results from the web become very difficult and classification o f web pages into r elevant categories i s the current research t opic. Web page classification i s the current research problem which focuses on c lassifying the documents into different categories which is used by search engines for producing the result. In this chapter we focus on different machine learning techniques and how web pages can be classified using these machine learning techniques. Automatic classification o f web p ages u sing machine learning techniques is the most efficient way used b y search e ngines t o provide accurate results to the users

S.No	Terms	No. of Occuences
1.	Web	7
2	Internet	2
3	users	3
4	classification	3
5	categories	2
6	machine	3
7	learning	3
8	techniques 3	

indicates a certain concept in the document. Formally, a web page is represented by a vector d_i with words $t_1, t_2, …, t_M$ as the features, each of which associates with a weight w_{ij} That is,

$$d_i = (w_{i1}, w_{i2}, w_{i3}, …, w_{iM})$$

where M is the number of indexing words and w_{ij} (1=j=M) is the importance (or weight) of word t_j in the web page d_i Since a phrase usually contain more information than a single word, the bag-of-words representation can be enriched by adding new features generated from word sequences, also known as n-grams. We refer to the enriched bag-of-words representation as bag-of-terms, where a term can be a single word or any n-gram.

The process of feature generation is performed in passes over documents, where i-grams are generated in the ith pass only from the features of length i-1 generated in the previous pass .Deciding the weights of terms in a web page is a term-weighting problem. The simplest way to define the weight w_j of term t_j in a web page is to consider the binary occurrence as following:

$$W_j = \{ \begin{array}{l} 1 \quad \text{if term } t_j \text{ in the web page} \\ 0, \quad \text{otherwise} \end{array}$$

Word Sense Representation

The problem with the bag-of-words or bag-of-terms representation is that using word occurrence omits the fact that a word may have different word senses (or meanings) in different web pages or in the same web page. For instance, the word "bank" may have at least two different senses, as in the "bank" of America or the "bank" of Mississippi river. However using a bag-of-words representation, these two "bank" are treated as a same feature. Rather than using a bag-of-words, using word senses to represent a web page can improve web page classification. By using word senses to be features of a web page vector, a web page d_i is represented as:

$$d_i = (w_{i1}, w_{i2}, w_{13}, \ldots, w_{iM})$$

Term Frequency Inverse Document Frequency

One of the most successful term weighting methods is TF-IDF (Term Frequency Inverse Document Frequency) which is obtained by the product of the local term importance (TF) and the global term importance (IDF). The term frequency (wherein the term frequency (tf) is a number of times a term appears in a particular electronic document) measure tf.

Where tf can be defined as

$$tf(t_i, d_j) = \#(t_i, d_j)$$

where $\#(t_i, d_j)$ denotes the number of times the term t_i occurs in document d_j.

The inverse document frequency is one by which a document containing certain term which is not present in other corpus is given higher importance. The weighting method is given by

$$W_{ij} = TF(t_j, d_i) . IDF(t_j)$$

STEPS IN WEB PAGE CLASSIFICATION

The task of web page classification is divided into three major phases:

1. Data collection
2. Preprocessing and feature extraction
3. Machine learning.

These parts are also phases in the overall process of knowledge extraction from the web and classification of web documents (tagging). As this process is interactive and iterative in nature, the phases may be included in a loop structure that would allow each stage to be revisited so that some feedback from later stages can be used. The parts are well defined and can be developed separately and then put together as components in a semi-automated system or executed manually. Web pages are submitted to search engines or retrieved by search engines and each and every day search engines have a voluminous data collection to be classified. Machine learning classifiers require training set and so already classified examples of each category of web pages are collected by search engines and they are used to train all the machine learning classifiers. Phase 2 involves feature extraction and data preparation. During this phase the web documents will be represented by feature vectors, which in turn are used to form a training/test data set for the Machine Learning stage. Phase 3 is the machine learning phase. Machine learning algorithms are used to create models of the data sets. These models are used for two purposes. The accuracy of the initial topic structure is evaluated and secondly, new web documents are classified into existing topics.

Collecting Sets of Web Documents

Most of the search engines get the help of human experts to classify the web pages into categories to form the training set. Sometimes other search engines categories may be used as training set. Most of the web pages are submitted to the search engines. To understand the process, let us start collecting some data from the existing web. Collect at least 50 pages for each category for 6 categories. Check whether all the pages have some textual information representing its category. i.e Check for the keywords that represent the category of the web page. Now the data collection phase is completed.

Feature Extraction and Data Preparation

During this phase the web documents will be represented by feature vectors, which in turn are used to form a training data set for the Machine Learning stage.

Preprocessing and Feature Selection

The web page classification needs a lot of preprocessing work because of the presence of hyperlinks and large number of HTML tags. It is estimated that 80% of the preprocessing is needed before the classification of web pages. Preprocessing can be achieved by the following ways.

a) Removing HTML Tags

HTML tags indicate the formats of web pages. For instance, the content within <title> and </title> pair is the title of a web page; the content enclosed by <table> and </table> pair is a table. These HTML tags may indicate the importance of their enclosed content and they can thus help weight their enclosed content. The tags themselves are removed after weighting their enclosed content.

b) Removing Stop Words

Stop words are frequent words that carry little information, such as prepositions, pronouns, and conjunctions. They are removed by comparing the input text with a "stop list" of words. There are so many lists available in the Internet and you can find one that suits you.

c) Removing Rare Words

Removing words whose number of occurrences in the text are less than a predefined threshold can do it. Rare words don't help to categorize the web page it represents most of the times and hence can be removed to reduce the high dimensionality.

d) Performing Word Stemming

Stemming is the process for reducing inflected (or sometimes derived) words to their stem, base or root form, generally a written word form. The stem need not be identical to the morphological root of the word; it is usually sufficient that related words map to the same stem, even if this stem is not in itself a valid root. The process of stemming, often called conflation, is useful in search engines for query expansion or indexing and other natural language processing problems. Word stemming is done by grouping words that have the same stem or root, such as computer, compute, and computing. The Porter stemmer is a well-known algorithm for performing this task.

The Porter stemming algorithm (or 'Porter stemmer') is a process for removing the commoner morphological and inflexional endings from words in English. Its main use is as part of a term normalization process that is usually done when setting up Information Retrieval systems.

Feature Selection

Feature selection is one of the most important steps in pattern recognition or pattern classification, data mining, machine learning and so on. Generally speaking, only classification information is included sufficiently in the eigenvector, classifier can classify the classification rightly. However, it is difficult to measure classification information in all features. Data preprocessing is an indispensable step in effective data analysis. It prepares data for data mining and machine learning, which aim to turn data into business intelligence or knowledge. Feature selection is a preprocessing technique commonly used on high dimensional data. Feature selection studies how to select a subset or list of attributes or variables that are used to construct models describing data. Its purposes include reducing dimensionality, removing irrelevant and redundant features, reducing the amount of data needed for learning, improving algorithms' predictive accuracy, and increasing the constructed models' comprehensibility. Feature-selection methods are particularly welcome in interdisciplinary collaborations because the selected features retain the original meanings domain experts are familiar with. The rapid developments in computer science and engineering allow for data collection at an unprecedented speed and present new challenges to feature selection. Wide data sets, which have a huge number of features but relatively few instances, introduce a novel challenge to feature selection.

Keyword Extraction

The next step is to extract keywords from each web document that identifies the topic. These keywords will need to represent the web document well. Select a number of terms (words) whose presence or absence in each document can be used to describe the document topic. This can be done manually by using some domain expertise for each topic or automatically by using a statistical text processing While extracting the keywords from the documents the following points should be keep in mind.

- The selected documents should have at least 5 keywords that identify the topic.
- Each document should have around 200 words. However, it is acceptable to select a document with fewer words if the document

has a high concentration of keywords.
- Avoid the documents that have no enough text to classify them.
- Some of these documents have an 'introduction' type link that fully describes the topic. In this case, select the web document pointed to by such a link to represent that topic.
- Each two pages under the same topic must share 5-10 keywords

During this phase, create the vector space model, a N x N matrix, which serves as a representation of the N web documents. These documents will serve as our training and learning set in the machine learning phase. Use the selected keywords as features (attributes) and represent those features as vector model representation.

Machine Learning

Machine learning refers to a system capable of the autonomous acquisition and integration of knowledge. This capacity to learn from experience, analytical observation, and other means, results in a system that can continuously self-improve and thereby offer increased efficiency and effectiveness. (Tom Mitchell. M, 1999). After features of training web pages have been selected to form concise representations of the web pages, various machine learning methods and classification algorithms can be applied to induce the classification to induce representations for categories from the representations of training web pages. When a new web page is to be classified, the classifiers use the learned function to assign the web page to categories. Many of the classification algorithms are used for supervised learning – decision lists, decision trees, artificial neural networks, Bayesian classifiers, SVM classifiers etc. Machine learning has a wide spectrum of applications including natural language processing, syntactic pattern recognition, search engines, medical diagnosis, bioinformatics, detecting credit card fraud, stock market analysis, classifying DNA sequences, speech and handwriting recognition, object recognition in computer vision, game playing and robot locomotion.

MACHINE LEARNING TECHNIQUES

There are a lot of machine learning techniques available in the literature. Most of the machine learning algorithms is commonly used for web applications. Some of them are discussed here.

SVM Based Classifiers

Support Vector Machine (SVM) has been demonstrated its excellent performance in terms of solving document classification problem. SVM is the first choice for web page classification because of its advantage on non-effective of feature dimension scale. In its simplest form, a linear SVM is a hyperplane that separates a set of positive examples from a set of negative examples with maximum margin. The margin is the distance from the hyperplane to the nearest of the positive and negative examples. For problems that are non linearly separable, kernel methods can be used to transform the input space so that some non-linear problems can be learned. SVM is used mostly with other classifiers for better performance.(Aixin Sun,EePeng Lim and WeeKeong Ng 2002, Gautam Pant and Padmini Srinivasan 2006, Jiu-Zhen Lung 2004)

Bayesian Classifiers

Bayesian methods provide the basis for probabilistic learning methods that accommodate and require knowledge about the prior possibilities of alternative hypotheses and about the probability of observing various data given the hypothesis. Bayesian methods allow assigning a posterior probability to each candidate hypothesis, based on these assumed priors and the observed data. Among Bayesian classifiers Naïve Bayes classifier

is mostly used for web page classification process.(Yong Wang, Julia Hodges, Bo Tang 2003)

a) Naïve Bayes Classifiers

The Naïve Bayes classifier is the simplest instance of a probabilistic classifier. The output $p(c|d)$ of a probabilistic classifier is the probability that a pattern d belongs to a class c after observing the data d (posterior probability). It assumes that text data comes from a set of parametric models (each single model is associated to a class). Training data are used to estimate the unknown model parameters. During the operative phase, the classifier computes (for each model) the probability $p(d|c)$ expressing the probability that the document is generated using the model. The Bayes theorem allows the inversion of the generative model and the computation of the posterior probabilities (probability that the model generated the pattern). The final classification is performed selecting the model yielding the maximum posterior probability. In spite of its simplicity, a Naïve Bayes classifier is almost as accurate as state-of-the-art learning algorithms for text categorization tasks. The Naïve Bayes classifier is the most used classifier in many different Web applications such as focus crawling, recommending systems, etc (Yong Wang, Julia Hodges, Bo Tang 2003)

Artificial Neural Networks

The study of Artificial Neural Networks has been inspired in part by the observation that biological learning systems are built of very complex webs of interconnected neurons. In rough analogy, artificial neural networks are built out of a densely interconnected set of simple units, where each unit takes a number of real-valued inputs (possibly the outputs of other units) and produces a single real-valued output (which may become the input to many other units).(Ali Selamat and Sigeru Omatu 2003) The basic computational element (model neuron) is often called a node or unit. It receives input from some other units, or perhaps from an external source. Each input has an associated weight w, which can be modified so as to model synaptic learning. The unit computes some function f of the weighted sum of its inputs:

$$y_i = f(\Sigma \, w_{ij} \, y_j)$$

Inductive Logic Programming

Inductive logic programming (ILP) is a subfield of machine learning which uses logic programming as a uniform representation for example, background knowledge and hypotheses. Given an encoding of the known background knowledge and a set of examples represented as a logical database of facts, an ILP system will derive a hypothesized logic program which entails all the positive and none of the negative examples.

Schema: positive examples + negative examples + background knowledge => hypothesis.

Inductive Logic Programming learns a general hypothesis H from a set of given examples E and possibly available background knowledge B. The set of examples E contain both positive E+ and negative E- examples.(Witold Pedrycz and Zenon Sosnowski, A., 2000, Heiner Stuckenschmidt, Jens Hartmann and Frank van Harmelen 2002). Inductive logic programming is particularly useful in bioinformatics and natural language processing

Instance-Based Learning

Instance-based learning generates classification predictions using only specific instances. Instance-based learning algorithms do not maintain a set of abstractions derived from specific instances. This approach extends the nearest neighbor algorithm, which has large storage requirements. While the storage-reducing algorithm performs well on several real-world databases, its performance degrades rapidly with the level of attribute noise in training instances. Instance-based learning methods differ from other approaches to function approximation because they delay processing of training examples until they must label a new instance.(Jiuyong Li 2006)

Decision Tree Learning

Decision trees are tree structures geared to solving classification problems. It is mainly used to identify decision rules for the particular problem or application. Decision tree learning provides a practical method for concept learning and for learning other discrete-valued functions. The trees usually consist of nodes and edges. The nodes of the decision tree represent the attributes of the problem. The edges of the tree are associated with the finite collections of the values of the attributes. The decision tree algorithm should be designed in such a way that it should give simple decision rules. It depends on how we have selected the attributes for the decision trees. The attributes must be prioritized for getting the best decision rules. Several approaches have been explored for finding the best attributes. The most well-known is Quinlan's which involves calculating the entropy of the distribution of the positive/negative instances resulting from splitting on each of the remaining attributes and then using the attribute which achieves the lowest entropy distribution. The entropy measure is based on the information theory of Shannon. According to this theory we can calculate the information content of the training set, and consequently, of any decision tree that covers this set of examples. The information gain is a probabilistic measure and it can be defined as

$$I = (p_i) \log (p_i)$$

The tree is grown starting from the most meaningful attribute and proceeding with other attributes at lower nodes of the tree. The choice of the attribute is made based upon its classification abilities. A measure of relevance of the attribute has an entropy-like flavor meaning that we are interested in attributes producing nodes of the highest homogeneity. Once the tree has been designed, any new pattern (datum) can be classified by traversing the tree moving down from the top node.(Witold Pedrycz and Zenon A. Sosnowski 2000)

RECENT TRENDS IN CLASSIFYING THE WEB PAGES

Semantic Web

Accessing documents and services on today's Web requires human intelligence. The interface to these documents and services is the Web page, written in natural language, which humans must understand and act upon. The Semantic Web will augment the current Web with formalized knowledge and data that computers can process. Like the Web, the Semantic Web is not an application; it is an infrastructure on which many different applications (such as e-commerce) will develop. Following the intense interests in Semantic Web, research on extracting and integrating information from the Web has become more and more important over the past decade. This is because it helps to tackle the urgent business problem of collating, comparing, and analyzing business information from multiple sites

In this section we discuss some of the more important techniques and methods in Semantic Web Area.

Ontology learning uses machine learning techniques, such as classification, clustering, inductive logic programming, association rules, concept induction, and Naive Bayes to construct ontologies and semantic annotations. Discovering the complicated domain ontologies, which could provide a detailed description of the concepts for a restricted domain, is an important subtask of ontology learning.

The other type of automated approaches includes metadata generation tools, such as screen scraping and metadata harvesting. Web page cleaning has been developed to identify redundant, useless, or irrelevant components (e.g., ads bar and category) in a Web page that the users would not be interested in. Another study emphasizes the development of an automated approach to detect the important portion (OREG) rather than to eliminate the unimportant components in complex Web pages.

Wrapper is a program that extracts data from Web pages and stores them in a database. The wrapper could either be generated by a human being or learned from labeled data. Wrapper generation techniques are used to generate wrappers which provide the required semantic knowledge about the underlying data which is useful for future classification of web pages.

Web Page Classification without the Webpage

It is interesting to show that web pages can be classified without accessing the web page itself from where it is stored. This provides the faster classification of web pages and in this section we discuss the techniques used by the researchers to classify it into categories without retrieving it.

Min-Yen Kan and Hoang Oanh Nguyen Thi (2005) demonstrate the usefulness of the uniform resource locator (URL) alone in performing web page classification. This approach is faster than typical web page classification, as the pages do not have to be fetched and analyzed. Their approach segments the URL into meaningful chunks and adds component, sequential and orthographic features to model salient patterns. The resulting features are used in supervised maximum entropy model.

Luis Gravano , Panagiotis G. Ipeirotis and Mehran Sahami (2003) describe QProber, which automates the categorization of searchable Web databases into topic hierarchies. QProber uses a combination of machine learning and database querying techniques. They use machine learning techniques to initially build document classifiers. Rather than actually using these classifiers to categorize individual documents, they extract classification rules from the document classifiers, and transform these rules into a set of query probes that can be sent to the search interface of the available text databases. The algorithm then simply uses the number of matches reported for each query to make classification decisions, without having to retrieve and analyze any of the actual database documents. This makes the approach very efficient and scalable.

PRIVACY PRESERVING DATA MINING

All the above machine learning classifiers may be trained to classify the personal information and any unauthenticated request for the information can easily be found and informed to the authorities. Another way is all the personal details may be stored in the encrypted form and the authenticated user only having the decryption key can get the relevant details. Others may get very irrelevant information. For banking, e-commerce and mobile applications where personal details are to be stored in the database, there is a possibility to get this information using data mining methods. To avoid this, data may be stored in a distorted form in the database and only secured, authenticated applications can retrieve the true data, but for others that may be impossible. Machine learning classifiers may be trained to find outliers, queries intend for fraudulent action and this would be very useful to avoid the undesirable outcomes.

CONCLUSION

In this article we mainly focus on machine learning methods used for Web Page Classification problems and show how researchers used different machine learning algorithms for Web page classification. We also discuss what the various issues in web page classification are and how machine learning techniques overcome this problem. We also discuss how the volume or large number of web pages can be taken as an advantage for the web page classification problem in the classification with unlabeled data section. Finally we conclude that the machine learning techniques play a key role in the classification of web pages. It is also better than the Knowledge Engineering approach for the classification of web pages.

REFERENCES

Aixin, S. , E. L., & Ng, W. K. (2002, November). Web Classification Using Support Vector Machine. *Proceedings of the 4th international workshop on Web Information and Data Management held in conj. With CIKM.*

Altingövde, I. S. & Ulusoy, O. (2004). Exploiting Interclass Rules for Focused Crawling. *IEEE Intelligent Systems,* pp. 66 – 73

Anagnostopoulos I., Kouzas G. Anagnostopoulos C., Vergados D., Papaleonidopoulos I., Generalis A., Loumos V., & Kayafas E., (2004). Classifying web pages using a probabilistic Neural Network. *IEEE Proceedings on Software. 151*(3).

Asirvatham, A. P., & Ravi, K. K. (2001). Web Page Categorization based on document structure. *Proceedings of ACM.*

Chan, C-H., Sun, A., & Lim, E-P.(2001). Automated Online News classification with Personalization. *Proceedings of the 4th international conference of Asian Digital Library (ICADL 2001),* pp. 320-329, Bangalore, India

Drori, O. (2005). Using frequently occurring words to identify the subject of a document. *Journal of Information Science, 31*(3), 164-177.

Dumais, S., & Chen, H. (2000). Hierarchical Classification of Web Content. *SIGIR 2000*, ACM, pp. 256 –263.

Gravano, L., Ipeirotis, P. G., & Sahami, M. (2003, January). QProber: A System for Automatic Classification of Hidden-Web Databases. ACM *Transactions on Information Systems, 21*(1), 1-41.

John, P. M. (2001). On the Automated Classification of Web Sites. *Link¨oping Electronic Articles in Computer and Information Science. 6*, 1-15.

Kan, M-Y., & Thi, H. O. N. (2005, October 31-November 5). Fast Webpage Classification Using URL Features. *CIKM'05*, Bremen, Germany. ACM.

Kwon, O-H., & Lee, J-H. (2000). Web Page Classification Based on k-Nearest Neighbor Approach. *Proceedings of the 5th International Workshop Information Retrieval with Asian Languages, 2000*, ACM, pp. 9- 15

Liang, J-Z. (2003). Chinese Web Page Classification Based on Self-organizing Mapping Neural Networks. *Proceedings of the Fifth International Conference on Computational Intelligence and Multimedia Applications (ICCIMA'03)*, IEEE.

Li, J. (2006, August). Robust Rule-Based Prediction. *IEEE Transactions on Knowledge and Data Engineering, 18*(8), 1043 – 1054.

Lung, J-Z. (2004, August 26-29). SVM Multi-Classifier And Web Document Classification. *Proceedings of the Third International Conference on Machine Learning and Cybernetics*, pp. 1347 – 1351.

Mitchell, T. M., (1999). The Role of Unlabeled data in Supervised Learning. *Proceedings of the Sixth International Colloquium on Cognitive Science.*

Pant, G., & Srinivasan, P. (2006). Link Contexts in Classifier-Guided Topical Crawlers. *IEEE Transactions on Knowledge and Data Engineering, 18*(1), 107 – 122.

Pedrycz, W., & Sosnowski, Z. A. (2000, March). Designing Decision Trees with the Use of Fuzzy Granulation. *IEEE Transactions on Systems, Man, and Cybernetics—Part A: Systems and Humans, 30*(2 151-159.

Riboni, D. (2002). Feature Selection for Web Page Classification. *Proceedings of ACM Workshop (EURASIA-ICT 2002).*

Sebastiani, F. (2002). Machine learning in Automated Text categorization. *ACM Computing Surveys, 34*(1), 1-47.

Selamat, A., Yanagimoto, H., & Omatu, S. (2002). Web News Classification Using Neural Networks Based on PCA. *SIC€* 2002 Auk 57,Osaka

Stuckenschmidt, H., Hartmann, J., & van Harmelen, F. (2002). Learning Structural Classification Rules for Web-page Categorization. *Proceedings of Fifteenth International conference on Artificial Intelligence*, Flairs-2002 , American Association for Artificial Intelligence,(www.aaai.org)

Wang, Y., Hodges, J., & Tang, B. (2003). Classification of Web Documents Using a Naive Bayes Method. *Proceedings of the 15th IEEE International Conference on Tools with Artificial Intelligence (ICTAI'03)*, 2003 IEEE.

KEY TERMS

Feature Extraction: Feature extraction is the preceding step to feature selection. It includes the collection of features from the web pages. It can be done using any of the feature extraction techniques. All the collected features during the feature extraction phase need not be relevant.

Feature Selection: Feature selection is a process of selecting the relevant features needed for classification purposes. Feature selection is the most important step because the selected features determine the classification accuracy.

HTML Structure: HTML refers to Hypertext Markup Language. It is used for the design of web pages. Most of the web pages contain html tags enclosed.

Machine Learning: Machine Learning is a technique commonly used for automatic classification of web pages. It includes both the training phase and the testing phase. The training phase is used to learn from examples. Based on the learning the classifier classifies during the testing phase.

Preprocessing: Preprocessing is the process of removing unnecessary information before the classification of web pages. It includes removing common words, rare words, removing HTML tags and stemming.

Web Page Classification: Web page classification is a process of determining whether the web pages belong to a particular category or not. It can be done by considering the various features like URL, head, title and the body contents of the web page.

World Wide Web: The World Wide Web means net of networks. It contains a large amount of information needed for the Internet browsers. Boundless amount of information can be downloaded at any point of time.

Chapter IX
U.S. Federal Data Mining Programs in the Context of the War on Terror:
The Congress, Court, and Concerns for Privacy Protection

Shahid M. Shahidullah
Virginia State University, USA

Mokerrom Hossain
Virginia State University, USA

ABSTRACT

This chapter examines the issues and concerns raised in the context of the recent growth of federal mining programs. The chapter argues that in the context of the war on terror, intelligence gathering on terrorist activities both within and outside the United States has emerged as one of the core strategies for homeland security. The major national security related federal agencies such as the Department of Justice, Department of Homeland Security, and the Department of Defense have developed a number of data mining programs to improve terrorism intelligence gathering and analysis in the wake of the events of September 11, 2001. Some data mining programs have, however, raised a number of issues related to privacy protections and civil liberties. These issues have given birth to a wider debate in the nation and raised new tensions about how to search for a balance between the needs for the protection of privacy and civil liberties, and the needs for national security. The authors believe that the future of this debate is intimately connected to the future of the war on terror. Currently, Congress and the federal courts seem to be more in favor of supporting the preeminent needs of protecting national security. Through a number of enactments, Congress has broadened the federal power for collecting terrorism intelligence both at home and abroad. In a number of cases, the federal courts have ruled in favor of the doctrines of the "state secret privilege" and the "inherent power of the President" to emphasize the overriding need for protecting national security in the context of the war on terror. As America has embarked on a long and protracted ideological war against radical militant Islam, issues of national security and the need for data mining for detecting and analyzing terrorist activities are likely to remain dominant for a long time.

INTRODUCTION

The birth of the computer and the Internet, and the rise of the information revolution have brought some fundamental transformations in the way information can be created, organized, analyzed, stored, and shared. A new generation of information technology has emerged today that made us able to gather an unfathomable amount of data about the mysteries of the space and the galaxies, the baffling nature of the earth and the seas, and the complexities of the human bodies, brains, minds, and behavior. The everyday life in the information society is a bundle of digital texts, bits, and bytes that can travel through space and time without much control of those who own and produce them. In our everyday life, we participate in the digital economy and roam around cyber space with the computer sitting in the privacy of our home and family (Tapscott, 1999). The unseen and the boundless cyber space, however, knows no privacy. Our information in cyber space is virtually opened to the world, and it is irretrievable. Through our participations in the digital economy and our use of the Internet, we create a series of virtual data structures about our daily activities—our work, education, health, home, travel, and entertainment. These data structures remain stored in various places such as telephone companies, Internet service providers, banks, credit card companies, hotels, airlines, travel agencies, and tourist organizations. Information scientists describe data warehousing as the process of organizing and storing data structures. By creating these data structures, we, in fact, create a digital profile of our habits, choices, preferences,

and prejudices. Through these data structures, one can even glean through the profiles of our families, friends, and relatives who live across different regions and countries. These data structures can lead to the discoveries of our habits and identities. They can lead to the discoveries of our patterns of thoughts, beliefs, and associations. Information technology or the methodology that makes these analyses and discoveries possible is known as data mining.

Data mining has opened up a new horizon of possibilities for growth and expansion in information science, artificial intelligence, super-computing, human genetics, neurology, medicine, earth science, and many other areas of scientific research (McCue, 2006; Wang, 2005). A variety of marketing, advertising, and business organizations today use data mining to create profiles of the habits and preference of their consumers (Perner, 2002). The use of data mining by business organizations and governmental agencies, however, has raised a number ethical and moral questions related to privacy, democracy, and civil liberties.

A debate is currently growing in America about the use of data mining by many federal agencies, particularly about the ones that are being conducted in the context of the war on terror. Federal agencies working with national security and homeland protections find in data mining a new weapon of intelligence to combat and prevent terrorist activities both within and outside the United States. In the larger society, however, concerns are being raised about how federal data mining programs undermine the notions of privacy and civil liberties (Carafano,, 2007; DeRosa, 2004; Heymann & Kayyem, 2005; United States

Senate, January 10, 2007). In the context of this debate, this chapter examines the extent of the use of data mining related to the war on terror by federal organizations, the development of federal enactments related to data mining and privacy, and the role of the federal court in protecting the rights of privacy in the wake of the expanding growth of data mining technology in general and its use by federal agencies in the context of national security in particular.

BACKGROUND

The Nature of Data Mining Technology

Data mining is a process of understanding the themes and relationships in a vast amount of discrete, descriptive, and disconnected digitalized data. The history of data gathering and data analysis for public policy-making goes back to the past. In the early 1600, "a census was taken in Virginia, and people were counted in nearly all of the British colonies that later became the United States" (United States Census, 2003, p. 1). The first systematic U.S. Census was taken in 1790 under the directions and planning of the then Secretary of State, Thomas Jefferson, and Congress created the United States Bureau of Census in 1902. The Uniform Crime Reporting Program to collect crime data was created by the International Chiefs of Police in 1927, and Congress made it a law by an act of legislation in 1930. Charles Booth's survey on life and poverty in England in the middle of the nineteenth century has been a great historical legacy for research and analysis in social science. In the 1950s and 1960s, in the context of post-World War II reconstruction, a new movement for survey research began in America under the leadership of Columbia University, University of Michigan, University of Chicago, and many other research and academic institutions. The General Social Survey (GSS)

conducted by the National Opinion Research Center at the University of Chicago is one of the major achievements of America's social science for advancing the tradition of data-based and research-based policy-making. In addition, there has recently been a great proliferation of public opinion polls including such organizations as the Gallup Poll, The PEW Research Center, and the Harris Poll that assess public opinion on diverse issues related to policy-making across different times and different groups.

The policy-makers' search for data for effective policy-making is old. But the contemporary phenomenon of using data mining for federal policy-making is recent in origin—it is barely a decade old. Using data mining in policy-making in the federal government came primarily with the development of the technology of data mining in information science and computing, on the one hand, and its relatively effective and productive use in business and industries, on the other. Data mining is a planned, deliberate, and goal-oriented search for meanings and relationships hidden in data structures. It is essentially a four-fold process of discovery—data, information, knowledge, and effective policy-strategies. Traditionally, data are presented in policy-making in the form of descriptive information. The discoveries of new knowledge and new patterns of relationships are usually left for policy-makers to assume and hypothesize. Modern data mining is a computer-based statistical and mathematical process of generating data-based knowledge structures, patterns, and predictabilities (Ye, 2003; Wang, 2003). Before the birth of modern information science and computing, it was not possible to organize, synthesize, cluster, and classify hundreds of thousands, and even millions of bits and bytes of data for discovering new knowledge and new patterns of meanings hidden in data structures. As one data mining expert describes: "*Data mining is the nontrivial extraction of implicit, previously unknown, interesting and potentially useful information (usually in the form of knowledge patterns* or models) from data. The extracted knowledge is used to describe the hidden regularity of data, to make prediction, or to aid human users in other ways" (Chen, 2001, p. 12).

Data mining in an archaic form existed in federal policymaking for a long time. The policy-analysts, particularly those who work for law enforcement organizations, national security agencies, foreign affairs departments or the U.S. Bureau of Census and the Department of Labor, regularly explain and analyze data for new knowledge and understanding. The recent technology of data mining, however, is based on sophisticated computer software programs that search "the data base by itself and finds significant patterns for knowledge discovery" (Chen, 2001, p. 21). Data mining represents "*a difference in kind rather than degree ….* Data mining utilizes a discovery approach, in which algorithms can be used to examine several multidimensional data relationships simultaneously, identifying those that are unique and frequently represented" (Congressional Research Service, 2007a, p. 1). The key goals of data mining are "to understand behaviors; to forecast trends and demands; to track performance; and, to transform seemingly unrelated data into meaningful information" (United States Department of Homeland Security, 2006, p. 5). In recent years, there has been a massive proliferation of software programs, and private vendors and companies related to data mining such as IBM Intelligent Miner Family, IBM Knowledge Management Solutions, KnowledgeMiner, Acxiom Corporation, The Data Mining Group, Norkom Global, Raptor International, and Data Mind Corporation (Matignon, 2007).

Data Mining in U.S. Federal Departments and Agencies

The use of data mining by federal agencies from the middle of the 1990s began primarily for the improvement of agency performance, human resource management, and the detection of fraud,

waste, and abuse of federal grants and resources. In 2004, the United States General Accounting Office (2004a) conducted the first systematic survey on the nature and prevalence of data mining in U.S. federal departments and agencies. The survey studied 128 federal departments and agencies, and found that "52 agencies are using or are planning to use data mining. These departments and agencies reported 199 data mining efforts, of which 68 are planned and 131 are operational" (p. i). The survey also found that most of these federal data mining programs (122 out of 199 programs) used personal information and that the primary purposes of data mining "were improving service or performance; detecting fraud, waste, and abuse; analyzing scientific and research information; managing human resources; detecting criminal activities or patterns; and analyzing intelligence and detecting terrorist activities" (United States General Accounting Office, 2004a, p. i).

Before September 11, 2001, the use of data mining by federal agencies was mostly for improving agency-specific public service delivery functions and performance. The U.S. General Accounting Office, for example, has been regularly using data mining as an important tool for "audits and investigations of federal government credit card programs" (United States General Accounting Office, 2003, p. 1). The U.S. Department of Education uses a number of data mining programs to study the citizenship background of its PLUS loan borrowers, to examine the Department of Education's Personal Data System, to identify patterns and trends in identity theft cases involving loans for education, and to understand the demographic trends in federal student loan applications. The Department of Health and Human Services uses several data mining programs to monitor the nation's public health, blood supply, and food and drug safety. Similar agency-specific service delivery and performance improvement related data mining programs exist in almost all federal departments and agencies (United States General Accounting Office, 2004a). The existence of federal data mining programs before September 11, 2001 did not draw much public attention or raise any significant legal and political controversies. It was generally seen as another contribution of information technology for improvement in public policy and governance.

Federal data mining programs entered into a new phase of growth and expansions after September 11, 2001 in the context of the war on terror and heightened concerns for homeland security. The doctrine of pre-emption, developed as an overall approach to fight the war on terror, led to the development of a new and wider series of governmental surveillance strategies including the expansion of data mining programs for the detection of terrorist activities by all federal departments and agencies. In the context of the events of September 11, a consensus has emerged within the government that one of the key strategies for fighting global terror is to overhaul the nation's security intelligence activities. From the trails left behind by the September 11 terrorists, the nation began to ponder that many of the same are probably still roaming around the country, driving along the highways, studying in colleges and universities, or living in the dark of the terrorist sleeper cells. It is estimated that about "80 million passengers [fly] into the United States per year on 823,757 commercial flights and [on] 139,650 private flights; 330 million people [come] across the Canadian and Mexican boarders by auto, train, and truck; 18 million by sea; and almost 200,000 cargo ships [unload] some 10 million containers in U.S. ports—all this per annum" (de Borchgrave, March 16, 2005, p. 1). One estimate shows that in 2004, about 700,000 foreign students and foreign exchange visitors were enrolled in America's 7,000 colleges and universities (Dougherty, February 25, 2004). Tracking terrorists who enter the United States, and plan and continue their terrorist activities in collaboration with their counterparts living both in the United States and abroad became a significant challenge for law enforcement and national

security agencies in the aftermath of the events of September 11. As President Bush said: "They blend in with the civilian population. They get their orders from overseas, and then they emerge to strike from within. We must be able to quickly detect when someone linked to al Qaeda is communicating with someone inside of America. That's one of the challenges of protecting the American people, and it's one of the lessons of September the 11" (The White House, 2006b, p. 1). Congress responded to this challenge through the enactment of the USA PATRIOT Act of 2001 (Uniting and Strengthening America by Providing Appropriate Tools Required to Intercept and Obstruct Terrorism Act of 2001- PL 107-56) and the Homeland Security Act of 2002 (PL 107-296). The Act of 2002 created a new Department of Homeland Security, by combining a number of federal agencies such as the Immigration and Naturalization Service, Department of Custom, Border Patrol, Coast Guard, Department of Transportation, and the Federal Aviation Authority, to focus on foreign terrorist threats in the America's homeland with a wider network of surveillance, intelligence gathering, and data analysis.

The USA PATRIOT Act of 2001 broadened the scope and power of domestic surveillance. Title II of the PATRIOT Act—Enhance Surveillance Procedures—created a new power for law enforcement and intelligence agencies to intercept wire and electronic communication, install trap and trace devices, collect foreign intelligence, and share terrorism investigation information. One of the major issues addressed by the USA PATRIOT Act was to improve the connectivity between and among different intelligence gathering agencies both at home and abroad (Congressional Research Service, 2002). To further streamline the federal intelligence activities, Congress created a separate Office of National Intelligence within the Executive Office of the President through the enactment of the Intelligence Reform and Terrorism Act of 2004 (PL 108-458). The prime mandate for the Office of National Intelligence is to function as a central coordinating unit for all federal intelligence agencies and activities.

In the context of the events of September 11 and in compliance with the USA PATRIOT Act of 2001, Homeland Security Act of 2002, and the Intelligence Reform and Terrorism Act of 2004, federal data mining efforts from the beginning of this decade began to be designed in almost all federal departments and agencies, particularly in law enforcement and public and national security related agencies, not just for improvement in internal performance and human resource management. It began to be designed also as a tool to fight the war on terror (Seifert, 2004). Some of the major federal data mining programs designed to detect and analyze terrorist activities include the Department of Justice's Foreign Terrorist Tracking Task Force (FTTTF), STAR Initiative (System-to-Assess-Risk), and the SCOPE Program (Secure Collaborative Operational Prototype Environment); Department of Homeland Security's ADVISE Technology Framework (Analysis, Dissemination, Visualization, Insight, and Semantic Enhancement), Automated Targeting System (ATS), MATRIX System (Multistate Anti-terrorism Information Exchange), SEVIS System (Student and Exchange Visitor Information System), US-VISIT (U.S. Visitor and Immigration Status Indicator Technology), Automated Export System Data Mart, Incident Data Mart, Case Management Data Mart, and Analyst Notebook 12; National Security Agency's (NSA) Phone Tracking Program; Department of Defense's TIA Program (Total Information Awareness), Insight Smart Discovery, Pathfinder, Verity K2 Enterprise, and Autonomy; Transportation Security Administration's CAPPS II Program (Computer Assisted Passenger Prescreening System), International Revenue Services' Reveal System; Department of Education's Project Strike Back; and the Centers for Disease Control and Prevention's BioSense (Congressional Research Service; 2003; Congressional Research Service 2004; United States Department of Justice, 2007;

United States Department of Homeland Security, 2007; United States General Accounting Office, 2004a)

The Department of Justice's Foreign Terrorist Tracking Task Force (FTTTF) was the first federal data mining program specifically designed and created to track and analyze data on foreign terrorists entering and living in the United States. It was created in October, 2001, and it is operated by the Federal Bureau of Investigation (FBI) in collaboration with the Department of Homeland Security's Bureaus of Immigration and Customs Enforcement and Customs and Border Protection, Department of Defense, Department of State, Department of Energy, Central Intelligence Agency, Social Security Administration, and the Office of U.S. Personnel Management. In the words of former FTTTF's Director Mark Tanner (2003): "The mission of the FTTTF is to provide information that helps keep foreign terrorists and their supporters out of the U.S. or leads to their removal, detention, prosecution or other legal action" (p. 1). The President's Homeland Security Presidential Directive-2 mandated that FTTTF uses all kinds of advanced information technology "to facilitate the rapid identification of aliens who are suspected of engaging in or supporting terrorist activity, to deny them access to the United States, and to recommend ways in which existing government databases can be best utilized to maximize the ability of the government to detect, identify, locate, and apprehend potential terrorists in the United States" (The White House, October 29, 2001, p. 1). FTTTF's major responsibility "is to identify and track both known and suspected terrorists inside the United States or as they attempt to enter this country. The information derived from FTTTF's assessments is then reported to U. S. Intelligence agencies and federal law enforcement officials" (United States Department of Justice, 2007, p. 8).

The Department of Justice's STAR Initiative (System-to-Assess-Risk) is an extension of its FTTTF Program. STAR is a process of subject-based data mining that has the ability to analyze a large number of data from multiple databases related to specific terrorists and terrorist threats and prioritize the need for immediate law enforcement and intelligence interventions. The STAR Program examines and analyzes "voluminous FTTTE data in a timely and efficient manner by leveraging a data analysis system that is designed to assess the risk potential of possible terrorist threats. The intent of the system is to increase the efficiency and effectiveness of the FTTTE analysts" (United States Department of Justice, 2007, p. 8). Data mining by the STAR Program is particularly focused to "determine whether an individual or group of interest may be associated with terrorism by producing risk assessment score based on a series of indicators of potential terrorist behaviors" (United States Department of Justice, 2007, p. 9).

After September 11, the Department of Justice (DOJ) has also started a data mining program titled IDW (Investigative Data Warehouse). The goal of IDW is to create a central repository of terrorist data from all conceivable sources—data that can be analyzed for pattern recognition and trends of terrorist threats and activities both at home and abroad. As of March 2005, according to one report (Herold, October 29, 2006), the IDW database contained "more than 100 million pages of terrorism-related documents, and billions of structured records such as addresses and phone numbers" (p. 1). In May 2006, FBI Director Robert S. Mueller testified to Congress that the IDW "contains over 560 million FBI and other agency documents ... Nearly 12,000 users can access [the IDW] via the FBI's classified network from any FBI terminal throughout the globe" (Herold, October 29, 2006, p. 1).

The Department of Homeland Security (DHS), since its inception in 2002, has focused on developing an extensive surveillance system for the control and containment of terrorist activities inside the United States (Congressional Research Service, 2007a; United States Department of Homeland

Security, 2007; Rosenzweig & Ahren, 2007). The Homeland Security Act of 2001 made it mandatory for DHS to use advanced data mining technologies for analyzing and detecting terrorist activities. ADVISE (Analysis, Dissemination, Visualization, Insight and Semantic Enhancement), initiated by the Science and Technology Division of the DHS in 2003, is one of the first generation data mining programs that DHS has planned to put in place. ADVISE is a technology framework that can identify and analyze, and visually represent the "potential relationships between people, places, and events" (United States Department of Homeland Security, 2007, p. 14). It is estimated that ADVISE has the capability of analyzing one billion pieces of structured data (such as computerized database information and watch list), and unstructured data (such as email texts, banking activity, financial transactions, countries visited, activities funded, phone records, organization affiliation, travel information, and hotel reservations) per hour (Hansen, 2007). The datasets that were entered into various ADVISE pilot projects in recent years included no-fly list of people barred from air traveling, more than 3.6 million shipping records, suspected terrorists who entered into the United States through the U.S-Canadian border, classified intelligence reports on groups and individuals engaged in trafficking of illicit drugs and weapons of mass destructions, lists of foreign exchange students and visitors under investigation, lists of people from special interest countries who must register with the DHS, and lists of foreign visitors who overstayed after the expiration of their U.S. visas (Sniffen, 2007). Both structured and unstructured data enable the ADVISE analysts to "search for patterns in data, including relationships among entities (such as people, organizations, and events), and to produce visual representations of these patterns, referred to as semantic graphs" (United States General Accounting Office, 2007, p. 3). The Department of Homeland Security has planned to use the ADVISE system as an overall approach to or an overall framework of analysis of its all data mining programs. "To promote the possible implementation of the tool within DHS component organizations, program officials have made demonstrations (using unclassified data) to interested officials, highlighting the tool's planned capabilities and benefits" (United States General Accounting Office, 2007, p. 6).

The Department of Homeland Security's Automated Targeting System (ATS) was developed by the Bureau of Customs and Border Protection (CBP). It was originally developed by CBP in response to the Anti-Terrorism and Effective Death Penalty Act of 1996 (PL 104-132) and the Title VII of the Omnibus Consolidated Appropriations Act of 1997 to detect and analyze suspicious activities of the ships and cargos leaving from and entering into the United States. "The risk assessments for cargo are also mandated under section 203 of the Security and Accountability for Every Port Act of 2006" (United States Department of Homeland Security, 2007, p. 17). In 2006, the DHS broadened the scope of ATS and decided to deploy it to screen all "travelers entering into the United States by car, plane, ship, or rail" (Congressional Research Service, 2007a, p. 17). The Aviation and Transportation Security Act of 2001 (PL 107-71) made it mandatory for the CBP to collect PNR (Passenger Name Records) from all airlines. Under the new law, all carriers flying from and entering into the United States must give electronic access to CBP for PNR data. PNR includes electronic data on all passengers entering into or leaving the United States through airways. PNR could contain more than fifty pieces of information on a traveler including data on seat assignments, travel plans, reservations, form of payment, contact phone numbers, and destinations. "CBP is currently collecting PNR data from 127 airlines, which represent all major carriers operating to and from the United States" (Rosenzweig & Ahern, 2007, p. 4). PNR and other travel data collected by the CBP form the core of ATS analysis.

In 2002, the Transportation Security Administration (TSA) of the Department of Homeland Security, in compliance with the Aviation and Transportation Security Act of 2001, initiated a new data mining program titled as CAPPS II (Computer-Assisted Passenger Prescreening System). The Computer Assisted Passenger Prescreening System (CAPPS), developed in the 1990s, is currently used by almost all U.S. airlines and airport authorities. The present system classifies all passengers into two categories: those who do not require additional screening and those who require additional screening called "selectees." In the CAPPS system, the airline's reservation authority decides, on the basis of the passenger's travel itinerary and government supplied watch list, which passenger requires additional screening (General Accounting Office, 2004a, p. 5). The CAPPS II system proposed by the TSA was designed to further extend and refine the existing process of screening by including four pieces of information in the Passenger Name Record (PNR): home phone number, home address, home phone, and date of birth. These data are to be supplied to CAPPS II system by commercial airliners and data providers. The CAPPS II will then analyze those data, provide an identity authentication scores to all passengers, and conduct a risk analysis. The system is designed to divide all passengers into three categories: passengers with acceptable risk (green score), passengers with unknown risk (yellow score), and passengers with unacceptable risk (red score). The airline check-in counters will have the risk scores of all passengers sent by the CAPPS II system at the time of the passengers' boarding. While the passengers with unknown risk will receive additional screening, the passengers with unacceptable risk will be detained and handed over to law enforcement for further investigation. In 2004, the Transportation Security Administration, however, decided to discontinue the CAPPS II program for the lack of data and other legal and privacy concerns. A new Secure Flight System analysis was planned, but it was also discontinued in 2006 (Congressional Research Service, 2007a, p. 11; United States General Accounting Office, 2004).

The Office of Inspector General of the Department of Homeland Security has conducted a survey of the existing data mining programs within the Department of Homeland Security in 2006. The survey identified 12 major data mining programs, 9 of which are in operation and 3 are under development. These 12 programs perform five types of analysis: expert systems analysis (ACE S1, FAS); association processes analysis (DARTTS, CEPIC, NETLEADS, and CVS); threat and risk assessment analysis (RMRS); collaboration and visualization analysis (I2F, NIPS, QID, TISS); and advanced analysis (ADVISE System). The programs under development include I2F, ADVISE, and FAS (see Table 1).

Along with the Department of Justice and the Department of Homeland Security, the Department of Defense (DOD) started also a number of new data mining programs in the context of the events of September 11 and the war on terror. One of the widely known and discussed programs initiated by DOD's Information Awareness Office is described as Total Information Awareness Program (TIA). TIA's mission was to create a system of total information awareness "useful for preemption, national security warning, and national security decision-making" (as quoted in Congressional Research Service, 2007a, p. 5). Different TIA projects aimed to develop a system of automated translation of foreign languages documents, a new generation of pattern recognition technologies for data mining, and a new system of collaborative decision-making between and among different federal agencies. Congress, however, decided to discontinue the funding of the TIA project in 2004.

The 2004 Survey of federal data mining programs by the General Accounting Office included five DOD data mining programs specifically focused on analyzing and preventing terrorist activities. These programs are: Insight Smart Discovery, Verity K2 Enterprise, PATHFINDER, Autonomy, and National Cargo Tracking Plan (United States General Accounting Office, 2004a). Out of these five programs, PATHFINDER is widely known and used in both private and public sectors for its capacity to quickly search, compare, and analyze large databases. "Project Pathfinder is an evolutionary, user-driven, Army-sponsored software R&D project pursuing the development of advanced data mining and visualization tools for intelligence analysts. Pathfinder is also a deployed system in use in over 40 organizations in the intelligence community (IC) and Armed Services" (Hendrickson, 2007, p.1). Many observe that "Pathfinder has become a core enabling technology in the War on Terrorism. These tools and techniques are now part of the Intelligence Community's DNA" (Hendrickson, 2007, p. 2). DOD is also developing, with the help of Lockheed Martin, a new Automated Biometric Identification System (ABIS) that will have the capacity to electronically store and analyze the fingerprint data collected from all over the world by DOD.

In October 2001, President Bush, through an Executive Order, gave the National Security Agency (NSA) an urgent task and a new responsibility of mobilizing all its expertise and technology to collect and analyze foreign intelligence related to terrorism, particularly the activities of Al-Qaeda inside the United States. In his Radio Address in 2005, President Bush clearly stated the goal of his 2001 Executive order: "In the weeks following the terrorist attacks on our nation, I authorized the National Security Agency, consistent with U.S. law and the Constitution, to intercept the international communications of people with known links to al Qaeda and related terrorists organizations" (as quoted in Congressional Research Service, 2007a, p. 18). NSA, in compliance with this Executive Order, started immediately to develop two major data mining programs: Terrorist Surveillance Program (TSP) and Novel Intelligence from Massive Data Program (NIDM). The goal of the Terrorist Surveillance Program is to collect and

Table 1. Selected data mining programs: Department of Homeland Security

Data Mining Activity	Agency, Purpose and Mission
ACE S1 (Automated Commercial Environment Screening	Bureau of Customs and Border Patrol - Prevents terrorists and terrorists' weapons from entering the United States. It uses the ATS system to search for high-risk cargo entering into the United States.
FAS (Freight Assessment System)	Transportation Security Administration - Protects and secures the nation's transportation system. FAS conducts a prescreening analysis of the cargos entering into the United States.
DARRTS (Data Analysis and Research for Trade Transparency System)	Immigration and Customs Enforcement - Identifies and analyzes terrorists' money laundering and financial transactions including illegal drug trafficking; tracks all commercial goods imported into and exported from the United States.
NETLEADS (Law Enforcement Analysis Data System)	Immigration and Customs Enforcement – Analyzes suspected individuals, groups and organizations for understanding terrorist activity trends and patterns.
RMRS (Risk Management Reporting System)	Transportation Security Administration – Protects the nation's transportation system through risk analysis and by generating a risk-based scoring system
I2F (Intelligent and Information Fusion)	Office of Intelligence and Analysis – Will develop integrated intelligence and information analysis capability through the use of advanced computing and data mining technology
ADVISE	Office of Science and Technology – Currently under development. Will analyze and visually represent relationships between and among different types of data and produce and discover new knowledge about suspected terrorists and terrorist activities.

Sources: Congressional Research Service, 2007a; United States Department of Homeland Security, 2007; United States General Accounting Office, 2004a

analyze data on international telephone calls. "The Program is designed," the Department of Justice described, "to target a key tactic of al Qaeda: infiltrating foreign agents into the United States and controlling their movements through electronic communication, just as it did leading up to the September 11 attacks" (as quoted in Congressional Research Service, 2007a, p. 19). The Terrorist Surveillance Program has collected data on millions of international telephone calls from three major U.S. telephone companies: AT&T, Verizon, and BellSouth to conduct "social network analysis." AT&T, Verizon and BellSouth "are the three largest telecommunication companies in the United

States, serving more than 200 million customers, accounting for hundreds of billions of calls each year" (Congressional Research Service, 2007a, p. 20). Since much of the world's international telephone calls flows through the U.S., the Terrorist Surveillance Program has been able to gather millions of data on international calls coming into and going out from United States during the last few years, particularly with the help of NSA's Center for Advanced Research and Development Activity in Information Technology (Arkin, May 12, 2006; Roberge, September, 2004).

The Novel Intelligence from Massive Data Program (NIDM) of the National Security Council was also established with the goal of helping the federal intelligence community with knowledge on trails and activities of the international terrorists in the United States. NIDM has the technological ability to search a massive database—a database that is complex, heterogeneous, and prolifering containing up to one quadrillion bytes— for new knowledge discoveries. "NIDM is one of several cutting-edge data mining technologies that not only has the capability of finding keywords among millions of electronically monitored communications, but can find hidden relationships among data point" (Center for Grassroots Oversight, 2007, p. 1)

Outside the mainstream national security related organizations, data mining programs for analyzing terrorist activities exist, as mentioned earlier, in many other federal departments and agencies. In 2002, the Internal Revenue Service created a data mining program, titled Reveal System, to track and analyze tax and financial information of people who are suspected to have engaged in terrorist and money laundering activities by the FBI and other security related organizations. The Reveal Program mines tax returns and financial records of the nation's hundreds of thousands of banks, accountants, and casinos, particularly the tax returns of suspected non-profit and charitable organizations. "Using programs called Visual links and the Digital Information Gateway, Reveal can detect and visually depict connections buried in mountains of tax documents" (Naamani-Goldman, 2007, p. 4). Under a new U.S. Tax Code made after September 11, 2001, the Internal Revenue Service is legally obligated to make tax information disclosures to the FBI and other national security and intelligence organizations.

After the events of September 11, keeping track of the activities of foreign students and visitors studying in U.S.'s colleges and universities became also one of the major priorities for national security organizations including the Department of Homeland Security. As John Miller, an As-

sistant Director of FBI stated: "During the 9/11 investigation and continually since, much of the intelligence has indicated terrorists have exploited programs involving student visas and financial aid" (as quoted in New York Times, p. 1). Each year, about 14 million students apply for federal loans, grants, and work-study programs. In the academic year 2005-2006, about 143,000 foreign students were enrolled in U.S. colleges and universities. In 2007, according to a source from the U.S. Department of State, about 600,000 thousand visas have been granted to foreign students and visitors (Anders, 2007). Ten days after September 11, 2001, the Department of Education's Office of Inspector General, in collaboration with the FBI, created a new data mining program, described as "Project Strike Back," to screen and monitor the activities of foreign students and visitors. During the last few years, the FBI and other national security organizations received hundreds of thousands of disclosures of information on foreign students and academic visitors from the Project Strike Back.

It is generally shared by national security and counterterrorism policy-makers that the use of biological weapons such as the spread of Anthrax, Small Pox, Ebola, and other infectious diseases and microorganisms by terrorists can cause the death of hundreds of thousands or even millions of Americans within a short period of time. Combating bioterrorism is an integral part of the war on terror. Congress passed the Public Health and Bioterrorism Response Act in 2002 (PL 107-188), and the Project BioShield in 2004 (PL 108-276). Through a Presidential Directive, a new program, titled BioDefense, was created in 2004 as a national framework to combat bioterrorism (The White House, April 2004). The Centers for Disease Control and Prevention's BioSense is one of the nation's largest data mining programs on bioterrorism. The main goal of BioSense is to develop "enhanced capabilities to rapidly detect and monitor bioterrorism .... The surveillance methods in BioSense address the need for identification, tracking, and management of rapidly spreading naturally occurring events and potential bioterrorism events by using advance algorithms for data analysis" (Centers for Disease Control and Prevention, 2006, p. 1).

MAIN FOCUS OF THE CHAPTER

Federal Data Mining Programs, Privacy Concerns, and the Role of the Congress

With the rapid growth of federal data mining programs, particularly those that have evolved in the context of the war or terror, there has been also a rapid spread in recent years of intense concerns for the protection of privacy and civil liberties. Both within and outside the government, concerns have been raised that many data mining programs collecting and analyzing personal information, such as telephone calls, emails, bank accounts, records of financial transactions, credit card information, data of birth, and social security numbers, may have been violating the citizens' rights to privacy. During the last few years, for some of the data mining program described above, different federal agencies have collected millions of personal information from private data collection agencies, particularly from ChoicePoint, Dunn & Brad Street, and LexisNexis. In many cases, private companies are given contracts to do the data mining for the federal government. ChoicePoint—a Georgia-based company that has a dominant share in the U.S. commercial data broker market—sells data on police records, motor vehicle records, employment background checking records, vital record services, credential verification, credit information, and public record searches. It can also provide data on DNA. Dunn & Brad Street, whose global database has about 115 million business records, specializes in providing information on business and financial transactions. LexisNexis has the expertise in data

management and data-based knowledge discovery. The IRS's Reveal Program, during the period from 2002 to 2005, spent about $15.7 million to buy data from ChoicePoints, and $10.6 million to buy data from LexisNexis (Naamani-Goldman, 2007). "Criminal investigators who have access to Reveal also have access to ChoicePoint" (Naamani-Goldman, 2006, p. 3). In 2005, ChoicePoint reported that "its government services group earned 14 percent of its annual revenue, or $148 million, up from $69 million, or 9 percent, of total revenue in 2002" (Medill School of Journalism, August 16, 2006, p. 1). The increased use of commercial data by federal data mining programs has further intensified concerns for the protection of privacy by federal data mining programs.

Transportations Security Administration's CAPPS II program was discontinued in 2004, as mentioned earlier, for alleged violations of privacy rights and civil liberties. The CAPPS II program received passenger data from many major airlines such as Delta Airlines, Northwest Airlines, Continental, Jet Blue Airlines, and the American West (Seifert, 2004). "In April 2004, it was revealed that American Airlines agreed to provide passenger data on 1.2 million of its customers to TSA" (Congressional Research Service, 2007a, p. 10). TSA Director, David M. Stone, in his Testimony before the Senate Committee on Government Affairs in 2004 stated that in 2002-2003, "four airlines; Delta, Continental, American West, and Frontier, and two travel reservations companies; Galileo International and Sabre Holdings, provided passenger records to TSA" (Congressional Research Service, 2007a, 2007, p. 10). For similar concerns about the protection of privacy and civil liberties, the Department of Defense's Total Information Awareness Program (TIA) was discontinued by Congress in 2004. The Technology and Privacy Advisory Committee of the Department of Defense in its 2004 report on *Safeguarding Privacy in the Fight against Terrorism* recognized that the TIA Program raised controversies and eventually was discontinued by

Congress because DARPA (Defense Advanced Research Projects Agency) failed to "build protections for privacy into TIA technologies as they were being developed" (United States Department of Defense, 2004, p. 20).

Between 2005 and 2007, the United States General Accounting Office has conducted three major studies on federal data mining programs and privacy issues for the members of the Congress. The first report of the United States General Accounting Office (2005), *Data Mining: Agencies have Taken Key Steps to Protect Privacy in Selected Efforts, but Significant Compliance Issues Remain,* was presented to the U.S. Senate Subcommittee on Oversight of Government Management, Committee on Homeland Security and Governmental Affairs. The second report of the United States General Accounting Office (2006), *Personal Information: Key Federal Privacy Laws Do Not Require Information Resellers to Safeguard all Sensitive Data*, was presented to the U.S. Senate Committee on Banking, Housing, and Urban Affairs. The United States General Accounting Office (2007) presented the third report, *Data Mining: Early Attention to Privacy in Developing a Key DHS Program Could Reduce Risks*, to the Committee on Appropriations, House of Representatives. These three GAO reports present an overview of the privacy issues being raised by different federal agencies related to their data mining programs and the rules and institutional safeguards they developed to remain fully in compliance with the federal laws related to privacy and civil liberties. GAO's 2005 report that reviewed 12 data mining programs related to war on terror activities of five federal departments and agencies—the Department of Homeland Security, Department of Justice, Department of State, Department of Defense, and Internal Revenue Service—concluded that these agencies "took many of the key steps required to protect privacy and security of the personal information they used. However, none of the agencies followed all the key privacy and security provisions" (United States

General Accounting Office, 2005, p. 28). All the agencies complied with requirement of public notification, but most of them (three of the five) did not conduct privacy impact assessment strictly in terms of the guidelines given by the Office of Management and Budget. The report further added "Until agencies fully comply with the Privacy Act, they lack assurance that individual privacy rights are appropriately protected" (United States General Accounting Office, 2005, p. 28).

There are two major federal enactments that govern the nature of the use and collection of personal information by private sector companies. These are the Fair Credit Reporting Act of 1970 (PL 91-508), as amended in 2003, and the Gramm-Leach-Billey Act of 1999 (PL 106-102). GAO's 2006 study for the Senate Committee on Banking, Housing, and Urban Affairs was a survey on the nature of compliance to these enactments by ten major information resellers, fourteen financial institutions, and some consumer lending companies. GAO's study found that "the applicability of the primary federal privacy and data security laws—the Fair Credit Reporting Act (FCRA) and Gramm-Leach-Billey (GLBA)—to information resellers is limited" (United State General Accounting Office, 2006, p. i). Banks and Financial institutions generally depend on the data supplied by information resellers such as Equifax, ChoicePoint, LexisNexis, Experian, and TransUnion.

The GAO's 2007 report to the House Committee on Appropriations examined the privacy issues related to the ADVISE Program of the Department of Homeland Security. GAO found that the ADVISE Program could lead to many privacy violations including "erroneous association of individuals with crime or terrorism, the misidentification of individuals with similar names, and the use of data that were collected for other purposes" (United States General Accounting Office, 2007, p. 3). The report concluded that the "Use of the ADVISE tool raises a number of privacy concerns. DHS has added some security control to the ADVISE tool, including access restrictions, authentication procedures, and security auditing capability. However, it has not assessed privacy risks" (United States General Accounting Office, 2007, p. 3).

From the beginning of the 1970s—the time of the beginning of the information revolution—concerns began to grow about the future of privacy rights in general in the face of advancing technology. In the 1980s and 1990s, with the rise of the digital revolution and the expansion of the cyber economy and e-governance, privacy concerns became more intensified. Many began to argue that the digital revolution will significantly endanger the privacy rights of the citizens, and that new laws are urgently needed to protect them (Agre & Rotenberg, 1998; Brin, 1999; Diffie & Landaw. 2007; Garfinkel, 2001; Solove, 2006; Solove, Rotenberg, & Schwartz, 2006). Federal laws on the protection of privacy rights by federal agencies are based on both federal statutory laws made by Congress and the judicial decisions of the federal courts. Federal statutory laws regarding privacy are based on seven major congressional enactments made between 1973 and 2007. These enactments are the Privacy Act of 1974 (PL 93-579), the Foreign Intelligence Surveillance Act of 1978 (PL 95-511), the Electronic Communications Act of 1986 (PL 99-508), the USA PATRIOT Act of 2001, the Intelligence Reform and Terrorism Act of 2004, the USA PATRIOT Improvement and Reauthorization Act of 2005 (PL 109-177), and the Protect America Act of 2007 (PL 110-55). There are two distinct phases in the evolution of these federal statutes enacted to protect the rights of privacy by federal agencies. The first phase of evolution was from 1974 to 2000, and the focus of the debates on privacy concerns at that period was to search for a balance between privacy and technology. The second phase of evolution began from September 2001 in the context of the war on terror. The focus of the debates since then is how to achieve a balance between the rights of privacy and the needs for national security.

The Privacy Act of 1974, signed into law by President Gerald Ford, promulgated a "No Disclosure without Consent Rule. The rule prohibited the disclosure of any private record maintained by federal agencies, by any means of communication, to any person or agency without a written consent of the individual to whom the record pertains." The Privacy Act of 1974 severely restricted the sharing of personal records and information between federal agencies. The Act, however, exempted federal agencies from the rule if private records and information are needed for performing agency functions, collected under the Freedom of Information Act, obtained for use by law enforcement agencies, and requested by the court and Congress.

The Foreign Intelligence Surveillance Act of 1978 (FISA) further emphasized the need for protecting privacy rights by federal agencies in the context of collecting foreign and domestic intelligence. As Senator Edward Kennedy, in introducing the Bill in the Senate (S. 1566) said: "Electronic surveillance can be a useful tool for the Government's gathering of certain kinds of information; yet, if abused, it can also constitute a particularly indiscriminate and penetrating invasion of the privacy of our citizens" (as quoted in Congressional Research Service, 2007b, p. 4). In compliance with the search and seizure provision of the Fourth Amendment, FISA established a system of congressional oversight and judicial review for intelligence collection. The Act established a foreign intelligence surveillance court from which a warrant is needed, within a year, if a federal agency is gathering intelligence from foreign persons and foreign governments, and where American citizens are not involved. A FISA warrant is required within 72 hours if a federal agency is collecting intelligence from communications in which American citizens are involved. The surveillance of the activities of American citizens by federal agencies without judicial authorization is a violation of FISA.

In 1986, Congress enacted the Electronic Communications Privacy Act (ECPA) to address issues related to privacy in the context of electronic surveillance. The federal criminal codes related to Electronic Communications Interception (18 U.S.C 2510), and Electronic Communications and Transactional Record Access (18 U.S.C. 2701) originated from the Electronic Communication Act of 1986. The ECPA was enacted as a result of increased concerns about the erosion of privacy in the wake of the expanding digital revolution. It was essentially an amendment to the Title III of the Omnibus Crime Control and Safe Street Act of 1968. Title III of the 1968 Crime Control Act made spying on and wire tapping telephone conversions a federal crime. The ECPA extended the wire tapping statute to cover not just telephone conversations but also electronic and computer communications such as email and computer network communication systems. The ECPA also criminalized the wiretapping of cellular and cordless communication devices that use digitalized communication networks. The Act criminalized spying on electronic communications both when they are in transit (Title I) and when they are stored in computer networks (Title II). Title III of the ECPA prohibited the use of trap and traces devices to intercept electronic communications both in transit and stored.

It is thus observed that from 1974 to 2000, there was evolving a series of federal enactments that significantly expanded the limits of federal intrusions into privacy. This process of statutory development for the protection privacy rights by federal agencies, however, came to a new turning point after the events of September 11, and with the beginning of America's new war on terror. The USA PATRIOT Act of 2001, the Intelligence Reform and Terrorism Act of 2004, the USA PATRIOT Improvement and Reauthorization Act of 2005, and the Protect America Act of 2007 brought many significant amendments to the Privacy Act of 1974, the Foreign Intelligence Surveillance Act of 1978, and the Electronic Communications Privacy Act of 1986—amendments that extended broad powers to federal agencies for domestic and foreign surveillance, and for collecting and analyzing terrorism related activities of American citizens and foreign nationals. In the context of the war on terror, the boundaries between foreign and domestic terrorist activities have become blurred, and the issues of national security have taken prominence over those of privacy and civil liberties. These new realities are at the core of the current debates on federal data mining programs and their relations with privacy issues.

The USA PATRIOT Act of 2001 included five broad strategies for the protection of the America's homeland. These strategies, described in nine major titles, are: preemption, connectivity, use of the information technology, better collection of intelligence, and enhancement in penalties for terrorist activities. The first four strategies are directly related to the development of federal data mining programs related to the war on terror. The USA PATRIOT Act provided new power to federal agents and agencies to enter into all facets of life and activities of U.S. citizens and foreign nationals living in the United States—from prayer rooms to public libraries, and from banks to sleeper cells—in search of terrorist acts and activities and terrorist connections and conspiracies. The Act extended the law enforcement power to search computer fraud and abuse (Section 202), share criminal and terrorist investigation information (Section 203), intercept suspected wire or electronic communications (Section 206), seize suspected voice mail message (Section 209), enforce mandatory disclosures of information from Internet service providers (Section 212), obtain suspected email and Internet communications, as well as information from telephone conversations through pen register and trap and trace devices (Section 214), and disclose the content of any intercepted computer communications (Section 217). Through the USA PATRIOT Act of 2001, "Congress amended FISA so that it no longer requires a certification that the (primary) purpose of a search or surveillance is to gather foreign intelligence information (Congressional Research Service, 2002, p. 18).

It is generally shared by U.S. national security policy-makers that the events of September 11 were possible not because the CIA, FBI, and other national security agencies did not know about the threats of Al Qaeda. The threats were possible because there were no systematic efforts of analyzing intelligence from a holistic point of view in order to discover the connections between different terrorist groups and individuals, examine the patterns of terrorist activities that were unfolding since the 1993 bombing of the World Trade Center, and share knowledge and intelligence between and among the different federal agencies. This has been clearly recognized by the 9/11 Commission Report: "Across the government there were failures of imagination, policy, capability, and management" (United States Government Printing Office, 2004, p. 9). The 9/11 Commission recommended a new global approach for a more unified intelligence community, a core group of federal agencies responsible for detecting and analyzing terrorism information from the perspective of network-based information sharing system, strong FBI and homeland defenders, and extended congressional oversight for quality and accountability (United States Government Printing Office, 2004). It is to materialize some of these recommendations of the 9/11 Commission that Congress passed the Intelligence Reform and Terrorism Act of 2004. The Act created a new Office of National Intelligence to be headed by a Director appointed by the President. The Director of National Intelligence was given the task of developing, analyzing, and coordinating all federal intelligence activities related to the war on terror. The Act made also a provision for the creation of an Office of Civil Liberties within the Office of the Director of National Intelligence to ensure that the "protection of civil liberties and privacy is appropriately incorporated in the policies and procedures developed for and imple-

mented by the Office of the Director of National Intelligence" (United States Government Printing Office, 2006, p. 23).

Between 2001 and 2005, concerns were raised both within the government and by many privacy advocacy organizations about how the FBI and other law enforcement and security related organizations were implementing the USA PATRIOT Act of 2001, and the extent to which it has undermined the privacy rights the American citizens. In response, Congress enacted the USA PATRIOT Improvement and Reauthorization Act in 2005. The Act of 2005 made 14 Sections of the USA PATRIOT Act of 2001 permanent including the Sections, 201, 202, 203, 204, 207, 209, 212, 214, 217, 218, 220, 223 (Congressional Research Service, 2006). These Sections of the USA PATRIOT ACT were the ones that raised most of the concerns for the violations of privacy rights.

The USA PATRIOT Improvement and Reauthorization Act of 2005, however, "contains several provisions against abuse of section 215 authority, including greater congressional oversight, enhanced procedural protections, more elaborate [FISA] application requirements, and a judicial review process" (Congressional Research Service, 2006, pp. 4-5). Section 215 of the USA PATRIOT Act of 2001 provided broad powers to the FBI and other security organizations to investigate both foreign nationals and American citizens related to terrorist activities, and search and seize, not just business records, but all investigation related tangible items without a probable cause. The USA PATRIOT Improvement and Reauthorization Act of 2005 (Section 106) "directs the Attorney General to submit to Congress an annual report regarding the use of section 215 authority" (Congressional Research Service, 2006, p. 5). This new directive "was an attempt to allay concerns over federal authorities abusing 215 authority to obtain sensitive types of records" (Congressional Research Service, 2006, p. 6). Under the Act of 2005, the recipients of the Section 215 order were given a right "to challenge their legality before a judge selected from the pool of FISA court judges" (Congressional Research Service, 2006, p. 7).

The USA PATRIOT Improvement and Reauthorization Act of 2005 also established a judicial process to protect the privacy rights of the recipients of National Security Letters. A National Security Letter is a letter that can be issued by the FBI and other federal agencies to conduct national security related investigations. The increased use of National Security Letters in the context of the USA PATRIOT Act of 2001 and the war on terror has raised many privacy concerns. It is reported that the FBI "now issues more than 30,000 letters a year ... a hundredfold increase over historic norms" (Gellman, November 6, 2006, p. 2). The individuals, groups and organizations receiving National Security Letters are required by law to disclose the information requested, and the issuance of those letters do not need any prior judicial approval, or to be based on any probable cause. The National Security Letters may require the disclosure of information from all citizens on internet service providers, electronic communications, financial records, money transfers, credit records, and other consumer identification records (Federal Bureau of Investigation, 2007). Information received through National Security Letters is not classified, and they can be shared by all federal agencies.

Many privacy advocacy groups in recent years have raised concerns that National Security Letters have been violating the privacy rights of American citizens. The USA PATRIOT Improvement and Reauthorization Act of 2005 made an amendment that "the recipient of a NSL request may petition a U.S. district court for an order modifying or setting aside the request" (Congressional Research Service, 2006, p. 11). The Act, however, also protected the rights of federal authorities to enforce the mandate of the National Security Letters through the actions of the federal courts. "If a NSL recipient fails to respond to the request for information, the Attorney General may seek a federal district court order to compel compliance with the request" (Congressional Research Service, 2006, p. 11).

Since the creation of the Office National Intelligence in 2005, the leaders of the national security intelligence community have raised concerns about the limits and restrictions imposed on them by the Foreign Intelligence Surveillance Act (FISA) of 1978 for collecting and investigating foreign intelligence of immediate and critical national concerns. The Director of National Intelligence expressed concerns that intelligence professionals, operating under FISA, were "missing a significant amount of foreign intelligence that we should be collecting to protect our country" (as quoted in The White House, 2007, p. 1). In response, Congress enacted the Protect America Act in 2007. Under the new law, national security organizations are not required to take a prior FISA court approval for conducting foreign intelligence investigations both in foreign countries and in the United States, even in cases where targeted foreign nationals are living in the United States and United States citizens are involved in the investigation. The Act made it legal to collect information about e-mail messages, websites, electronic communications, and telephone conversation of American, either directly or through third party informants, by the national security agencies without any probable cause and without prior court approval. In signing the Protect America Act of 2007, President Bush said: "We know that information we have been able to acquire about foreign threats will help us direct and prevent attacks on our homeland. Mike McConnell, the Director of National Intelligence, has assured me that this bill gives him the most immediate tools he needs to defeat the intentions of our enemies" (The White House, 2007, p. 1).

What is thus observed is that between the Privacy Act of 1974 and the Protect America Act of 2007, Congress has made a series of enactments to ensure the protection of privacy rights and civil liberties by federal agencies. Before the events of September 11, during the first phase of the evolution of federal statutory protections of privacy rights, Congress was largely in favor of extending the limits of search and seizures of American citizens by federal agencies by requiring judicial approval, congressional oversights, and the development of rules and procedures within the executive agencies to comply with privacy rights and civil liberties.

During the second phase of the evolution of federal statutory protections of privacy rights—the phase that started in the context of the events of September 11 and the war on terror—Congress, with bipartisan support, has redefined the nature and the need for information, analysis, and knowledge about terrorism investigations. Congress has broadened the power of federal national security investigation agencies, particularly through the USA PATRIOT Act of 2001, USA PATRIOT Improvement and Reauthorization Act of 2005, and the Protect America Act of 2007, largely as a strategy to control and contain global terrorism and to protect America's homeland from the possible threats of nuclear, chemical, biological, and cyber terrorism. From the second phase of evolution of federal data mining programs, concerns for the protection of the homeland, and not privacy rights and civil liberties, became prominent. The growth of federal data mining programs related to terrorism investigation and analysis is an integral part of this larger process of expansion of the power of federal agencies responsible for protecting the homeland.

Federal Data Mining Programs, Privacy Concerns and the Role of the Federal Courts

The understanding of the complexities of the privacy and civil liberty issues related to federal data mining needs also an understanding of how the federal courts deal with the issues of relations between privacy and national security in the context of the war on terror. Four constitutional provisions—the First Amendment, the Fourth Amendment, the Fifth Amendment, and the Fourteenth Amendment— are particularly relevant to the protection of privacy rights and civil liberties of the American citizens. The First Amendment states that "Congress shall make no laws respecting an establishment of religion, or prohibiting the free exercise thereof; or abridging the freedom of speech." The Fourth Amendment states that "The right of people to be secure in their persons, houses, papers, and effects, against unreasonable searches and seizures, shall not be violated, and no Warrant shall issue, but upon a probable cause." Under the Fourth Amendment, search and seizures of American citizens without a valid warrant is a violation of the constitution. The Fifth Amendment protects the rights to have an indictment by grand jury, rights to be treated in terms of the due process of law, and rights against self-incrimination. The Fourteenth Amendment pertains to the due process of law and it states that "No State shall make or enforce any law which shall abridge the privileges or immunities of citizens of the United States; nor shall any State deprive any person of life, liberty, or property, without due process of law." The constitution has not particularly addressed the concept of privacy. Privacy and civil liberties issues, in general, are interpreted in terms of the above constitutional provisions, particularly in terms of the core principles of the First and Fourth Amendments.

From 1965 to 2003, the U. S. Supreme Court has considerably broadened the scope of privacy rights through a series of landmark decisions (Glenn, 2003). Some of those landmark decisions were made in the cases of the *Griswold v. Connecticut* in 1965, *Eisenstadt v. Baird* in 1972, *Roe v. Wade* in 1973, *Doe v. Bolton* in 1973, *Akron v. Akron Center for Reproductive Health*, Inc. in 1983, *Reno v. ACLU* in 1997, *Ashcroft v. The Free Speech Coalition* in 2003 and *Lawrence v. Texas* in 2003. But none of these cases were related to issues of privacy and national security.

A number of private citizens, lawyer groups, and privacy advocacy organizations such as the American Civil Liberties Union (ACLU), Electronic Privacy Information Center, and the Center for Constitutional Rights has recently challenged the federal data mining programs and has taken some of them to the federal courts (Electronic Frontier Foundation, 2006). Most of the cases filed in the federal courts against the federal data mining programs were based on their alleged violations of the First and Fourth Amendments. In recent years "hundreds of lawyers, journalists, telecommunications company customers, and civil rights groups have claimed that their privacy rights had been violated. About 50 lawsuits were filed against the government and telecommunication companies for allegedly turning over customer account information" (Chea, 2007, p. 1). The government—the Executive Branch—has been defending most of these cases in the federal courts on the basis of two major doctrines—the doctrine of "state secrets privilege" and the doctrine of "inherent power of the President." The federal courts in most of the federal data mining cases are primarily engaged in the determination of the nature and the meaning of these doctrines in the context of the war on terror. The core issue the federal courts are trying to examine and analyze is whether the use of the state secret privilege and the inherent power of the President doctrines are judicially and constitutionally justifiable defenses.

"In the last six years," the state secret privilege doctrine has been invoked by the Executive Branch "39 times, according to the best available count—or more than six times every year. Along with the numbers, the scope and definition of what constitutes a state secret [have] expanded" (Siegel, 2007, p. 1). The state secret privilege doctrine implies that the government, under some extraordinary circumstances, has the right to withhold the submissions of any document or evidence in a court of law that will jeopardize national security. On the basis of this privilege, a government can also request the dismissal of a case that will require the public disclosure of evidence unsafe

for national security. In the case of *United State v. Reynolds in 1953*, the U.S. Supreme Court ruled for the first time in favor of this doctrine. The Court, in its analysis noted that the "privilege belongs to the Government and must be asserted by it; it can neither be claimed nor waived by a private party. It is not to be lightly invoked. There must be a formal claim of privilege, lodged by the head of the department which has control over the matter" (as quoted in United States District Court for the District of Columbia, 2004, p. 7).

The doctrine of the inherent power of the President implies that the constitution vested the executive power in the hands of one person—the President. In times of national security crises, the President has the power to take extraordinary national security measures through such policy tools as Proclamations, Executive Orders, and National Security Directives—measures that might even be taken without an immediate and expressed consent of Congress (Vikki, 2007). The doctrine of the inherent power of the President has been in the debates on presidential powers and in the court of law since *Marbury v. Madison* in 1803. Chief Justice Marshall, in *Marbury v. Madison*, said that the "President is invested with certain important political powers, in the exercise of which he is to use his own discretion, and is accountable only to this country in his political character, and to his own conscience" (Lieberamn, 1999, p. 367).

In the context of the events after September 11 and the war on terror, the state secret privilege doctrine was first used by the Executive Branch in *Sibel Edmonds v. United States Department of Justice, et al.* in 2002. In 2002, the Department of Justice fired Sibel Edmonds, a Turkish American woman hired by the FBI after September 11 as a translator of Middle Eastern languages. The Department of Justice claimed that she was fired because of many of her allegations raised against the Department of Justice compromised national security. Sibel Edmonds filed a law suit with the United States District Court for the District of

Columbia on the grounds that the Department of Justice has violated her First and Fifth Amendment rights. The plaintiff's First Amendment claim was based on her assertion "that her complains about misconduct [within the FBI] constituted protected First Amendment conduct" (United States District Court for the District of Columbia, 2004, p. 5). The plaintiff's Fifth Amendment claim "asserts that the termination of her employment and interference with her ability to obtain future employment by the defendants violated her rights to procedural due process" (United States District Court for the District of Columbia, 2004, p. 5). In October 2002, the Department of Justice sent a Press Release that Attorney General Ashcroft "asserted the state secrets privilege in *Sibel Edmonds v. Department of Justice*" to prevent the public disclosure of classified national security information (United States Department of Justice, 2002, p. 1). On the basis of an analysis and appropriateness of the state secrets privilege doctrine in the context of *Sibel Edmonds v. United States Department of Justice,* the United States District Court of the District of Columbia dismissed the case. On appeal, the United States Court of Appeal of the District of Columbia concurred with the decision of the lower court. The case was brought into the U.S. Supreme Court by Sibel Edmonds, ACLU, and other privacy rights organizations. In November, 2005, the U.S. Supreme Court refused to hear the Edmonds' case.

The National Security Agency's (NSA) Terrorism Surveillance Program (TSP) is one of the major federal data mining programs that were recently challenged in the federal courts. In January 2007, ACLU and a group of journalist, academics, and lawyers filed a law suit with the federal District Court of the Eastern District of Michigan challenging the constitutional validity of TSP. The plaintiff argued that the warrantless wiretapping and data mining activities of TSP violated the First Amendment's provisions of free speech and free association, the privacy rights protected by the Fourth Amendment, the separation of power

doctrine, Title III of the Omnibus Crime Control and Safe Street Act of 1968, and the Foreign Intelligence Surveillance Act of 1978. In defense, the National Security Agency and the Executive Branch invoked the state secrets privilege and the inherent power of the President doctrines and asked the court for a summary dismissal of the case. "The NSA had invoked the State Secrets Doctrine to bar the discovery or admission of evidence that would expose [conditional] matters which, in the interests of national security, should not be divulged" (United States Court of Appeal for the Sixth Circuit, July 6, 2007, p. 3). The NSA and the Executive Branch also presented as a defense the doctrine that "the Constitution grants the President the 'inherent authority' to intercept the international telecommunications of those who are affiliated with al-Qadea" (United States Court of Appeal for the Sixth Circuit, July 6, 2007, p. 3).

The United States District Court for the Eastern District of Michigan ruled in favor of the plaintiffs and ordered the termination of TSP activities by NSA primarily on the grounds of its violation of the Fourth Amendment. On appeal, the United States Court of Appeals for the Sixth Circuit, however, vacated the order of the District Court and remanded "this case to the district court with instructions to Dismiss for lack of jurisdiction" (United States Court of Appeals for the Sixth Circuit, July 6, 2007, p. 35) As the Circuit Court Judge, Alice Batchelder, said: "The plaintiffs are a collection of associations and individuals led by the American Civil Liberties Union, and they cross-appeal. Because we cannot find that any of the plaintiffs have standing for any of their claims, we must vacate the district court's order and remand for dismissal of the entire action" (United States Court of Appeals for the Six Circuit, July 6, 2007, p. 2).

The United States Court of Appeals for the Ninth Circuit made a similar ruling in *Al-Haramain Islamic Foundation et al. v. George W. Bush, the President of the United States et al.* in

2007. In February 2006, Al-Haramain Islamic Charity, based in Oregon, filed a law suit with the United States District Court of Oregon against the President of the United States, George W. Bush. The plaintiff alleged that the National Security Agency's Terrorist Surveillance Program, ordered by the President, violated the First, Fourth, and the Sixth Amendments to the Constitution by secretly tracking the Charity's telephone conversations, emails, and other electronic communications. The Charity acknowledged the fact that it was under surveillance by NSA's Terrorist Surveillance Program based on a package of Sealed Document that was inadvertently given to the attorneys of the Charity by the Department of Treasury at the time of the hearing on the declaration of Al-Haramain as a member of the group of "Specially Designated Global Terrorists."

The government brought a motion for a summary dismissal of the case on the basis of the state secrets privilege doctrine. The government asserted that "the very subject matter of the action was a state secret" (United States Court of Appeals for the Ninth Circuit, November 16, 2007, p. 14964). The United States District Court of Oregon denied the government's request for a summary dismissal of the case. The Court accepted the state secrets privilege argument of the government but still made a decision that it would "permit Al-Haramain-related witness to file *in camera* affidavits attesting from the memory to the contents of the document to support Al-Haramain's assertion of the standing and its prima facie case" (United States Court of Appeals for the Ninth Circuit, November 16, 2007, p. 14965). The case was then transferred by the Multi-District Litigation Panel to the Northern District of California. On appeal by the government, the United States Court of Appeals for the Ninth Circuit agreed for an interlocutory review, and consolidated this appeal with *Tash Hepting et al. v. AT&T Corporation et al.* In *Tash Hepting et al. v. AT&T Corporation et al.* in 2006, the plaintiffs filed a similar suit against the AT&T Corporation claiming that it

violated the Fourth Amendment right of protection against unusual search and seizure by transferring millions of its customer phone calls data to the Terrorist Surveillance Program of the NSA. The Ninth Circuit reversed the decision of the District Court and dismissed the case. The Ninth Circuit Court argued that Al-Haramain cannot establish that it has standing without revealing the content of the Sealed Document, and the "sealed document is protected by the state secrets privilege" (United States Court of Appeals for the Ninth Circuit, November 16, 2007, p. 14961). The Ninth Circuit reversed the decision of the District Court that a standing for the case could be created by Al-Haramain on the basis of the reconstruction of the content of the Sealed Document through memory. "Once properly invoked and judicially blessed, the state secrets privilege", said the Ninth Circuit, "is not a half-way proposition" (United States Court of Appeals for the Ninth Circuit, November 16, 2007, p. 14961).

FUTURE TRENDS

The future of federal data mining programs is intimately connected to the future of the war on terror. The National Intelligence Council's (2004) 2020 Project "Mapping the Global Future," The 9/11 Commission Report of the National Commission on Terrorist Attack Upon the United States (2005), the Quadrennial Defense Review 2006 published by the United States Department of Defense (2006), the White House (2006a) Report on Strategy for Winning the War on Terror and a number of other national reports in recent years have claimed that America's engagement with the world has come to a new turning point after the events of September 11, 2001. They all share the perspective that the events of September 11 have drawn America into a "protracted, generational, or multigenerational" (Kilcullen 2007, p. 2) ideological war with militant radical Islam, particularly with the global jihad of Al Queda (Sookhdeo, 2007).

The 9/11 Commission Report stated that the America's "enemy is not just 'terrorism,' some generic evil. This vagueness blurs the strategy. The catastrophic threat at this moment in history is more specific. It is the threat posed by *Islamist* terrorism—especially the al Qaeda network, its affiliates, and its ideology" (National Commission on Terrorist Attack Upon the United States, 2005, p. 362). About the future of this emerging ideological struggle and the global war on terror, the 9/11 Commission Report was more emphatic. "It is not a position with which Americans can bargain or negotiate. With it there is no common ground—on which to begin a dialogue. It can only be destroyed or utterly isolated" (National Commission on Terrorist Attack Upon the United States, 2005, p. 362). The Department of Defense's Quadrennial Defense Review 2006 shared the same perspective about America's long and protracted ideological war with militant radical Islam and global jihad. The Quadrennial Defense Review begins with the statement that the "United States is a nation engaged in what will be long war" (United States Department of Defense, 2006, p. v).

The National Intelligence Council's report "Mapping the Global Future" made similar observations on the basis of a more thorough analysis of the emergence of various competing and conflicting forces related to globalization. The report predicted that "The key factors that spawned international terrorism show no signs of abating over the next 15 years. Facilitated by global communications, the revival of Muslim identity will create a framework for the spread of radical Islamic ideology inside and outside the Middle East" (National Intelligence Council, 2004, p.15). The report further claimed that by 2020 "al-Qa'ida will be superseded by similarly inspired Islamic extremist groups, and there is substantial risk that broad Islamic movements akin to al-Qa'ida will emerge with local separatist movement" (National Intelligence Council, 2004, p. 15). The report

also cautioned that "Strong terrorist interest in acquiring chemical, biological, radiological and nuclear weapons increases the risk of a major terrorist attack involving WMD. Our greatest concern is that terrorists might acquire biological agents or, less likely, a nuclear device, either of which could cause mass casualties" (National Intelligence Council, 2004, p. 16).

What all these studies suggest is that the war on terror and concerns for homeland security will continue to remain dominant in both foreign and domestic policy-making in United States in the coming decades. The continuing concerns for the war on terror and homeland security will further expand the growth of federal data mining programs related to terrorism intelligence. The major national security related federal data mining programs of the Department of Justice, the Department of Homeland Security, and the Department of Defense are still in their infancy. These programs are more likely to grow and expand in the context of the rapid growth of computing technology within the field of data mining, on the one hand, and the continuing emphasis of the government for improving intelligence gathering in the context of the growing war on terror, on the other. The further growth of federal data mining programs related to national security is likely to further intensify the tensions between the issues of privacy and security. The nature and the specific articulations of these tensions by different actors—the federal agencies, congress, the federal court, and the public—will largely depend on the progress in the war on terror.

Through a series of enactments made between 2001 and 2007, Congress, as mentioned earlier, has broadened the scope of federal power for terrorism investigation. Congress, however, has not ceased to search for balance between privacy and national security (Congressional Research Service, 2007a). In 2004, Congress, through the enactment of the Intelligence Reform and Terrorism Prevention Act of 2004, established a Privacy and Civil Liberties Oversight Board within the

Office of the President. The Board "is specifically charged with responsibility for reviewing the terrorism information sharing practices of executive branch department and agencies" (Executive Office of the President, 2008, p. 1). Similar statutorily required privacy oversight offices exist within the Department of Homeland Security (The Privacy Office), Department of Justice (Office of Information and Privacy), and the Department of Defense (Defense Privacy Office).

In January 2007, the Senate Committee on the Judiciary held a major congressional hearing on "Balancing Privacy and Security: The Privacy Implications of Government Data Mining Programs" (United States Senate, January 10, 2007). A major federal data mining Bill (S.236) titled "Federal Agency Data Mining Reporting Act of 2007," sponsored by Senator Russell Feingold (D-WI) and John Sununu (R-NH), is currently being debated in the 110th Congress. The Bill would require all federal agencies to send a yearly public report to Congress about the details of their data mining activities including privacy impact assessments. In February 2008, The Senate, however, passed a Bill (68-29) that again legalized eavesdropping on phone calls and emails by federal law enforcement agencies for tracking terrorist activities. The Bill also granted immunities to telecommunication companies that provided data to different federal data mining programs after September 11, 2001. A similar version of the Bill, without the provision of immunity for telecommunication companies, was passed by the House in 2007.

Tensions exist also in the minds of the public about the future of privacy in the context of the overriding governmental concerns for the war on terror and national security. A poll conducted by the Washington Post in 2005 found that "Americans overwhelmingly support aggressive government pursuit of terrorist threats even it may infringe on personal privacy but they divide sharply along partisan lines over the legitimacy of President Bush's program of domestic eavesdropping without court authorization" (Balz &

Deane, January 11, 2005, p. 1). About sixty six percent of percent of respondents said that "it is more important to investigate possible terrorist threats than to protect civil liberties" (Balz & Deane, January 11, 2005, p. 2).

A poll conducted by the Pew Research Center in 2006 found that public concerns about national security are deeper than those of civil liberties. In a survey of 1,503 adults, the Pew Research Poll found that in 2004 forty nine percent of Americans believed that the government did not go too far to protect the country. In 2006, forty six percent of Americans shared the similar views. Seventy three percent of respondents in the same Poll, however, were opposed to the idea of governmental eavesdropping on their phone calls, emails, and credit card records. But fifty two percent of Whites and twenty seven percent of Blacks agreed that it was right to monitor the terror suspects' phone calls and emails without a warrant (The Pew Research Center, 2006, pp. 2-4).

In a similar study, conducted by the Washington Post-ABC News Poll in 2006, sixty three percent of Americans said that they found the NSA program to be an "acceptable way to investigate terrorism" (CNET Forums, May, 2006, p. 1). In 2007, according to a FOX News/Opinion Dynamic Poll (August 21-22, 2007), ninety percent of Americans believed that there were members of Al Qaeda group in the United States. In 2003, ninety two percent of respondents expressed the similar views (PollingREport,Com, 2007). According to a Newsweek Poll, conducted in July, 2007, fifty two percent of Americans agreed that the FBI should wiretap mosques to track terrorist activities and radical preaching by Muslim clerics inside the United States (PollingREport. com, 2007).

CONCLUSION

After the events of September 11 and in the context of the war on terror, different federal agencies related to law enforcement and national security have created a number of data mining programs. The data mining programs of the Department of Justice, the Department of Homeland Security, the Department of Defense, and the National Security Agency have been particularly organized for detecting and analyzing terrorist information. These data mining programs are based on data generated within the agencies, and data brought and collected from private sector companies. The creation of the Department of Homeland Security, Office of National Intelligence and a variety of other federal agencies and programs after September 11, 2001 was based on the assumption of preemption. The core idea is that information and intelligence about the nature and patterns of terrorist activities must be gathered and analyzed, and policies for the control and containment of terrorism must be put in place before terrorist attacks are materialized. The 9/11 Commission has found that weakness in intelligence gathering and sharing was one of main reasons for the success of the September 11 terrorists. Different federal data mining programs have evolved in the context of these and other federal efforts to create a global data bank on terrorist networks and activities through the use of the state-of-the art of information technology.

The increasing numbers of private data that are collected, stored, and analyzed by federal agencies, however, have raised concerns for privacy and civil liberties. When reports began to come out that the National Security Agency has been conducting a Terrorist Surveillance Program ordered by the President immediately after September 11, 2001; major telecommunication companies such as the AT&T, Verizon, Bell South are sharing customer information with federal agencies; major airlines such as the American West, Delta, and Continental are handing over information on millions of passengers to Transportation Security Administration's CAPPS II data mining program; and federal agencies are collecting data also from private sector companies such as ChoicePoint,

Dunn & Brad Street, and LexisNexis, doubts and concerns began to escalate in the nation whether the federal data mining efforts are conducted in violations of the Constitution's First and Fourth Amendments, the Privacy Act of 1974, and the Foreign Intelligence Surveillance Act of 1978.

It was response to escalating doubts and concerns about privacy and civil liberties that the Congress discontinued the Department of Defense's Total Information Awareness Program (TIA) and the Transportation Security Administrations' CAPPS II Program. The General Accounting Office's 2005 report on *Data Mining: Federal Agencies Have Taken Key Steps to Protect Privacy in Selected Efforts, but Significant Compliance Issues Remain* found that all federal data mining programs have developed rules and procedures to protect the privacy rights but many gaps exist in compliance.

After the events of September 11 and the start of the war on terror, congress had enacted four major legislations related to intelligence gathering on terrorism activities both within and outside the United States. All these legislations—The USA PATRIOT Act of 2001, the Intelligence Reform and Terrorism Act of 2004, the USA PATRIOT Improvement and Reauthorization Act of 2005, and the Protect America Act of 2007—have broadened the scope of federal power for the search and surveillance of terrorist activities. The 110th Congress is currently debating a new Bill—Federal Agency Data Mining Reporting Act of 2007—to develop more congressional oversights on federal data mining programs. The future of this Bill, however, depends on the specific nature of success and evolution of the war on terror.

Many private individuals, lawyer groups, and privacy rights advocacy organizations in recent years have taken the President of the United States and various federal departments and agencies to the federal courts in connections with the federal data mining programs. The plaintiffs, in general, have alleged that many federal data mining programs are conducted in violation of privacy rights protected by the First and Fourth Amendments of the constitution, the Privacy Act of 1974, and the Foreign Intelligence Surveillance Act of 1978. In defense of almost all federal data mining and terrorism surveillance cases, the government has invoked the state secrets privilege doctrine and the doctrine of the inherent power of the President. An analysis of the decisions given in some of those cases by the Federal Court of Appeals for the District of Columbia, Federal Court of Appeals for the Ninth Circuit, and the Federal Court of Appeal for the Sixth Circuit shows that the federal courts are mostly in favor of the government's perspective of looking at the significance of terrorism surveillance and related data mining programs from the broader point of the threats of global terrorism and national security.

It seems, however, that the federal courts are still trying to grapple with the whole significance of the state secret privilege doctrine and the doctrine of the inherent power of the President in the context of the war on terror. The U.S. Supreme Court has not yet deliberated on federal data mining programs. In 2004, the U.S. Supreme Court in *Rasul et al. v. George W. Bush, the President of the United States, et al.* ruled, challenging the argument of the government, that the "United States courts have jurisdiction to consider challenges to the legality of the detention of foreign nationals captured abroad in connection with hostilities and incarcerated at Guantanamo Bay" (Supreme Court of the United States, 2004, pp. 1-2). In 2006, the U.S. Supreme Court said that the trial of the Guantanamo detainees by a special military commission cannot be authorized under the federal law, and it is also a violation of the Geneva Convention. Congress, in response, enacted a new legislation—Military Commission Act of 2006—to try the Guantanamo detainees by special military tribunals (In the Senate, 53 Republicans and 12 Democrats, and in the House, 218 Republicans and 32 Democrats voted in favor of the Bill).

In December 2007, the U.S. Supreme Court heard oral arguments on two cases—*Boumediene v. Bush* and *Al Odah v. Bush*—filed to challenge the legality of the Military Commission Act of 2006. The final decisions of the Supreme Court on these two cases are expected to be given in the summer of 2008. These cases about the rights and trials of the Guantanamo detainees are not directly related to federal data mining programs, but they point to the fact that tensions exist between different branches of the government, on the one hand, and between the government and private citizens, on the other, for achieving a balance between privacy and national security. The nature and future of federal data mining programs and the specific articulations of the balance between privacy and national security will depend on the progress of the war on terror.

REFERENCES

Agre, P. E., & Rotenberg, M. (Eds.). (1998). *Technology and privacy: The new landscape.* Cambridge: The MIT Press.

Anders, J. (2007). *U.S. student visas reach record numbers in 2007.* United States Department of State: International Information Program.

Arkin, W. M. (May 12, 2006). *NSA's multi-billion dollar Data mining effort.* Retrieved on December 15, 2007 from Washingtonpost.com

Balz, D., & Deane, C. (January 11, 2006). *Differing views on terrorism: Americans divided on eavesdropping program.* Retrieved January 2, 2008 from http://www.washingtonpost.com

Brin, D. (1999). *Transparent society: Will technology force us to choose between privacy and freedom?* Jackson, TN: Perseus Books Group.

Carafano, J. J. (January 10, 2007). *Promoting security and civil liberties: The role of data mining in combating terrorism* (Testimony before the Senate Judiciary Committee). Washington DC: U.S. Senate.

Centers for Disease Control and Prevention. (2006). *BioSense: Background.* Atlanta: Georgia: CDC.

Center for Grassroots Oversight. (2007). *National Security Agency begins huge data mining project similar to "Total Information Awareness."* Retrieved September 10, 2007 from www.cooperativeresearch.org

Chea. T. (2007 December 21). *Court deals blow to wiretapping case.* New York: The Associated Press, December 21, pp. 1-2. Retrieved November 3, 2007 from www.abcnews.com

Chen, Z. (2001). *Data mining and uncertain reasoning: An integrated approach.* New York: John Wiley and Sons.

CNET Forums. (2006, May 12). *Poll: Most Americans support NSA's efforts.* Retrieved January 10, 2008 from http://forums.cnet.com.

Congressional Research Service. (2007a). *Data mining and Homeland Security* (by J. W. Seifert). An overview. Washington DC: CRS.

Congressional Research Service. (2007b). *The Foreign Intelligence Surveillance Act: A brief overview of selected issues* (by E. B. Bazan). Washington DC: Congressional Research Service.

Congressional Research Service. (2006). *USA PATRIOT Improvement and Reauthorization Act of 2005: A legal analysis.* Washington DC: CRS.

Congressional Research Service. (2004). *Data mining: An overview* (by J. W. Seifert). Washington DC: CRS.

Congressional Research Service. (2003). *Privacy: Total Information Awareness Programs and related information access, collection, and protection laws* (by G. M. Stevens). Washington DC: CRS.

Congressional Research Service. (2002). *The USA PATRIOT Act: A Sketch.* Washington DC: CRS.

De Borchgrave, A. (March 16, 2005). *Likelihood of U.S. terrorist sleeper cells.* Retrieved September 3, 2007 from www.archive.newsmax.com

DeRosa, M. (2004). *Data mining and data analysis for counterterrorism.* Washington DC: Center for Strategic and International Studies.

Diffie, W., & Landaw, S. (2007). *Privacy on the line: The politics of wiretapping and encryption.* Cambridge: The MIT Press.

Dougherty, M. (February 25, 2004). *Testimony before the House Subcommittee on Immigration, Boarder Security and Claims.* Washington DC: United States House of Representatives.

Electronic Frontier Foundation. (2006). *FOIA Litigation: DOJ's Investigative Data Warehouse.* Retrieved December 5, 2007 from www.eff.org

Executive Office of the President. (2008). *Privacy & Civil Liberties Oversight Board.* Washington DC: The White House.

Federal Bureau of Investigation. (2007). *National Security Letters* (Press Release). Washington DC: Department of Justice. Retrieved December 2, 2007 from www.fbi.org

Garfinkel, S. (2001). *Database nation: The death of privacy in the 21st century.* New York: O'Reily Media, Inc.

Gellman, B. (November 6, 2006). The *FBI's secret scrutiny: In hunt for terrorism Bureau examines records of ordinary citizens.* Retrieved August, 2, 2007 from www.washingtonpost.com

Glenn, R. A. (2003). *The right to privacy: Rights and liberties under the law.* Santa Barbara, CA: ABC-CLIO Inc.

Hansen, B. (2007). ADVISE data mining program by Homeland Security. *The Register,* September 6, pp. 1-3.

Herold, R. (October 29, 2006). *Electronic Frontier Foundation sues the U.S. DOJ for FOIA information.* Retrieved January 2, 2008 from www.realtime.com

Hendrickson, T. (2007). *Innovation: 2005 Best Practice Award Winners.* Retrieved December 10, 2007 from www.tdwi.org

Heymann, P. B., & Kayyem, J. N. (2005). *Protecting liberty in an age of terror.* Cambridge, MA: The MIT Press.

Kilcullen, D. (2007). *New paradigm for 21st century conflict.* Retrieved February 2, 2008 from www.smallawarsjournal.com

Lieberaman. J. K. (1999). *A practical companion to the constitution: How the Supreme Court has ruled on issues from abortion to zoning.* CA: University of California Press.

Matignon, R. (2007). *Data mining using SAS Enterprise Minor.* New York: Wiley-Interscience.

McCue, C. (2006). *Data mining and predictive analysis: Intelligence gathering and crime* analysis. New York: Butterworth-Heineman.

Medill School of Journalism. (August 16, 2006). *Commercial data use by law enforcement raises questions about accuracy, oversight* (by N. Duarte). Retrieved December 19, 2007 from http://newsintiative.org

Naamani-Goldman, D. (2007). *The IRS war on terrorism: How it work.* The Los Angeles Times, January 15, p. 1-7.

Naamani-Goldman, D. (2006). *Revealing terror* (Medil School of Journalism). Retrieved December 17, 2007 from http://newsinitiative.org.

National Commission on Terrorist Attack Upon the United States. (2005). *The 9/11 Commission Report.* Washington DC: Government Printing Office.

National Intelligence Council. (2004). *Mapping the Global Future: Report of the National Intelligence Council's 2020 Project.* Washington DC: Government Printing Office.

New York Times. (2006). *Education Dept. shared student data with F.B.I* (by J. D. Glater). September 1, pp.1-2.

Perner, P. (Ed.). (2002). *Advances in data mining: Applications in e-commerce, medicine, and knowledge management.* New York: Springer.

PollinREport.Com. (2007). *War on terrorism: Nationwide surveys of Americans.* Retrieved January 5 from http://www.pollingreport.com/terror.htm

Roberge, B. (September, 2004). New research center focuses on IT and the intellectual community. *The MITRE DIGEST,* pp. 1-4. Retrieved November 10, 2007 from www.mitre.org/news/digest

Rosenzweig, P. S., & Ahern, J. P. (2007). *Testimonies before the Senate Subcommittee on Terrorism, Technology, and Homeland Security.* Washington DC: United States Senate.

Seifert, J. W. (2004). Data mining and search for security challenges for connecting the dots and databases. *Government Information Quarterly,* 21(4), p. 461-480.

Siegel, B. (2007). State-secret overreach. *Los Angeles Times,* September 16, pp. 1-2.

Solove, D. (2006). *The digital person: Technology and privacy in the information ag*e. New York: New York University Press.

Solove, D. J., Rotenberg, M., & Schwartz, P. M. (2006). *Privacy, information and technology.* New York: Aspen Publishers.

Sniffen, M. J. (2007). DHS ditches data mining program over privacy woes. *The Associated Press,* September, 5, p. 1-3.

Sookhdeo, P. (2007). *Global jihad: The future in the face of militant Islam.* New York Isaac Publisher: W. W. Norton & Company.

Supreme Court of the United States. (2004). *Rasul et al. v. George W. Bush, President of the United States, et al.* (No. 03-334). Washington DC: The U.S. Supreme Court.

Tanner, M. (October, 16, 2003). *Foreign Terrorist Tracking Task Force* (Testimony before the House Judiciary Subcommittee on Immigration, Border Security and Claims). Washington DC: United States House of Representatives.

Tapscott, D. (1999). *Growing up digital: The rise of the net generation.* New York, NY: McGrow Hill.

The Pew Research Center. (January 11, 2006). *Americans taking Abramoff, Alito and domestic spying in stride.* Retrieved January 5 from http://people-press.org

The White House. (2007). *Fact sheet: The Protect America Act of 2007.* Washington DC: The White House.

The White House. (2006a). *Strategy for winning the war on terror.* Washington DC: The Office of the President

The White House. (2006b). *President visits National Security Agency* (Press Release). Washington DC: The White House.

The White House. (April, 2004). *Biodefense fact sheet: President Bush signs Biodefense for the 21st century.* Washington DC: The White House.

The White House. (October, 29, 2001). *Homeland Security Presidential Directive-2.* Washington DC: The White House.

United States Census. (2003). *History.* Washington DC: Bureau of the Census, Department of Commerce.

United States Court of Appeals for the Sixth Circuit. (July 6, 2007). *American Civil Liberties Union et al. v. National Security Agency et al. (Nos. O6-2095.2140).*

United States Court of Appeals for the Ninth Circuit. (November 16, 2007). *Al-Haramain Islamic Foundation et al. v. George W. Bush, President of the United States et al.* (No. 03-36083).

United States Department of Defense. (2004). *Safeguarding privacy in the fight against terrorism* (Report of the Technology and Privacy Advisory Committee). Washington DC: DOD.

United States Department of Defense. (2006). *Quadrennial Defense Report.* Washington DC: Office of the Secretary of Defense, DOD.

United States Department of Homeland Security. (2007). *2007 Data Mining Report* (DHS Privacy Office Response to House Report 109-699). Washington DC: DHS.

United States Department of Homeland Security. (August, 2006). *Survey of DHS data mining activities.* Washington DC: DHS.

United States Department of Justice. (2007). *Report on data mining activities* (Submitted to the Congress Pursuant to Section 126 of the USA PATRIOT Improvement and Reauthorization Act of 2005). Washington DC: DOJ.

United States Department of Justice. (2002). Statement regarding today's filing in *Sibel Edmonds v. Department of Justice.* Washington DC: DOJ.

United States District Court for the District of Columbia. (2004). *Sibel Edmonds v. United States Department of Justice et al.* Washington DC (Case No. 02-1448).

United States General Accounting Office. (2007). *Data mining: Early attention to privacy in developing a key DHS Program could reduce risk.* Washington DC: GAO.

United States General Accounting Office. (2006). *Personal information: Key federal privacy laws do not require information resellers to safeguard all sensitive data.* Washington DC: GAO.

United States General Accounting Office. (2005). *Data Mining: Agencies have taken key steps to protect privacy in selected efforts, but significant compliance issues remain.* Washington DC: GAO.

United States General Accounting Office. (2004a). *Data mining: Federal efforts cover a wide range of uses.* Washington DC: GAO.

United States General Accounting Office. (February, 2004b). *Aviation security: Computer Assisted Passenger Prescreening System faces significant implementation challenges.* Washington DC: GAO.

United States General Accounting Office. (2003). *Results and challenges for government program audits and investigation* (Testimony of D. Katz before the Subcommittee on Technology, Information Policy, Intergovernmental Relations and the Census). Washington DC: United States House of Representatives.

United States Government Printing Office. (2006). *Congressional reports* (H.RPT. 108-796—Intelligence Reform and Terrorism Prevention Act of 2004). Washington DC: GPO.

United States Government Printing Office. (2004). *The 9/11 Commission Report (Executive Summary)*. Washington DC: GPO.

United States Senate. (January 10, 2007). *Balancing privacy and security: The privacy implications of government data mining programs* (Hearing before the Committee of the Judiciary). Washington DC: U.S. Government Printing office.

Vikki, G. (2007). *The law: Unilateral shaping U.S. national security policy: The role of National Security Directives.* Presidential Studies Quarterly, http://goliath.ecnext.com

Ye, N. (Ed.). (2003). *The handbook of data mining.* Mahwah, NJ: Lawrence Erlbaum Associate Publishers.

Wang, J. (2003). *Data mining: Opportunities and challenges.* London: Idea Group Publishers.

Wang, W., & Yang, J. (2005). *Mining sequential patterns from large data sets.* New York: Springer.

KEY TERMS

ADVISE: A new data mining program currently being developed by the Department of Homeland Security. ADVISE (Analysis, Dissemination, Visualization, Insight, and Semantic Enhancement) has the capability of analyzing one billion pieces of information per hour.

American Civil Liberties Union (ACLU): ACLU was established in 1920, and its mission is to protect the privacy rights and civil liberties of the American citizens. ACLU is the leader of the organizations and individuals who have taken federal data mining cases to the federal court for their alleged violations of the constitutional principles related particularly of the First, Fourth, and Fourteenth Amendments.

ATS: A new data mining program currently used by the Department of Homeland Security to screen all passengers who enter the United States by car, plane, ship, or rail. ATS (Automatic Targeting System) collects Passenger Name Record (PNR) from all airlines that leave from and enter into the United States. The ATS program was developed in 1997, but it was greatly improved and extended in compliance with the Aviation Security Act of 2001.

Data Mining: A general process of discovering forms and patterns hidden in a large set of descriptive, discrete, and disconnected data. In social science and policy-making, data mining is a new information technology to understand the patterns of habits, beliefs and behavior of people from the digital data they create through a number of activities in their ordinary life.

Electronic Frontier Foundation (EFF): An advocacy organization dedicated to the mission of protecting privacy in the age of digital information. EFF has taken a number of federal data mining programs to federal court for their alleged violations of privacy protection principles of the constitution.

Privacy Act of 1974: The Privacy Act of 1974 contains the statutory guidelines that regulate the collection, maintenance, use, disclosure, and sharing of personal information by federal executive branch agencies.

USA PATRIOT Act of 2001: The USA Patriot Act of 2001 is the main statutory basis of national security related data mining activities by different federal agencies. The Act broadened the power of federal law enforcement agencies to track and detect terrorist activities even without the authorization of a warrant. The USA Patriot Act of 2001 substantially amended the Foreign Intelligence Surveillance Act (FISA) of 1978.

War on Terror: A global strategy to control and contain the spread of radically militant Islam, particularly the global terrorist activities of Al Qaeda. It has become a common foreign policy and national security metaphor for almost all countries of the western world after the events of September 11, 2001.

Chapter X
Legal Frameworks for Data Mining and Privacy

Robert Sprague
University of Wyoming College of Business, USA

ABSTRACT

This chapter explores the foundations of the legal right to privacy in the United States, juxtaposed against the accumulation and mining of data in today's society. Businesses and government agencies have the capacity to accumulate massive amounts of information, tracking the behavior of ordinary citizens carrying out ordinary routines. Data mining techniques also provide the opportunity to analyze vast amounts of data to compile comprehensive profiles of behavior. Within this context, this chapter addresses the legal frameworks for data mining and privacy. Historically, privacy laws in the United States have adapted to changing technologies, but have done so slowly; arguably not keeping pace with current technology. This chapter makes clear that the legal right to privacy in the United States is not keeping pace with the accumulation, analysis, and use of data about each and every one of us.

INTRODUCTION

In the classic Grimm's fairy tale, Hansel and Gretel dropped bread crumbs as they walked through the forest so they could later follow them home. Of course, birds ate the crumbs, leaving Hansel and Gretel ultimately in the hands of the wicked witch. In modern society, we all leave crumbs wherever we go, only today's crumbs are electronic and they never seem to go away. Transactional data are tracked, cell phones are monitored, Web surfing is recorded, and our moves in public are recorded by surveillance cameras (Froomkin, 2000). "The small details that were once captured in dim memories or fading scraps of paper are now preserved forever in the digital minds of computers, vast databases with fertile fields of personal data" (Solove, 2001, p. 1394). Our purchases now leave indelible traces, and the accumulation of these isolated transactions ultimately creates a recognizable portrait of each consumer (Karas, 2002).

It is not only businesses that collect and analyze data about our activities. The government is becoming increasingly reliant on consumer transactional data, using companies that already track that data (O'Harrow, 2005). Federal officials reportedly are routinely asking courts to order cell phone companies to furnish real-time tracking data to pinpoint the whereabouts of suspects (Nakashima, 2007b), and the FBI has been accused of seeking grocery-store purchase records in an effort to locate domestic terrorists (Singel, 2007). And the federal government itself maintains some 2,000 databases (Solove, 2001).

"Surveillance ... has become a pervasive activity among both government and private organizations, as they rely on the details of peoples' records to shape their dealings precisely to the circumstances of each individual they confront" (Rule, 2007, p. xi). The scope of data mining activities was exemplified shortly after the September 11, 2001 terrorist attacks in the United States, when the Defense Department tried to create a computerized surveillance system (called Total Information Awareness) to track the everyday activities of all American citizens with the goal of ferreting out terrorists (McClurg, 2003). Although Congress essentially killed the program, it was really nothing more than what hundreds of private companies are already doing (McClurg, 2003).

The U.S. legal system has recognized a "right to privacy" for over one hundred years. While its origin was sparked by changes in technology, it has recently failed to keep pace with technological advances in data collection and use. The right to privacy protects facts and conduct one

wishes to keep private. But most data collected is publicly known or freely disclosed in individual transactions. As a result, the legal right to privacy does not adequately incorporate "informational privacy." It does not provide any protection for how accumulated data are used. The concern is that data mining techniques expose every aspect of an individual's life to businesses, the government, and possibly the public.

This chapter reviews privacy concerns arising from data mining used in two (overlapping) contexts—by businesses and by government entities. This dichotomy is based on the two principal aspects of privacy recognized within the U.S. legal system: a "civil" right to privacy that protects individuals from offensive conduct by other individuals (including businesses); and a constitutional right to privacy that protects individuals from government intrusions. While specific standards vary between these two aspects of privacy, they also incorporate parallel attributes—one of which is that there is no current legal framework to sufficiently restrict the use of data mining, by either businesses or the government, to protect individual privacy. There is also a third source of privacy protection, laws passed by Congress, which are briefly discussed later in this chapter. These privacy laws are only given a brief discussion because they are very specific in their application; covering only a small portion of data collection and mining activities.

Data mining techniques center on large databases, which often include data warehouses—multiple linked databases (Zarsky, 2002-2003). Therefore, many of the issues related to individual rights to privacy examined in this chapter relate not only to how data are used (data mining), but also how data are accumulated.

BACKGROUND

Data mining—a technique for extracting knowledge from large volumes of data—is increasingly being used by businesses and government to mine personal information from public as well as private sector organizations (General Accounting Office, 2004). Data mining is the application of database technology and techniques (such as statistical analysis and modeling) to uncover hidden patterns and subtle relationships in data and to infer rules that allow for the prediction of future results (General Accounting Office, 2004). Stated another way, "[d]ata mining provides its users with answers to questions they did not know to ask" (Zarsky, 2002-2003, p.6).

The amount of information collected is vast. One private company reportedly maintains databases of credit and demographic information for over 200 million Americans, while another company reportedly has over 14 billion records on individuals and businesses for uses such as pre-employment screening of job candidates (Tien, 2004). Corporations now routinely record consumer transactions, selling dossiers of personally identifiable information to direct marketers and data collectors (Karas, 2002).

Meanwhile, the U.S. government wants to mine the same or similar data for law enforcement and anti-terrorism purposes (Tien, 2004). In 2004, the General Accounting Office identified 52 federal agencies conducting (or planning to conduct) 199 data mining projects, of which 122 used personal information (including names, aliases, Social Security numbers, e-mail addresses, driver's license numbers, student loan application data, bank account numbers, credit card information, and taxpayer identification numbers) (General Accounting Office, 2004).

The Department of Homeland Security is developing a technology framework, called Analysis, Dissemination, Visualization, Insight, and Semantic Enhancement (ADVISE), with the goal of analyzing and visually representing relationships between different types of data (Department of Homeland Security, 2007). The General Accounting Office (2007) notes that ADVISE could raise privacy concerns because of the

potential for erroneous association of individuals with crime or terrorism and the misidentification of individuals with similar names.

With the collection of vast amounts of information, individuals are often unaware of the increasingly sophisticated methods used to collect information about them (In re DoubleClick, Inc. Privacy Litigation, 2001; Schwartz, 2004). Supermarkets track our purchases, the government tracks our travel and communications, insurers and employers track our medical histories, retailers track our Web site visits, and financial institutions track our credit histories (Rule, 2007).

Concerns about data aggregation go beyond the obvious. There is the risk of identity theft if data is stolen or misappropriated. From January 2005 through 2007, over 200 million records, many containing sensitive personal and financial account information, were potentially exposed through breaches and lapses in data security ("A Chronology of Data Breaches," 2007; Kerber, 2007). Weak data security ultimately results in the distribution of personal information beyond the bounds of consent and expectations (Warner, 2005). Credit may also be denied if data are inaccurate. Errors in personally identifying information decrease our control over what others know or think they know about us, and the more inadequate the error prevention and detection in these systems, the more control we lose (Warner, 2005). And there are even more serious concerns—stalkers have used data services to locate, attack, and even kill their targets (Remsburg v. Docusearch, Inc., 2003).

Are individuals' privacy being violated by data mining? Consider Corey Ciocchetti's example: the University of Denver professor provided his name, address, and $29.95 to an online investigations company; fifteen minutes later he received via e-mail a fairly comprehensive dossier, including an extensive address history (reaching back to his days as a second-grader), past and present property ownership records, political party affiliation, various information concerning his current neighbors and past relatives (including his father-in-law's ex-wife); and, if it had applied, the dossier would have also included known aliases, results of a nationwide criminal search, sexual offense conviction records, bankruptcies, tax liens and judgments, UCC filings, airplane and boat registrations, and hunting, fishing, and concealed weapons permits (Ciocchetti, 2007). According to Ciocchetti (2007): "Individually, each of these pieces of personal information represents a mere pixel of my life, but when pieced together, they present a rather detailed picture of my identity" (p. 56). In the past seven years, the only thing that has changed is that personal dossiers are available faster and cheaper—as a similar experiment conducted by a journalist revealed similar information in a week at a much greater price (Penenberg, 1999).

U.S. citizens do have some (though minimal) legal protection regarding the collection and use of personal information. In general, privacy protections from databases and data mining are dependent upon legal theories that have historically adapted to technological changes. The only problem, though, is that they have done so very slowly.

PRIVACY IN THE UNITED STATES

There are three legal sources of privacy in the United States. Individual state courts have recognized a civil right to privacy, protecting against invasions by private individuals (including business). And, although the U.S. Constitution does not expressly guarantee a right to privacy, the United States Supreme Court has recognized an implied right to privacy in the Fourth Amendment to the Constitution, protecting individuals from warrantless searches and overly-intrusive regulation by government entities. There are also a number of specific privacy-related laws which have been passed by Congress that provide only limited protection in specific circumstances.

The concept of privacy is, though, amorphous. Commentators have referred to it as "illusive" and "ill-defined" (Posner, 1984, p. 331); a "concept in disarray" for which no one can articulate a meaning (Solove, 2006, p. 477); with little agreement about its source as a right (Bostwick, 1976). In one sense, privacy protects against affronts to dignity by persons or entities who pry too deeply into our personal affairs (Bloustein, 1984), and it is considered vital to decisions of intimacy (Gerstein, 1984). Privacy also stands for the "right to be let alone" (Warren & Brandeis, 1890, p. 204).

Privacy is also contextual. A conversation whispered behind closed doors may be deemed private when surreptitiously listened to by an eavesdropper, compared to the same conversation shouted in front of open windows overheard by a passerby (cf., Thomson, 1975). The context centers on a person's subjective expectation of privacy in any given situation (Katz v. U.S., 1967). For example, the court in Nelson v. Salem State College (2006) found no invasion of privacy where a college employee was videotaped by a hidden camera while changing clothes in a locked office to which a number of employees had a key and which the court regarded as an "open work area" (p. 343). Even though the video camera was installed to thwart after-hour thefts, the court was unconcerned that the camera was recording twenty-four hours per day, focusing instead on the employee's subjective expectation of privacy within the office, with or without the camera, which was minimal at best since any employee could have walked in at any time (Nelson v. Salem State College, 2006).

Although the U.S. Supreme Court has stated there is no expectation of privacy, and hence no constitutional protection, for matters open to public observation (Bond v. U.S., 2000), that is not an absolute rule. For example, one court has held that night club dancers had no expectation of privacy regarding video surveillance of their dressing room (of which they were aware) by club security personnel, but did have an expectation of privacy as to government agents viewing the same surveillance without a warrant (Bevan v. Smartt, 2004). Loss of privacy in one context (such as undressing in one's home before an open window) does not necessarily lead to loss of privacy in other aspects (such an unwarranted search by police of that same home for illegal drugs) (Bevan v. Smartt, 2004).

Into this amorphous and contextual environment come massive databases and data mining, where any notion of rights to information privacy are fractured and incomplete (Reidenberg, 2003).

Privacy in the United States: Civil Laws

In 1890, Warren and Brandeis advocated the legal recognition of a "right to be let alone" (p. 193), arguing for a legal protection from "injurious disclosures as to private matters" (p. 204). Their main thesis was that individuals had the right to determine what information about themselves could be made public (Warren & Brandeis, 1890). It is reported the impetus for Warren and Brandeis' article (1890) was newspaper reports of Warren's daughter's wedding—in a time when the socially elite were not accustomed to their names and affairs being printed in local newspapers (Prosser, 1960). Warren and Brandeis (1890) worried that "[i]nstantaneous photographs and newspaper enterprise have invaded the sacred precincts of private and domestic life; and numerous mechanical devices threaten to make good the prediction that 'what is whispered in the closet shall be proclaimed from the house-tops'" (p. 195). In particular, Warren and Brandeis (1890) were concerned that new technology allowing instantaneous photography would allow strangers to surreptitiously photograph people in public places. What was required, according to Warren and Brandeis (1890), was a legally recognized protection from having private matters involuntarily made public by strangers.

During the next seventy years, state courts throughout the United States began to recognize a civil right to privacy on the basis of Warren and Brandeis' (1890) work. In analyzing the various state cases involving a right to privacy, Prosser (1960) identified four distinct types of invasion: (1) intrusion upon seclusion; (2) public disclosure of embarrassing private facts; (3) publicity which places a person in a false light in the public eye; and (4) commercial appropriation of a person's name or likeness.

Unfortunately, most of these civil rights to privacy do not directly apply to data mining techniques. When courts were first presented with claims of invasion of privacy, it was perhaps easier to recognize this new form of protection in severe cases, where a court was compelled to find a solution. For example, in the case of De May v. Roberts (1881) (the first reported instance of a U.S. court of law recognizing a right to privacy), a man had impersonated a doctor in order to be present when a woman gave birth. Given circumstances approximating an intrusion upon seclusion, the De May v. Roberts (1881) court acknowledged the woman's right to privacy during "a most sacred" occasion, ruling "[i]t would be shocking to our sense of right, justice and propriety to doubt even but that for such an act the law would afford an ample remedy." (p. 148-149). In Melvin v. Reid (1931) (an early case involving public disclosure of private facts), a former prostitute and murder defendant who had abandoned her "life of shame," married, and led a life in "respectable society" which was unaware of her past was facing the publication of these facts (p. 91). Expressing a similar tone as the De May v. Roberts (1881) court, the California Court of Appeal held that the publication "… of the unsavory incidents in the past life of [the woman] after she had reformed, coupled with her true name, was not justified by any standard of morals or ethics known to …" the court (Melvin v. Reid, 1931, p. 93). Similarly, under Prosser's (1960) third type of invasion (false light publicity), the situations in which it was applied by the courts involved objectionable uses of an individual's name or likeness. "[T]he hypersensitive individual will not be protected" (Prosser, 1960, p. 400). As such, an underlying requirement of offensive conduct has become ingrained in the first three of the four types of civil rights to privacy.

Under the first of Prosser's (1960) types of invasion, an invasion of privacy occurs when someone (including a business) "... intentionally intrudes, physically or otherwise, upon the solitude or seclusion of another or his private affairs ..., if the intrusion would be highly offensive to a reasonable person" (Restatement (Second) of Torts, 1976, § 652B). Because data mining techniques aggregate disparate pieces of information, the collection of the information is not considered highly offensive to a reasonable person because each particular instance of collection is often small and innocuous (Solove, 2001). As a result, courts have thrown out cases for intrusion involving the type of information that would likely be collected in databases (Solove, 2001). For example, courts have rejected a claim of intrusion for obtaining a person's unlisted phone number (Seaphus v. Lilly, 1988), for selling subscription lists to direct mail companies (Shibley v. Time, Inc., 1975), and for collecting and disclosing an individual's past insurance history (Tureen v. Equifax, Inc., 1978).

While it would appear that disclosing embarrassing private facts by selling information collected through data mining would be an actionable invasion of privacy, this second type of Prosser's (1960) invasion of privacy "... appears designed to redress excesses of the press, and is accordingly focused on the widespread dissemination of personal information ..." (Solove, 2001, p. 1433). This second type of invasion is also limited to public disclosure of highly offensive private facts (Restatement (Second) of Torts, 1976, § 652D). Most information in databases would not be considered highly offensive (Solove, 2001). This type of invasion recognizes the difference between a "... shrinking soul who is abnormally

sensitive about ... publicity" and "... details of sexual relations spread before the public gaze, ..." or highly personal portrayals of intimate private conduct (Prosser, 1960, p. 397).

In addition, the facts made public must first be private. Most information in databases often is derived from public records (Solove, 2001). "Certainly no one can complain when publicity is given to information about which he himself leaves open to the public eye..." (Prosser, 1960, p. 394). "With regard to databases, much information collection and use occurs in public, and indeed, many parts of cyberspace may well be considered public places" (Solove, 2001, p. 1433).

Prosser's (1960) third type of invasion, "false light," is a type of defamation, in that it injures a person's reputation by disclosing facts to the public in, again, a "highly offensive" manner (Restatement (Second) of Torts, 1976, § 652E). However, the type of information collected in databases often is not harmful to one's reputation (Solove, 2001).

Prosser's (1960) fourth and final type of invasion generally applies to using someone's name or likeness for a commercial endorsement (Restatement (Second) of Torts, 1976, § 652C). However, courts have not found an invasion of privacy when a company has sold a person's name to other merchants (Dwyer v. American Express Co., 1995), or when a magazine sold subscription lists to direct mail companies (Shibley v. Time, Inc., 1975), because the person whose information was sold was not used to endorse any product.

This issue did arise in late 2007, however, when the social networking Internet site Facebook implemented a new marketing technique known as Beacon. The key element of a social networking site (such as Facebook) is that individuals can share information with their friends (who are also members of the site). In late 2007, many Facebook users reportedly did not notice a small alert notifying them that their transactions on certain e-commerce sites would be broadcast to their Facebook friends (unless they selected an option preventing the broadcast) (Jesdanun & Metz, 2007). In addition, companies using this feature could also display the Facebook member's photograph (Jesdanun & Metz, 2007). Facebook's Beacon service raised the issue of the way personal data are disclosed for marketing purposes (Nakashima, 2007b).

Facebook's Beacon service also appears to be a situation when the sharing of information went too far, at least for Facebook's members. Within weeks of its implementation, Facebook revamped the Beacon service. The central issue was that, initially, users had to expressly select not to have their purchase information shared (i.e., "opt-out"), as opposed to expressly selecting to have the information shared (i.e., "opt-in"). Facebook modified Beacon so that members' purchases were not broadcast unless they opted in (Nakashima, 2007b).

Beyond the ruined Christmases (when a wife learns through Facebook of a diamond ring her husband bought for her—at a 51% discount no less) (Nakashima, 2007b), many privacy advocates also claimed Beacon invaded privacy by using Facebook members' names and likenesses for commercial purposes. This would be the case where members did not clearly consent to the use of their information for commercial endorsements.

Privacy in the United States: Constitutional Protections

Contemporaneous with the development of the civil right to privacy in state courts, another related right to privacy was also developing—that against unreasonable searches, seizures, and intrusions by the government. The Fourth Amendment to the U.S. Constitution grants "[T]he right of the people to be secure in their persons, houses, papers, and effects, against unreasonable searches and seizures …." Warrants authorizing a search or seizure must be based on probable cause and must describe with particularity the place to be searched, and the persons or things to be seized. The Fourth Amendment applies to the states through the Fourteenth Amendment (O'Connor v. Ortega, 1987).

In the late nineteenth century, the U.S. Supreme Court ruled that sealed letters (Ex parte Jackson, 1877) and private papers (Boyd v. U.S., 1886) were subject to Fourth Amendment warrant requirements. And it was technology which played a central role in the Supreme Court's decision in Ex parte Jackson (1877). Prior to the mid-nineteenth century, envelopes containing letters were sealed with wax, making them very easy to be opened and read. Indeed, there was such a lack of secrecy in letters sent through the early U.S. postal service that George Washington observed that sending a letter through the post office meant his words would become known to the world (Brenner, 2005). In the mid-1800's the self-sealing adhesive envelope was introduced, meaning letters could be truly sealed (Brenner, 2005). It was within the context of a fully sealed letter that the Supreme Court found a right to privacy (Brenner, 2005).

Technology drove another privacy issue in the early twentieth century as well—specifically whether authorities needed a warrant to surreptitiously listen to someone's telephone call. This was problematic because the Fourth Amendment's language refers to seizing people or things, or searching places. Since there was no entry, no search, and no seizure, the Supreme Court initially ruled that telephone conversations were outside the Fourth Amendment's warrant requirement (Olmstead v. U.S., 1928). In his dissent in Olmstead v. U.S. (1928), Justice Brandeis resurrected a theme from his earlier treatise with Warren (Warren & Brandeis, 1890), that technology had transformed the nature of communications from letters to conversations over wires. Brandeis argued that if sealed letters deserved protection, so did telephone conversations.

Following this theme, the Supreme Court reversed itself in Katz v. U.S. (1967), rejecting a requirement of physicality in a search or seizure. In Katz v. U.S. (1967), the Court held that the government's activities in electronically listening to and recording an individual's words violated the privacy upon which he justifiably relied while using a telephone booth, resulting in a "search and seizure" within the meaning of the Fourth Amendment (p. 353). The Supreme Court stated that while what a person exposes to the world is not protected by the Fourth Amendment, what a person seeks to preserve as private may be constitutionally protected (at least from an unwarranted search or seizure) (Katz v. U.S., 1967).

The Supreme Court appeared to support a general constitutional right to privacy in Griswold v. Connecticut (1965), holding there was a "penumbral" right to privacy emanating from the Constitution and its amendments (p. 484). In particular, the majority of Justices believed there was a "zone of privacy" relative to the intimate relation of a husband and wife, and their physician's role in that relation (Griswold v. Connecticut, 1965, p. 485). The right to privacy expressed in Griswold v. Connecticut (1965) was used as the basis to overturn laws banning interracial marriages (Loving v. Virginia, 1967), the possession of pornography in one's own home (Stanley v. Georgia, 1969), and the distribution of contraceptives (Eisenstadt v. Baird, 1972); as well as limits on sexual conduct of consenting adults in the privacy of their own homes (Lawrence v. Texas, 2003).

The main focus of the Supreme Court's penumbral zone of privacy is intimacy, while one's constitutional rights relative to the collection and dissemination of information derives from the Fourth Amendment. However, in Katz v. U.S. (1967), the Supreme Court specifically rejected the notion that the Fourth Amendment provides a general constitutional right to privacy. Any protection of a general right to privacy is up to the laws of the individual states (Katz v. U.S., 1967). In addition, the Supreme Court in Roe v. Wade (1973) noted that only personal rights that can be deemed "fundamental" or "implicit in the

concept of ordered liberty" are included in any constitutional guarantee of personal privacy (p. 152).

Similar to the civil right to privacy, application of the constitutional right to privacy depends on whether the person invoking its protection can claim a justifiable, a reasonable, or a legitimate expectation of privacy that has been invaded by government action. The Supreme Court uses a two-part analysis to make this determination: (1) whether the individual, by his or her conduct, has exhibited a subjective expectation of privacy; and (2) whether that subjective expectation of privacy is reasonable (objectively justifiable under the circumstances) (Smith v. Maryland, 1979). Once again, expectations of privacy are contextual. For example, in Whalen v. Roe (1977), the U.S. Supreme Court reviewed the constitutionality of a New York statute which required the collection, in a centralized computer file, of the names and addresses of all persons prescribed certain drugs associated with drug abuse. Patients were concerned that if the information in the database was disclosed, they would be labeled drug abusers and therefore were reluctant to use the particular drugs covered by the statute (Whalen v. Roe, 1977). The Supreme Court concluded that since disclosures of private medical information to doctors, hospital personnel, insurance companies, and public health agencies are an essential part of modern medical practice, even when the disclosures may reflect unfavorably on the character of the patient, requiring similar disclosures to a state agency having responsibility for the health of the community does not automatically invade patient privacy (Whalen v. Roe, 1977).

Under this approach, the Supreme Court has indicated that records are not a protectable privacy interest. For example, in Smith v. Maryland (1979), the Supreme Court ruled that the state of Maryland did not need a warrant to install a pen register on a person's home telephone line which recorded the phone numbers dialed from the telephone line, but not the actual conversations that took place. The

Court concluded phone customers have no legitimate expectation of privacy in the phone numbers they dial because that information is transmitted to the phone company, which uses and records that information for a number of legitimate business purposes (Smith v. Maryland, 1979). And at least one court, following Smith v. Maryland (1979), has ruled that using a "mirror port" (analogous to a pen register) to obtain from a criminal suspect's Internet Service Provider (ISP) account to/from addresses of e-mail messages, the Internet protocol ("IP") addresses of websites visited, and the total volume of information transmitted to or from the account, is not a Fourth Amendment search (U.S. v. Forrester, 2007).

The U.S. Supreme Court has also limited privacy rights in records maintained by third parties. In U.S. v. Miller (1976), the subject of a tax evasion investigation (Miller) tried to prevent the government from using his bank records in the investigation. The Supreme Court concluded that Miller had no privacy interest in his bank records because they were not his personal papers which he did not own or possess—they were the business records of the bank (U.S. v. Miller, 1976). As a general matter, the U.S. Supreme Court has concluded "…that when we convey information to a third party, we give up all constitutionally protected privacy in that information, for we assume the risk that the third party might relay it to others" (Thai, 2006, p. 1733). And following U.S. v. Miller (1976) and Smith v. Maryland (1979), the federal courts have adopted the position that "…internet users have no reasonable expectation of privacy in their subscriber information, the length of their stored files, and other noncontent data to which service providers must have access" (U.S. v. D'Andrea, 2007, p. 120).

However, government authorities cannot necessarily review transaction records of third parties to collect evidence regarding a suspect. For example, a Wisconsin federal court refused to enforce an FBI subpoena seeking the identities of thousands of people who bought books through the online retailer Amazon.com (Foley, 2007). The FBI was investigating a public official who was running a used-book business out of his government office; since the official had sold a number of books through Amazon.com, the FBI wanted to search Amazon.com records to locate potential witnesses (Foley, 2007). In quashing the subpoena, a federal magistrate stated, "It is an unsettling and un-American scenario to envision federal agents nosing through the reading lists of law-abiding citizens while hunting for evidence against somebody else" (Foley, 2007).

Courts have also made specific distinctions between surveillance of conduct in public places (particularly automobiles) versus the home. For example, when authorities used an electronic tracking device inside a container of chemicals to track the container during its travels over the road, the U.S. Supreme Court found no violation of the Fourth Amendment (U.S. v. Knotts, 1983), whereas when authorities used an electronic tracking device to track a container after it was located inside a suspect's home, the Supreme Court ruled a warrant was required under the Fourth Amendment (U.S. v. Karo, 1984). In the former case, the Court believed the agents obtained no more information than they would have through physical surveillance—"[a] person travelling in an automobile on public thoroughfares has no reasonable expectation of privacy in his movements" (U.S. v. Knotts, 1984, p. 281). Hence, the ability of the government to record and analyze images from surveillance cameras in massive databases without a warrant. In the latter case, the Court believed the surveillance went too far once the container was moved into the suspect's home—"private residences are places in which the individual … expects privacy … and that expectation of privacy is plainly one that society is prepared to recognize as justifiable" (U.S. v. Karo, 1984, p. 714).

Rosen (2000) believes, particularly as to surveillance, the subjective expectation of privacy is a tautology: "as advances in the technology of monitoring and searching have made ever more intrusive surveillance possible, expectations of privacy have naturally diminished, with a corresponding reduction in constitutional protection" (pp. 60-61). In his dissent, Justice Marshall recognized a similar dilemma in the holding in Smith v. Maryland (1979)—the government could control the level of privacy expectation, and therefore the extent of protected privacy, simply by announcing an intent to monitor certain communications, such as phone calls and mail. On a more general matter, therefore, as data accumulation becomes a more routine part of our daily lives, the less privacy expectation—and protection—we will have.

Privacy in the United States: Congressional Enactments

While the civil and constitutional rights to privacy are the principal legal protections for privacy in the United States, there are a variety of federal privacy laws passed by Congress, but which apply only in specific circumstances. Based on the fear of the growth of databases by the federal government in the 1960's and 1970's, Congress passed the Privacy Act of 1974, which regulates the collection and use of records by federal agencies. While the Privacy Act, on its face, appears to provide broad privacy protection—giving individuals the right to access and correct information about themselves held by federal agencies, and restricting the use of information by federal agencies only for relevant and necessary purposes—in reality, its exceptions provide minimal protections—it only applies to federal (not state or local) agencies; information can be disclosed to law enforcement entities and consumer reporting agencies; and information may be disclosed for any "routine use" that is "compatible" with the purpose for which the agency collected the information (Solove, 2002a, p. 1167). The "routine use" exception is a significant loophole which has done little to bar external disclosure of personal information (Solove, 2002a).

In 1986, Congress enacted the Electronic Communications Privacy Act (ECPA). While the name of the Act promises privacy protection, it actually provides very little. The strongest part of the Act, Title I (the Wiretap Act), requires that government entities obtain a warrant before they can intercept communication transmissions. And current technology allows for a wider array of types of communication transmissions. For example, in In re Order for Roving Interception of Oral Communications (2003), the FBI obtained an order to intercept communications from a vehicle's on-board system that communicates with the vehicle's manufacturer (normally used for purposes such as directions and emergency roadside assistance). The FBI realized the on-board system could be used like a "roving bug" to intercept conversations taking place inside the vehicle (In re Order for Roving Interception of Oral Communications, 2003, p. 1134). The court ultimately voided the court order, but only because use of the on-board system for the FBI's purpose would incapacitate the system for its normal purposes, meaning the FBI interception would excessively interfere with the service in violation of the Wiretap Act (In re Order for Roving Interception of Oral Communications, 2003).

Title II of the ECPA, the Stored Communications Act (SCA), promises to protect communications stored by telephone companies and ISPs. However, the SCA requires a warrant only to obtain "temporarily" stored communications. If the communication is stored for a more permanent purpose, copies can then be obtained without a warrant (Solove, 2002b). On this basis, courts have determined that the use of cookies to store users' Web site visits, which are then used to direct advertising to users, does not violate the ECPA. For example, DoubleClick stores information about which Internet Web pages individuals visit in computer files (called "cookies") on the individuals' computer hard drives (In re Double-Click, Inc. Privacy Litigation, 2001; cf., White, 2007). DoubleClick specializes in collecting, compiling, and analyzing this information about Internet users to create profiles of users in order to place customized advertisements in the Web pages they visit (In re DoubleClick, Inc. Privacy Litigation, 2001). The cookies, however, are stored indefinitely; they are therefore outside the scope of the ECPA (*In re DoubleClick*, 2001). Indeed, according to the In re DoubleClick, Inc. Privacy Litigation court (2001), the primary purpose of the ECPA is "... to prevent hackers from obtaining, altering or destroying certain stored electronic communications. It creates ... sanctions ... against persons who gain unauthorized access to communications facilities and thereby access electronic communications stored incident to their transmission" (p. 507).

Title III of the ECPA, the Pen Register Act, limits the holding in Smith v. Maryland (1979), requiring the government to obtain a court order before installing and using a pen register device. However, probable cause is not required for the court order, only a showing that the information to be gained is relevant to an ongoing criminal investigation. The target does not even have to be a criminal suspect. As a result, courts have little discretion in issuing Title III orders (Solove, 2002b).

A substantial amount of personal data are stored in credit reporting databases. The Fair Credit Reporting Act (FCRA) of 1970 regulates credit agencies, but has minimal restrictions regarding disclosures of information (Solove, 2001). In § 1681i the FCRA does, though, provide mechanisms for individuals to review their credit records and request corrections of inaccurate information.

There are other privacy protection laws that prohibit the sale or sharing of personal information without prior consent, but they are limited to very specific circumstances. For example, the Gramm-Leach-Bliley Act of 1999 limits information sharing by financial institutions with third parties without prior consent by customers. However, under the Gramm-Leach-Bliley Act, "consent" is automatic unless an individual expressly opts out of the sharing of information. Additional privacy-related laws include: the Family Educational Rights and Privacy Act of 1974, which limits the accessibility of student records; the Right to Financial Privacy Act of 1978, which requires government officials to obtain a warrant or subpoena to obtain financial information, and was enacted in direct response to the U.S. Supreme Court's decision in U.S. v. Miller (1976) that customers had no expectation of privacy in records held by their banks and other financial institutions; the Privacy Protection Act of 1980, which restricts the search or seizures of work product materials in the possession of third parties; the Cable Communications Policy Act of 1984, which restricts disclosure of the viewing habits of cable customers; the Video Privacy Protection Act of 1988, which prohibits video rental stores from disclosing customer video rental and purchase information; the Computer Matching and Privacy Protection Act of 1988, which regulates the federal government's practice of comparing individual information stored across different agency computer databases; the Driver's Privacy Protection Act of 1994, which prohibits states from selling driver's license information without prior consent; and the Health Insurance Portability and Accountability Act of 1996, which regulates the disclosure of health information.

Returning to the Facebook Beacon service, one commentator has suggested that its interaction with the movie rental firm Blockbuster probably (initially) violated the Video Privacy Protection Act of 1988 (Grimmelmann, 2007). If Blockbuster reported back to Facebook (alone for Facebook's own data collection, or for distribution to other Facebook members) which movies its members had rented, without the members' express permission, then violations of the Act probably occurred (Grimmelmann, 2007).

These various privacy-related laws do provide some protection against data collection and mining activities. But, as Solove (2002b) points out, these privacy laws miss a vast amount of data stored by merchants and various businesses, and, in particular, they often apply only to various types of information based on the particular types of third parties that possess them rather than on the types of information themselves.

This review of U.S. privacy laws demonstrates a desire to update protections as technology evolves—incorporating sealed letters, instantaneous photographs, telephone conversations, and Internet communications. However, with only limited exceptions for certain types of information, data accumulation and mining activities are not subject to substantive privacy-based restrictions.

FUTURE TRENDS

It is apparent there is no legal right to privacy regarding most data collection and mining efforts. In 1970-1971, the National Academy of Sciences sponsored a project that profiled 55 private and government entities transferring paper records to computer databanks (Westin & Baker, 1972). The project concluded that "... computer usage has not created the revolutionary new powers of data surveillance predicted by some commentators[,]" and that "... organizational policies which affect individual rights are still generally following the precomputer patterns in each field of record-keeping[]" (i.e., where rights to privacy had been recognized in the past, these rights were being carried over into the computerized systems) (Westin & Baker, 1972, p. 341). Members of the project can be excused for not being prescient enough to predict some thirty years later GPS tracking in cars and cell phones, surveillance cameras throughout cities, every non-cash transaction being recorded, all in interconnected computer systems (cf., Garfinkel, 2000). Technology appears to have outpaced legal rights to privacy.

Time and again, legal rights to privacy have expanded with advances in technology, albeit slowly. We appear to once again to be in a period of transition. "Advances in technology and corporations' unquenchable thirst for consumer information have substantially eroded the ability of individuals to control their personal data. Scholars have suggested a wide variety of ways of combating the problem, but have not developed a satisfactory conceptual framework for protection of mundane consumer information" (Johnson v. Bryco Arms, 2004, p. 541). Although computer databases have been viewed as problematic for rights of privacy, "... the problem is often not well defined" (Solove, 2001, p. 1394-1395).

Many commentators have equated massive data collections, even by private companies, with the notions of Big Brother, George Orwell's oppressive dictatorship that was always watching and listening (Orwell, 1949; Hatch, 2001; Solove, 2001; Hoofnagle, 2004). The principal argument is that the collection of massive amounts of data "creates a potential for suppressing a capacity for free choice: the more that is known about an individual, the easier it is to force his obedience" (Schwartz, 1995, p. 560) And some are concerned that features such as Facebook's Beacon, for example, cross the line into being Big Brother (Story & Stone, 2007).

Underlying the Big Brother concern is a loss of individual self-identity (Schwartz, 1995). Others, such as Solove (2001), argue that massive data collection fosters "a state of powerlessness and vulnerability created by people's lack of any meaningful form of participation in the collection and use of their personal information" (p. 1423).

Future trends do not bode well for privacy advocates. Although Facebook quickly modified its Beacon feature, which broadcasts members' e-commerce transactions to other Facebook members, to make it easier for members to opt out of the feature (Vara, 2007), some critics complain that Beacon goes further that most members realize—reporting back to Facebook its members' e-commerce transactions even if the members have opted out of having Beacon broadcast their purchases to other members of the service (Perez, 2007).

Courts have already found that tracking Internet activities of individuals is not an invasion of privacy (In re DoubleClick, Inc. Privacy Litigation, 2001). But DoubleClick's cookie technology is dependent upon users visiting particular Web sites in order to collect data (In re DoubleClick, Inc. Privacy Litigation, 2001; cf., White, 2007). The next iteration of Internet use data collection is "deep-packet inspection boxes" in which ISPs track every Web page viewed by their users—potentially delivering far more detailed information to advertisers (White, 2007).

The difference in these technologies is that DoubleClick knows nothing more about Internet users beyond certain Web pages they view, whereas ISPs know a lot more, in addition to every Web page viewed—for example, name and address (White, 2007). This latest technology allows for the combining of online and offline information (White, 2007) to create a more detailed profile of Internet users. In addition, users can block tracking through cookies using Web browser software settings. With deep-packet inspection, users will have to request to opt out of tracking by ISPs (White, 2007).

One may argue that this is all innocent tracking and a benefit to Internet users—they'll only be presented with advertising that appeals to them. And these same tracking technologies can protect the public—for example, by identifying an individual who anonymously posts a message on a blog primarily used by college students threatening to shoot students at a particular university (Schwartz, 2007). But this same information could be used by the government, to review, say, whether an individual has visited Web sites that espouse certain political views. What is to stop local authorities from trying to identify potential pedophiles by monitoring who visits Web sites identified as having pedophile-related material? Will it identify someone as a pedophile simply because he or she accidentally clicked on a link to

a particular site that turned up in a Google search? Federal authorities have already tried to obtain search records from Google in order to determine whether a federal law aimed at protecting children from being exposed to sexually explicit Internet material was more effective than filtering software (Kopytoff, 2006). While Google refused to turn over the data, Yahoo! and Microsoft turned over millions of search records under similar requests (Kopytoff, 2006).

There is no clear path for increasing individual privacy protection from data collection and mining techniques, nor even agreement as to the extent of the threat (cf., DeMarco, 2006). As to the government's use of commercial data, Solove (2002b) suggests a regulatory scheme that addresses minimization (keeping government information gathering to a minimum), particularization (limiting data gathering efforts to specific individuals suspected of criminal involvement), and control (supervision over the government's information gathering activities). In contrast, Slobogin (2005) recommends a regulatory scheme more attuned to the underlying expectation of privacy in the information recorded—e.g., allowing public records and catalogic data (transactional records) to be accessible on less than probable cause.

Brenner and Clarke (2006), specifically as to government access to private databases, recommend focusing on the relationship between the provider of data and its collector. The mere fact that a collector possesses data should not automatically enable the government to obtain it (Brenner & Clarke, 2006). They recommend, however, the government should have access to data the consumer "... has set adrift in the stream of commerce ..." in that the same information would have been disclosed to casual observers or employees of the collector in comparable real-world transactions (Brenner & Clarke, 2006, p. 269).

As to commercial use of personal information, commentators have offered a variety of approaches to protect individual privacy, some of them conflicting. Hatch (2001) argues for opt-in legislation, in which personal information cannot be shared unless individuals expressly agree. In contrast, Tindall (2003) argues that the United States continue its opt-out approach, in which personal information will be shared unless individuals expressly give notice of their objection. Tindall (2003) contends that an opt-out scheme, coupled with improved notice provisions, will balance consumers' privacy needs with the conveniences associated with data collection and sharing. While Ciocchetti (2007) does not advocate an absolute opt-in or opt-out approach (recognizing that requiring companies to gain consent for every informational use would be prohibitively expensive), he argues for clearer, more uniform privacy policies that allow individuals to more easily make informed choices regarding data collection and sharing. Basho (2000), on the other hand, recommends a licensing scheme in which individuals negotiate the terms under which they will allow their information to be used. Similarly, Bergelson (2003) argues for a recognition of property rights in personal information, granting individuals the right to demand the correction of errors and the deletion of inaccurate information, as well as the power to transfer information for commercial use.

There is no clear path for protecting personal information from collection and mining techniques. The only clear future trend is that data collection and mining will continue on an expanding basis.

CONCLUSION

There is no question that individuals living in the United States are subject to vast array of tracking, whether through their movements on the street, on the Internet, or their purchases in a store. And there is no doubt there is a corresponding loss of privacy—a lot can be learned from all this collected data. Although privacy laws in the U.S. have adapted over time to technology, it appears

technology is now far outstripping the capability of the legal system to adjust to new threats to privacy. At the same time, there is little agreement as to how much privacy protection should be afforded and how to provide it. When it comes to data accumulation and mining, the solution for increasing individual privacy is just as amorphous as the concept of privacy itself.

REFERENCES

A Chronology of Data Breaches. Privacy Rights Clearinghouse. Retrieved Oct. 25, 2007, from http://www.privacyrights.org/ar/ChronDataB-reaches.htm.

Basho, K. (2000). The licensing of our personal information: Is it a solution to Internet privacy? *California Law Review, 88*, 1507-1545.

Bergelson, V. (2003). It's personal but is it mine? Toward property rights in personal information. *U.C. Davis Law Review, 37*, 379-451.

Bevan vs. Smartt, 316 F.Supp.2d 1153 (D.Utah 2004).

Bloustein, E.J. (1984). Privacy as an aspect of human dignity: An answer to Dean Prosser. In F.D. Schoeman (Ed.) *Philosophical dimensions of privacy: An anthology* (pp. 156-202) New York: Cambridge University Press.

Bond vs. U.S., 529 U.S. 334 (2000).

Bostwick, G. L. (1976). A taxonomy of privacy: repose, sanctuary, and intimate decision. *California Law Review, 64*, 1447-1483.

Boyd vs. U.S., 116 U.S. 616 (1886).

Brenner, S.W. (2005). The fourth amendment in an era of ubiquitous technology. *Mississippi Law Journal, 75*, 1-84.

Brenner, S. W., & Clarke, L. L. (2006). Fourth amendment protection for shared privacy rights in stored transactional data. *Journal of Law and Policy, 14*, 211-280.

Cable Communications Policy Act of 1984, 42 U.S.C. § 551(2007).

Ciocchetti, C. A. (2007). E-commerce and information privacy: Privacy policies as personal information protectors. *American Business Law Journal, 44*, 55-126.

Computer Matching and Privacy Protection Act of 1988, Pub. L. No. 100-503.

DeMarco, D.A. (2006). Understanding consumer information privacy in the realm of Internet commerce: Personhood and pragmatism, Pop-Tarts and six-packs. *Texas Law Review, 84*, 1013-1064.

De May v. Roberts, 9 N.W. 146 (Mich. 1881).

Department of Homeland Security. (2007). *2007 data mining report*. Retrieved Feb. 5, 2008, from http://www.dhs.gov/xlibrary/assets/privacy/privacy_rpt_datamining_2007.pdf.

Driver's Privacy Protection Act of 1994, 18 U.S.C. §§ 2721-25(2007).

Dwyer vs. American Express Co., 652 N.E.2d 1351 (Ill. App. Ct. 1995).

Eisenstadt v. Baird, 405 U.S. 438 (1972).

Electronic Communications Privacy Act, Title I, 18 U.S.C. §§ 2510-22 (2007).

Electronic Communications Privacy Act, Title II, Stored Communications Act, 18 U.S.C. §§ 2701-2711 (2007).

Electronic Communications Privacy Act, Title III, 18 U.S.C. §§ 3121-27 (2007).

Ex parte Jackson, 96 U.S. 727 (1877).

Fair Credit Reporting Act of 1970, 15 U.S.C. § 1681 (2007).

Family Educational Rights and Privacy Act of 1974, 20 U.S.C. § 1232g (2007).

Foley, R. J. (2007). Feds cancel Amazon customer ID request. Associated Press. Retrieved Nov. 28, 2007, from http://ap.google.com/article/ALeqM5gz0slCB4SYJCVk2J3xbYH-M6R55oAD8T66FAG0.

Froomkin, A. M. (2000). The death of privacy? *Stanford Law Review, 52*, 1461-1543.

General Accounting Office. (2007). *Data mining: Early attention to privacy in developing a key DHS program could reduce risks*. Retrieved Feb. 5, 2008, from http://www.gao.gov/new.items/d07293.pdf.

General Accounting Office. (2004). *Data mining: Federal efforts cover a wide range of uses.* Retrieved Nov. 13, 2007, from http://frwebgate.access.gpo.gov/cgi-bin/getdoc.cgi?dbname=gao&docid=f:d04548.pdf.

Garfinkel, S. (2000). *Database nation: The death of privacy in the 21st century*. Sebastopol, CA: O'Reilly.

Gerstein, R. S. (1984). Intimacy and privacy. In F.D. Schoeman (Ed.) *Philosophical dimensions of privacy: An anthology* (pp. 265-271). New York: Cambridge University Press.

Gramm-Leach-Bliley Act of 1999, 15 U.S.C. §§ 6801-09 (2007).

Grimmelmann, J. (2007, Dec. 10). Facebook and the VPPA: Uh-Oh. Retrieved Dec. 11, 2007, from http://laboratorium.net/archive/2007/12/10/facebook_and_the_vppa_uhoh.

Griswold v. Connecticut, 381 U.S. 479 (1965).

Hatch, M. (2001). The privatization of big brother: Protecting sensitive personal information from commercial interests in the 21st century. *William Mitchell Law Review, 27*, 1457-1502.

Health Insurance Portability and Accountability Act of 1996, Pub. L. No. 104-191.

Hoofnagle, C.J. (2004). Big brother's little helpers: How Choicepoint and other commercial data brokers collect and package your data for law enforcement. *North Carolina Journal of International Law and Commercial Regulation, 29*, 595-637.

In re DoubleClick, Inc. Privacy Litigation, 154 F. Supp.2d 497 (S.D. N.Y. 2001).

In re Order for Roving Interception of Oral Communications, 349 F.3d 1132 (9th Cir. 2003).

Jesdanun, A. & Metz, R. (2007). Facebook users complain of new tracking. Associated Press. Retrieved Nov. 16, 2007, from http://ap.google.com/article/ALeqM5jktmzai0_n_sMBgH_jfy-6QXNS_6gD8T299HG0.

Johnson v. Bryco Arms, 224 F.R.D. 536 (E.D. N.Y. 2004).

Karas, S. (2002). Privacy, identity, databases. *American University Law Review, 52*, 393-445.

Katz vs. U. S., 389 U.S. 347 (1967).

Kerber, R. (2007, Oct. 24). Court filing in TJX breach doubles toll. *Boston Globe*, p. A1 (Business).

Kopytoff, V. (2006, Jan. 20). Google says no to data demand. *San Francisco Chronicle*, p. A1.

Lawrence vs. Texas, 539 U.S. 558 (2003).

Loving vs. Virginia, 388 U.S. 1 (1967).

McClurg, A. J. (2003). A thousand words are worth a picture: A privacy tort response to consumer data profiling. *Northwestern University Law Review, 98*, 63-143.

Melvin vs. Reid, 297 P. 91 (Cal. 1931).

Nakashima, E. (2007a, Nov. 23). Cellphone tracking powers on request. *Washington Post*, p. A1.

Nakashima, E. (2007b, Nov. 30). Feeling betrayed, Facebook users force site to honor their privacy. *Washington Post*, p. A1.

Nelson vs. Salem State College, 845 N.E.2d 338 (Mass. 2006).

O'Connor vs. Ortega, 480 U.S. 709 (1987).

O'Harrow Jr., R. (2005). *No place to hide*. New York: Simon & Schuster, Inc.

Olmstead v. U.S., 277 U.S. 438 (1928).

Orwell, G. (1949). *Nineteen eighty-four*. New York: Harcourt, Brace and Company.

Penenberg, A. (1999, Nov. 29). The end of privacy. *Forbes*, p. 182.

Perez, J. C. (2007, Nov. 30). Facebook's Beacon more intrusive than previously thought. *PC World*. Retrieved Dec. 4, 2007, from http://www.pcworld.com/article/id,140182-c,onlineprivacy/article.html.

Posner, R. A. (1984). An economic theory of privacy. In F.D. Schoeman (Ed.) *Philosophical dimensions of privacy: An anthology* (pp. 333-345). New York, NY: Cambridge University Press.

Privacy Act of 1974, 5 U.S.C. § 552a (2007).

Privacy Protection Act of 1980, 42 U.S.C. § 2000aa (2007).

Prosser, W. L. (1960). Privacy. *California Law Review, 48*, 383-423.

Reidenberg, J. R. (2003). Privacy wrongs in search of remedies. *Hastings Law Journal, 54*, 877-898.

Remsburg vs. Docusearch, Inc., 816 A.2d 1001 (N.H. 2003).

Restatement (Second) of Torts (1976), § 652B.

Restatement (Second) of Torts (1976), § 652C.

Restatement (Second) of Torts (1976), § 652D.

Restatement (Second) of Torts (1976), § 652E.

Right to Financial Privacy Act of 1978, Pub. L. No. 95-630.

Roe vs. Wade, 410 U.S. 113 (1973).

Rosen, J. (2000). *The unwanted gaze*. New York: Random House.

Rule, J. B. (2007). *Privacy in peril*. New York: Oxford University Press.

Seaphus vs. Lilly, 691 F. Supp. 127, 132 (N.D. Ill. 1988).

Schwartz, N. (2007, Dec. 9). Blogger threatens LA campus shooting. *Denver Post*. Retrieved Dec. 9, 2007, from http://www.denverpost.com/breakingnews/ci_7674486.

Schwartz, P. M. (1995). Privacy and participation: Personal information and public sector regulation in the United States. *Iowa Law Review, 80*, 553-618.

Schwartz, P. M. (2004). Property, privacy, and personal data. *Harvard Law Review, 117*, 2055-2128.

Shibley vs. Time, Inc., 341 N.E.2d 337 (Ohio Ct. App. 1975).

Singel, R. (2007, Nov. 6). FBI mined grocery store records to find Iranian terrorists, CQ reports—Updated. Retrieved Nov. 10, 2007, from http://blog.wired.com/27bstroke6/2007/11/fbi-mined-groce.html.

Slobogin, C. (2005). Transaction surveillance by the government. *Mississippi Law Journal, 75*, 139-190.

Smith vs. Maryland, 442 U.S. 735 (1979).

Solove, D. J. (2001). Privacy and power: Computer databases and metaphors for information privacy. *Stanford Law Review, 53*, 1393-1462.

Solove, D. J. (2002a). Access and aggregation: Public records, privacy and the Constitution. *Minnesota Law Review, 86*, 1137-1218.

Solove, D. J. (2002b). Digital dossiers and the dissipation of Fourth Amendment privacy. *Southern California Law Review, 75*, 1083-1167.

Solove, D. J. (2006). A taxonomy of privacy. *University of Pennsylvania Law Review, 154*, 477-564.

Stanley vs. Georgia, 394 U.S. 557 (1969).

Story, L., & Stone, B. (2007, Nov. 30). Facebook retreats on online tracking. *New York Times*, p. C1.

Thai, J. T. (2006). Is data mining ever a search under Justice Stevens's fourth amendment? *Fordham Law Review, 74*, 1731-1757.

Thomson, J. J. (1975). The right to privacy. *Philosophy and Public Affairs, 4*, 295-314.

Tien, L. (2004). Privacy, technology and data mining. *Ohio Northern University Law Review, 30*, 389-415.

Tindall, C. D. (2003). Argus rules: The commercialization of personal information. *Journal of Law, Technology & Policy, 2003*, 181-202.

Tureen vs. Equifax, Inc., 571 F.2d 411 (8th Cir. 1978).

U.S. Constitution, amendment IV.

U.S. Constitution, amendment XIV.

U.S. vs. D'Andrea, 497 F. Supp.2d 117 (D. Mass. 2007).

U.S. vs. Forrester, 495 F.3d 1041 (9th Cir. 2007).

U.S. vs. Karo, 468 U.S. 705 (1984).

U.S. vs. Knotts, 460 U.S. 276 (1983).

U.S. vs. Miller, 425 U.S. 435 (1976).

Vara, V. (2007, Dec. 6). Facebook rethinks tracking. *Wall Street Journal*, p. B4.

Video Privacy Protection Act of 1988, 18 U.S.C. §§ 2710-11(2007).

Warner, R. (2005). Surveillance and the self: Privacy, identity, and technology. *DePaul Law Review, 54*, 847-871.

Warren, S. D., & Brandeis, L. D. (1890). The right to privacy. *Harvard Law Review, 4*, 193-220.

Westin, A. F., & Baker, M. A. (1972). *Databanks in a free society: Computers, record-keeping and privacy.* New York: Quadrangle Books.

Whalen vs. Roe, 429 U.S. 589 (1977).

White, B. (2007, Dec. 6). Watching what you see on the web. *Wall Street Journal*, p. B1.

Zarsky, T. Z. (2002-2003). "Mine your own business!": Making the case for the implications of the data mining of personal information in the forum of public opinion. *Yale Journal of Law & Technology, 5*, 1-56.

KEY TERMS

Civil Right to Privacy: A form of the legal right to privacy that protects individuals from offensive conduct by other individuals (including businesses).

Constitutional Right to Privacy: A form of the legal right to privacy, derived from the Fourth Amendment to the U.S. Constitution, that protects individuals from government intrusions.

Cookies: Computer files stored on Internet users' computers by Web sites visited by the users. Cookies allow Web sites to track Internet activity of users and to customize advertisements shown to individual users.

Data Mining: The application of database technology and techniques (such as statistical analysis and modeling) to uncover hidden patterns and subtle relationships in large amounts of data and to infer rules that allow for the prediction of future results.

Expectation of Privacy: The legal right to privacy is dependent upon a reasonable expectation of privacy for any given situation. One should not expect a right to privacy in openly public information.

Fourth Amendment to the U.S. Constitution: "The right of the people to be secure in their persons, houses, papers, and effects, against unreasonable searches and seizures, shall not be violated, and no Warrants shall issue, but upon probable cause, supported by Oath or affirmation, and particularly describing the place to be searched, and the persons or things to be seized." The U.S. Supreme Court has found an implied right to privacy from certain government intrusions based upon the Fourth Amendment.

Right to Privacy: An amorphous and contextual legal right; commonly described as the right to be left alone.

Transactional Data: Records associated with individual commercial transactions, particularly a purchase made using a credit card.

Chapter XI
Privacy in Trajectory Data

Aris Gkoulalas-Divanis
University of Thessaly, Greece

Vassilios S. Verykios
University of Thessaly, Greece

ABSTRACT

In this era of significant advances in telecommunications and GPS sensors technology, a person can be tracked down to proximity of less than 5 meters. This remarkable progress enabled the offering of services that depend on user location (the so-called location-based services—LBSs), as well as the existence of applications that analyze movement data for various purposes. However, without strict safeguards, both the deployment of LBSs and the mining of movement data come at a cost of privacy for the users, whose movement is recorded. This chapter studies privacy in both online and offline movement data. After introducing the reader to this field of study, we review state-of-the-art work for location and trajectory privacy both in LBSs and in trajectory databases. Then, we present a qualitative evaluation of these works, pointing out their strengths and weaknesses. We conclude the chapter by providing our point of view regarding the future trends in trajectory data privacy.

INTRODUCTION

Privacy is a fundamental right for every human being. As well stated in Alderman & Kennedy (1997), "Privacy covers many things. It protects the solitude necessary for creative thought. It allows us the independence that is part of raising a family. It protects our right to be secure in our own homes and possessions, assured that the government cannot come barging in. Privacy also encompasses our right to self-determination and to define who we are. Although we live in a world of noisy self-confession, privacy allows us to keep certain facts to ourselves if we so choose. The right to privacy, it seems, is what makes us civilized". However, as technology increasingly permeates society, new means are becoming available that in the wrong hands can lead to the breach of people's privacy. The currently available technological equipment along with the recent achievements in computational analysis, enable the collection, storage and in-depth analysis of huge piles of personal data in a matter of a few minutes. As an effect, it has become now more important than it was ever before, to identify new ways to protect the individuals' right to privacy. This chapter deals with a specific form of privacy that involves the collection and analysis of location and trajectory data, and discusses privacy preservation techniques by means of modern technology. The location/trajectory privacy, as is called, refers to the right of individuals to keep their whereabouts unknown to untrusted third entities. In what follows, we discuss the currently available means for the collection and the analysis of both location and trajectory data, we indicate the severe threats that these can pose to user privacy and we motivate the rest of this work.

Database management systems (DBMSs) are typically capable of collecting, storing and analyzing millions of data in an efficient manner. In the majority of the cases, the involved data is relational, consisting of transactions that are building upon a set of basic data types (e.g., integer/floating point numbers and variable length strings) and organized in tables with references among them. To efficiently handle this data, the database engine contains various functions that can be applied either to manipulate or to query the stored information. Soon enough, the necessity for storing and analyzing more complex information, than the one adhering to the basic types, became apparent and led the DBMS vendors to upgrade the functionality of their products. A first major extension regarded the handling of temporal data, such that the stored transactions can carry timestamps denoting the date and/or time of an event. This extension made possible e.g., the issuing of queries regarding events that took place over a given period of time or calculations involving date/time data. It also made possible the storing and efficient manipulation of time series data, such as information related to weather forecasting, to banking transactions or to

financial data. A second, and much more recent, extension of DBMSs regarded the appropriate handling of spatial data. This was made possible through the use of spatial geometries that support either Euclidean (flat-earth) data, or geography, ellipsoidal (round-earth) data, involving GPS latitude and longitude coordinates. To allow for the storing and manipulation of spatial data, a new data type, known as (*spatial*) *geometry*, was employed in the database products of vendors such as Oracle, IBM and Microsoft. Through the use of this data type, a transaction can contain information regarding e.g., the location of a store, or the extent of a football field. Furthermore, the handling of the spatial data through the DBMS functions, allows for creating queries that return the nearest neighbors of a given geometry, depict the spatial relations that exist among a set of geometries (e.g., overlap, disjoint, contains, etc) or calculate non-spatial information, such as the perimeter or the area of a geometry. The most recent extension of DBMSs is in academic stage and regards the handling of spatio-temporal data, where an entity is referenced both in space and time (Pelekis & Theodoridis 2006). This extension allows a DBMS to manipulate movement data, such as moving vehicles, and is expected to be officially supported in the future releases of all the major commercial database products.

Apart from the advances in the database industry, significant advances have also taken place in telecommunications and in GPS sensors technology. The offering of personalized Location Based Services (LBSs) is one of the most remarkable evidence of this progress by allowing mobile subscribers, equipped with positioning devices, to access a set of high-end spatially-aware services. In the typical use of such a service, the mobile subscriber communicates his or her position to the telecom provider and asks for a location based service, such as the nearest pharmacy or routing instructions to a certain place (e.g., a restaurant). Upon receiving this information, the telecom provider performs a query to the database to reveal the respective geometries and processes them appropriately in order to offer the requested service to the user.

Finally, nowadays there exist numerous data mining techniques that offer in depth analysis of both location and movement data. From the spatial perspective, approaches such as Estivill-Castro & Murray (1998) analyze location data to identify spatial relationships. On the other hand, from the temporal perspective, approaches like the work of Ale & Rossi (2000) provide insight on the temporal dimension of the movement data. Other approaches, like the one of Peuquet & Wentz (1994) are capable of analyzing both the spatial and the temporal dimension of the movement data.

With all this plethora of available means, it becomes evident that the new computing paradigm is challenging the way people live and work. However, it also poses a series of challenges as it touches upon delicate privacy issues. The European directive 2002/58/EC, as well as the US Privacy Act, require telecom providers to adopt techniques to ensure data security and privacy. For example, the EC directive states, among others, that "the provider of a publicly available electronic communication service must take appropriate technical and organizational measures to safeguard the security of its services having regard to the state of the art", and also that "when location data relating to users can be processed, such data can only be processed when they are made anonymous or with the consent of the user".

As is evident, without the existence of strict safeguards, the deployment of LBSs comes at a cost of privacy for the user, whose location is transmitted to the provider of the service. Especially in the case of dynamic routing, where traffic and other related information need to be taken into account when guiding the user to his or her target, the necessity of consecutive location transmissions causes the whole user trajectory to become exposed to the telecom provider. This fact constitutes a serious threat to the privacy of the user, since his or her identity along with certain behavioral aspects, can easily be revealed. For example, consider a user who everyday travels from home to work and for whom the telecom provider has knowledge of his or her itinerary. By utilizing this knowledge, one can easily track the user down to his or her house and thus reveal his/her identity. Furthermore, by utilizing information regarding the places that a person regularly visits, it is possible to identify personal preferences and create a user profile. Such a profile can lead to abuse scenarios that range from unsolicited advertising to 24 hour surveillance.

A similar situation can occur when datasets containing user location or movement data, collected by a trusted service, are disclosed to untrusted third parties. As an example, consider the Octopus smart RFID card, commonly used by Hong Kong residents both for transportation and for selected point-of-sale payments at convenience stores, supermarkets, on-street parking meters, etc. Currently, the Octopus company accumulates, for internal purposes, a large amount of movement data on a daily basis. Consider the scenario that this movement data is made accessible to a shopping chain, such as Wal-Mart, even after properly hiding the IDs of the customers included in the data. Then, whenever a person uses his or her Octopus card to pay at a Wal-Mart store, this transaction will be recorded both in the Wal-Mart's database and in the database of the Octopus company. After a number of visits at any Wal-Mart store, the person will be easily matched to the appropriate entry of the Octopus database. As a result, a large portion of the person's activities during each day, involving multiple and different locations, will be made known to employees at Wal-Mart. Clearly, this constitutes an important privacy breach.

In what follows, we define privacy for both location and trajectory data, and we present some of the most commonly followed research directions to address this issue. Through a set of research works, the reader is introduced to this fascinating field of study and is informed about the capabilities and the limitations of the current state of the art approaches. After presenting the existing research directions, we perform a qualitative evaluation of the presented methodologies and highlight their strengths and weaknesses. Finally, we discuss over the open issues and the future trends in the field of trajectory privacy, based on the existing and unmet privacy requirements.

BACKGROUND

The collection of location data through mobile devices, such as cellular phones, can be achieved with an accuracy that ranges from a few meters to a few hundred meters, depending on the existence of any special hardware to the mobile device. A transmission of the current location of a user, through his or her mobile device, is known as a *location update*, and reflects the x, y-coordinates where the user resides at current time t. Given a set of consecutive location updates transmitted by the same individual, it is possible to approximate the itinerary that the user followed at the respective time period. This approximation is called a *trajectory* of the user and in its simplest form is found by joining together the consecutive location updates. Generally speaking, the quality of the achieved approximation is an immediate consequence of the rate and the accuracy of the transmitted location updates.

Prior to defining trajectory privacy, we proceed to define the notion of location privacy. In *location privacy* the location of a user needs to be appropriately concealed from unauthorized entities. In the case of LBSs, this can be achieved either by refraining from reporting this information to the unauthorized entities or by appropriately blurring the information prior to releasing it. In the latter case, the so-called cloaking methodologies reduce the accuracy / granularity of the information that is transmitted to the third parties, such that it can no longer be used to trace the corresponding user.

On the other hand, in *trajectory privacy*, parts of users' trajectories instead of specific locations, have to be protected from disclosure. Privacy methodologies for trajectory data (e.g., Gidofalvi, Huang & Pedersen 2007, Abul, Bonchi & Nanni 2008) aim at obfuscating a user trajectory such that it becomes indistinguishable from a set of other trajectories. In this way, it becomes almost impossible for an adversary to accurately match a set of user trajectories to the respective users. An interesting insight regarding location and trajectory privacy is that these two types of privacy are strongly related. This is due to the definition of a trajectory as the approximation of the user movement based on a series of location updates. As it becomes evident, there are situations at which location privacy techniques (e.g., Gruteser & Grunwald 2003, Gkoulalas-Divanis, Verykios & Mokbel 2007) can be applied on consecutive location updates, building up a trajectory, to offer trajectory privacy. Due to this strong relation that exists among these two types of privacy, in what follows we present approaches that belong in either of these fields.

LOCATION AND TRAJECTORY PRIVACY MODELS

In this section, we review the basic research directions in the field of location and trajectory privacy. As presented in Figure 1, the existing approaches can be classified into four broad categories: (i) hardware policy-based approaches, (ii) K-anonymity approaches, (iii) confusion-based approaches, and (iv) trajectory hiding approaches. The first three categories collect methodologies that are suitable for systems which handle online requests for location data. The last category involves approaches that are specifically targeted for offline trajectory data.

Figure 1. A classification of the available privacy approaches for trajectory data

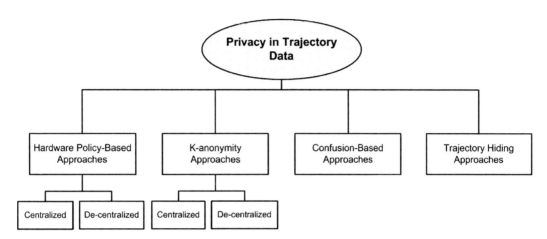

Hardware Policy-Based Approaches

The first generation of location privacy techniques was mostly based on assumptions regarding the properties of specific types of networks, especially the GSM (e.g. Kesdogan, Reichl & Junghartchen 1998). They operated by controlling the access to individuals' location data based on what is known as a *location policy*. Location policies state who and when a subject is allowed to get location information concerning a specific individual. Currently, there are several known types of policies, as well as special languages for their specification. Existing policy-based approaches can be classified as either centralized or decentralized.

An example of a centralized approach that relies on special-purpose equipment appears in the work of Smailagic & Kogan (2002). The authors consider a private wireless LAN that consists of a series of access points and a central server. The LAN interconnects a set of users and resources in the Carnegie Mellon University. Each user, based on his or her current location, is assigned to an access point. As the users move between access points, these assignments change and the information has to be accordingly updated and recorded in the central server. To communicate,

the individuals need to have knowledge regarding the location of the user that they wish to contact. This is made available through the central server that provides the access point of the target user. By utilizing this information, along with the signal strength of the user devices, the central server infers the distance between the client and the access points. The location privacy of the individuals is achieved by having the user decide to whom will allow access to his or her location information and thus to control whether the central server will disseminate this information to the requesting parties. This is accomplished through the specification of user policies.

Priyantha, Chakraborty & Balakrishnan (2000) present Cricket, an indoor, decentralized system that consists of special hardware user mobile devices equipped with location sensors. In Cricket, users can determine their position through the location sensors that exist in their devices, as opposed to the building infrastructure. Without the need for centralized tracking, the users can conceivably decide when and to whom this data should be advertised. Moreover, through an active map, sent from a map server application, the users gain knowledge regarding the available services in their vicinity and can choose the ones they wish to use. On the negative side, this solution does not address the scenario when location information is intentionally reveled in order to provide for LBS. Furthermore, it requires users to carry powerful, special designed devices.

Location K-Anonymity Approaches

The second category of privacy approaches collects methodologies that make use of the location K-anonymity principle. Anonymity techniques operate by depersonalizing the data prior to its release. They are based on the premise that the precise location information that is transmitted by the user cannot be used to re-identify the subject. Each user through his or her mobile device can issue a request, defined as a tuple in the form of $R = (sid, x, y, t, data)$, where sid is the identification number of the requested service and data is an optional field that contains service specific information. A user is said to be *K-anonymous* when sending a request R, if the location information that is released to an untrusted third party points to at least K individuals (one of whom is the requester) who may have issued this request. These K individuals are said to comprise the anonymity set of the requester. Depending on the properties of the anonymity set, such as its extent and the location of the users within its region, in the best case scenario, the actual requester can be identified with a probability of only $1/K$. This is the best privacy that can be offered by an anonymity set of size K. In what follows, we present two approaches for the offering of location anonymity in LBSs.

Gruteser & Grunwald (2003) are the first to propose the offering of location anonymity in LBSs through the reduction of both the spatial and the temporal resolutions of the user location. In this work, the authors assume the existence of a central trusted server, whose task is to anonymize location data prior to sending it to the telecom provider. To do so, it first applies a spatial <u>cloaking</u> strategy whose purpose is to generalize the location of request to reduce its resolution. This is achieved by recursive subdivision of the total area that is covered by the anonymizer into equi-size quadrants. At each point, the quadrant that contains the requester is subdivided into new quadrants, until the selected area contains K subjects who may be using location services within this area (and therefore may have sent this request). This last quadrant is the one that is forwarded as part of the user request to the telecom provider. An orthogonal approach to spatial cloaking is temporal cloaking. The proposed methodology allows for a higher accuracy in the spatial domain, by reducing the temporal accuracy related to the time of request. The key idea is to delay the servicing of the request until K-1 other users have visited the (generalized) area of the requester. This area is captured by performing limited spatial <u>cloaking</u> to achieve a pre-specified spatial resolution. Then, the actual time of request is substituted with a time interval starting at some moments before the actual time of request R and ending at the current time of the system. The cloaked request is then forwarded to the service provider.

Chow, Mokbel & Liu (2006) identify two shortcomings regarding the centralized privacy preserving algorithms. First, the trusted server that is assigned the anonymization task can easily become the system bottleneck or single point of failure. Second, since the trusted server collects the exact locations of the users, it may pose a serious privacy threat when being attacked by adversaries. For these reasons, the authors propose a decentralized, peer-to-peer (P2P) approach for the offering of location privacy. Unlike centralized approaches, in the decentralized setting the peers handle themselves the task of privacy preservation through a set of mutual communications. The proposed P2P spatial cloaking algorithm proceeds as follows. First, the entire system area is divided into a grid and the mobile user that wants to issue a request for an LBS, searches the network for the location of K-1 peers in order to achieve

K-anonymity. To do so, it broadcasts a special type of request, along with the hop distance to its neighboring peers, and waits for the reply from its neighboring peers. Then, it forms a group with the identified peers and blurs its exact location into the corresponding spatial region where all the K peers move. If the formulated region of the K subjects falls below a given minimum area threshold, the mobile device of the user extends this area to satisfy this requirement. Finally, to address the issue of locating the querying mobile device by using cellular positioning techniques, a mobile user (among the K-1) is randomly selected by the requester, in order to conduct all the necessary communications on his or her behalf and to communicate to the requester the outcome of the service. The P2P spatial cloaking algorithm operates in two modes: on demand and proactive. When operating on demand, the mobile user executes the algorithm when it needs to request an LBS. On the other hand, in proactive mode, the mobile user periodically executes the algorithm in the background and thus is capable of immediately cloaking its location into a spatial region, when in need to request an LBS. Through experimental evaluation, the authors demonstrate good scalability properties of their methodology and its effectiveness in providing high quality services without the need of exact location information.

A different centralized K-anonymity approach can be found in the work of Gkoulalas-Divanis, Verykios & Mokbel (2007). An interesting decentralized methodology can be found in the work of Ghinita, Kalnis & Skiadopoulos (2007). It is important to mention that all these approaches assume that the telecom provider is capable of servicing imprecise queries for LBSs.

Confusion-Based Approaches

Confusion-based approaches can be classified to the field of privacy preservation in adversarial data mining (Aggarwal, Pei & Zhang 2006). These approaches operate by devising simple ways to blur the actual location of the users through fuzification techniques that reduce the confidence of the telecom provider regarding the real location of the user. There are several ways that this can be accomplished. For example, Beresford & Stajano (2003) propose a strategy to split user movement trajectories into unlinkable segments. They introduce the concept of a mix zone, a spatial region in which none among a set of users has registered any application callback. Assuming a trusted station that periodically collects the location of the users, the proposed approach utilizes mix zones to frequently change the pseudonyms of the users (that is the ids that the users have in the system), thus protect their privacy. Since applications do not receive any location information from the users that are in a mix zone, the trusted station achieves to "mix" the user identities. As an effect, when a user exits the mix zone, the applications are unable to tell who the user is, among the users that entered the zone. In that sense, a mix zone is an analogy of a black box that protects the user identities, offering location privacy to the users.

Kido, Yanagisawa & Satoh (2005) propose an anonymous communication technique that protects the location privacy of individuals by introducing several false position data (dummies) along with the true location updates of the users. As an effect, even if the service providers store location data, they cannot be certain about the whereabouts of the real users. On the client side, the mobile device of the user is capable of disregarding answers sent from the service provider that involve dummies and present to the user only the answers involving his or her true location updates. The challenge in the proposed methodology is to achieve realistic dummy movements that will confuse an adversary to identify the actual user movement, and to minimize the communication overhead that is introduced by the dummies on the server side, i.e. the telecom provider. To achieve the first target, the authors propose two dummy generation algorithms that attempt to model real user movement. In both algorithms, the initial locations of the dummies are randomly selected. In the first algorithm, the next position of a dummy is tight to be in the neighborhood of the current position of the dummy. To achieve that, the user device memorizes the last location of the dummy and generates dummies around this location. On the other hand, the second dummy generation algorithm is applicable when the mobile device of the user can acquire and receive the location of other users. In this case, the dummies are generated in the vicinity of these users, while special care is taken to ensure that the density of the users in the generated region remains within acceptable bounds. To minimize the communication overhead that is introduced by the dummies on the server side, the authors propose a compression technique along with four strategies that a user can follow to send information unrelated to position data to the service provider.

Trajectory Hiding Approaches

Trajectory hiding approaches operate on offline movement data, recorded for a set of individuals. The target of these methodologies is to sanitize an input database, such that the trajectories that it contains can no longer be associated to specific individuals. This research direction is relatively new and few approaches have been proposed so far. In this section, we investigate a recent approach that uses trajectory K-anonymity along with clustering (Jain & Dubes 1988) to construct the sanitized database.

Abul, Bonchi & Nanni (2008) propose a trajectory K-anonymity technique that anonymizes a database of trajectories by exploiting the inherent uncertainty regarding the whereabouts of the moving objects. As the authors state, due to the inherent imprecision of sampling and positioning systems, trajectories of moving objects can no longer be considered as 3D polylines, consisting of (x, y, t) elements. Instead, the authors represent the uncertainty of a trajectory using a cylindrical volume that consists of a series of disks, defined for the different time intervals of user movement. The sampling time is assumed to be the same for all trajectories and within each time interval the object is assumed to move linearly and at a constant speed. Depending on the radius of the cylinder, it is possible that more than one trajectories fall into the same cylinder. If this so happens for K trajectories, then the cylinder that contains them formulates an anonymity set of size K. To enforce trajectory anonymity in the database, the authors consider a variant of the greedy clustering technique that constraints the radius of the identified clusters and represents the best trade-off between effectiveness and efficiency.

The proposed clustering algorithm proceeds as follows. First, the farthest trajectory from the dataset center is selected. Second, a sequence of pivot trajectories are chosen, such that each one is the farthest trajectory from the previous pivot. Third, the K-1 trajectories that are nearest to each selected pivot are captured as a cluster. Given a threshold of maximum radius for a cluster, the algorithm ensures that the co-clustered objects do not produce a cluster that violates the threshold. Finally, each remaining (unclustered) trajectory is included to the cluster of its nearest pivot, provided once again that it does not violate the maximum radius threshold. In any case, if a trajectory is selected to be added to a cluster and this leads to the violation of the maximum radius threshold, the trajectory is simply trashed. Another interesting trajectory hiding approach can be found in the work of Gidofalvi, Huang & Pedersen (2007).

QUALITATIVE EVALUATION

In this section, we provide a qualitative comparison of the approaches presented so far, in order to demonstrate their strengths and weaknesses, and when each of these should be used. Table 1

Table 1. A short summary of the pros and cons of the various privacy methodologies

Methodology	Strengths	Weaknesses
Hardware policy-based	excellent choice for confined environments with specific needs	hardware limitations, costly equipment, low scalability
Location K-anonymity	cheap equipment, adequate scalability, can be personalized to cover the privacy needs of each individual	decentralized approaches suffer from large communication overhead; centralized approaches have a single point of failure (trusted server)
Confusion-based	efficiency, adequate scalability,	reliance on somewhat unrealistic assumptions, not very practical
Trajectory Hiding	high efficiency, shown to perform well in various tested settings	unrealistic assumptions of users' movement, high dependence on parameters/thresholds

presents a short summary of the pros and cons in the various privacy methodologies.

The special hardware policy-based approaches depend highly on a set of assumptions regarding the hardware that is used for the client mobile devices, the type of wireless network and the other components of the system. These approaches are shown to operate well in small scale systems involving few users and limited network coverage. However, their dependence on hardware makes them inappropriate for a larger scale deployment, both due to the cost of the equipment and to their low scalability. On the other hand, these approaches are excellent choices in confined environments with specific needs. The Cricket system of Priyantha, Chakraborty & Balakrishnan (2000) is more appropriate for a larger number of users, since its decentralized architecture enables it to cope with several concurrent requests. On other hand, Cricket requires expensive client devices that need to conduct powerful calculations in order to conform to the adopted communication protocol. This is an immediate consequence of its decentralized nature, a fact that is avoided in the centralized system of Smailagic & Kogan (2002).

As in the case of policy-based approaches, the location K-anonymity methodologies are either centralized or decentralized. The basic advantage of a decentralized architecture is that it avoids the use of a trusted server that is usually the single point of failure in a large scale system, involving thousands of users. However, decentralized approaches require extra communication overhead, since each user has to identify his or her anonymity set and formulate the corresponding request that is then forwarded to the telecom provider. This overhead can be substantial, and thus special measures need to be applied to reduce it. The proactive mode of operation, presented by Chow, Mokbel & Liu (2006) is one possible measure. On the other hand, centralized approaches assume the existence of a trusted server who has knowledge of the user locations for all the users of the system at any time instant. Thus, the calculation of the anonymity set of the requester is a straightforward process, involving fewer operations than in the case of a decentralized architecture. The limitation of the centralized approaches, such as the one of Gruteser & Grunwald (2003), becomes evident when multiple requests for LBSs have to be processed simultaneously by the trusted server, which has limited computational and communication resources.

Confusion-based approaches offer an alternative to K-anonymity that is independent of the used hardware. The mix zones of Beresford & Stajano (2003) "mix" the identities of the users that cross them, such that the identity of users exiting the mix zone cannot be safely matched to that of users entering the zone. Although the proposed idea is interesting, it suffers from several shortcomings. First, it relies on a rather unrealistic assumption; the existence of regions where no user has registered any application callback. This is a rather uncommon situation and, when considered along the fact that many users should coincide in the mix zone in order to make sense to perform the mix, it constitutes the approach even less applicable. Another shortcoming is based on the fact that the entry point of a user in the mix zone, considered together with the previous movement of the user, usually provides a good estimate on the exit point of the user from the mix zone. Thus, the privacy that is offered by this approach is directly related not only to the number of the users that are simultaneously in the mix zone but also to the entry points of the users and their previous movement behavior. On the positive side, the algorithm that performs the mix is efficient and scalable, even in the case of too many people being within the mix zone.

Compared to this approach, the methodology of Kido, Yanagisawa & Satoh (2005) does not suffer from these shortcomings. However, its applicability to real world problems is also limited. First of all, since the real location of the user is hindered through the false location of the dummies, an equivalent of K-anonymity would be offered by this approach when K-1 dummy locations are generated along the real location of a request. This means that K messages should be served by the service provider, among which only one is actually useful to the user. As an effect, both the communication overhead on the client and the server side, and the computation overhead

on the server side (which needs to process all the K requests) will be very high. This fact makes unrealistic the use of the technique in a large scale system. Another issue involves the dummy generation algorithm. The generated dummies should resemble as much as possible the real user and their movement should be continued for as long as the user moves in order to adequately protect his or her privacy. Furthermore, the dummies should interact with the actual user movement (e.g., by creating some crossings between the real user trajectory and those of the dummies) in order to create a vicinity where the adversary can be confused regarding the actual user location. This means that the user mobile device should be powerful enough to execute the dummy generation algorithm, to produce the necessary amount of dummies, and to handle their movement. A final point regards the practicality of the approach. In a real case scenario the use of LBSs comes at a cost based on the number of times that an LBS is used. By using this approach, when a user requests a single LBS he or she will be charged for K requests.

In contrast to the previous methodologies that involve online requests for LBSs, the trajectory hiding approach of Abul, Bonchi & Nanni (2008) operates on offline movement data, collected in a database of moving objects. On the positive side, to the best of our knowledge this is the best approach so far for the offering of privacy in offline trajectory data and is proved to experience high efficiency. For instance, compared to the work of Gidofalvi, Huang & Pedersen (2007), the representation of uncertainty by means of a cylinder rather than a grid serves much better the model of trajectory anonymity and introduces less distortion to the trajectory data. However, the algorithm of Abul, Bonchi & Nanni (2008), suffers from several shortcomings and is based on some unrealistic assumptions. First, unlike in Gidofalvi, Huang & Pedersen (2007), the sampling time is assumed to be the same for all the trajectories. This is far from realistic, since it would mean that users start and end their movement at certain, common time. The authors propose the allowance of small time gaps or the selection of coarser time samplings to circumvent this problem; however both proposed solutions have limited usefulness. Another shortcoming involves the assumption of linear movement and constant speed of the objects within each considered time interval. Finally, the clustering approach that is followed to identify the anonymity sets in the dataset can lead to solutions where many trajectories are trashed, since they violate the maximum radius threshold for the clusters. The maximum radius threshold is highly related to the quality of the hiding solution. When small, it leads to coherent clusters, where the trajectories are near each other and formulate a representative anonymity set; however, it can potentially lead to a large amount of trajectories being trashed. On the other hand, when the threshold is large, it leads to few trajectories being trashed but the quality of the produced anonymity sets (equiv. clusters) is expected to be low. As one can observe, the selection of this threshold is of vital importance for the success of the methodology and the best value of the threshold is bound to change from dataset to dataset.

FUTURE TRENDS

The offering of privacy in trajectory data is an emerging field with a wide variety of applications, ranging from the handling of online trajectory data in LBSs to the sanitization of offline movement data. It is our belief that this field of study is bound to proceed in two principal research directions: (i) handling of online trajectory data in LBSs, and (ii) handling of offline trajectory data stored in databases. In what follows, we discuss open research issues and provide a roadmap for each of these directions.

Online Trajectory Data in LBSs

The offering of online user trajectory privacy is considered as the offspring of location privacy methodologies for LBSs. According to our opinion, research in this direction will proceed along, at least, two lines. First, the proposal of novel algorithms that offer trajectory privacy in LBSs. Second, the incorporation of such algorithms, along with security-based approaches, into unified frameworks that can be employed by telecom providers that offer LBSs.

Along the first line, we expect in the future to witness trajectory privacy approaches that make use of the properties of the underlying networks of user movement, such as the one of Gkoulalas-Divanis, Verykios & Mokbel (2007), instead of being based on the simplistic assumption of a free terrain. Furthermore, we believe that more efficient approaches will be devised, with a scalability that will allow them to be used in a real world scale. Relevant questions that need to be properly addressed in future work, include the following (i) if a location is anonymous, how can we ensure that a sequence of locations, occupied by the same individual, also remain anonymous? (ii) how can we measure and quantify trajectory K-anonymity? (iii) in K-anonymity approaches, what is a reasonable value of K and which parameters influence its selection?

Along the second line, approaches like the work of Damiani & Bertino (2006) that share several characteristics of both access control-based and policy-based methodologies are expected to appear. Access control (Hengartner & Steenkiste 2003) is the mechanism that guarantees the security of individuals' information after its collection and storage in the system. It achieves this goal by controlling the access of individuals to the sensitive resources and by defining the type of operations that each individual is allowed to accomplish. On the other hand, policy-based methodologies protect the privacy of an individual's information pre data collection. As we demonstrated earlier, this is typically achieved by restricting the granularity of the returned location information regarding a user's current location. Approaches that combine the characteristics of access control-based and policy-based methodologies achieve to provide a solution on both the issues of individual privacy and security of collected sensitive data. However, a comprehensive and flexible architectural framework is still missing. Such architecture should integrate different functionalities including, but not limited to, user authentication, service customization, privacy preservation, and system administration and control.

Offline Trajectory Data in Databases

The hiding of user trajectory data collected in a database is the most recent research direction in trajectory data privacy. Very few works have been proposed so far, each considering a different type of privacy and using different measures to evaluate the quality of the approach. The work of Abul, Bonchi & Nanni (2008) is certainly a good start point for future research proposals on this domain. However, we believe that the reason that constitutes this research direction so unexplored is the fact that several properties related to movement data are currently under investigation. For example, to perform clustering one need to have knowledge of a similarity or distance metric that defines when objects are similar enough to be clustered together. However, little research has been performed so far on computing the nearest neighbors of a trajectory (Frentzos, Gratsias, Pelekis & Theodoridis 2007), thus finding a commonly acceptable similarity measure that is suitable for moving object trajectories. On that grounds, an approach like the one of Abul, Bonchi & Nanni (2008) that reduces to trajectory clustering, cannot make use of a publicly acceptable measure to identify the clusters.

We believe that light should be shed on several issues that are also currently under investigation. For instance, (i) when are two trajectories similar and how can this similarity being quantified? (ii) how should the uncertainty regarding the actual user movement, that is inherent in a trajectory, be modeled? (iii) how can we avoid to make unreal assumptions regarding user movement (such as linearity of movement and/or constant speed between consecutive location updates) and still be capable of accurately manipulating the data? (iv) what happens when trajectories partially overlap in time (e.g., T_1 = [5, 10], T_2 = [9-12]). Can such trajectories be co-clustered? and finally, (v) since trajectories represent user movement and different users are bound to experience different requirements for privacy and to follow different routes on a daily basis, isn't it sensible to use different degrees of privacy to protect each individual's trajectories (or to automatically identify and protect the sensitive parts of their trajectories) ?

CONCLUSION

In this chapter we provided an introduction to the field of privacy in trajectory data and presented a selection of the state of the art research works that cover different research directions. Since privacy of trajectory data is a new research field, to better familiarize the reader with its special requirements, we included in our presentation research works that offer location privacy in LBSs. After presenting current research, we provided a qualitative evaluation of the approaches to highlight their strengths and weaknesses. Finally, we discussed open research issues and future trends in trajectory privacy along two basic lines: privacy in online and privacy in offline trajectory data.

REFERENCES

Abul, O., Bonchi, F., & Nanni, M. (2008). Never walk alone: Uncertainty for anonymity in moving objects databases. In *24th International Conference on Data Engineering,* IEEE press.

Aggarwal, C., Pei, J., & Zhang, B. (2006). On privacy preservation against adversarial data mining. In *12th ACM SIGKDD International Conference on Knowledge Discovery and Data Mining*, ACM press.

Alderman, E., & Kennedy, C. (1997). *The right to privacy.* Vintage press.

Ale, J. M., & Rossi, G. H. (2000). An approach to discovering temporal association rules. In *ACM Symposium on Applied Computing*, ACM press.

Beresford, A., & Stajano, F. (2003). Location privacy in pervasive computing. *IEEE Pervasive Computing, 2*(1), 46-55.

Chow, C.-Y., Mokbel, M., & Liu, X. (2006). A peer-to-peer spatial cloaking algorithm for anonymous location based services. In *14th Annual ACM International Symposium on Advances in Geographic Information Systems,* ACM press.

Damiani, M., & Bertino, E. (2006). Access control and privacy in location-aware services for mobile organizations. In *7th International Conference on Mobile Data Management,* IEEE press.

Estivill-Castro, V., & Murray, A. T. (1998). Discovering associations in spatial data-an efficient medoids based approach. *In 2nd Pacific-Asia Conference on Research and Development in Knowledge Discovery and Data Mining (PAKDD '98).* Springer-Verlag press.

Frentzos, E., Gratsias, K., Pelekis, N., & Theodoridis, Y. (2007). Algorithms for nearest neighbor search on moving object trajectories. In *Geoinformatica, 11*(2), 159-193.

Ghinita, G., Kalnis, P., & Skiadopoulos, S. (2007). Prive: Anonymous location-based queries in distributed mobile systems. In *16th International Conference on World Wide Web,* ACM press.

Gidofalvi, G., Huang, X., & Pedersen, T. (2007). Privacy-preserving data mining on moving object trajectories. In *10th ACM International Workshop on Data Warehousing and OLAP,* ACM press.

Gkoulalas-Divanis, A., Verykios, V., & Mokbel, M. (2007). A network aware privacy model for online requests in trajectory data. Technical Report, University of Thessaly.

Gruteser, M., & Grunwald, D. (2003). Anonymous usage of location based services through spatial and temporal cloaking. In *1st International Conference on Mobile Systems, Applications and Services,* ACM press.

Hengartner, U., & Steenkiste, P. (2003). Protecting access to people location information. In *1st International Conference on Security in Pervasive Computing,* LNCS, Springer-Verlag press.

Jain, A. K., & Dubes, R. C. (1988). Algorithms for clustering data. Prentice-Hall, Inc.

Kesdogan, D., Reichl, P., & Junghartchen, K. (1998). Distributed temporary pseudonyms: A new approach for protecting location information in mobile communication networks. In *5th European Symposium on Research in Computer Security.* Springer-Verlag press.

Kido, H., Yanagisawa, Y., & Satoh, T. (2005). An anonymous communication technique using dummies for location based services. In *International Conference on Pervasive Services,* IEEE press.

Pelekis, N., & Theodoridis, Y. (2006). Boosting location-based services with a moving object database engine. In *5th ACM International Workshop on Data Engineering for Wireless and Mobile Access (MobiDE)*, ACM press.

Peuquet, D., & Wentz, E. (1994). An approach for time-based analysis of spatiotemporal data. In *6th International Symposium on Spatial Data Handling*, Advances in GIS Research.

Priyantha, N., Chakraborty, A., & Balakrishnan, H. (2000). The cricket location-support system. In *6th Annual International Conference on Mobile Computing and Networking*, ACM press.

Smailagic, A., & Kogan, D. (2002). Location sensing and privacy in a context-aware computing environment. *IEEE Wireless Communications,* 9(5), 10-17.

KEY TERMS

Anonymity Set: An anonymity set is the set of participants who satisfy the property of K-anonymity. In the context of relational data, an anonymity set is the set of records that satisfy relational K-anonymity. In the context of location data, an anonymity set is the set of participants who (probably) have sent a certain request, as seen by a global observer, during a given time period and from a location that is close to the actual requester. Finally, in the context of trajectory K-anonymity, the anonymity set is defined as the set of trajectories that could belong to a certain user, based on the spatial and the temporal details of the user's movement.

K-Anonymity: We consider three variants of K-anonymity. *Relational K-anonymity* is the state of being indistinguishable along a set of attributes (known as *quasi-identifiers*) from a set of at least K-1 records that are stored in a dataset. *Location K-anonymity* is the state of being indistinguishable from a set of at least K-1 individuals who have send (or could have send) a certain request for an LBS, as seen by a global observer, from within an area that is near to the requester and within a time period that is close to the time of the actual request. *Trajectory K-anonymity* is the state of being indistinguishable from a set of at least K-1 other user trajectories, as seen by a global observer, from within a certain time period.

Location Based Services (LBSs): LBSs are services targeted at mobile subscribers, which provide location specific information to the users. Their use requires knowledge of the current location of the user, typically captured through his or her mobile device. Depending on the type of service, an LBS can be completed within a single or multiple location updates.

Sanitization: Sanitization is the process of applying a hiding methodology on an input dataset in order to produce its privacy-aware version that can safely be disclosed. The privacy-aware version of the dataset (a.k.a. *sanitized* dataset) achieves to protect the sensitive patterns.

Spatial Geometry: A (spatial) geometry is the spatial data type used by DBMSs that offer spatial features, to store spatial data in a database. In that sense, geometry can be any spatial object that the DBMS supports, such as a point, a line, or a polygon. Recent DBMSs support a wide variety of both basic and advanced spatial geometries.

Telecom / Service Provider: A telecom or service provider is the actual content provider of LBSs. In all presented methodologies, the telecom / service provider is considered to be an untrusted third party to whom sensitive data should not be disclosed.

Trusted Server: A trusted server is a component (middleware) in the centralized architecture of a privacy preserving system that is assigned the duty of processing the incoming user requests for LBSs such that the resulting requests satisfy anonymity and can be safely disclosed to untrusted third parties. The server needs to be trusted since it handles sensitive private data.

Chapter XII
Feature Selection for Web Page Classification

K. Selvakuberan
Tata Consultancy Services, India

M. Indra Devi
Thiagarajar College of Engineering, India

R. Rajaram
Thiagarajar College of Engineering, India

ABSTRACT

The World Wide Web serves as a huge, widely distributed, global information service center for news, advertisements, customer information, financial management, education, government, e-commerce and many others. The Web contains a rich and dynamic collection of hyperlink information. The Web page access and usage information provide rich sources for data mining. Web pages are classified based on the content and/or contextual information embedded in them. As the Web pages contain many irrelevant, infrequent, and stop words that reduce the performance of the classifier, selecting relevant representative features from the Web page is the essential preprocessing step. This provides secured accessing of the required information. The Web access and usage information can be mined to predict the authentication of the user accessing the Web page. This information may be used to personalize the information needed for the users and to preserve the privacy of the users by hiding the personal details. The issue lies in selecting the features which represent the Web pages and processing the details of the user needed the details. In this chapter we focus on the feature selection, issues in feature selection, and the most important feature selection techniques described and used by researchers.

INTRODUCTION

There are an estimated 15 to 30 billion pages available in the World Wide Web with millions of pages being added daily. Describing and organizing this vast amount of content is essential for realizing the Web's full potential as an information resource. Automatic classification of Web pages is needed for the following reasons. (a) Large amount of information available in the internet makes it difficult for the human experts to classify them manually (b) The amount of Expertise needed is high (c) Web pages are dynamic and volatile in nature (e) More time and effort are required for classification. (f) Same type of classification scheme may not be applied to all pages (g) More experts needed for classification. Web page classification techniques use concepts from many fields like Information filtering and retrieval, Artificial Intelligence, Text mining, Machine learning techniques and so on. Information filtering and retrieval techniques usually build either a thesauri or indices by analyzing a corpus of already classified texts with specific algorithms. When new text is to be classified, thesaurus and index are used to find the similarity with already existing classification scheme to be associated with this new text.

Until the late 1980s, the most effective approach to Web page classification seemed to be that of manually by building classification systems by means of knowledge-engineering techniques, i.e. manually defining a set of logical rules that encode expert knowledge on how to classify Web page documents under the given set of categories. In the 1990s this perspective has been overturn, and the machine learning paradigm to automated Web page classification has emerged and definitely superseded the knowledge-engineering approach. Within the machine learning paradigm, a general inductive process automatically builds an automatic text classifier by "learning", from a set of previously classified Web documents, the characteristics of the categories of interest. The advantages of this approach are accuracy comparable to human performance and a considerable savings in terms of expert manpower, since no intervention from either knowledge engineers or domain experts is needed. Currently Web page categorization may be seen as the meeting point of machine learning and information retrieval. As Machine Learning aims to address larger, more complex tasks, the problem of focusing on the most relevant information in a potentially overwhelming quantity of data has become increasingly important. For instance, data mining of corporate or scientific records often involves dealing with both many features and many examples, and the internet and World Wide Web have put a huge volume of low-quality information at the easy access of a learning system. Similar issues arise in the personalization of filtering systems for information retrieval, electronic mail, net news, etc.

The main objective of this chapter is to focus on the feature selection techniques, need for feature selection, their issues in Web page classification, feature selection for privacy preserving data mining and the future trends in feature selection.

LITERATURE SURVEY

Rudy Setiono and Huan Liu (1997) proposed that Discretization can turn numeric attributes into discrete ones. χ^2 is a simple algorithm. Principal Component Analysis-compose a small number of new features. It is improved from simple methods such as equi-width and equal frequency intervals. For each and every attributes calculate the χ^2 value for each and every interval. Combine the lowest interval values while approximation.

Shounak Roychowdhury (2001) proposed a technique called granular computing for processing and expressing chunks of information called granules. It reduces hypothesis search space, to reduce storage. Fuzzy set based feature elimination techniques in which subset generation and subset evaluation are employed. For optimal feature selection brute force technique is employed.

Catherine Blake and Wander Pratt (2001) suggested the relationship between the features used to represent the text and the quality model. A comparison of association rules based on three different concepts: words, manually assigned keywords, automatically assigned concepts are made. Bidirectional association rules on concepts or keywords are useful than the words used. Each individual feature should be informative. The quality of features should be meaningful. The concepts and keywords also represent fewer than 90% of the words used in the medical diagnosis.

Martin, Mario and Anil (2004) discuss the various algorithms of clustering and the issues of feature selection such as what attributes and data should be selected. Feature saliency should be maintained. EM algorithm and mixture based clustering are employed. Minimum message length-saliency of irrelevant features is reduced to zero. Methods based on variance (PCA) need not produce best features. The Filter and Wrapper approaches are also employed for feature classification.

Christoph, Nidal Zeidat, and Zhenghong Zhao (2004) proposed an algorithm called supervised clustering. The goal is to identify the class uniform clusters that have high probability densities.

Four algorithms have been suggested.

1. A greedy algorithm with random restart
2. SRIDHCR, that seeks for solutions by inserting and removing single objects from the current solution
3. SPAM (a variation of the clustering algorithm PAM),
4. An evolutionary computing algorithm named SCEC, and a fast medoid-based top-down splitting algorithm, named TDS. The four algorithms were evaluated using a benchmark consisting of four UCI machine learning data sets. Fitness function and Impurity and number of clusters are also taken into account.

Huang, McCullagh, Black (2004) used ReliefF as a feature mining technique that is sensitive to the definition of relevance. It is computationally expensive in handling large data sets. They proposed an optimization algorithm (Feature Selection via Supervised Model Construction) for data transformation and starter selection, and evaluate its effectiveness with C4.5. Frequency based encoding scheme is employed for transforming categorical data into numerical data. The number of instances sampled from the data set determines the selection of features. Experiments are performed on UCI Repository data set and concluded that their proposed supervised model outperforms the other models

WEB PAGE CLASSIFICATION

Web page classification, also known as Web page categorization, is the process of assigning a Web page to one or more predefined category labels. Classification is often posed as a supervised learning problem in which a set of labeled data is used to train a classifier which can be applied to label future examples. The general problem of Web page classification can be divided into multiple sub-problems: subject classification, functional classification, sentiment classification, and other types of classification. Subject classification is concerned about the subject or topic of a Web page. For example, Classifying whether a page is about "arts", "business" or "sports" is an instance of subject classification. Functional classification cares about the role that the Web page plays. For example, deciding a page to be a "personal homepage", "course page" or "admission page" is an instance of functional classification. Sentiment classification focuses on the opinion that is presented in a Web page, i.e., the author's attitude about some particular topic. Based on the number of classes in the problem, classification can be divided into binary classification and multi-class classification, where binary classification categorizes instances into exactly one of two classes positive or negative; or multi-class classification deals with more than two classes. Based on the number of classes that can be assigned to an instance, classification can be divided into single-label classification and multi-label classification. In single-label classification, one and only one class label is to be assigned to each instance, while in multi-label classification, more than one class can be assigned to an instance. If a problem is multi-class, say four-class classification, it means four classes are involved.

Classification plays a vital role in many information management and retrieval tasks. In case of the Web, classification of page content is essential to focused crawling, to the assisted development of Web directories, to topic-specific Web link analysis, and to analysis of the topical structure of the Web. Web page classification can also help improve the quality of Web search. Earlier surveys in Web page classification typically lack a detailed discussion of the utilization of Web specific features. In this chapter, we carefully examine the Web-specific features and algorithms that have been explored and found to be useful for Web page classification. The contributions of this chapter are:

- A detailed review of useful Web-specific features for classification;
- Various feature selection techniques used in classification; and,
- A discussion of future research directions.

WHAT IS FEATURE SELECTION?

Feature extraction or selection is one of the most important steps in pattern recognition or pattern classification, data mining, machine learning and so on. Generally speaking, if only classification information is included sufficiently in the eigenvector, classifier can classify the classification rightly.

However, it is difficult to measure classification information in all features. Data preprocessing is an indispensable step in effective data analysis. It prepares data for data mining and machine learning, which aim to turn data into business intelligence or knowledge. Feature selection is a preprocessing technique commonly used on high dimensional data. Feature selection studies how to select a subset or list of attributes or variables that are used to construct models describing data. Its purposes include reducing dimensionality, removing irrelevant and redundant features, reducing the amount of data needed for learning, improving algorithms' predictive accuracy, and increasing the constructed models' comprehensibility. Feature-selection methods are particularly welcome in interdisciplinary collaborations because the selected features retain the original meanings domain experts are familiar with. The rapid developments in computer science and engineering allow for data collection at an unprecedented speed and present new challenges to feature selection. Wide data sets, which have a huge number of features but relatively few instances, introduce a novel challenge to feature selection.

Need for Feature Selection

The Web pages need 80% of the preprocessing work since the Web pages have large amount of useless information. Data preprocessing describes any type of processing performed on raw data to prepare it for another processing procedure. Commonly used as a preliminary data mining practice, data preprocessing transforms the data into a format that will be more easily and effectively processed for the purpose of the user for example, in a neural network. There are a number of different tools and methods used for preprocessing, including: sampling, which selects a representative subset from a large population of data; transformation, which manipulates raw data to produce a single input; denoising, which removes noise from data; normalization, which organizes data for more efficient access; and feature extraction, which pulls out specified data that is significant in some particular context.

In a customer relationship management (CRM) context, data preprocessing is a component of Web mining. Web usage logs may be preprocessed to extract meaningful sets of data called user transactions, which consist of groups of URL references. User sessions may be tracked to identify the user, the Web sites requested and their order, and the length of time spent on each one. Once these have been pulled out of the raw data, they yield more useful information that can be put to the user's purposes, such as consumer research, marketing, or personalization.

Preprocessing makes it possible for complex homepages to be delivered lightning fast, and lets you significantly increase the number of pages served in an extremely cost-effective manner. The idea of preprocessing content for Web pages grew out of necessity. Preprocessing can be achieved by the following ways:

a. **Removing HTML tags:** HTML tags indicate the formats of Web pages. For instance, the content within <title> and </title> pair is the title of a Web page; the content enclosed by <table> and </table> pair is a table. These HTML tags may indicate the importance of their enclosed content and they can thus help weight their enclosed content. The tags themselves are removed after weighting their enclosed content.

b. **Removing stop words:** Stop words are frequent words that carry little information, such as prepositions, pronouns, and conjunctions. They are removed by comparing the input text with a "stop list" of words.

c. **Removing rare words:** Removing words whose number of occurrences in the text is less than a predefined threshold.

d. **Performing word stemming:** Word stemming is done by grouping words that have the same stem or root, such as computer,

compute, and computing. The Porter stemmer is a well-known algorithm for performing this task.

Issues in Feature Selection

Feature extraction or selection is one of the most important steps in pattern recognition or pattern classification, data mining, machine learning and so on. But the increasing feature brings disadvantages for classification problem. On one hand, feature increased gives difficulties to calculate, because the data occupy more amount of memory space and computerization time, on the other hand, a lot of features include certainly many correlation factors respectively, which results to information repeat and waste. Therefore, we must take measures to decrease the feature dimension under not decreasing recognition effect; this is called the problems of feature optimum extraction or selection. On the other hand the number of features needs to be constrained to reduce noise and to limit the burden on system resources. The number of features needs to be constrained to reduce noise and to limit the burden on system resources.

Characteristics of Selected Features

For the purposes of automated text categorization, features should be:

1. Relatively few in number
2. Moderate in frequency of assignment
3. Low in redundancy
4. Low in noise
5. Related in semantic scope to the classes to be assigned
6. Relatively unambiguous in meaning

DIMENSIONALITY REDUCTION BY FEATURE SELECTION

In statistics, dimension reduction is the process of reducing the number of random variables under consideration, and can be divided into feature selection and feature extraction. Feature selection, also known as variable selection, feature reduction, attribute selection or variable subset selection, is the technique, commonly used in machine learning, of selecting a subset of relevant features for building robust learning models. . By removing most irrelevant and redundant features from the data, feature selection helps improve the performance of learning models by:

- Alleviating the effect of the curse of dimensionality.
- Enhancing generalization capability.
- Speeding up learning process.
- Improving model interpretability.

Feature selection also helps people to acquire better understanding about their data by telling them that which are the important features and how they are related with each other. Feature selection selects a subset of the original feature space based on some criteria. Two broad approaches for feature selection have been presented in the literature: the wrapper approach and the filter approach. The wrapper approach employs a search through the space of feature subsets. It uses an estimated accuracy for a learning algorithm as the measure of goodness for a particular feature subset. Thus the feature selection is being "wrapped around" a learning algorithm. For example, for a neural network algorithm the wrapper approach selects an initial subset of features and measures the performance of the network; then it generates an "improved set of features" and measures the performance of the network. This process is repeated until it reaches a termination condition (either a minimal value of error or a number of iterations). While some wrapper based methods have encountered some success for classification tasks, they are often prohibitively expensive to run and can break down when a very large number of features are present. For the filter approach, feature selection is performed as a preprocessing step before applying machine learning. Thus the method of feature selection is independent to the learning algorithm. The filter algorithm does not incur the high computational cost and is commonly used in classification systems even in a very high feature space.

Feature extraction is a special form of dimensionality reduction.

When the input data to an algorithm is too large to be processed and it is suspected to be notoriously redundant (much data, but not much information) then the input data will be transformed into a reduced representation set of features (also named features vector). Transforming the input data into the set of features is called *features extraction*. If the features extracted are carefully chosen it is expected that the features set will extract the relevant information from the input data in order to perform the desired task using this reduced representation instead of the full size input. Feature extraction involves simplifying the amount of resources required to describe a large set of data accurately. When performing analysis of complex data one of the major problems stems from the number of variables involved. Analysis with a large number of variables generally requires a large amount of memory and computation power or a classification algorithm which overfits the training sample and generalizes poorly to new samples. Feature extraction is a general term for methods of constructing combinations of the variables to get around these problems while still describing the data with sufficient accuracy

Jun Yan, Benyu Zhang, Ning Liu, Shuicheng Yan, Qiansheng Cheng, Weiguo Fan, Qiang Yang, Wensi Xi, and Zheng Chen (2006) give an overview of the popularly used feature extraction and selection algorithms under a unified framework. They propose two novel dimensionality reduction algorithms based on the Orthogonal Centroid algorithm (OC). The first is an Incremental OC (IOC) algorithm for feature extraction. The second algorithm is an Orthogonal Centroid Feature Selection (OCFS) method which can provide optimal solutions according to the OC criterion. Both are designed under the same optimization criterion. Experiments on Reuters Corpus Volume-1 data set and some public large-scale text data sets indicate that the two algorithms are favorable in terms of their effectiveness and efficiency when compared with other state-of-the-art algorithms.

FEATURE SELECTION STEPS

Preprocessing of Web pages is the first step for the Web page classification problem. Web pages cannot be processed as such because of the size, content and nature of the Web pages. Dimensionality reduction is an essential data preprocessing technique for large-scale and streaming data classification tasks. It can be used to improve both the efficiency and the effectiveness of classifiers. Traditional dimensionality reduction approaches fall into two categories: Feature Extraction and Feature Selection. Techniques in the feature extraction category are typically more effective than those in feature selection category. Feature extraction refers to the extraction from the various features of the Web page such as Title, Meta and URL of the Web page.

Feature selection is a process that selects a subset of original features. The optimality of a feature subset is measured by an evaluation criterion. A typical feature selection process consists of four basic steps namely, subset generation, subset evaluation, stopping criterion, and result validation. Subset generation produces candidate feature subsets for evaluation based on a certain search strategy. Each candidate subset is evaluated and compared with the previous best one according to a certain evaluation criterion. If the new subset turns out to be better, it replaces the previous best subset. The process of subset generation and evaluation is repeated until a given stopping criterion is satisfied.

FEATURE SELECTION TECHNIQUES

PCA

Principal Component Analysis (PCA) involves a mathematical procedure that transforms a large number of correlated variables into a smaller number of uncorrelated variables called principal components. The objectives of principal component analysis are to discover (or reduce) the dimensionality of the data set and identifies new meaningful underlying variables. The mathematical technique used in PCA is called eigen values. PCA is a classical statistical method that transforms the data to a new coordinate system such that the greatest variance by any projection of the data comes to lie on the first coordinate (called the first principal component), the second greatest variance on the second coordinate, and so on. PCA is theoretically the optimum transform for a given data in least square terms.

Principal Component Analysis is a feature selection technique that searches for c k-dimensional orthogonal vectors that can be used to represent the data, where c<=k. The original data are those projected into a smaller space, resulting in data compression. PCA can be used as a form of dimensionality reduction. The input data are normalized, so that each attribute falls within the same range. It helps to ensure that attributes with large domains do not dominate the smaller domains. It uses a special coordinate system that depends upon the cloud of points. Place the first axis in the direction of greater variance of the points to maximize the variance along that axis. The second axis is perpendicular to it. It is also a technique used to reduce multi dimensional data sets to lower dimensions for analysis.

PCA is a non-parametric analysis and independent of any hypothesis about data probability distribution. PCA compression and decompression are easy operations to perform given the model parameters. However, the latter two properties are regarded as weakness as well as strength, in that being non-parametric, no a-priori assumptions can be incorporated and that PCA compressions often incur loss of information. When used for the applications of clustering, the main limitation of PCA is that it does not consider class separability since it does not take into account the class label of the feature vector. PCA simply performs a coordinate rotation that aligns the transformed axes with the directions of maximum variance. There is no guarantee that the directions of maximum variance will contain good features for discrimination

Fei Wu, Yonglei Zhou and Changshui Zhang proposed a general iterative framework for relevant linear feature extraction that efficiently utilizes both the side information and unlabeled data to enhance gradually algorithms performance and robustness. Both good relevant feature extraction and reasonable similarity matrix estimation can be realized. They adopt Relevant Component Analysis (RCA) under this framework and get the derived Iterative Self-Enhanced Relevant Component Analysis (ISERCA) algorithm. The experimental results on several data sets show that ISERCA outperforms RCA. Side-information represents some equivalence constraint between pair of samples, indicating whether the two samples originate from the same but unknown category (positive constraint) or from two different categories (negative constraint). They use "labeled data" to denote the samples involved in the given side-information

Information Gain

Information Gain is a method that removes the less informative attributes, collecting the more informative ones for use in concept description analysis. It is a dimension based data analysis method. An arbitrary sample belongs to class C_i with the probability s/S where S is the total number of samples. The expected information gain is given by:

$$I(s_1, s_2, \ldots, s_m) = -\sum s/S \log s/S$$

and the gain is given by

$$\text{Gain} = I(s_1, s_2, \ldots, s_m) - E(A)$$

Information theoretic methods are also used to evaluate features: the mutual information between a relevant feature and the class labels should be high. Nonparametric methods can be used to compute mutual information involving continuous features. Although information gain is usually a good measure for deciding the relevance of an attribute, it is not perfect. A notable problem occurs when information gain is applied to attributes that can take on a large number of distinct values.

Mark Last and Oded, Maimon (2004) proposed an algorithm called Information theoretic algorithm that is based on minimal subset features. Information Network, is a tree like structure is formed by input features and the targeted classification. Unlike other decision-tree models, the information network uses the same input attribute across the nodes of a given layer (level). The input attributes are selected incrementally by the algorithm to maximize a global decrease in the conditional entropy of the target attribute. They employ the pre pruning approach: When no attribute causes a statistically significant decrease in the entropy, the network construction is stopped. More information implies higher accuracy of classification.

TF-IDF

Each document is represented in the term space, such that d = {$w_1, w_2, \ldots, w_n$}, where w_i, i = 1, ..

. , n, is the weight of term i in the document. The weight of a term could be simply calculated as the frequency of the term in that document ($w_i = tf_i$); i.e. how many times it appeared in the document. A more popular term weighting scheme is TF×IDF (Term Frequency ×Inverse Document Frequency), which takes into account the document frequency of a term (df_i), the number of documents in which the term appears. A typical inverse document frequency (idf) factor of this type is given by $\log(N/df_i)$. Thus the TF×IDF weight of a term is $w_i = tf_i \times \log(N/df_i)$. In other words, terms that appear more frequently in a certain document but less frequently in other documents are given higher weights in that document, since it has higher correlation with that document than others. On the other hand, terms that appear frequently in all documents are penalized in all documents since they have less discrimination power.

Daniele Riboni(2005) conducted various experiments on a corpus of 8000 documents belonging to 10 Yahoo! categories, using Kernel Perceptron and Naive Bayes classifiers. They introduce a new method for representing linked pages using local information that makes hypertext categorization feasible for real-time applications. Experimental results show that the local words with a hyper textual one can improve classification performance.They tested five different text sources for Web page representation namely:

BODY, META, TITLE, MT, the union of META and TITLE content and BMT, the union of BODY, META and TITLE content.

Alexandros Kalousis, Julien Prados, Melanie Hilario (2005) suggested that study is an attempt to fill the gap by quantifying the sensitivity of feature selection algorithms to variations in the training set. The authors assess the stability of feature selection algorithms based on the stability of the feature preferences that they express in the form of weights scores, ranks or a selected feature subset. They examine a number of measures to quantify the stability of feature preferences and propose an empirical way to estimate them.

Chi-Square (CHI)

In probability theory and statistics, the chi-square distribution (also chi-squared or χ^2 distribution) is one of the most widely used theoretical probability distributions in inferential statistics, i.e. in statistical significance tests. It is useful because, under reasonable assumptions, easily calculated quantities can be proven to have distributions that approximate to the chi-square distribution if the null hypothesis is true. The chi-square distribution has one parameter: *k* - a positive integer that specifies the number of degrees of freedom (i.e. the number of X_i). The chi-square distribution is a special case of the gamma distribution. The best-known situations in which the chi-square distribution is used are the common chi-square tests for goodness of fit of an observed distribution to a theoretical one, and of the independence of two criteria of classification of qualitative data. However, many other statistical tests lead to a use of this distribution. Chi-square measures the lack of independence between a term t and a category c_i and can defined as

$$\chi^2(t, c_i) = \frac{N[P(t, c_i)P(\bar{t}, \overline{c_i}) - P(t, \overline{c_i})P(\bar{t}, c_i)]^2}{P(t)P(\bar{t})P(c_i)P(\overline{c_i})}$$

Hongjun Lu, Sam Yuan Sung and Ying Lu (1996) propose Conflict analysis that is finding a set of attributes having perfect association with the class labels contingency table analysis is used with the nominal variables –the variables whose values are from an unordered set used chi square statistics.

Correlation Coefficient (CC)

Correlation is a measure to identify the relationship between the attributes. For that purpose,

221

correlation coefficients are introduced. The correlation coefficient is a number between -1 and 1 which measures the degree to which two variables are linearly related. If there is perfect linear relationship with positive slope between the two variables, we have a correlation coefficient of 1; if there is positive correlation, whenever one variable has a high (low) value, so does the other. If there is a perfect linear relationship with negative slope between the two variables, we have a correlation coefficient of -1; if there is negative correlation, whenever one variable has a high (low) value; the other has a low (high) value. A correlation coefficient of 0 means that there is no linear relationship between the variables.

Wen-Zhou Chen and Lei Li (2004) proposed a model of Correlation based Modified SVM, which ranks the features according to the correlation measures. Forward selection search with correlation based method to form a feature subset, labeled training examples each with a feature vector and a class are used.

Correlation coefficient of a word t with a category c_i and can be defined as

$$CC(t, c_i) = \frac{\sqrt{N}[P(t, c_i)P(\bar{t}, \overline{c_i}) - P(t, \overline{c_i})P(\bar{t}, c_i)]}{\sqrt{P(t)P(\bar{t})P(c_i)P(\overline{c_i})}}$$

Odds Ratio (OR)

The odds ratio is one of a range of statistics used to assess the risk of a particular outcome if a certain factor (or exposure) is present. The odds ratio is a relative measure of risk, telling us how much more likely it is that someone who is exposed to the factor under study will develop the outcome as compared to someone who is not exposed. Odds are a way of presenting probabilities. The odds of an event happening is the probability that the event will happen divided by the probability that the event will not happen. It is a measure used for selecting terms for relevance feedback. The basic idea is that the distribution of features

on the relevant documents is different from the distribution of features on the non-relevant documents. It is defined as follows:

$$OR(t, c_i) = log\frac{P(t|c_i)[1 - P(t|\overline{c_i})]}{[1 - P(t|c_i)]P(t|\overline{c_i})}$$

Filters and Wrappers

The filter approaches evaluate the relevance of each feature (subset) using the data set alone, regardless of the subsequent learning algorithm. The filter model relies on general characteristics of the training dataset to select some features without involving any learning algorithm. The wrapper model requires one predetermined learning algorithm in feature selection and uses its performance to evaluate and determine which features are selected. It invokes the learning algorithm to evaluate the quality of each feature (subset). Specifically, a learning algorithm (e.g., a nearest neighbor classifier, a decision tree, a naive Bayes method) is run on a feature subset and the feature subset is assessed by some estimate of the classification accuracy. Wrappers are usually more computationally demanding, but they can be superior in accuracy when compared with filters, which ignore the properties of the learning task at hand. Wrapper models tend to find features better suited to the predetermined learning algorithm resulting in superior learning performance, but it is also computationally expensive compared to the filter model.

Huan Liu and Lei Yu proposed that feature selection algorithms for classification and clustering, groups and compares different algorithms with a categorizing framework based on search strategies, evaluation criteria, and data mining tasks, reveals unattempted combinations, and provides guidelines in selecting feature selection algorithms. With the categorizing framework, an integrated system for intelligent feature selection is built up. For employing feature selection, wrapper, filter and hybrid model are adopted.

Elı́as , Elena Montane´ s, Irene Dı́az, Jose´ Ranilla, and Ricardo Mones (2005) suggested that to select the relevant features by a family of linear filtering approaches. The feature selection approaches are bag of words representation, filter and wrapper approaches, term frequency, document frequency, inverted document frequency and the Information Gain indicates the presence of word in the category or not. The distribution of documents over the categories is considered by introducing the concept of canonical or unconditional rule which says that any document belongs to the category. This rule is used as a reference for the rest of rules of the same category. SVM classifier is employed with Reuters 21578 collections as the experimental data.

Decision Tree Based Feature Selection

The basic decision tree induction is a greedy algorithm that constructs decision trees in a top-down recursive divide and conquer manner. Nodes in the decision tree involve testing a particular attribute. The test at a particular node compares the attribute values with a constant.

A decision tree can be constructed top-down using the information gain in the following way:

1. begin at the root node
2. determine the attribute with the highest information gain which is not used in an ancestor node
3. add a child node for each possible value of that attribute
4. attach all examples to the child node where the attribute values of the examples are identical to the attribute value attached to the node

5. if all examples attached to the child node can be classified uniquely add that classification to that node and mark it as leaf node
6. go back to step two if there is at least one more unused attribute left, otherwise add the classification of most of the examples attached to the child node

Philip Laird Ronald Saul (1994) proposed that each object is represented in the form of vector of attribute values. Genetic based algorithm includes decision trees, feed forward neural networks and Bayesian classifiers. Value-class pair(x,C) is generated. Based on the value-class pair decision tree is constructed. At each node in the tree, a feature is tested for inclusion in two or more sets or in ranges. Minimum message length (MML) is used to determine the mutual information gain. Fringe technique is employed to identify the identical sub trees and the determination of the root.

Heuristic Search Trees

The predominant state-space planning methods in artificial intelligence are collectively known as heuristic search. Heuristic search is not concerned with changing the approximate, or "heuristic," value function, but only with making improved action selections given the current value function. In other words, heuristic search is planning as part of a policy computation. In heuristic search, for each state encountered, a large tree of possible continuations is considered. The approximate value function is applied to the leaf nodes and then backed up toward the current state at the root. The backing up stops at the state-action nodes for the current state. Once the backed-up values of these nodes are computed, the best of them is chosen as the current action, and then all backed-up values are discarded. In conventional heuristic search no effort is made to save the backed-up values by changing the approximate value function. In fact, the value function is generally designed by people and never changed as a result of search.

In conventional heuristic search, this process computes backed-up values of the possible actions, but does not attempt to save them. Thus, heuristic search can be viewed as an extension of the idea of a greedy policy beyond a single step. Search methods traverse the attribute space to find a good subset. Quality is measured by the chosen attribute subsets. Subsets that have been cached are evaluated.

Pat Langley (1994) proposes that the Heuristics search through a space of feature set. Search Space specifies a subset of original feature. First determine the starting point and next the direction in which they are applied .It includes forward selection & backward elimination greedy approach (BFS)

Clustering with Tree Representation

Clustering is the classification of objects into different groups, or more precisely, the partitioning of a data set into subsets (clusters), so that the data in each subset (ideally) share some common trait - often proximity according to some defined distance measure. Data clustering is a common technique for statistical data analysis, which is used in many fields, including machine learning, data mining, pattern recognition, image analysis and bioinformatics. Data clustering algorithms can be hierarchical or partitional. Hierarchical algorithms find successive clusters using previously established clusters, whereas partitional algorithms determine all clusters at once. Hierarchical algorithms can be agglomerative ("bottom-up") or divisive ("top-down"). Agglomerative algorithms begin with each element as a separate cluster and merge them into successively larger clusters. Divisive algorithms begin with the whole set and proceed to divide it into successively smaller clusters. Two-way clustering, co-clustering or biclustering are clustering methods where not only the objects are clustered but also the features of the objects, i.e., if the data is represented in a data matrix, the rows and columns are clustered simultaneously

An algorithm for feature selection that clusters attributes using a special metric and, generates clusters that are placed in a cluster tree. Clustering is obtained by extracting those clusters that are situated at a given height in this tree.

Richard Butterworth, Gregory Piatetsky-Shapiro and Dan (2005) devised an algorithm for feature selection that clusters attributes using a special metric and then makes use of the dendrogram of the resulting cluster hierarchy to choose the most relevant attributes. The main interest of our technique resides in the improved understanding of the structure of the analyzed data and of the relative importance of the attributes for the selection process. Hierarchical algorithms generate clusters that are placed in a cluster tree, which is commonly known as a dendrogram. Clusters are obtained by extracting those clusters that are situated at a given height in this tree.

Hierarchical Trees

A hierarchical method creates a hierarchical decomposition of the given set of objects. A hierarchical method can be classified as agglomerative or divisive approach which is based on how the hierarchical decomposition is formed. The agglomerative approach is a bottom-up approach. The divisive approach is a top-down approach.

Shou-Bin Dong (2004) proposed a technique of hierarchical classification of Web content based on the combination of both textual and visual features. Images can be ignored during classification. Combination of multiple classifiers is employed. The most widely used approach typically combines the classifier outputs directly by means of simple combining rules or functions. It relates to techniques like majority vote, threshold voting, averaged Bayes classifier, different linear combinations of a posteriori probabilities, maximum and minimum rules, product rule. Page, summary, title, image related text are also taken into account.

Suresh, Jitender ,Vijay and Heyeri Sever (1996) use four feature selection algorithms-all the algorithms start with the same feature space but the heuristic used for pruning is different. The objective is to find a small amount of features that are sufficient and necessary for describing the feature space

1. **Best fit SBS:** Start with all the features and the features are removed one at a time
2. **Hybrid Heuristic SBS:** The current node is considered as the root node. The root nodes are expanded in such a way that the successors have one less condition attributes than its predecessors
3. **Alternating heuristic SBS:** The current node is assigned as the root node. Alternately BFS and first fit can be employed to find the next node of detail.
4. **k-level best SBS:** It divides the search space into k-groups starting from the root node to the leaf node. The last stage contains less than k-levels.

FUTURE TRENDS IN FEATURE SELECTION APPROACH

Hybrid Feature Selection

Hybrid feature selection combines different feature selection algorithms. It took the best characteristics of each and every algorithm and combines them effectively. Now –a-days the researchers used to combine the multiple feature selection algorithms for classification.

Yi Lu Murphey and Hong Guo (2000) proposed a model called hybrid feature selection algorithm using three different statistical measurements such as class pair-wised distance, linear separability, and overlapped feature histogram. They applied Bayes EM algorithm to select a sub-optimal set. The hybrid feature selection algorithm can be used as a preprocessing in a classification system

and it is independent of the classifier to be used in the subsequence stage.

Hwanjo Yu, Kevin Chen-Chuan Chang and Jiawei Han (2002) propose a model that eliminates the need for negative training data and they concluded that the classification accuracy is increased by using two learners.

Sampling Technique and Correlation

Sampling is a reduction technique as it allows a large data set to be represented as small samples of data. The samples are thus correlated and the results are validated. Sampling is that part of statistical practice concerned with the selection of individual observations intended to yield some knowledge about a population of concern, especially for the purposes of statistical inference. Each observation measures one or more properties (weight, location, etc.) of an observable entity enumerated to distinguish objects or individuals.

Sriharsha Veeramachaneni Paolo Avesani (2004) proposed a technique of sampling the feature values with the ultimate goal of choosing between alternative candidate features with minimum sampling cost. Their heuristic algorithm is based on extracting candidate features in a region of the instance space. An experimental evaluation on a standard database shows that it is possible outperform a random sub sampling policy in terms of the accuracy in feature selection. The basic idea is to prescribe an iterative policy that chooses the next instance on which the candidate features are to be probed.

PRIVACY PRESERVING DATA MINING USING FEATURE SELECTION TECHNIQUES

Data mining is usually performed for applications not having personal details like weather forecasting, GPSS, etc. But data mining for banking, e-commerce, mobile and the like applications involve databases with personal details. Here the security aspects have to be taken into account while retrieving the features used to find the required Web page by the user. One way to achieve this is by using a multilevel authentication system. The user giving the query must be an authenticated user to pose that query. Another way is to distort the data by inserting noise so that no one can access the personal details only the results or prediction can be shown. Yet another way is encrypt the information stored in the database so that if more than one person/company involved in the data mining, no one can get the other person/company details. Data mining can also be used to detect susceptible queries that intend to retrieve the personal information and also can be used to detect the person/program who did it. All the above feature selection techniques can be used to deal the security issues and to find the best features.

CONCLUSION

In this chapter we focus on various feature selection methods and how they are used by many researchers for selecting optimal feature set for Web page classification problem. We mainly concentrate on the various ways a particular method is used for the purpose rather than giving references that solve the problem in the same way. This chapter may be incomplete in the aspect that it does not refer all the papers in the feature selection area but this is a useful research work for researchers who do research in the Web page representation and Web page classification areas.

REFERENCES

Blake, C., & Pratt, W. (2001). Better rules, fewer features: A semantic approach to selecting features from text. IEEE-2001, 59-66.

Butterworth, R., Piatetsky-Shapiro, G., & Simovici, D. A. (2005). On Feature Selection through Clustering. *Proceedings of the Fifth IEEE International Conference on Data Mining (ICDM'05).*

Chen, W-Z., & Li, L. (2004). Correlation and MSVM-based Feature Selection. *Proceedings of the Third International Conference on Machine Learning and Cybernetics*, Shanghai, 26-29 August 2004.

Combarro, E. F., Montanes, E., Díaz, I., Ranilla, J., & Mones, R. (2005). Introducing a Family of Linear Measures for Feature Selection in Text Categorization. *IEEE Transactions on Knowledge and Data Engineering, 17*(9), 1223-1232.

Eick, C. F., Zeidat, N., & Zhao, Z. (2004). Supervised Clustering – Algorithms and Benefits. *Proceedings of the 16th IEEE International Conference on Tools with Artificial Intelligence (ICTAI 2004).*

Kalousis, A., Prados, J., & Hilario, M. (2005). Stability of Feature Selection Algorithms. *Proceedings of the Fifth IEEE International Conference on Data Mining (ICDM'05).*

Huang, Y., McCullagh, P. J., & Black, N. D., (2004). Feature Selection via Supervised Model Construction. Proceedings of the Fourth IEEE International Conference on Data Mining (ICDM'04).

Langley, P. (1994). Selection of Relevant Features on Machine Learning. *Proceedings of AAAI conference on Relevance-1994.*

Last, M., & Maimon, O. (2004, February). A Compact and Accurate Model for Classification. *IEEE Transactions on Knowledge and Data Engineering, 16*(2), 203-215.

Law, M. H. C., Figueiredo, M. A. T., & Jain, A. K. (2004, September). Simultaneous Feature Selection and Clustering Using Mixture Models. *IEEE Transactions on Pattern Analysis and Machine Intelligence, 26*(9), pp1154-1166.

Liu, H. & Yu. L. (2005). Towards Integrating Feature Selection Algorithms for Classification and Clustering. *IEEE Transactions on Knowledge and Data Engineering, 17*(4), 491-502.

Lu, H., Sung, S. Y., & Lu, Y. (1996). On Pre-processing Data for Effective Classification. *Workshop on Research Issues on Data Mining, Proceedings of ACM.*

Murphey, Y-L., & Guo, H. (2000). Automatic Feature Selection - A hybrid statistical approach. *IEEE-2000,* 382-385.

Riboni, D. (2005). Feature Selection for Web Page Classification. *Proceedings of International Conference on Data Mining, ICDM'05.*

Roychowdhury, S. (2001). Feature Subset Selection using Granular Information. *IEEE-2001,* 2041-2045

Saul, P. L. R. (1994). Automated Feature Extraction for supervised Learning, 674-679.

Scherf, M., & Brauer, W. (1997). Feature Selection by Means of a Feature Weighting Approach. Technical Report No. FKI-221-97, Forschungsberichte kunstliche Intelligenz, Institut fur Informatik, Technische Universitat Munchen, http://citeseer.ist.psu.edu/scherf97feature.html

Shou-Bin, D. (2004). The Hierarchical Classification of Web content by the combination of Textual and Visual Features. *Proceedings of the Third International Conference on Machine Learning and Cybernetics,* Shanghai, 26-29 August 2004, 1524-1529.

Setino, R., & Liu, H. (1997). Feature Selection via Discretization. *IEEE Transactions on Knowledge and Data Engineering, 9*(4), 642-645.

Suresh, K., Jitender, C., Deogun, S., Vijay, V., Raghavan, & Sever, H. (1996). A comparison of Feature Selection Algorithms in the context of Rough Classifiers. *Proceedings of Fifth IEEE conference on Fuzzy Systems, 2*(8-11), 1122-1128.

Wu, F., Zhou, Y., & Zhang C. (2004). Relevant Linear Feature Extraction Using Side-information and Unlabeled Data. *Proceedings of the 17th International Conference on Pattern Recognition (ICPR'04).*

Yan, J., Zhang, B., Liu, N., Yan, S., Cheng, Q., Fan, W., Yang, Q., Xi, W., & Chen, Z. (2006). Effective and Efficient Dimensionality Reduction for Large-Scale and Streaming Data Preprocessing. *IEEE Transactions on Knowledge and Data Engineering, 18*(3), 320-333.

Yu, H., Chen-Chuan Chang, K., & Han, J. (2002). Heterogeneous Learner for Web Page Classification. *Proceedings of International Conference on Data Mining 2002.*

KEY TERMS

Feature Extraction: Feature extraction is the preceding step to feature selection. It includes the collection of features from the Web pages. It can be done using any of the feature extraction techniques. All the collected features during the feature extraction phase need not be relevant.

Feature Selection: Feature selection is a process of selecting the relevant features needed for classification purposes. Feature selection is the most important step because the selected features determine the classification accuracy. Feature selection is a preprocessing technique commonly used on high dimensional data. Feature selection studies how to select a subset or list of attributes or variables that are used to construct models describing data. Its purposes include reducing dimensionality, removing irrelevant and redundant features, reducing the amount of data needed for learning, improving algorithms' predictive accuracy, and increasing the constructed models' comprehensibility.

HTML Structure: HTML refers to Hypertext Markup Language. It is used for the design of

Web pages. Most of the Web pages contain html tags enclosed.

Machine Learning: Machine learning usually refers to the changes in systems that perform tasks associated with artificial intelligence. Such tasks involve recognition, diagnosis, planning, robot control and prediction etc. It is a technique commonly used for automatic classification of Web pages. It includes both the training phase and the testing phase. The training phase is used to learn from examples. Based on the learning the classifier classifies during the testing phase. Machine learning has a wide spectrum of applications including natural language processing, syntactic pattern recognition, search engines, medical diagnosis, bioinformatics, detecting credit card fraud, stock market analysis, classifying DNA sequences, speech and handwriting recognition, object recognition in computer vision, game playing and robot locomotion

Preprocessing: Preprocessing is the process of removing unnecessary information before the classification of Web pages. It includes removing common words, rare words, removing HTML tags and stemming.

Web Page Classification: Web page classification, also known as Web page categorization, may be defined as the task of determining whether a Web page belongs to a category or categories. It can be done by considering the various features like URL, head, title and the body contents of the Web page.

World Wide Web: The World Wide Web (commonly shortened to the Web) is a system of interlinked hypertext documents accessed via the Internet. With a Web browser, a user views Web pages that may contain text, images, videos, and other multimedia and navigates between them using hyperlinks. The World Wide Web is also called as net of networks. It contains a large amount of information needed for the Internet browsers. Boundless amount of information can be downloaded at any point of time.

Chapter XIII
Agricultural Data Mining in the 21st Century

E. Arlin Torbett
AgriWorld Exchange Inc., USA

Tanya M. Candia
Candia Communications LLC, USA

ABSTRACT

Data on the production, sale, repackaging, and transportation of fresh produce is scarce, yet with recent threats to national safety and security, forward and backward traceability of produce is mandatory. Recent advances in online marketing of fresh produce, a new international codification system and use of advanced technologies such as Radio Frequency Identification (RFID) and bar coding are working together to fill the gap, building a solid database of rich information that can be mined. While agricultural data mining holds much promise for farmers, with better indications of what and when to plant, and for buyers, giving them access to improved food quality and availability information, it is the world's health organizations and governments who stand to be the biggest beneficiaries. This chapter describes the current state of fresh produce data collection and access, new trends that fill important gaps, and emerging methods of mining fresh produce data for improved production, product safety and public health through traceability.

INTRODUCTION

Agriculture has always been, and continues to be, a key industry in the world's economy. In spite of its vital role in the world's economy, until very recently most data on production, brokerage, transportation, processing and consumption of agricultural products has been available only in the aggregate, rather than in a form that lends itself to investigation and learning. This is largely due to the fact that the majority of growers, shippers and buyers around the world are small businesses doing business by phone, fax or word of mouth.

Similarly, food traceability data related to product as it moves through the supply chain has been difficult to obtain with any certainly. Individual lots of fruits or vegetables are broken up, repackaged, and trans-shipped without any means of tracing forward or backward. This has profound implications for food safety and hygiene, and indeed to national defense.

Recent advances in online collection and maintenance of data related to fresh produce trading and exchange, as well as product inspection in the field and agricultural practices investigation, coupled with proposed standards for classification and Radio Frequency Identification (RFID) and other advanced tracking mechanisms have brought us to the point at which it becomes feasible to engage in effective data mining of agricultural data.

This ability has never been more important to a nation's and the world's interests. Such information can help to inform import and export policies; it can aid in efforts to ensure that agricultural workers receive fair pay for the fruits of their labor. Similarly, it can provide actionable information in the event of a food safety crisis. It can even assist governments to avoid or react to bioterrorism attacks. By correlating disparate data sources, agricultural data mining can finally lead to both forward and backward traceability, a thorny and hitherto unsolvable problem given the nature of the industry.

This chapter provides background and a review of the literature surrounding the topic, followed by an in-depth treatment of the recent historical context of agricultural data and problems associated with the lack of agricultural data repositories representing real-time data. It then discusses some important recent trends and issues that argue for development of online data bases related to agricultural production, movement and consumption. With a strong focus on the branch of agriculture related to fresh produce, the chapter discusses solutions and recommendations with regard to this highly demanding environment, where issues of determining optimal planting time, product and quantity relate to expected supply and demand; where product quality is inextricably tied to shelf life which drives pricing; where solid traceability is a key requirement for protection of the common good. Finally, the chapter presents future trends that will be important to research in the coming years.

BACKGROUND

As of 2006, an estimated 36 percent of the world's workers are employed in agriculture (International Labour Organization, 2007), down from 42% in 1996, making it by far the most common occupation across the globe. Although agricultural production accounts for less than five percent of the gross world product (an aggregate of all gross domestic products), it has been the world's key industry for centuries. It is the sale and purchase of agricultural products that has long provided the financial foundation for this industry.

Early History

Early agricultural transactions took place locally, between small growers and equally small buyers. Information about product quality, growing conditions, preparation and, especially, grower reputation was easy to come by, since eyewitness accounts and local knowledge served as the local data repository. Due to the perishable nature of fresh produce, it was almost always the case that buyers and sellers were in close geographic proximity. It was impossible to hide or distort information related to the specifics of which field a given lot was produced in, what types of pest control were in use, whether fertilizers were used, and other detailed data related to product quality or condition.

Over time, distributors took on an important role in moving goods to more remote markets, aggregating and consolidating product for larger buying communities. Whether within a country or among various countries, the distribution of food products has become the norm rather than the exception. Recent agreements such as the North American Free Trade Agreement (NAFTA) have had a profound effect on the flow of fresh fruits and vegetables among the relevant regions (Mexico, the United States and Canada). This agreement, which took effect on January 1, 1994, eliminated most trade barriers among the three countries. It thus became easy for buyers in the United States and Canada to take advantage of extended growing seasons in Mexico, augmenting their national supplies with easily-obtainable produce from neighboring countries.

In addition to regional trade agreements, advances in production, storage, packaging, refrigeration and shipping methods over the past 20 years have made it possible to extend the reach of even small growers. An example is the controlled atmosphere technique in maritime transport which came into play in the 1980's. When this technique is used, fresh produce is shipped in an atmosphere where all key elements: oxygen, nitrogen, carbon dioxide, humidity and temperature are maintained at the precise levels necessary to preserve food quality during the voyage.

With greater reach came less specific information on product and circumstances of production. In many cases, the distributor remained a repository of information. By collecting specific information about lots and loads of produce, the distributor became the "historian" of the data. However, the quality and reliability of that information was often somewhat less reliable than that produced by face-to-face interaction.

Today's Complex Transactions

Today's agribusiness has come to involve complex commercial transactions with many participants and multiple steps. Fresh produce is grown, harvested, prepared, packaged, shipped, processed and sold – and again bought and sold - with many iterations during the supply chain. Prices paid by the ultimate consumer often bear no resemblance to the price paid to the grower. Product produced in one geographical region will often be commingled with product from other, far-removed areas with different standards and regulatory requirements. The very "identity" of fresh produce becomes extremely difficult to ascertain.

Yet the problem is no less serious. Solid, auditable information on product, quality, quantity and price is vitally important to farmers, agricultural organizations, local governments and even entire countries and regions. Farmers need information on prices paid, trends, specialty product requirements, buying habits and the consumer. Food service and food processing industry members need information on availability, quality, location and reputation of growers/shippers. Government agricultural ministries and governmental health organizations need information about product source, growing conditions, processing environment and, above all, full traceability of product from consumer back to the source, and every step in between. In fact, in many countries the choice of trade partners is increasingly being impacted by the role played by phytosanitary measures as imposed by governmental organizations. Such measures, related to plant health, are designed to prevent the spread of pests or diseases.

Missing Elements

This type of information – on product quality, price, requirements, growing conditions, safety and other important issues - is in short support. There are three primary reasons for this situation:

1. There has been no central location in which to store such information
2. There has been no method of codifying such information
3. There has been no method of tracking product as it moves along the supply chain

Each of these three issues will be addressed in turn, and the impact will be explored.

Lack of Central Repository

The first issue stems from the historical method by which people have been buying and selling fresh produce for centuries. In the past and even today, agricultural transactions take place in a complex environment where solid information about the product (its source, growing conditions and history during its sometimes extended path from grower to buyer) is hard to find, and the need for much more specific data relative to the product, price, quantity and quality is in high demand. This is due not so much to any lack of deliberation on the part of the buyer and the seller, but rather because of the nature of the transaction itself.

Unlike the financial market, where the audit trail for transactions is normally clear and comprehensive, most agricultural transactions take place in an informal setting. A seller phones possible buyers with whom he has dealt in the past, offers his product, and the seller agrees to the purchase during the phone conversation. A confirmation is faxed to the buyer, and any further negotiations take place by phone. There is no electronic record of the transaction. At best, there is a faxed document that may or may not be stored in a physical

file. As such, there is no electronic method to easily retrieve the document. Even more difficult is the task of re-creating a series of telephone conversations where the only notation might be a scribble in a notebook.

Lack of Codification Scheme

The second issue also stems from the historical and localized roots of fresh produce sales. Until very recently, the industry lacked even a rudimentary method of describing fresh produce in universally-understood terms. The typical method used by a buyer and seller, engaged in a phone transaction, is often very informal. The buyer describes the product he wants to purchase, and the seller agrees that his product matches that description. The Produce Marketing Association describes the normal process thus: "a combination of attributes and descriptions, sometimes accompanied by an internal reference number, is used to order an item". The organization further explains "…these attributes and descriptions are defined and used differently throughout the produce industry, and…the inconsistent use of these characteristics often results in failed expectations or mis-shipments, both of which strain relationships, add costs to the supply chain, result in loss of business, and require additional handling. Additionally, these inconsistencies and interpretations make it extremely difficult to categorize produce items." (Produce Marketing Association, 2005).

Lack of Product Integrity through the Supply Chain

The third issue is somewhat more recent in nature, and relates to the fact that lots may not maintain their integrity all along the supply chain. While a truckload of a commodity such as broccoli might be produced in a single field, it can move into the supply chain and be altered in any number of ways. The truckload might be combined with other truckloads at a terminal market, and from there be shipped to a food processor that mixes the broccoli with still other loads and produces broccoli soup. It might be broken up by a packer into smaller lots or cartons, and shipped to markets across the country. In the case of leaf vegetables such as lettuce and spinach, product from a number of fields might be combined at a processing location where the lettuce is cleaned and bagged.

Soon after the produce is harvested, its origins become cloudy. This makes it extremely difficult for health officials to determine the actual source of product. In cases where the food is suspected of being tainted, such lack of integrity can lead to widespread recalls in the interest of safety. However, in reality perhaps only a small quantity of the product is really tainted.

The need for such information has recently moved out of the realm of nice-to-have to the position of must-have. The world is reliant on its food supply chain, yet is increasingly vulnerable to it. A May 12 2007 United Press International (UPI) science news story reports: "Since Sept. 11, bioterrorism became the federal government's number one priority. The subject includes food security--protecting the nation's food supply from a bioterrorism attack......advanced technology and a decentralized food supply make it possible for terrorists to contaminate the U.S. food supply and sicken or even kill thousands of citizens." (Dyckman, 2003)

Even when viewed on a more mundane level, such information is needed. It is also vitally important for growers and buyers to have access to such information. Growers, constantly struggling to achieve a profit in the face of uncertainty, need to be able to determine the best variety to plant and the best time at which to plant. In addition, they need information on buying and consumer trends. Buyers need information on actual prices paid, quantity of product on offer, sources and, above all, safety and quality information.

AGRICULTURAL DATA MINING BECOMES POSSIBLE

Three factors are converging to enable, for the first time ever, collection and analysis of data related to fresh produce: its origins (along with field safety factors), quality, variety, production methods, movements through the supply chain, and eventual disposition, These factors include a new method of classifying fresh produce data, new methods of tracking fresh produce along the supply chain, and an innovative method of collecting such information and making it available for data mining. Each of these will be discussed in detail.

Brief Overview of Agricultural Data Mining

Data mining can be defined in any number of ways. The definition used by the U. S. Congressional Research Service and the Government Accountability Office is:

"Data mining involves the use of sophisticated data analysis tools to discover previously unknown, valid patterns and relationships in large data sets. Data mining consists of more than collecting and managing data; it also includes analysis and prediction." (Cooney, 2006).

Data mining involves a series of steps, the first of which is to define the problem to be solved. Next, the task is to collect or aggregate data into large data sets. Then the data undergoes a cleansing process, eliminating inaccurate or incomplete data. Subsequently, models are built with which to detect patterns in the data, validate them, and predict future events and behaviors. The models must then be validated, and deployed to the field. At this point, rules must be implemented to ensure proper data ownership and maintenance. The process is iterative, as new information learned is fed back into the process at any of the above steps.

In the case of agricultural data mining, there are a number of types of data that become relevant when collected in sufficient quantity. Examples include data related to general agricultural production, as well as those specific to individual plant, animal and crop issues. Other relevant data might cover different types of soils, climates and microclimates, and growing conditions. In addition, data might also cover the use of soil amendments, fertilizers, pesticides, herbicides and similar methods of influencing growing conditions and the resultant products.

The following sections discuss various types of data that are now being collected, due to recent advances in electronic commerce, classification schemes and emerging businesses that address heretofore neglected opportunities for data collection.

Food and Food Safety Classification Codes

Today's agricultural transaction encompasses a vast variety of data types: product type and sub-type, species, growing location, packing location, planting date, harvest date, method of harvesting, post-harvest processing, packing type, quantity, weight, quality, and a host of other data types. Once the produce is harvested, it moves along the supply chain, where the original information can be, and often is, modified. Lots can be broken up into smaller lots, combined with other lots, processed, packaged and even transformed completely, such as happens when broccoli makes its way into canned soup.

It is vitally important to a nation and to the world community to be able to collect, store, track and mine such information for the reasons stated previously. As an example, the U. S. Department of Agriculture oversees the health of products imported into the United States through a service called the Animal and Plant Health In-

spection Service (APHIS). This service governs the importation of fresh produce through phytosanitary certificates, rules about importation, and inspections. The Economic Research Service of the USDA (Huang, 2007) explains that under authority of Title 7 Code of Federal Regulations (CFR) 319.56, APHIS demands written permits for importing fresh produce. The regulations also call for foreign quarantine notices for fruit and vegetables.

The problem occurs when a government, rather than interrogating a rich database of information about specific products and their quality and safety, must instead apply blanket measures to all such products. In the U.S., the USDA takes such action on specific commodities it suspects might be contaminated. An example can be seen with grapes grown in countries where the Mediterranean fruit fly is present. All such grapes must be subjected to cold treatment as outlined in CFR 319-2d.

The situation is changing. While past approaches to buying and selling fresh produce relied on a combination of attributes and descriptions, today vital food-related information is collected and stored through a variety of newer methods that will someday make agricultural data mining possible.

Some of the most important methods include the Produce Marketing Association codes, farm safety categorization, field inspection data and the proposed new Global Trade Item Number (GTIN) coding system. Each of these is briefly discussed in turn, and finally a new method of aggregating such data is presented as a means of providing a rich base for data mining.

ASAP

The U.S. Produce Marketing Association (PMA) has devised a set of commodity codes related to fresh produce. Known as ASAP (A Standardized Attributes Product), or more commonly as the Produce Standard Attributes, the codes are intended to assist the industry with database standardization in order to help increase e-commerce efficiencies. This necessary foundation is leading to standardization across the industry, which in turn is making automation possible.

A great deal of work, on the part of a task force made up of mathematicians, industry participants and produce organizations, was done over a period of time to gather standard values for each of a number of attributes. The main purpose of the task force was to standardize the data used in the produce supply chain, to make it more efficient and enable the use of e-commerce, data integration, data synchronization and data alignment. (Produce Marketing Association, 2005) The key item in the scheme is the attribute, a short descriptive term used to identify individual produce characteristics.

Attributes in the ASAP system include:

- Type (the category in which a commodity can be placed, such as Produce, Nut, Dried Produce)
- Commodity (the name of the industry-recognized grouping of species by the consumer, buyer and seller, such as Apple or Potato)
- Variety Group (used for grouping sets of like varieties for a specific commodity, such as: Commodity=Watermelon; Variety Group=Seedless)
- Variety (the name of a subspecies for a commodity, such as: Commodity=Apple, Variety=Red Delicious)
- Variety Refinement (used to further define the characteristics of a variety, such as: Commodity=Tomato, Variety=Roma, Variety Refinement=On the Vine)
- Grade (grade of commodity as established by the USDA (United States Department of Agriculture) or CFIA (Canadian Food Inspection Agency) as well as those of specific states, such as U.S. #1, U.S. Fancy)
- Origin
  - Origin – Country
  - Origin sub-attributes (such as State/Province)
- Growing Method (description of growing characteristics, such as Conventional, Organic, Genetically Modified, Kosher)
- Growing Region (user-defined region that further describes the origin)
- Size (generally accepted numeric industry sizes, or count where used)
- Size Unit of Measure (e.g. in, cm)
- Size Group (used when not referring to size as a numeric value, such as Small, Jumbo)
- Shipping Container (type of container in which the trade item is shipped, e.g. carton)
- Net Weight (gross weight less packaging materials)
- Net Weight Unit of Measure
- Inner Pack (refers to the items found inside the Trade Item that would be used as the consumer unit; uses four sub-attributes)
  - Pack Style (packaging style of units held within the Trade Item Pack, such as Clamshell, Bunch, Bag, 3-Layer, etc)
  - Pack Quantity (number of consumer units held within the Trade Item)
  - Pack Size (the size of the units held in the packaged format; e.g. "5" would indicate bags are 5-lbs each)
  - Pack Size Unit of Measure (UOM – a two-character code describing unit of measure for the Pack Size)
- Quantity (number of consumer units within the Trade Item
- Size (size of units held in the packaged format within the Trade Item Pack)
- Pack Size Unit of Measure (used to describe the pack size)
- Storage/Handling (a method used when harvesting, handling and/or storing a product, such as Controlled Atmosphere, Hydrocooled, Hand-Picked)

- Treatment (topical application of a type of treatment on a product, occurring after the product has been harvested, such as Waxed, Smart Fresh, Taste Mark)
- Maturity (process used to enhance the maturity level of an item or the level at which it is actually ripened, such as Tree Ripened, Gassed, Jet Fresh)

Since the ASAP codes were first introduced in 2005, they have been adopted by growers, shippers, packers, wholesalers, the food service industry and buyers around the world, First used in catalogs, they quickly made their way onto purchase orders, invoices, advanced ship notices, electronic payments and the like. The codes likewise became popular in buyer catalogs, creating a common nomenclature across the industry. While originally developed by the United States Produce Marketing Association, the codes are today well-understood by sellers and buyers in virtually every country in the world. PMA's ASAP Produce allows buyers and suppliers to have the same information in both of their databases.

This necessary first step has established a common vocabulary that enables the collection, rationalization and interpretation of basic produce movements. However, it is only a first step. There is a wealth of additional data that comes into play when making decisions about planting schedules, varieties, agricultural methods, forward and backward traceability of produce, and the like. Some of it is collected today through private organizations and enterprises that have been established to enhance food safety and foster good agricultural practices. This type of data is currently being aggregated into common databases that should prove valuable in a variety of ways, as are discussed below.

Farm Safety Categorization Data

Until recently, data related to individual farms and even the specific fields in which fresh produce is grown has not been gathered in a systematic manner. However, a number of organizations have come into being with the express charter of testing for farm safety, and reporting on the results. This specific data, when gathered in commonly-accessible databases, will help greatly in providing vital information that can be used in the event of contamination, food safety issues or other health-related concerns.

One example of this type of data collector organization is Primus Labs (Primus, 2008), a Santa Maria, CA-based organization that tests farm and field water for biological and chemical contamination, reporting on the presence of fertilizer, pesticides and/or biological products in the water. In addition, the organization inspects the growing practices on the farm. Such practices might include the requirement that farm workers wear hair covering while harvesting, that fields are fenced off to prevent intrusion by animals, irrigation and waste water processing practices, and the like.

The organization can perform three different types of sampling. The first is a pre-harvest sampling and analysis program in which personnel collect a representative sample of the commodity from the field and maintain a strict chain of custody from the field to the laboratory for analysis. A product is "Certified" when it meets applicable government standards.

A second type of sampling occurs post-harvest; personnel collect a representative sample from the loading dock, cooler or distribution center, again utilizing the chain of custody from the sample collection point to the laboratory. Based upon favorable findings, this program can warrant that any pesticide residues detected within the lot analyzed are within established government tolerances.

A third program is available to any individual or firm concerned with possible pesticide residues that may be present on a specific shipment or commodity. A sample provided to the organization by the client is analyzed and the results are then reported to the client.

Specific data collected at Primus Labs includes both microanalysis and pesticide analysis data.

Micro Analysis

Environment
- Total Plate Count
- Listeria
- Yeast & Mold

Water Sources
- Total Coliform
- E.coli

Final Product
- Total Plate Count
- Total Coliform
- E.coli
- Yeast & Mold
- Analyses for specific pathogens, such as Salmonella, E.coli 0157:H7, Listeria, Staphylococcus aureus, Clostridium perfringens, Shigella and other

Special Services
- Shelf life
- Challenge studies
- Sensory evaluations
- Evaluation of spoilage cause

Pesticide Analysis

Using the Food and Drug Administration (FDA), Environmental Protection Agency (EPA) and AOAC International methodologies, coupled with internal Standard Operating Procedures and adherence to the Chain of Custody for all samples from sample collection to analysis, Primus Labs is able to test for a variety of pesticides. More than 250 compounds can be analyzed for and recovered, representing

- Organochlorines
- Organophosphates
- Organonitrates
- Organosulfates
- Methyl carbamates

While such farm safety data is not collected for all or even a majority of US-based farms, the practice is becoming more common. The need for such information was clearly seen in the recent E. coli outbreak linked to spinach grown in California, where fresh produce contamination resulted in more than 200 illnesses and the deaths of three people. According to the FDA, fresh produce has caused more food-borne illnesses than meat and poultry in the past ten years. The sources of such contamination are multiple: in an individual field, the produce may come in contact with bird or animal droppings, manure, flood water, irrigation or sewage, or may be contaminated through human handling both before and after harvesting. Farm safety data helps to isolate suspect produce and enables inspectors to target their investigations.

While many of the outbreaks have resulted from poor safety practices on the part of the producers, the fact is that microbial contamination can come from multiple sources at various steps in the production chain. (Loaharanu, 2006) Fresh spinach, lettuce and other leafy greens are often harvested from many fields, brought together in centralized facilities, washed together and then bagged. This practice can confuse the issue when trying to trace back to a given farm or field. With the advent of new technologies such as RFID (see below), the industry will be better equipped to trace a product from its original field, through the entire production chain to the ultimate consumer.

Field Inspection Data: Grading of Product

A third category of agricultural data augments the produce quality data specified by ASAP, above.

This type of information comes from independent third-party inspectors who grade the product as it is harvested. Since fresh produce is a perishable commodity, and the grade determines the transportability and the shelf life, a reliable source of information on grades is invaluable. A number of companies across the United States provide such independent inspection services. Based on their assessment of the quality and freshness of the product, grades are assigned that can then be interpreted by the buyer and the shipper.

An example of fresh produce grading could show that some strawberries from the Central Valley in California are grade 2, meaning they are only suitable for transporting within California due to the quality and appearance of the berries. Others might rate a grade of 3, indicating they can be shipped as far as Nevada without danger of early spoilage, while still others might be graded 5 and can be shipped as far as the East Coast of the US.

Most fresh produce, depending on the commodity, will last between five and 20 days. Buyers need to know how many days the product will last, since they must subtract transportation time in order to arrive at the shelf life. Naturally, such information is needed precisely at the time the product is offered for sale. Organizations such as the ones described here can provide much-needed information on the quality of the product. However, unless this information is collected, transported with the product, and made available for later investigation, it becomes useless after the fact.

New Methods of Tracking Fresh Produce Movement

Fresh fruits and vegetables harvested in a given field or orchard often enter the supply chain and are broken into smaller lots, processed, mixed with other product and, in the end, lose all information related to their source. Unless there is a method of identifying such products on a very granular level, it becomes difficult if not impossible to trace product back to its source. Two such methods are bar coding and the use of radio frequency identification tags, or RFID tags.

Bar Codes

Bar coding is a relatively new method that is being adopted by agribusiness to help in the traceability effort. The use of bar coding has become more widespread in recent years. This "revolution" began in Troy, Ohio on June 26, 1974 when a pack of gum was scanned at a supermarket and the cash register automatically displayed the price. Now, more than 30 years later, some five billion bar codes are scanned each day. (Varchaver, 2004)

Bar codes are generally applied to boxes, crates or pallets and provide a means of tracking produce from a specific grower and often from a specific field. This information can be scanned in by the grower, shipper, food processor, retailer or wholesaler, to begin to provide an audit trail of sorts. Use of bar codes along the supply chain calls for both printers and readers at various places, with associated costs for printers and readers.

RFID

Radio frequency identification tags represent another new method for tracking produce. The use of RFID tags enables the identification of individual units of produce: an apple, a head of lettuce or a watermelon. Use of RFID scanners can provide the same precision of tracking as bar codes, but with far more granularity. However, the cost is quite a bit higher. According to RFID Radio, "Barcoding is more advantageous from a cost standpoint. It will cost about $0.005 to implement a barcode. RFID costs about $0.07 to $0.30 per tag." (Boeck, 2007) Nevertheless, the RFID market is calculated to represent $4.93 Billion in 2007, growing to $5.29 Billion in 2008. (IDTechEx 2008)

Food producers in Australia are in the vanguard of those investigating RFID for a number of uses. Major producer Moraitis is undergoing an important IT system overhaul, and is pioneering an RFID system. In fact many major buyers are mandating the use of RFID, chief among them Woolworths and Coles. By 2004 four out of five Australian retailers had begun investigating the use of RFID to improve their inventory systems and streamline workflows. (Head, 2004) Likewise, the use of RFID to track livestock has begun to enter the mainstream thanks largely to new laws for RFID tagging of cattle, especially in Australia. This requirement, as well as mandates to tag food, initially at the pallet and case level in Europe and the US, has been driven by giants such as Woolworth and Target. (IDTechEx, 2007)

The Woolworth requirement stipulates that each pallet supplied from January 2005 must have two human-readable barcode labels that conform to the EAN-128 standard, based on the European Article Number (EAN). Information contained in the bar code must include the serial shipping container code, the traded unit number describing the product on the pallet, the number of boxes or crates on the pallet, and the pack date, with additional information being optional.

In the case of fresh produce, growers and shippers are taking steps to mark their packed product (in boxes, cases or the like) with bar codes. The introduction of RFID tags promises to allow the growers to mark products on an individual basis, rather than packed in boxes or on pallets. Thus, individual product items can be tracked throughout the supply chain, even if original harvested lots are broken up along the way.

This scheme can only apply to non-leafy vegetables, since it will be impossible and impractical to use RFID to identify individual leaves. However, leafy vegetables are being put into plastic bins that are themselves bar coded, to allow for some traceability and movement from field to field, and within packing facilities. Similarly, this approach is not practical for fresh herbs or flowers. Nevertheless, when it comes to almost all other types of fresh vegetables and fruits, RFID promises to finally provide the missing link that will allow both backward and forward traceability.

CENTRALIZED DATABASE TO HOUSE CATEGORY, QUALITY, SAFETY AND MOVEMENT DATA

The third aspect related to the ability to do agricultural data mining relates to the need for a centralized database that can house all relevant data. While no such database exists today, recent movements in agricultural e-commerce hold the promise to build such a base in the near future. When viewed in light of the above advances in categorization and data collection along the supply chain, the possibility exists that such a database could be a reality within the next two years.

One company in California, AgriWorld Exchange (AgriWorld Exchange, 2008) based in Menlo Park, has recently introduced an online fresh produce exchange that initially handles transactions across the US, Canada, Mexico and Central and South America. Using a simple interface, buyers post product for sale and sellers make offers to buy. All information regarding the commodity for sale is entered and tracked using the aforementioned ASAP Product codes, which leads to standardization of description. In addition, information from farm safety inspection organizations is linked into the online system, making it both possible and easy to track the safety data related to a given lot of produce. Similarly, data on food quality and grading are linked to the database, as well as other subjective data related to individual transactions. Finally, information on the actual sale price, bid prices, quantity on offer and other economic issues is tracked and stored.

The data stored by AgriWorld Exchange includes:

- Source of the product
- Product (as specified by the above ASAP codes)
- Farm
- Date harvested
- Quality (as specified by code or text fields)
- Quantity (for each specific transaction)
- Asking price
- Bid price
- Quantity on offer by day
- Nutritional value (as specified by codes or text fields)
- Specific information such as "locally grown", "organic", "fair trade", "fair wage", "shade grown", "specialty food", etc.

After introducing the system in late 2007, the company collected data on more than 20 tons of fresh produce in the first three months. Based on extrapolations by company management, the exchange expects to handle more than 20 percent of the US fresh produce transactions within two years, as well as some ten percent of transactions from Mexico, Central and South America. When compared with the much smaller amount of data collected by the US Department of Agriculture, this database holds the promise of finally providing the rich source of information that has been lacking in the industry.

DATA MINING AND FRESH PRODUCE DATA

The Data Mining and Information Engineering Conference 2007, held at the Wessex Institute of Technology (WIT) in the New Forest, UK, revealed that data mining is growing in importance, especially in the agricultural industry. According to Dr. Alessandro Zanasi, "...data mining is seen not only as an exciting area of research but also as a technology that may solve European citizens' current concerns with problems such as security." He goes on to state that, "a recent analysis about the growth rate of the text mining market estimates it to be between 30 and 60% per year." (Zanasi, 2007)

However, data warehousing and data mining are new areas for agricultural research. Because the three key ingredients – codification schemes, information on fresh produce in motion, and a data warehouse with sufficient depth – are only now coming into being, few scholarly studies exist to show the potential uses and benefits. A few relevant studies are presented in the following sections.

Data Management for Site-Specific Farming

The Illinois Laboratory for Agricultural Remote Sensing undertook a research program to develop effective technologies to process the massive data set generated by precision farming production and research. One of the main purposes of the research program was to try to find ways to apply data mining to help farmers improve their use of precision farming tools. Today, although sophisticated machinery makes it possible to very precisely target treatment of crops and fields, a lack of quality data has slowed the adoption of new farming techniques. One very specific manifestation of this phenomenon is summed up by Lei Tian, Assistant Professor of Agricultural Engineering, University of Illinois: "In the normal field, only about 20 to 30 percent of the field has weed problems, which means you should only have to spray 20 to 30 percent. But in reality, we spray 100 percent. Farmers just don't have the information they need for precision farming." (Tian, 2001)

Data used in the program came from the University of Illinois Morrow Plots, for a 30-year period for which consistent data were available involving modern production practices. The team used a feed-forward, completely connected, back-propagation artificial neural network to approximate the nonlinear yield function relating corn yield to factors influencing yield. The back-propagation, feed-forward neural network predicted corn yields with 80% accuracy. The team working on the project plans to set up a high-tech data management environment for the application of ground-based and remote sensing data to precision farming.

Innovative Agricultural Applications Using Data Mining

Another example is seen in the work done at the University of Waikato in Hamilton, New Zealand. There, the Waikato Environment for Knowledge Analysis (WEKA) research team set out to mine information from existing agricultural datasets, and to perform basic research in data mining by developing new algorithms. The system used by the team includes a set of data pre-processing routines, classifiers and other data mining algorithms, metaclassifiers, experimental support and benchmarking tools. During the project, the team analyzed more than 50 data sets, primarily agricultural. The current version contains ten classifiers, a clustering algorithm and an association rule learner. The following types of classifiers are supported:

- ZeroR
- OneR
- NaiveBayes
- DecisionTable
- Instance-based learning schemes
- J48
- Part
- SMO
- Numeric Prediction (LWR, Linear Regression & M5 Prime)
- DecisionStump

The group constructed metaclassifiers via boosting (using the AdaBoost.M1 boosting algorithm and LogitBoost), and bagging. Clustering methods involved use of the EM clustering algorithm.

Information mined from the data provided insights into the domain that actually ran counter to conventional wisdom. A case study in mushroom grading proves the point. The issue was whether fresh products such as mushrooms could be graded into three broad quality bands more effectively when the product was inspected in person, than when photographs of the products were examined. According to the study, "The results indicate that visually-based attributes, which can be automatically extracted from digitized images, are sufficient for good separation of mushrooms into three broad quality bands (where 'good' is measured in comparison to human grading standards.) The subjective attributes, commonly believed to play a crucial role in grading, are apparently irrelevant to the task." (Cunningham, 1999)

Although these examples are disparate and tangential to the issue of tracking and mining data about agricultural production and shipment, they serve to point out the fact that data mining is at last making its way into the agricultural world. However, in reality the field is still quite new. As an example, a publication by the U.S. Federal Government's General Accounting Office states that data mining efforts cover a wide range of uses, with federal agencies using data mining for a variety of purposes - improving service, increasing productivity, and even analyzing and detecting terrorist patterns and activities.

It is interesting to note, however, that among the 60 departments and agencies that reported no operational or planned data mining efforts in 2004 were the following:

- Department of Agriculture
- Agricultural Marketing Service
- Agricultural Research Service

- Animal and Plant Health Inspection Service
- Cooperative State Research, Education and Extension Service
- Foreign Agricultural Service
- National Agricultural Statistics Service
- Food Safety and Inspection Service
- Forest Service
- National Agricultural Statistics Service
- International Trade Administration
- Administration for Children and Families
- National Institutes of Health
- Science and Technology Directorate
- Bureau of Land Management
- Fish and Wildlife Service
- Department of Transportation
- National Science Foundation

In fact, the instances of data mining cited in the report show very early adoption of the concept. Applications include tracking travel expenses, grantee information, and the like. Clearly, the area of agricultural data mining is in its infancy. (Government Accounting Office, 2004)

FUTURE TRENDS

Two important trends should be studied closely over the next five to ten years to ensure safety, security and economic viability for the world's food supply. These are 1) the economic impact of requirement for automated methods of tracking, such as bar codes and RFID, and 2) the promise of the emerging GTIN coding system.

Economics of Bar Codes and RFID

The incipient requirement for the use of bar codes and, soon, RFID labels for tracking and controlling fresh produce movement will bring significant challenges to producers of fruits and vegetables at a time when profits are already squeezed by all other participants in the supply chain. Woolworths, as mentioned above, is rolling out a program requiring bar code labels. This program, called "Mercury", demands of each supplier that each pallet supplied from January 2005 on must bear two human-readable bar code labels that conform to the EAN-128 standard. Each label must contain information such as the serial shipping container code, the traded unit number describing the product on the pallet, the number of boxes or crates on the pallet, and the pack date. Suppliers must not only comply with this current requirement, they must also prepare to handle the demands of RFID when it becomes mandated.

According to experts in the fresh produce industry, two main challenges occur when a company becomes RFID-ready. First, the company will face the challenge of needing to purchase or build middleware that can accommodate data flowing into its enterprise resource planning system from the RFID readers; second, it must undertake a study to determine what information to collect on the tags, and how to store and access it. While these efforts will become costly (see previous estimates of the cost of a single bar code or RFID tag), the benefits may eventually outweigh the cost of infrastructure and modified workflows. Data integrity, expected to be a byproduct of RFID, may well facilitate effective trade and deliver labor efficiencies and reduced waste. (Head, 2004)

Forward and Backward Traceability

An intriguing use of agricultural transaction information involves the issue of traceability: the ability to determine exactly where a given item was produced, and exactly where a given item ends up – for example, in which supermarket a given lot of spinach or pears was eventually sold. The Produce Marketing Association (PMA) and the United States Department of Agriculture (USDA) are very interested in forward and backward traceability, as is the World Trade Organization where food traceability has played a part in recent negotiations. (Golan, 2004) Today, vital information is lost each time a food commodity changes hands, are lots are broken up, reformed and processed. The recent spinach recall caused a massive reaction – to some, an overreaction – because forward traceability was not possible. The spinach industry in California is estimated to have lost well over $100 Million after regulators warned consumers not to eat bagged spinach following three deaths and several hundred cases of illness.

In order to ensure both forward and backward traceability, we need both a workable model and sufficient raw data. A recent workshop conducted by the University of California, Davis Agricultural Issues Center and the Department of Agricultural and Resource Economics provides an interesting model for traceability. (Cal-Med, 2007)

The other part of the equation, sufficient codified data, requires a more comprehensive and sophisticated system than the current ASAP codes or the disparate information collected and maintained in private corporate databases. A proposal for a new set of codes, called Global Trade Identification Number, or GTIN, describes a family of GS1 (EAN.UCC) global data structures that employ 14 digits and can be encoded into various types of labels such as bar codes and RFID. This family includes 8-, 12-, 13- and 14-digit numbers. The 14-digit code, GTIN-14 (EAN/UCC-14 or ITF-14) is a 14-digit number used to identify trade items, products or services including information about various packaging levels. (Produce Marketing Association, 2008)

It is believed that the use of GTIN codes could greatly augment the amount of information that can be tracked throughout the lifecycle of fresh produce. Such expanded codes could be included in RFID tags or bar codes, and could include information on who produced the commodity, when, where and how. Each time the lot changes hands or is modified, broken up or regrouped, the

GTIN information would be similarly modified. All this information could be tracked in a worldwide database such as that being constructed by organizations like AgriWorld Exchange, making data mining and full traceability possible for the first time in the history of produce trading.

CONCLUSION

Food producers, packers, shippers, wholesalers, retailers and consumers around the globe have begun to pay much closer attention to the source, quality, characteristics and flow of fresh produce along the supply chain. Key issues at stake relate to the overall economics of food production, the challenges inherent in dealing with a perishable product, and food safety and, indeed, national security issues related to this vulnerable commodity.

Past efforts to collect and investigate such data were stymied by the lack of a central database, the paucity of information collected, and the absence of an internationally-accepted, sophisticated coding system that would be able to track individual produce items with sufficient granularity. While in the past some of this information was collected in individual databases, the systems were varied and of unequal quality, and the resulting data mining efforts were almost absent. Today, efforts are underway to build the massively-scalable systems and data warehouses that will need to come into play if we are to successfully trace the origin, safety and quality of the food we eat.

Today's new precise systems all have an important role to play in changing the status quo. The use of bar codes and RFID tags provides us the ability to do much more in-depth data collection and tracking of agricultural products, down to the individual item level. New centralized data repositories will allow us to track information related to production and handling of agricultural commodities. Similarly, they will allow us to track shipments of product – even as original lots are broken up and re-formed - along the entire supply chain. Massively scalable electronic commerce systems will enable us to track food products from the moment of production, and pinpoint the precise location within a field where they are grown. We will be able to understand all aspects of production, including chemical and biological agents used in food production. Perhaps most importantly, we will be able to track food all the way from initial production to the end consumer. Because of these advances, the future for agricultural data mining looks bright.

REFERENCES

AgriWorld Exchange (2008). AgriWorld Exchange Web site; www.agriworldexchange.com

Boeck, H., RFID Podcast. RFID Radio; June 4, 2007

Cal-Med Workshop (2007, October 26). *Traceability and Incentives for Food Safety and Quality: Implications for Mediterranean Crops*; Sonoma California.

Cooney, M. (2006, July 6). Data Mining *Report: Department of Homeland Security Privacy Office Response to House Report 108-774*

Cunningham, S., & Holmes (1999). Developing innovative applications in agriculture using data mining. University of Waikato, Department of Computer Science. *SEARCC 1999 Conference Proceedings.*

Dyckman, L. (2003). *Bioterrorism: A Threat to Agriculture and the Food Supply.* United States General Accounting Office: Testimony Before the Committee on Governmental Affairs, U.S. Senate.

Golan, E., Krissoff, B., Kuchler, F., Calvin, L., Nelson, K., & Price, G. (2004). *Traceability in the U.S. Food Supply: Economic Theory and Industry Studies.* Economic Research Service, U.S. Department of Agriculture, Agricultural Economic Report No. 830.

Government Accounting Office (2004). Data Mining: Federal Efforts Cover a Wide Range of Uses. GAO-04-548.

Head, B. (2004). Fresh Produce. CIO Magazine. Retrieved January 2008 from http://www.cio.com.au/index.php/id;282160542

Huang, S., & Huang, K. (2007). *Increased U.S. Imports of Fresh Fruit and Vegetables.* United States Department of Agriculture publication FTS-328-01. September 2007.

IDTechEx Ltd. (2007). Animals and Farming. *The RFID Knowledgebase.* Retrieved January 25, 2008 from http://rfid.idtechex.com/knowledgebase/en/nologon.asp

IDTechEx Ltd. (2008). *RFID Market Projections.* IDTechEx Ltd. Retrieved February 2008 from http://www.idtechex.com/

International Labour Organization (2007). International Labour Organization. Key Indicators of the Labour Market Programme. *International Labour Organization, 4,* 6.

Loaharanu, P. (2006). *Don't Fear Spinach – Irradiate It.* American Council on Science and Health. Health Facts and Fears.com. Retrieved from http://www.acsh.org/factsfears/newsID.865/news_detail.asp

Produce Marketing Association (2005, May). *ASAP Implementation Guide/* Produce Marketing Association publication. Newark Delaware USA.

Produce Marketing Association (2008). *GTIN – A Case for Streamlining the Supply Chain.* Publication of the Produce Marketing Association.

Primus (2008). Primus Labs Web site; www.primuslabs.com

Tian, L., Bullock, D., & Westervelt, J. (2001). *Developing an Agricultural Remote Sensing Program at the University of Illinois.* Illinois Laboratory for Agricultural Remote Sensing.

VandenBos, G., Knapp, S., & Doe, J. (2001). Role of reference elements in the selection of resources by psychology undergraduates. *Journal of Bibliographic Research, 5*, 117-123. Retrieved October 13, 2001, from http://jbr.org/chapters.html

Varchaver, N. (2004). Scanning the Globe. Fortune Magazine May 31, 2004.

Zanasi, A. (2007). *Data Mining and Information Engineering Conference 2007. Wessex Institute of Technology.* Retrieved January 2008 from http://www.wessex.ac.uk/conferences/2007/data07/index.html

KEY TERMS

Data Mining: Data mining is an information extraction activity whose goal is to discover hidden facts contained in databases. Using a combination of machine learning, statistical analysis, modeling techniques and database technology, data mining finds patterns and subtle relationships in data and infers rules that allow the prediction of future results. Typical applications include market segmentation, customer profiling, fraud detection, evaluation of retail promotions, and credit risk analysis.

Hidden Nodes: Hidden nodes are the nodes in the hidden layers in a neural net. Unlike input and output nodes, the number of hidden nodes is not predetermined. The accuracy of the resulting model is affected by the number of hidden nodes. Since the number of hidden nodes directly affects the number of parameters in the model, a neural net needs a sufficient number of hidden nodes to enable it to properly model the underlying behavior. On the other hand, a net with too many hidden nodes will overfit the data. Some neural net products include algorithms that search over a number of alternative neural nets by varying the number of hidden nodes, in the end choosing the model that gets the best results without overfitting.

Metadata: Metadata are data about data. An item of metadata may describe an individual datum, or content item, or a collection of data including multiple content items. Metadata (sometimes written 'meta data') are used to facilitate the understanding, use and management of data. The metadata required vary with the type of data and context of use. In the context of an information system, metadata about an individual data item would typically include the name of the field and its length. Metadata about a collection of data item - a computer file, for example – might include the name of the file, the type of file and the name of the data administrator.

Model: An important function of data mining is the production of a model. A model can be descriptive or predictive. A descriptive model helps in understanding underlying processes or behavior. For example, an association model describes consumer behavior. A predictive model is an equation or set of rules that makes it possible to predict an unseen or unmeasured value (the dependent variable or output) from other, known values (independent variables or input). The form of the equation or rules is suggested by mining data collected from the process under study. Some training or estimation technique is used to estimate the parameters of the equation or rules.

Neural Network: A neural network is a complex nonlinear modeling technique based on a model of a human neuron. A neural net is used to predict outputs (dependent variables) from a set of inputs (independent variables) by taking linear combinations of the inputs and then making nonlinear transformations of the linear combinations using an activation function. It can be shown theoretically that such combinations and transformations can approximate virtually any type of response function. Thus, neural nets use large numbers of parameters to approximate any model. Neural nets are often applied to predict future outcome based on prior experience. For example, a neural net application could be used to predict who will respond to a direct mailing.

Predictive Modeling: Predictive modeling is the process by which a model is created or chosen to try to best predict the probability of an outcome. In many cases the model is chosen on the basis of

detection theory, to try to guess the probability of a signal given a set amount of input data. An example would be predicting how likely it is that a given email is spam. Models can use one or more classifiers in trying to determine the probability of a set of data belonging to another set.

Traceability Systems: Traceability systems are recordkeeping systems designed to track the flow of product or product attributes through the production process or supply chain.

Chapter XIV
A Case Study in Data Mining for Automated Building of Teams

Robert K. McCormack
Aptima Inc., USA

Andrew Duchon
Aptima Inc., USA

Alexandra Geyer
Aptima Inc., USA

Kara Orvis
Aptima Inc., USA

ABSTRACT

This chapter highlights a case study involving research into the science of building teams. Accomplishment of mission goals requires team members to not only possess the required technical skills but also the ability to collaborate effectively. The authors describe a research project that aims to develop an automated staffing system. Any such system requires a large amount of personal information about the potential team members under consideration. Gathering, storing, and applying this data raises a spectrum of concerns, from social and ethical implications, to technical hurdles. The authors hope to highlight these concerns by focusing on their research efforts which include obtaining and using employee data within a small business.

INTRODUCTION

Data mining of customer information is now wide-spread throughout the business world, however systematic data mining of employee information is less common. Thus, while the opinions of consumers have driven much of the effort to protect their data, the opinions of employees have often been ignored. The attitude of employees towards the use of their personal data is greatly affected by their perceptions of the company's intentions. If the employer makes the effort to obtain permission from individual employees and carefully explain the goals of the data collection, negative perceptions may be reduced (Long & Troutt, 2003). Even when legal restrictions are observed, data mining within one's own organization can have far-reaching social and ethical implications. Any process which can be considered invasive to personal data requires sensitivity to all stakeholders, including both the employees and the company itself (Saban, 2001).

This chapter highlights the approach taken by one company in gathering, storing, and using employee data to automatically staff teams for new projects. The company described herein is a privately owned research and development firm with approximately 100 employees. The majority of the staff is comprised of scientific researchers with graduate degrees in psychology, cognitive science, human-system engineering, modeling and simulation, and computer science.

Much of the business performed by the company is supported by dozens of small government contracts obtained by responding to quarterly requests for proposals (RFPs) and winning follow-on work. Currently, teams for writing the proposals and carrying out the project work are created by word of mouth. This chapter focuses on one such project, TeamBuilder, conducting research into the science of building teams automatically from employee data. The goal of the project is to make the process of staffing teams more efficient and the projects more successful by automatically finding people that both have the requisite skills and would work best together as a team. It was decided by the TeamBuilder research team to use their own company as a test bed, due to familiarity with team processes within the organization and availability of data. It was determined early in the project that, in order to establish whether each given candidate possesses the necessary skills and abilities that are required for a specific team, large amounts of personal data would be needed.

Using employee data for any purpose has both drawbacks and benefits. Clearly, the employer would like to use all available information about employees that would make them more efficient, productive and successful. A well-conducted data analyses could also help build better relationships between employees and the organization, increase the opportunities and choices available to individuals, and in general help build a better understanding of the organization as a whole. Additionally, automated interpretation of the data could help management reach conclusions beyond the ability of human analysis and avoid inefficient word-of-mouth processes. On the other hand, there is the ever-present concern about invasion of privacy. Exploiting personal information also brings the risks of false conclusions being drawn, abuse of information to the detriment of individuals or organizations, and misapplication of erroneous data. These risks must be weighed against the benefits (Cook & Cook, 2003).

The organization of the chapter is as follows. We will first discuss the scientific and theoretical issues of staffing teams that are the basis for the TeamBuilder project. Then we will describe how we gathered the data for our case study while addressing privacy, ethical, legal and security concerns of the organization (both employees and management). Because the goal of the project is to create teams automatically, the integrity of the data must be high in order to obtain the trust of both management for using the tool and employees for understanding their assignments. We therefore describe a number of processes undertaken to ensure data integrity. Finally, we briefly discuss some of the computational methods we use to operationally define team theoretical constructs and employee abilities, in order to automatically staff teams with people who both have the skills to do the task and will work well together. There are issues with applying any automated process to assess human behavior and we provide some details of how we mitigate these concerns.

BACKGROUND

TeamBuilder Overview

Teams are an integral part of almost every organization. The use of teams allows consideration of expertise in multiple areas (Rouse, Cannon-Bowers, & Salas, 1992) as team members are often brought together with diverse knowledge, skills, and abilities. With technological advancements in communication, teams can now be formed across barriers of time and space, as project requirements dictate. The greater wealth of information that exists in teams, in comparison to any one individual member, has prompted a plethora of research dedicated to better understand the nature of teams (see Kozlowski & Ilgen, 2006, for a review). The area of team research that is very relevant to the TeamBuilder project is concerned with the understanding of team composition.

Traditionally teams have been staffed by matching individual demographic characteristics (training, rank, experience) to generic functional roles and known project requirements (Klimoski & Jones, 1995; Klimoski & Zukin, 1999). However, little research or practical attention has been directed to evaluating the efficacy of particular staffing strategies or determining how well team members, selected under certain strategies, actually work together as a team on given projects and within specific mission parameters. Ideally, team composition should reflect the full range of performance requirements posed by both the task itself and the collaborative quality of teamwork. **Taskwork skills** are the capabilities necessary to effectively complete all of the performance requirements for a particular task or project. **Teamwork skills**, on the other hand, are capabilities that allow individuals to operate effectively in a multi-person environment. Teamwork skills are the mix of attitudes, personality, and values that would optimize teamwork effectiveness and group cohesion among a particular set of individuals working within particular contexts. (Cannon-Bowers, Tannenbaum, Salas, & Volpe, 1995; Klimoski & Zukin, 1999; Morgan & Lassiter, 1992; Salas, Burke, & Cannon-Bowers, 2002).

A team staffing strategy should also reflect the most effective means of matching available human capital with the full range of requisite taskwork and teamwork skills demanded by the team's mission. While traditional staffing strategies have considered taskwork requirements, few, if any, have similarly acknowledged teamwork needs (Klimoski & Jones, 1995; Klimoski & Zukin, 1999). For example, if a project required a lot of interaction between the team members, then one might want to staff that project with people who have the generic teamwork skill of *cooperation* (Kerr, 1983).

The purpose of this research and development effort is to create a team staffing tool which assists managers in automatically forming teams that fulfill both taskwork and teamwork requirements. One of the sub-goals of this project is to capitalize on existing organizational resources (e.g. resumes, project information, and employee communication logs) to help identify the individuals who possess the skills required by project. A major aspect of this effort then is to determine the computational means by which to link the raw data to abstract taskwork and teamwork skills. Additionally, we discuss the ethical, legal, privacy and social implications that arose as various data resources were mined and applied in this context.

GATHERING, STORING, AND USING DATA FOR STAFFING TEAMS

Gathering the Data

Before the data-gathering process began, we first needed to address several issues regarding the ethical, legal, privacy, and social implications of collecting and using employee data. Although the company owns many of the data sources we wanted to utilize for TeamBuilder, such as time-card records, email, instant messaging, and phone logs, it was quickly decided that participation in the project would be strictly on an "opt-in" basis. With the support of the executive management, and assistance from legal professionals, a consent form was given to each employee describing the purpose of the project, their rights, and the types of data being collected. While many employees had concerns about privacy and the creation of an Orwellian atmosphere, explanation of the purpose and processes of the project allayed most of these fears. In the end, an overwhelming majority of employees chose to participate and allow access to their data. In this section, we will discuss the data gathering process for this project, including ethical and legal hurdles, the types of data collected, and the social implications of gathering data.

Addressing Privacy, Ethical, and Legal Risks of Data Gathering

Prior to gathering data, an effort was made to identify the risks and stakeholders in order to mitigate future problems. The data that had to be implemented in TeamBuilder could be divided into two categories: information about employees and information about projects. In general, gathering and using employee and project information introduces a variety of concerns. Whereas the exposure of project data poses little risk to individual employees, it could prove detrimental to the company itself. Use of employee data, on

the other hand, raises many issues, including privacy concerns for both the individual and the company as a whole. In order to alleviate some of the privacy issues, it was decided not to collect personal information regarding age, gender, race, performance, or pay because they were not essential for the purpose of this effort. Only employee and project data deemed absolutely necessary for TeamBuilder would be collected.

In order to create a version of TeamBuilder which would aid company staffers in putting together the best teams for proposals, projects, and special committees, it was necessary to obtain and analyze several data resources. Among these resources, resumes and biographies provide textual descriptions of individual professional skills, educational background, and employment history. This type of information is vital when it comes to matching the needs of the mission to the capabilities of the employees. Resources such as e-mail, phone, and instant messaging logs provide insight into the communication network among company employees. Rather than affording skill-based assessments of each individual, the communication logs can be used to determine teamwork skills. Timecards provide historic snapshots of project teams, the level of involvement by various employees, and how much groups of employees have worked together (which also touches on teamwork skills).

Project data supplies detailed information regarding all the past projects and teams that have been formed in the company. Spreadsheets on projects and proposals feature titles of the efforts, names of managers, budget information, period of performance, and other important facts. Descriptions of project requirements are obtained from government RFPs (Requests for Proposals). These requests describe the technical needs, dates, and provide names and contact information of customers for the given project. RFPs are used in TeamBuilder as a basis for matching project requirements to individual skills. Table 1 illustrates the data resources utilized in the

Table 1. Summary of data resources

	Data Resource	Description	Format
Employee Information	Resumes	Resumes for current and past employees with information on skills, past employment, and education	Unstructured text; format varies widely from person to person
	Biographies	Short description of employees' current and past work	Unstructured text
	Hire dates	Dates of hire and termination (if applicable) for current and past employees	Structured spreadsheet
	Communication logs	E-mail, phone, and instant messaging (IM) logs with information on sender, recipient, date/time, and size/duration (content not gathered)	SQL database
Project Information	Timecards	Hours charged by each employee to various projects broken down month by month	Structured spreadsheet
	Project information	Summary information on each project, including title, dates, customer, budget, and manager	Structured spreadsheet
	Proposal information	Summary information on each proposal, including title, dates, customer, and proposal leader	Structured spreadsheet
	Request for proposals (RFP)	Government issued requests with descriptions of desired work	Unstructured text

initial development of TeamBuilder, as well as their individual description.

Taking under consideration the social and ethical concerns that might be raised by gathering above data resources, efforts were made ensure that the collection was handled with utmost sensitivity and respect for privacy. It has been shown that individual's perceptions of fairness and invasion of privacy are affected by his or her ability to authorize or disallow disclosure of information (Eddy, Stone, & Stone-Romero, 1999). Even though all data required for the TeamBuilder project is the legal property of the company (since it is maintained on company computer equipment, systems and/or networks and used for business purposes), the company decided to extend a professional courtesy to its employees by allowing them to decide if they

wanted the data related to them to be used in this study. As Cook and Cook (2003) point out, ethics are more restrictive than the law and adhering to the law does not always mean being ethical. Even though the company was not legally obligated to obtain consent forms from its employees, it was done regardless.

The consent form was handed out to all company employees and contained relevant information about the project (e.g. funding source, purpose, benefits) as well as reasons for needing to collect the data. Several of the possible risks were identified, and the steps that would be taken to prevent them were described. It was also noted that participants could at any time during the course of the study revoke their consent, and withdraw without prejudice, and that refusing to participate would involve no penalty or loss of benefits to which they were entitled as employees. If a participant chose to withdraw from the experiment, personal data from that participant would be removed from all databases.

The following points illustrate some of the risks and concerns, as well as the mitigation strategies, as they were presented in the consent form.

1. Your signing of the informed consent form does NOT allow us to use the data for any other application/reason than building and testing the validity of our TeamBuilder approach.
2. If TeamBuilder proves to be a useful tool, it will NOT be the ultimate decision maker for all teams created. It is intended to be a decision support tool that can help people choose members for teams (whether that would be proposal teams, special interest teams, project teams, etc.). The decision to use it would be strictly up to you. Currently we build teams by word of mouth and employee expertise is sometimes overlooked. Our hope is that it will open more opportunities up to company employees, and not less. In addition, functionality is built into the tool which allows novices to try new roles/projects. Therefore, TeamBuilder will not stunt employee growth.
3. We are not gathering any content from E-mail, IM, and phone. Even if we wanted to look at the content of those messages, we couldn't feasibly do it. We have absolutely no access to it whatsoever. We are using the "to-from" data for social network analysis, to see who is communicating with whom. This may serve as selection criteria if the "mission" required a team that could hit the ground running. In that case, you might want to pull together people who have worked together many times in the past.
4. Your data will not be shared with anyone outside of the organization. We are creating "dummy data" for the customer.

This approach was successful in that about 93% of the company's employees signed the consent form granting us access to their data. Of those who did not participate, some stated that they made this decision because they felt uncomfortable sharing their private data, even if it was only for the purpose of the TeamBuilder project. Overall, the key concerns for many employees were with respect to accessing the content of their e-mail, IM, and/or phone conversations. We reassured people that this would not be the case. We also stressed to everyone that refusal to sign the consent form would not result in any type of penalty or loss of benefits.

For several members of the staff, it was deemed in the best interest of the individuals, the company, and the TeamBuilder project not to include them in the data collection process. These employees included several members of the human resources staff who regularly send and receive highly sensitive emails and communications. Even though we were not gathering content of these communications, the frequency or amount of emails between HR staff and individual employees may itself be highly sensitive and raise privacy concerns. As Fule and Roddick (2004) explain, data at different levels of sensitivity can be represented in a hierarchy of interest. The frequency with which email is sent may be less sensitive than the full content of the messages, but these levels of sensitivity can vary among different groups.

Gathering Project and Employee Data

With the help of the human resource staff, contracts management, and information systems groups, gathering the various data resources was a straightforward procedure. Based on the list of identified resources as well as the list of participating and excluded employees, data resources were collected and stored in a central computer. Since employee biographies (displayed on the company website) and government RFPs are publicly available, they were easily obtained.

Project and proposal information, while containing somewhat sensitive company data, is available to all employees. With the approval of the executive management, these resources were obtained for the TeamBuilder project. Resumes, hire dates, timecards, and communication logs were collected and filtered to exclude the non-participating employees.

Storing and Organizing the Data

After obtaining consent and collecting the various data sources, the next step in the TeamBuilder project was to incorporate the data into a single relational database. In this section we will discuss the technical challenges in transferring data from raw formats into a cohesive database structure while preserving the integrity of the data. This includes structured data such as email logs and timecards, as well as unstructured text, as found in resumes and project abstracts. We will delve into the process of correlating disparate data sources in which identifiers do not always match (e.g. names spelled differently in separate data sources). In addition, we will discuss the steps taken to ensure privacy of the data.

In all, we identified and gathered eight different types of data, as described in Table 1. Because each data source varied widely in the type and format of information contained within, individual data extractors were created to parse out the relevant information from the source and store it in a relational database table. Note that this is inherently an ad hoc process. Extractors were tailored for the individual idiosyncrasies of each data source and relied on us recognizing the repeating patterns, if any. Once the desired data were identified in the text, they were inserted into the proper fields of the database.

Figure 1 displays a sample of the database tables derived from timecard data used for this project. Each box represents a table in the TeamBuilder database. The column names and data types (e.g., INTEGER vs. TEXT) are defined for each table. The data types used for each table were often dictated by the original data source.

The timecard data is broken out into three separate tables: employees, projects, and a relational table describing the hours each employee worked on a given project during a particular month. Because the timecard management system uses automated record keeping, it was decided that this data would serve as the canonical list of both employees and projects. That is, the timecard data is taken as the standardized list of all employees and projects to which other data resources are mapped. The correlation of disparate data resources is discussed shortly. Now, we briefly describe how each data resource was mined, and the types of information extracted.

Figure 1. Example tables in the TeamBuilder database

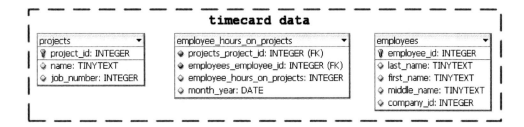

Parsing and Storing Unstructured Textual Data

Much of the data needed for TeamBuilder is stored in unstructured documents. These include resumes, biographies, and government RFPs. Each of these types poses unique challenges for extracting data. Because they consist mainly of free text and have little consistency in format between documents, locating relevant information can be time consuming. Here we describe the general approach to data extraction from each unstructured data source.

- **Resumes:** Employee resumes vary widely in their formats, but generally contain the same types of information. For this project, we were interested in the skills and past education of each employee. In the analysis and use of resume data, text analytic techniques are used (as described in the next section). Therefore, it is not necessary to manually identify and categorize different features of the text, such as specific skills, because the text analytic algorithms operate on raw text. However, sections of the resumes which describe skills, education, etc. must be tagged and stored in the database for inclusion in the algorithms. Because the resumes lacked a cohesive format, much of data tagging was done by hand.
- **Biographies:** Employee biographies are short, one to two paragraph descriptions of current and past projects and skills, used mainly for marketing (e.g. placement on the public website or attaching to proposals). Like the resumes, biographies are used to identify individual skills and experience using text analysis. Thus, while not necessary to manually extract individual pieces of data, sections containing pertinent information were tagged.
- **Requests for Proposals:** Government RFPs in general include a title, objective,

and description, along with metadata such as a solicitation code and technical point of contact. The majority of RFPs follow a consistent format and therefore the sections of raw text identifying metadata, objectives and topic descriptions can be found.

Parsing and Storing Structured Data

Structured data comes in several forms, most notably in this case, spreadsheets and databases. Dates of hire, proposal and project information, and timecard data are all accessible via standard spreadsheets. Communication data from email, phone, and instant messaging are automatically stored in a database. Parsing this data and inserting it into the database is accomplished in a fairly straightforward manner. We describe the data extracted from these structured resources.

- **Hire Dates:** The dates of hire and, for former employees, termination, were maintained in a spreadsheet, and only minor algorithmic steps were necessary to ensure dates were formatted correctly for the database.
- **Timecards:** Timecard information for each employee is collected by an automated system. Monthly reports are generated as structured spreadsheets. We were able to extract specific pieces of data from the spreadsheets and insert them into the database. This data included each employee's name, the total number of hours logged for each month, and the total hours charged to each project during each month.
- **Proposal Information:** High-level information on submitted job proposals is stored in a structured spreadsheet. Included in this information are reference numbers, proposal titles, proposal managers, customer information, proposed budget, and likelihood of winning.
- **Project Information:** As with proposal information, high-level information on

each project at the company is stored in a structured spreadsheet. This information includes internal job numbers, the job number of the proposal which led to the project, the project title, the customer, the budget, begin and end dates, and the project manager.

- **Communications Data:** Data regarding e-mail, phone, and IM conversations is automatically logged and stored by the company's Information Systems division. This data includes the sender, recipient, timestamp, and size/duration of the communication. It does not, however, include information on the content of the messages or conversations. The IS system stores all of the logs in a database, so it was a simple matter of importing that information into the central TeamBuilder database.

Correlating the Database

After each data resource was formatted and inserted into the database, the next step was to correlate the information across different sources. Because the various data resources are maintained in different ways, by different people, and for different purposes, there is often no direct link between corresponding entities within different sources. Records between databases may not match for several reasons including: letter transpositions, omission of letters, misspellings, changes in personal information, use of nicknames, or even fraud (Cook & Cook 2003). Additionally, the manner in which entries are stored in different databases can make it difficult to match corresponding entities. For example, an employee's name might be stored as "John Smith" in one resource and as "JSMITH" in another.

In general, the task of matching multiple references to the same entity is referred to as record linkage. First introduced in the late 1950's, the theory of record linkage was later formalized by Felligi and Sunter (1969). In their article, Felligi and Sunter classify the decisions made when

comparing entity data as either a link (the data refers to the same entity), a non-link (the data does not refer to the same entity), or a possible link (manual review is required). An optimal linkage rule can then be defined which attempts to minimize the error when assigning links and non-links, as well as minimize the number of possible links for manual review. The actual rules and processes which are used to match the data can vary. The most straightforward approach to record linkage is a rules-based method. Here, common rules for matching entities are defined and then revised as exceptions occur. While this approach is relatively easy to implement, the number of rules and exceptions can grow very quickly. Standardization of the data can help mitigate many of the exceptions and rules (Welker 1993). Statistical and machine learning approaches to record linkage, such as Bayesian networks, offer more robust solutions, but require labeled training data (Gu 2003, Welker 2002).

For the TeamBuilder project, the decision was made to use a **mixed-initiative interaction** approach based on rules-based methodologies to correlating the data.

A mixed-initiative approach combines the strengths of the computer agent with the strengths of the human agent, applying each when appropriate (Hearst 1999). The goal of Day, et. al. (1997) in their mixed-initiative approach to language processing was to "transform the process of manual tagging to one dominated by manual *review*." Likewise with TeamBuilder, our aim is to push the burden for correlating entities onto the computer and leave the process of reviewing to the human user. This process takes advantage of the ability of the computer to quickly match similar entities across data resources along with any added knowledge that the user has which isn't explicitly formalized in either the computer program or data. For example, if an employee was to get married and changed her name, the computer may have difficulty linking the different name references to the same person. The human operator can inject that knowledge in the review process to make the correlation.

This mixed-initiative approach was deemed appropriate for this application for a number of reasons. First, the time constraints placed on this portion of the project did not allow implementation of complex statistical methods for linking data. Instead, a rules-based approach was used in which individual data fields were matched across resources. The process of matching entities was accomplished through the text matching capabilities of the database. When possible matches were identified, the user was tasked with approving or rejecting the matches. In the case of incorrect matches, the user was asked to choose the correct match from the list of all entities. This approach is sub-optimal by Felligi and Sunter's definition, due to the fact that to the number of possible links identified is not minimized. But, once the constraint of time was considered, this approach proved to be more desirable. Additionally, due to the size of the data (approximately 100 entities to be correlated), this particular mixed-initiative rules-based approach was manageable. With larger data sets this approach can still be applied, but caution is necessary to ensure that the burden on the user remains minimal. Using the computer to find possible matches and presenting the user with the ability to accept or reject the match is less time consuming than manually matching entities especially when dealing with large sets of data. However, when dealing with larger quantities of entities, optimizing the rules of automated matching to better identify positive links becomes increasingly important. Statistical methods are better suited to large data sets, and the time spent applying them is easily made up by the decrease in time spent during manual review.

Figure 2. Correlation tables in the TeamBuilder database

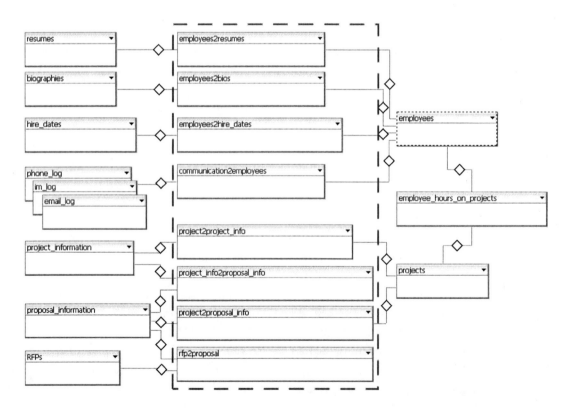

The first step to this approach to correlating tables within the database is to identify specific corresponding fields within each table. As stated previously, the employees and projects tables (derived from the timecard data) are taken to be the canonical repositories of employee names and project names and codes. Thus, all tables containing information about employees are correlated back to the employees table, and likewise for projects. A program was developed for the TeamBuilder project which allows the user to specify the rules for matching entities. For example, in the table for hire dates, employee names are stored in a single field by last name, first name. In the employees table, names are stored in separate fields for first and last. After the user has configured these values, the program finds the closest matches between the tables. Using a mixed-initiative approach, the results are displayed to the user who can then select the correct matches. Figure 2 illustrates the tables used for correlating different data sources within the database.

Privacy and Security Perspectives in Data Storage

In general, there are many techniques for protecting stored data. Based on the proposed application of the data and level of security required, one or more can be implemented to mitigate misuse of the data. Limiting access of the data resources to trusted users is a common approach (Clifton and Marks, 1996). At one end of the spectrum, access control mechanisms can be used to completely allow or deny access to the data. At a finer resolution, users can be given rights of use to only certain portions of the database to prevent full exposure of the information. Aggregation is another technique in which data is combined either within or across individuals. This can often be done in such a way as to prevent undesired uses of the data, while still enabling the planned applications (Verykios, et. al., 2004). Elimination

of unnecessary groupings can prevent unwanted information from being exposed. For example, when storing employee phone numbers, the use of the area code can be used to determine general locations of individuals. If the area code is not necessary for the intended application of the data, it should be eliminated from the database. Adding misleading entries to the database can obfuscate the data to unwanted queries. This must be done in such a way, though, so the intended access algorithms will only retrieve correct information. For example, suppose extra, fictitious people were added to a company phone book. It would still be possible to find the phone number of a known individual, but queries to find all individuals in a particular group would return additional fictitious people. This technique makes it more difficult to distinguish actual data points from the added noise. Perturbation of the data, through alteration by a known value or addition of noise, can limit access to users who know the perturbation scheme (Clifton and Marks, 1996).

To mitigate the risk of exposure of any information in TeamBuilder, it was deemed sufficient to implement access control procedures. A small subgroup of the development team was given admission to the database. Access was further limited by only giving users access to the portion of the data required for their research. While for some researchers it was necessary to allow full access to the data, others were, for example, allowed to view resumes, but denied privileges to the communication logs.

In addition to accidental exposure of private data, inaccurate correlation of disparate data resources can have undesirable social consequences. In the case of TeamBuilder specifically, if incorrect data is correlated to individuals it can bring about sub-optimal team assignments. Teams which are ill-equipped to face their missions, in terms of either teamwork or taskwork competencies, can lead to stressful social environments. A mixed-initiative approach to handling the data diminishes this risk by taking advantage of the speed and capabilities of the computer along with human oversight.

Using the Data

Once the data has been organized into a common database, the TeamBuilder algorithms can operate on the data to provide measures of individual and team skills and competencies, and ultimately assemble near-optimal teams. The various algorithms which operate on the data include natural language processing, social-network analysis, and multivariate optimization. Each of these will be described along with other issues such as dealing with missing data. At this stage of the process, again, individual privacy is an important issue. Additionally, there are social implications involved in using TeamBuilder. While the system does incorporate a wide range of data, there are still exogenous factors that can influence the assignment of teams. We will discuss the steps taken to mitigate social concerns.

TeamBuilder analyzes three types of data. The first type of data is textual descriptions of the mission and of the skills of the employees: the taskwork skills needed and available. The second type of data is relationships between employees, as well as an employee's people skills as determined by social network analysis: the teamwork skills. Social network analysis (SNA) examines the social structure formed between individuals and applies mathematical techniques to derive measures such as *centrality* of leadership and *cohesion* of individuals or groups. The third type of data are the constraints associated with putting together any particular team due to availability, cost, and the like.

TeamBuilder is designed to be as unobtrusive, yet helpful, as possible. This requires that the analysis of these three types of data be done automatically with minimal input by supervisors and employees. In addition, the outputs of the system must make sense and be trusted by both parties. To enable this process, we take advantage of a number of recent advancements in text analytics, social network analysis and multivariate utility assessment.

Assessing the Taskwork Skills of the Team

To match the skills of employees to the requirements of a mission, we use an unsupervised machine-learning technique called **Probabilistic Latent Semantic Analysis** (PLSA; Hoffman, 2001). PLSA produces a probabilistic multinomial model of the domain of interest – in this case the team and task-relevant characteristics of personnel. Although PLSA was initially developed as a word-focused tool for information retrieval that could function without dependence upon a dictionary, thesaurus, or a predefined taxonomy of concepts (Hofmann, 2001), it is a far more flexible methodology. Any type of discrete (i.e. count) data, such as elements in personnel bio-data, documents dealing with performance on projects, and more, can also be used in PLSA to assist in mapping the space of interest – here, taskwork skills. These skills are defined by "topics" which are simply distributions of words or other features.

As an example, consider the RFPs from a recent batch of Department of Defense Small Business Innovation Research program. These RFPs, which are generally one page, single-paced, represent the mission data. They describe the general objective to be achieved, a small background section and description of the problem, then the specific goals of the contract. For employee data, we have biographies (typically 1-2 paragraphs) and resumes of current and previous company employees and consultants. Both the RFPs and the bio-data were analyzed with the PLSA technique using a 40-topic model.

Table 2 illustrates the top ten most probable features from four of the topics in the model, in this case the features are words and their stems (e.g., materials, material, and materialization, would all

Table 2. Topics extracted from a corpora of text using PLSA

Topic 10	Topic 12	Topic 16	Topic 37
Materi	Health	Cultur	Human
Composit	Medic	Cultural	Factors
Materials	Diseas	Train	Factor
Composite	Care	Game	Design
Parachut	Clinic	Training	Interaction
Polym	Medical	Behaviors	Interfac
Textil	Clinical	Interactions	Interact
Composites	Blood	Behavior	Usabl
Fiber	Food	Cultures	Usability
Parachute	Ahlta	Interact	interface

be stemmed to "materi"). Even with this small amount of data some very clear topics emerge. Topic 10 is about composite materials for making parachutes. Topic 16 is about game-based training of cultural behaviors and interactions. Topic 37 is concerned with human factors and interface usability. Thus, PLSA is able to automatically extract the "gist" of a document, in this case an RFP or employee biography/resume. That is, after reading an RFP and being asked what it is about, the first few content words one would say would be in the topic, e.g., "Oh, it's something to do with human factors and designing an interface."

The topics create a layer of abstraction between the documents and the words in the documents. Thus, when comparing documents, matches can be made even when the individual words within the documents are mutually exclusive. For example, if the RFP uses only the terms "human factors design" and a person's resume only uses "interface usability," even though they refer to the

same skill, the two documents will be recognized as highly related because they both score high on Topic 37 in Table 2. Using these definitions of the topics, every RFP and biography/resume can be characterized by a "topic profile," i.e., the extent to which the document is concerned with each topic. This information can then be used to determine the relevance of an employee to a particular RFP. This is achieved by directly comparing the topics of the employee with the topics of the RFP.

No one employee is likely to have all the necessary skills, so multiple employees will typically be required to achieve the goals of a mission. At the same time, one does not want skills duplicated between employees, therefore TeamBuilder aims to minimize the overlap between employees, while maximizing the match to the mission tasks.

Assessing the Teamwork Skills of the Team

In an organization, many employees are likely to have some of the same requisite skills, and teams of them can be created that have little overlap among those skill sets; but another aspect of team performance is how well the team members will work together to accomplish the task. Of the teams of people that do have all the skills required, which team would work together best and be most likely to succeed? To assess this, TeamBuilder takes advantage of a variety of analyses of the data.

Simple measures of success rates for individuals can fairly easily be derived directly from the data. Examining the percentage of projects an individual has been involved in that have had follow-on work can provide some insight into the past performance and success of that person. Combining measures such as this with other data, for instance percentage of total project hours worked by each team member, can further differentiate individual success from overall team success. More interesting information can be obtained by looking at other, "softer" aspects of an individual's work behavior. For example, an employee's "dependability" could be ascertained by looking at the frequency or speed with which they return emails to other people on the team when they are working on a project together versus when not (to account for more general friendship between them).

To further illustrate how measures of individual behaviors can be ascertained from the given data, consider the skill of **conflict management**. We define this as managerial experience in resolving potential disputes among team members. In the absence of data documenting past disputes, we operate under the hypothesis that functionally diverse teams (i.e. teams composed of individuals with different technical skills and backgrounds) are more likely to have conflict than teams composed of similar individuals. Conflict, in this sense, is related to disagreements over technical approach, goals, etc., rather than personality conflicts. To measure the functional diversity of a team, some value of similarity between individual members is needed. PLSA provides a means of comparing team members. The resumes of individuals are used to train a PLSA model, and thereby comparisons can be made between each pair of team members. The functional diversity of the team is derived from these calculations. Teams with highly dissimilar members will be more functionally diverse.

To determine a manager's experience in conflict management, we can therefore examine the functional diversity of all the teams he or she has managed in the past. To further refine this measure, the functional diversity of teams can be weighted by the project's success. Thus, highly diverse teams that succeeded in their mission indicate higher conflict management skills of the manager than teams which were diverse but failed their mission.

Other kinds of specific teamwork skills may be required for a leader of the team. For example, a mission may require a leader that is good at direction-setting. That is, he or she is capable of determining the end state or specific end product. Information about this skill could be ascertained by a number of means such as looking at the number of previous projects they have led (a more general assessment), or looking at the number and length of email chains they initiate to project team members.

TeamBuilder will also assess measures of the team as a whole, such as cohesiveness using **social network analysis**. These analyses would, for example, examine the timecard data showing who has worked on what projects at the same time. High correlations between people indicate that they work on a lot of the same projects, and over time would suggest that they work well together. Measures of this type could also be weighted by the success of the projects to eliminate people who work together a lot by circumstance but do not accomplish their tasks as well.

However, a fully-connected network of team members with previous experiences together may not be the ideal team design. Rather, a few individuals with many prior connections, and most with little or no prior connections, have been shown to enhance team functioning (Lazer & Katz, 2000). Further, a recent study on free-riding /social loafing in teams investigated the association between network ties and the amount of effort individuals invested in their teams. Their surprising finding was that although previous relationships with other team members was *not* related to team effort, the extent of common third-party relationships of team members (knowing the same people in common *outside* the team) was strongly related to team effort. The more people team members knew in common, the more effort they invested in their team work (Lazer & Katz, 2005).

Centrality, or the relative importance of individual nodes in a network, is an essential measure used in social network analysis. However, there is no single agreed upon conceptual definition or procedure to measure centrality (Freeman, 1979). We propose a measure based on email communications between team members. For each past project, we derive a value of centrality of each team member. By examining the total number of recipients on emails that an individual receives, the exclusiveness in communications for that individual can be determined. That is, we measure the degree to which team members send emails to an individual where he or she is the only (or one of a few) recipient. The centrality of a single team member can then be derived from his or her measures of communications exclusiveness with other members. Our hypothesis is that individuals who receive many communications addressed only to them play an important and central role on the team. This measure can be used to determine the functional leaders or the highly knowledgeable members of the team.

Taskwork skill assessment can be explained in a more straightforward manner, and gaps or overstatements of skills probably due to a lack of information by the TeamBuilder system that can be overcome. Teamwork skills and social connections however, may be more difficult to explain and thus less trusted by supervisors and employees. For example, no one will want to be labeled as less "dependable" than someone else, even if these measures reflect people's (unstated) perceptions of others. To mitigate problems with such measures, supervisors will actually see this information only at the team level, e.g., the average dependability of one team versus another. In this manner, individuals maintain a certain (though not complete) amount of anonymity.

In addition, what relative weight should be put on dependability, or direction-setting or any other teamwork skill, versus taskwork skills is a matter of empirical research which we are conducting. This research will walk-forward through historical data to determine which of these parameters are best at determining a team's success. In any case, as with the task skills, the supervisor will have the final say on who will be assigned to the team.

Assessing Constraints on the Team

After determining who, among those groups of people who have the right skills, would work well together and have a high probability of success, we must determine if these individuals are actually available to work at the right time, for the right amount of money, and at the least cost to other projects. These logistical constraints can be satisfied, and combined with the other two types of measures using the "**multivariate utility assessment algorithm**" (Levchuk, 2003) to assess the projected overall quality of the mission, based on projected quality of each task, past history of team members' performance, and the relative cost in time, dollars and other projects' probabilities for success.

The complexity of combining these different kinds of information is one reason for our development of TeamBuilder. No supervisor would be able to weigh all of these factors, let alone have access to the information on which they are based. At the same time, the reasons behind the ranking of teams given a mission must make some intuitive sense in order to be useful for supervisors to use. That is, if a supervisor had access to all the information, could figure out what weight each factor should have, then determine the costs and other constraints, then he or she should come to the same conclusion. As TeamBuilder is developed and deployed we will constantly monitor its "sanity" such that both supervisors and subordinates will trust its results enough to not be threatened.

There are several social implications to keep in mind resulting from this process. Depending on the accuracy of the data, TeamBuilder may not suggest perfectly capable individuals for a particular mission. To mitigate the consequences of the automatic assignments, we always present to the supervisor the list of potential team members and their skills/topics. The supervisor can at this point always add team members that might be appropriate, or remove those that are not. Thus, the system itself is merely a suggestion tool, performing triage, with ultimate responsibility up to supervisor. Allowing human override of the systems suggestions can have either positive or negative consequences, depending on the motives of the user. Ultimately, we feel that employees will be more comfortable with the final decision if it is derived from both the human and computer, rather than from one independently.

FUTURE TRENDS

Transitioning to Novel Organizations

Because the data mining conducted in this project was completely internal to the company, the legal hurdles faced in collecting employee data were relatively few. Additionally, the types of personal data collected, such as resumes and timecards, were less invasive than other sources, such as performance reviews or pay scales. Transitioning a project such as TeamBuilder to new organizations presents a new set of problems.

Most organizations have strict data privacy policies in place and will allow access to different types of information. The way in which data is stored and used can depend on a number of factors, such as the size of the business or the type of business (government, military, private).

To cope with the different types and sources of data, TeamBuilder is designed to be adaptable to different situations. By creating a layer of abstraction between the teamwork and taskwork measures needed to drive the tool and the underlying data resources, the tool can handle changes in data availability. For example, measures of specific taskwork skills can be derived from resumes or biographies through natural language processing. If those sources are not available, other resources, such as surveys or skill assessment tests, can be substituted.

The greatest challenge to introducing Team-Builder to novel environments will be the social, ethical, and legal issues involved with the particular organization. By bringing to light these concerns, strategies can be formulated to mitigate the risks involved in such a process. Ultimately, successful integration of a tool like TeamBuilder requires buy in from both the organization and the employees.

CONCLUSION

Traditional methods of assembling teams are based on manual matching of individual skills to the requirements of the mission tasks. These methods often do not consider the quality and mix of the teamwork and collaboration skills across the team members. This can lead to poor performance even when each individual is technically qualified to accomplish his or her tasks. By automating the selection of teams and considering taskwork and teamwork competencies, the team members will be better prepared tackle the mission goals in a collaborative manner. In this chapter we provided insight into the technical challenges of such an endeavor, as well as the social and ethical implications of automatically assigning teams.

The automated process of assigning teams requires large amounts of personal data about the potential team members. Using employee data can greatly enhance the quality of the product, but introduces many concerns. The ethical and social challenges associated with obtaining personal information are often more difficult than the legal concerns. Obtaining employee buy-in in order to use their data requires a careful approach and explanation of intentions. The technical issues inherent in dealing with disparate data resources are challenging, but can be dealt with through a systematic approach. This is required to ensure the integrity of the data and the soundness of automated assessments of employees and their assignment to projects. Through understanding of the risks involved in projects like the one described here, both individuals and organizations can benefit from strategic use of employee information.

ACKNOWLEDGMENT

This work was supported under Air Force contract FA8650-07-C-4510 with approval WPAFB 08-3088.

REFERENCES

Cannon-Bowers, J. A., Tannenbaum, S. I., Salas, E., & Volpe, C. E. (1995). Defining competencies and establishing team training requirements. In *Team effectiveness and decision making in organizations,* Guzzo & Salas (Eds.), Jossey-Bass, San Francisco, 333–380.

Clifton, C., & Marks, D. (1996). Security and privacy implications of data mining. In *Proc. 1996 SIG-MOD'96 Workshop on Research Issues on Data Mining and Knowledge Discovery (DMKD'96),* Montreal, Canada., pp. 15-20,

Cook, J. S., & Cook, L. L. (2003). Social, ethical, and legal issues of data mining. In *Data Mining: Opportunities and Challenges,* Wang, J. (Ed.), Idea Group Publishing, Hershey, PA, 395-420.

Day, D., Aberdeen, J., Hirschman, L., Kozierok, R., Robinson, P., & Vilain, M. (1997). Mixed-Initiative Development of Language Processing Systems. *Fifth Conference on Applied Natural Language Processing, Association for Computational Linguistics,* 348-355.

Eddy, E. R., Stone, D. L., & Stone-Romero, E. F. (1999). The effects of information management policies on reactions to human resource systems: An integration of privacy and procedural justice perspectives. *Personnel Psychology, 52,* 335-358.

Fellegi, I. P., & Sunter, A. B. (1969). A Theory for Record Linkage. *Journal of the American Statistical Association, 64,* 1183-1210.

Freeman, L. C. (1979). Centrality in Social Networks, Conceptual Clarification. *Social Networks, 1,* 215-239.

Fule, P., & Roddick, J. F. (2004). Detecting privacy and ethical sensitivity in data mining results. Appeared at *Twenty-Seventh Australasian Computer Science Conference* (ACSC2004), Dunedin, New Zealand.

Gu, L., Baxter, R., Vickers, D., & Rainsford, C. (2003). Record Linkage: Current Practice and Future Directions. CMIS Technical Report No. 03/83, CSIRO Mathematical and Information Sciences, GPO Box 664, Canberra 2601, Australia.

Hearst, M. (1999). Trends & Controversies: Mixed-initiative interaction. *IEEE Intelligent Systems, 14*(5), 14-23.

Hoffman, T. (2001). Unsupervised Learning by Probabilistic Latent Semantic Analysis. *Machine Learning Journal, 42*(1), 177-196.

Kerr, N. L. (1983). Motivation losses in small groups: A social dilemma analysis. *Personality and Social Psychology, 45*, 819-828.

Klimoski, R., & Jones, R. G. (1995). Staffing for effective group decision making: Key issues in matching people and task. In *Team effectiveness and decision making in organizations,* Guzzo & Salas (Eds.), Jossey-Bass, San Francisco, 292-332.

Klimoski, R., & Zukin, L. (1999). Selection and staffing for team effectiveness. In *Supporting work team effectiveness: Best management practices for fostering high performance,* E. Sundstrom & Associates (Eds.), Jossey-Bass, San Francisco.

Kozlowski, S. W. J., & Ilgen, D. R. (2006). Enhancing the effectiveness of work groups and teams. *Psychological Science in the Public Interest, 7,* 77–124.

Lazer, D., & Katz, N. (2000). Putting the Network into Teamwork. Presented at the Academy of Management annual meeting, Toronto, Canada.

Levchuk, G. M., Feili, Y., Pattipati, K. R., & Levchuk, Y. (2003). From hierarchies to heterarchies: Application of network optimization to design of organizational structures. *Proceedings of the 8th International Command and Control Research and Technology Symposium,* Washington, DC.

Long, L. K., & Troutt, M. D. (2003). Data mining for human resource information systems. In *Data Mining: Opportunities and Challenges,* Wang, J. (Ed.), Idea Group Publishing, Hershey, PA, 366-381.

Morgan, B. B., & Lassiter, D. L. (1992). Team composition and staffing. In *Teams: Their training and performance,* R. Sweezy & E. Salas (Eds.), Kluwer, Norwood, Mass., 75–100.

Rouse, W. B., & Morris, N. M. (1986). On looking into the black box: Prospects and limits in the search for mental models. *Psychological Bulletin, 100,* 350–363.

Rouse, W., Connon-Bowers, J., & Salas, E. (1992). The role of mental models in team performance in complex systems. *IEEE Trans. On Sys., man, and Cyber, 22*(6), 1296-1308.

Saban, K. (2001). The data mining process: At a critical crossroads in development. *Journal of Database Marketing, 8,* 157-167.

Salas, E., Burke, C. S., & Cannon-Bowers, J. A. (2002). What we know about designing and delivering team training. In *Creating, implementing, and managing effective training and development: State-of-the-art lessons for practice,* K. Kraiger (Ed.), Jossey-Bass, San Francisco, 234–259.

Verykios, V. S., Bertine, E., Fovino, I. N., Provenza, L. P., Saygin, Y., & Theodoridis, Y. (2004). State-of-the-art in Privacy Preserving Data Mining. *ACM SIGMOD Record, 33*(1), 50-57.

Winkler, W. E. (1993). *Matching and record linkage.* Washington, D.C.: Bureau of the Census.

Winkler, W. E. (2002) *Methods for Record Linkage and Bayesian Networks.* Washington, D.C.: Statistical Research Division, Bureau of the Census.

KEY TERMS

Centrality: A commonly used measure in social network analysis which determines the relative importance of a node within a network. There is no single, agreed-upon method to measure centrality; different methods are used depending on the application. In the case of building and assessing teams, centrality within the communication network can be used to determine the functional leaders or knowledgeable members of the team.

Conflict Management: A measure of a leader's ability to successfully manage functionally diverse teams. When creating teams with members of highly varied backgrounds and skills, conflict management is an important managerial skill for resolving disputes related to goals and technical approaches. This is an example of a teamwork skill that can be derived from employee data.

Mixed-Initiative Interaction: An approach which combines the strengths of the computer agent and strengths of the human agent, applying each when appropriate. In record linkage, or the correlation of entities across data sources, mixed-initiative approaches can take advantage of the pattern matching abilities of the computer, leaving the task of reviewing the matches to the user.

Multivariate Utility Assessment: A mathematical optimization technique to assess the projected overall quality of the mission, based on projected quality of each task, past history of team members' performance, and the relative cost in time, dollars and other projects' probabilities for success.

Probabilistic Latent Semantic Analysis (PLSA): A statistical natural language processing technique for analysis of co-occurrence data within large corpora of text. PLSA finds the underlying topics, or "gist", of a document and can be used for searching or comparing documents.

Social Network Analysis (SNA): An analysis technique which examines the social structure formed between individuals and applies mathematical techniques to derive measures such as centrality of leadership and cohesion of individuals or groups

Taskwork Skills: Capabilities necessary to effectively complete all of the performance requirements for a particular task or project.

Teamwork Skills: The mix of attitudes, personality, and values that would optimize teamwork effectiveness and group cohesion among a particular set of individuals working within particular contexts.

Chapter XV
Basic Principles of Data Mining

Karl-Ernst Erich Biebler
Ernst-Moritz-Arndt-University, Germany

Bernd Paul Jäger
Ernst-Moritz-Arndt-University, Germany

Michael Wodney
Ernst-Moritz-Arndt-University, Germany

ABSTRACT

This chapter gives a summary of data types, mathematical structures, and associated methods of data mining. Topological, order theoretical, algebraic, and probability theoretical mathematical structures are introduced. The n-dimensional Euclidean space, the model used most for data, is defined. It is executed briefly that the treatment of higher dimensional random variables and related data is problematic. Since topological concepts are less well known than statistical concepts, many examples of metrics are given. Related classification concepts are defined and explained. Possibilities of their quality identification are discussed. One example each is given for topological cluster and for topological discriminant analyses.

INTRODUCTION

Data mining is up to a point a self-guided data-evaluating process and influenced by accompanying activity of the user. In comparison to data analysis, it describes an in-advance-defined process of the data evaluation. Data mining describes explorative procedures most of the time. Hypoth-eses being in connection with the examined data are sought. One must presuppose nothing about the methods of the collection of the data.

The concluding procedures pursue another aim position: A given hypothesis shall be checked with data. The collection of the data then must be carried out according to certain principles, however.

As a rule, if statistical procedures are used, the data must be able to be regarded as samples.

More exact definitions of the concepts of information and hypothesis are not looked here. Contributions to the methods of data mining are from different branches, for example computer science, logic, learning theory, artificial intelligence, also from the application fields like medical informatics, financial analysis etc.

Basic concepts of data mining shall be explained in the following. The concepts used are part of different areas of mathematics. They are defined and illustrated as examples.

One has to distinguish data of different types. According to this, the mathematical methods of data evaluation have to be designed. The mathematical structures are of basic importance. They correspond with the respective data types. The result interpretations must refer to it.

If one can calculate the pair wise distances for the objects of a data set, then so-called topological methods of data mining can be designed.

Statistical methods of data mining are based on observations of random variables. It is presupposed mostly that the data are a sample. If this is not the case, statistical methods are considered only in exceptions. It is not a trivial problem of deciding whether data are a sample of a random variable. Therefore, we point to not statistical methods of data mining.

Methods of data mining are mathematical procedures. Its variety is exceptionally broad. We therefore confine ourselves to some classification methods and different possibilities of their treatment.

The reader is able thus in principle to recognize the connection of data type, observation strategy, structure of the data as well as the data-mining method. This is essential for any result interpretation.

Transformations of the original data can influence the results of data mining. It is therefore recommended always to refer to the original data.

DATA TYPES

Observations at objects are informed about as data. One can receive these observations as measuring, numbers or verbal descriptions, for example. Sometimes they concern a quality, often also more qualities. Also more complicated facts can be included concerning the objects, such as relations. It is therefore required to distinguish data types. Data types relevant for the data analyses are described in the following.

One knows data types also from programming languages. These shall not be treated here.

A set X in the set-theoretical meaning consists of elements x_i, $X = \{x_i, i \in I\}$. The index I may be finite or infinite. According to this one distinguishes finite and infinite sets. The sets $\{x_1, x_1, x_1, x_2\}$ and $\{x_1, x_2\}$ are the same in the set-theoretical meaning. This means all elements of a set are different.

Data sets are collections of elements of a set. The data sets $\{x_1, x_1, x_1, x_2\}$ and $\{x_1, x_2\}$ have to be distinguished. The same element of a set can appear repeatedly in a data set.

String data are signs or character strings (e.g. letters, words, abstract words). Numerical data are numbers (e.g. 3, 324, 2.1482). Dates are not regarded as numeric data. They form a type of their own.

Categorical data are collections of elements of a set X, e.g., {red, red, red, green, green} is collected from X = {red, green, blue}. Categorical data can be string data or numerical data.

Ordinal data is data which can be ordered. One can order numbers after their size. The words of a language are string data and can be ordered in a dictionary.

Metric data are collections of elements of an interval X of real numbers, e.g., {2.001, 13.2, 1.008, 200.23} shall have been collected from X = [0; 225]

Symbolic data are collections of compositions of elements of different sets, e.g.,

$$\{S3, \text{Sunshine}, (C1,C2), 23, (\text{Boston } 3/4, \text{ Cambridge} 1/4), (10,26)\}$$

is one observation from the composition of sets

$$\{\text{supplier, company, customer, working time, town , number}\}$$

The first and the second variable are string variables. The third one is a multivariate variable. "Working time" is a numeric variable. The variable "town" is multivariate with evaluating weights, "number" is multivariate.

The analysis of symbolic data is a relatively new field of data mining. One finds more to this at (Bock & Diday, 2000), for example.

STRUCTURES

The qualities of data types are obviously different. With numeric data one can execute algebraic operations. An example is the calculation of the average weight of objects. Of course such a calculation is not possible for string data. The methods required for the evaluation of data are dependent on the qualities of the data. Structures serve for the description of such qualities on sets. We look at the structures practically most important to data mining in the following.

Algebraic Structures

The majority of the data-mining methods calculate using the data itself. One consequently needs an algebraic structure for the data. This is only possible for data of the numeric type.

Let $\mathbb{R}$ denote the set of real numbers and $\mathbb{R}^n = \mathbb{R} \times \mathbb{R} \times ... \times \mathbb{R}$ its n-fold product. The element $x \in \mathbb{R}^n$, $x = (x_1, ..., x_n)$ is called row vector.

The representation

$$x = \begin{pmatrix} x_1 \\ \vdots \\ x_n \end{pmatrix}$$

is a column vector. The real numbers $x_i \in \mathbb{R}$ are the coordinates of the vector $x = (x_1, ..., x_n)$. $\mathbb{R}^n$ with the addition $x + y = (x_1 + y_1, ..., x_n + y_n)$ for $x = (x_1, ..., x_n)$ and $y = (y_1, ..., y_n)$ from $\mathbb{R}^n$ and the scalar multiplication $\alpha x = (\alpha x_1, ..., \alpha x_n)$ for $\alpha \in \mathbb{R}$ is called vector space.

$y = \alpha_1 x_1 + ... + \alpha_k x_k$ with $\alpha_i \in \mathbb{R}$ is called a linear combination of the elements $x_i \in \mathbb{R}^n$, $i = 1, ..., k$.

A row vector $x = (x_1, ..., x_n)$ and a column vector

$$y = \begin{pmatrix} y_1 \\ \vdots \\ y_n \end{pmatrix}$$

of the equal length n can be multiplied. One gets the scalar product

$$\langle x, y \rangle = \sum_{i=1}^{n} x_i y_i .$$

The column vector y is written comfortably in the transposed form $y' = (y_1, ..., y_n)$.

A rectangular scheme $A_{m \times n} = (a_{ij})$ of real numbers a_{ij} with $i = 1, ..., m$ rows and $j = 1, ..., n$ columns is called matrix of type (m, n). If the rows and the columns of a matrix $A_{n \times m}$ of type (n, m) are exchanged, then one gets the transposed matrix $A'_{m \times n}$ of type (m, n).

The addition of two matrices $A = (a_{ij})$ and $B = (b_{ij})$ of the same type (m, n) is defined element wise, $A + B = C = (c_{ij})$, and $c_{ij} = a_{ij} + b_{ij}$ for $i = 1, ..., m; j = 1, ..., n$. If a matrix $A_{mxn} = (a_{ij})$ has just as many rows as the number of columns in the matrix $B_{nxp} = (b_{jk})$, then one can form its product $A_{m \times n} B_{n \times p} = C_{m \times p}$. The elements of $C_{m \times p}$ are

$$c_{ik} = \sum_{j=1}^{n} a_{ij} b_{jk}$$

for $i = 1, ..., m$ and $k = 1, ..., p$.

The inverted matrix regarding the multiplication of a matrix $\mathbf{A}$, the so-called inverse matrix $\mathbf{A}^{-1}$, can be calculated under certain assumptions. The explanations to this would be too extensive here. Interested readers are referred to textbooks on linear algebra.

We can explain the concept data matrix now. A number of p metric features are observed in n objects, $xr_i = (x_{i1}, ..., x_{ip})$ and $i = 1, ..., n$. These are the row vectors of the observations. They form the data matrix X of type (n, p)

$$\mathbf{X} = \begin{pmatrix} x_{11} & x_{12} & \cdots & x_{1p} \\ x_{21} & x_{22} & \cdots & x_{2p} \\ \vdots & \vdots & \vdots & \vdots \\ x_{n1} & x_{n2} & \cdots & x_{np} \end{pmatrix} = \begin{pmatrix} xr_1 \\ xr_2 \\ \vdots \\ xr_n \end{pmatrix}.$$

The column vector $xc_j' = (x_{1j}, ..., x_{nj})$ represents the n observed values for feature j, $j = 1, 2, ..., p$. The vector of the arithmetical means $\overline{x} = (\overline{x}_1, ..., \overline{x}_p)$ of the features can be calculated from the data matrix as:

$$\overline{x} = (\overline{x}_1, ..., \overline{x}_p) = \frac{1}{n} \mathbf{1} X.$$

The symbol $\mathbf{1}$ describes the vector $\mathbf{1} = (1, ..., 1)$ of the length n here. The matrix $S_{p \times p} = (s_{jk})$ of squared deviances:

$$s_{jk} = (x_{1j} - \overline{x}_j, ..., x_{nj} - \overline{x}_j)(x_{1k} - \overline{x}_k, ..., x_{nk} - \overline{x}_k)'$$

permits the calculation of the matrix of empirical covariances of the p features as

$$C = \frac{1}{n-1} S.$$

The empirical covariance matrix $C = (c_{ij})$ is of type (p, p) and symmetric regarding its main diagonal.

The calculation of C is explained in another way now.

The vector $xc_j' = (x_{1j}, ..., x_{nj})$ is associated to the feature m_j. Its mean is:

$$\overline{x}_j = \frac{1}{n} \sum_{i=1}^{n} x_{ij}.$$

The vector of centralized observations $(xc_j^z)' = (x_{1j} - \overline{x}_j, ..., x_{nj} - \overline{x}_j)$ can be calculated with that. The empirical covariance $c_{jk} = \widehat{\text{cov}}(xc_j, xc_k)$ of two features is then calculated from the data $xc_j' = (x_{1j}, ..., x_{nj})$ and $xc_k' = (x_{1k}, ..., x_{nk})$ under use of the scalar product of vectors as:

$$\widehat{\text{cov}}(xc_j, xc_k) = \frac{1}{n-1} (xc_j^z)' xc_k^z = \frac{1}{n-1} \langle xc_j'^z, xc_k'^z \rangle$$

The empirical variance of $xc_j = (x_{1j}, ..., x_{nj})$ is $\widehat{\text{var}}(xc_j) = \widehat{\text{cov}}(xc_j, xc_j)$, the empirical standard deviation is:

$$s(xc_j) = \sqrt{\widehat{\text{cov}}(xc_j, xc_j)}.$$

The matrix X^z of data, centralized regarding the features $m_1, ..., m_p$, is

$$\mathbf{X}^z = \begin{pmatrix} x_{11} - \overline{x}_1 & x_{12} - \overline{x}_2 & \cdots & x_{1p} - \overline{x}_p \\ x_{21} - \overline{x}_1 & x_{22} - \overline{x}_2 & \cdots & x_{2p} - \overline{x}_p \\ \vdots & & \vdots & \vdots & \vdots \\ x_{n1} - \overline{x}_1 & x_{n2} - \overline{x}_2 & \cdots & x_{np} - \overline{x}_p \end{pmatrix}.$$

The empirical covariance matrix C is then the matrix product of X^z with its transposed matrix,

$$C = \frac{1}{n-1} (X^z)' X^z.$$

One gets the standardized observation vectors

$$\left(xc_j^s\right)' = \frac{\left(xc_j^z\right)'}{s\left(xc_j\right)} = \left(\frac{x_{1j} - \bar{x}_j}{s\left(xc_j\right)}, \; ..., \; \frac{x_{nj} - \bar{x}_j}{s\left(xc_j\right)}\right), j = 1, \; ..., \; p$$

with that. The empirical correlation $\widehat{\mathrm{corr}}\left(x_j, x_k\right)$ is

$$r_{jk} = \widehat{\mathrm{corr}}\left(xc_j, xc_k\right) = \frac{\left(xc_j^s\right)'xc_k^s}{n-1} = \frac{\widehat{\mathrm{cov}}\left(xc_j, xc_k\right)}{s\left(xc_j\right)s\left(xc_k\right)}$$

The matrix of the empirical correlations $\boldsymbol{R} = \left(r_{jk}\right)$ is of type (p, p) and symmetric. It can be calculated as

$$\boldsymbol{R} = \frac{1}{n-1}\left(\boldsymbol{X}^s\right)'\boldsymbol{X}^s.$$

$\boldsymbol{X}^s$ is the standardized data matrix here,

$$\boldsymbol{X}^s = \begin{pmatrix} (x_{11}-\bar{x}_1)/s(xc_1) & (x_{12}-\bar{x}_2)/s(xc_2) & \cdots & (x_{1p}-\bar{x}_p)/s(xc_p) \\ (x_{21}-\bar{x}_1)/s(xc_1) & (x_{22}-\bar{x}_2)/s(xc_2) & \cdots & (x_{2p}-\bar{x}_p)/s(xc_p) \\ \vdots & \vdots & \vdots & \vdots \\ (x_{n1}-\bar{x}_1)/s(xc_1) & (x_{n2}-\bar{x}_2)/s(xc_2) & \cdots & (x_{np}-\bar{x}_p)/s(xc_p) \end{pmatrix}$$

.

Its columns are the standardized observation vectors. $r_{jj} = 1$ holds for the elements of the main diagonal of the matrix $\boldsymbol{R}$.

The concepts covariance, standard deviation and correlation have a probability theoretical character. The calculations put on here are also feasible if the data are not sample results, of course. One must then confine himself to the algebraic and the geometrical interpretations. If two vectors are empirically uncorrelated, for example, then this means its orthogonal in the $\mathbb{R}^n$. In the two dimensional space $\mathbb{R}^2$ orthogonal means geometrically two straight lines which include a right angle.

Topological Structures

A topological structure on a set permits the description of the position of the elements of the set to each other. The distance of two objects which lie on the table is measured.

Distance and proximity are ideas of our geometrical experience. If we ask for the distance between San Francisco and Berlin, the answer is no longer trivial. How shall the distance be measured? Lengthways the imaginary direct connecting line? Along a line on the surface of the earth? Which line on the earth's surface is chosen? So there are different methods of the distance measuring between points on a spherical surface.

Obviously the concept distance must be defined abstractly. This is done in the following way: Let be X a set and d: $X \times X \to \mathbb{R}$ a real function with the properties

1. $d\left(x, y\right) \geq 0$,
2. $d\left(x, y\right) = d\left(y, x\right)$ (symmetry),
3. $d\left(x, y\right) \leq d\left(x, z\right) + d\left(z, y\right)$ (triangle inequality),

for all $x, y, z \in X$. Then d is called a distance.

A distance with the property

4. $d\left(x, y\right) = 0$ if and only if $x = y$

is called a metric. X gets a metric structure by d, (X, d) is called a metric space.

With the following examples the variety of metric structures shall be indicated. This gives a certain idea on the scale of the class of the topologically founded data-mining methods. The qualities of these methods are determined by the used metric fundamentally. According to the data and the aim of data mining a metric can be chosen.

Examples of Distances in Different Sets

1. Let be X the set of all matrices of type (m, n). The distance between two elements $A = A_{m \times n} = \left(a_{ij} \right)$ and $B = B_{m \times n} = \left(b_{ij} \right)$ of X can be measured by $d\left(A, B \right) = \left| a_{11} - b_{11} \right|$.

   This distance is not a metric, because $d\left(A, B \right) = 0$ if and only if $a_{11} = b_{11}$. But of course it is possible to define a metric:

   $$d\left(A, B \right) = \max_{i=1,\ldots,m; j=1,\ldots,n} \left| a_{ij} - b_{ij} \right|$$

   or

   $$d\left(A, B \right) = \sum_{i=1}^{m} \sum_{j=1}^{n} \left| a_{ij} - b_{ij} \right|.$$

   These expressions can be zero only, if all $a_{ij} = b_{ij}$, $i = 1, \ldots, m$ and $j = 1, \ldots, n$.

2. Let be X the set of all continuous functions over the interval [a, b]. The distance $d\left(f, g \right) = \left| f(x_0) - g(x_0) \right|$ is not a metric again, if x_0 is an arbitrary but fixed point of the interval [a, b]. A metric we obtain by the definition $d\left(f, g \right) = \max_{x \in [a,b]} \left| f(x) - g(x) \right|$.

   The metric is a very important concept. If one have a set with a metric, it is possible to define other terms like convergence or continuity.

Examples of Metrics for Numeric Data

1. The set $\mathbb{R}$ equipped with the distance

   $$d_1\left(\alpha, \beta \right) = \left| \alpha - \beta \right| \text{ for } \alpha, \beta \in \mathbb{R},$$

   the absolute value of the difference, is a metric space. Especially, $d_1\left(\alpha, 0 \right) = \left| \alpha \right|$ is valid. The absolute value of a number is its distance from zero.

2. The Euclidean metric

   $$d^E\left(x, y \right) = \sqrt{\sum_{i=1}^{n} \left(x_i - y_i \right)^2}$$

   is defined for $x = \left(x_1, \ldots, x_n \right)'$ and $y = \left(y_1, \ldots, y_n \right)' \in \mathbb{R}^n$. $\left(\mathbb{R}^n, d^E \right)$ is called the Euclidean space. The Theorem of Pythagoras illustrates geometrically the Euclidean metric in the two dimensional $\mathbb{R}^2$. The distance of the point $x = \left(x_1, x_2 \right)$ from the origin $\mathbf{0} = (0, 0)$ is given by $d^E(x, 0) = \sqrt{x_1^2 + x_2^2}$, the length of the connecting line. All points with Euclidean distance 1 from the origin form a circle. The equation

   $$\left(d^E\left(\mathbf{x}, \mathbf{y} \right) \right)^2 = \left(x_1 - x_2 \right)^2 + \left(y_1 - y_2 \right)^2$$
   $$= \left\langle \mathbf{x} - \mathbf{y}, \mathbf{x} - \mathbf{y} \right\rangle$$

   gives a relation of the Euclidean distance and the scalar product of two vectors. It can be extended without any problems to higher dimensional spaces. This way topological structure and algebraic structure are connected.

3. The so-called Manhattan metric

   $$d\left(x, y \right) = \sum_{i=1}^{n} \left| x_i - y_i \right|,$$

   defined on $\mathbb{R}^n$, measures the distance of two points parallel to the coordinate axes. This is the sum of the lengths of the legs of a right triangle in the two-dimensional case.

4. The first three examples are special cases of the so-called L_p-metrics

   $$d^{Lp}\left(x, y \right) = \sqrt[p]{\sum_{i=1}^{n} \left| x_i - y_i \right|^p},$$

   $x, y \in \mathbb{R}^n$ and a real number $0 < p < \infty$. This traditional name p is not in a relation with the feature number p used for the data matrix above! One gets the Manhattan metric for $p = 1$. The Euclidean metric gives up for $p = 2$.

5. The Canberra metric

$$d^{CANB}(x, y) = \sum_{i=1}^{n} \frac{|x_i - y_i|^s}{|x_i| + |y_i|}.$$

is defined on $\mathbb{R}^n$ for a real number $s \geq 1$.

6. A metric on $\mathbb{R}^n$ is defined by

$$d(x, y) = \max\{|x_i - y_i|, \ i = 1, ..., n\}.$$

7. The Mahalanobis metric on the data matrix is of special significance for data mining. It is defined by

$$d_{ij}^M = d_{ij}^M(xr_i, xr_j) = \sqrt{(xr_i - xr_j)\, C^{-1}\, (xr_i - xr_j)'}, \ i, j = 1, ..., n$$

$xr_i = (x_{i1}, ..., x_{ip})$ and $xr_j = (x_{j1}, ..., x_{jp})$ describe observation vectors and C^{-1} the inverse empirical covariance matrix here. The Mahalanobis metric is defined in dependence of the data matrix. This is a remarkable peculiarity!

The special case of a data matrix of the type $(n, 2)$ is looked at in the following. Two features m_x and m_y are watched. The vectors of observations shall be called $xc = (x_1, ..., x_n)'$ and $yc = (y_1, ..., y_n)'$. Abbreviating one normally writes $\widehat{\text{cov}}(xc, yc) = s_{xy}$, $\widehat{\text{var}}(xc) = s_x^2$, $\widehat{\text{var}}(yc) = s_y^2$. For the empirical covariance matrix

$$C = \begin{pmatrix} s_x^2 & s_{xy} \\ s_{xy} & s_y^2 \end{pmatrix}$$

one has the inverse matrix

$$C^{-1} = \frac{1}{s_x^2 s_y^2 - s_{xy}^2} \begin{pmatrix} s_y^2 & -s_{xy} \\ -s_{xy} & s_x^2 \end{pmatrix}.$$

One calculates the quadratic Mahalanobis distance

$$(d_{ij}^M)^2 = (xr_i - xr_j) C^{-1}(xr_i - xr_j)$$
$$= \frac{(x_i - x_j)^2 s_y^2 - 2(x_i - x_j)(y_i - y_j)s_{xy} + (y_i - y_j)^2 s_x^2}{s_x^2 s_y^2 - s_{xy}^2}$$

for the observations $xr_i = (x_i, y_i)$ and $xr_j = (x_j, y_j)$ with that. All points of a Mahalanobis distance one from the zero form an ellipse. In cases where the sample covariance matrix is the unit matrix

$$\begin{pmatrix} 1 & 0 \\ 0 & 1 \end{pmatrix},$$

Mahalanobis distance and Euclidean distance coincide. This is exactly the case then if the two columns of the standardized data matrix are orthogonal.

Do data transformations influence the distance measuring? Scale changes that are multiplications of all observed values of a feature by the same number, translations, reflections or rotations of the observation vectors are examples of data transformations. The Euclidean distance is translation invariant, invariant regarding reflection and rotation of the vectors. It is not invariant against scale change. The Mahalanobis distance is invariant regarding all mentioned data transformations. The L_p-metrics are not scale invariant, in general.

Binary data and metrics: Categorical features can always be coded as binary vectors. One writes "1" if the category was watched, otherwise one writes "0". One uses special metrics in the case that the objects are characterized by binary variables. Some of them are introduced here. The symbolism is explained in the Table 1.

The $\alpha, \beta, \gamma, \delta$ are the numbers of coordinates of two binary vectors $x = (x_1, ..., x_n)$ and $y = (y_1, ..., y_n)$ of length n, respectively, for which the entries of 0 or 1 are in the given relation. α is the number of coordinates in which both

Table 1.

		y_i	
		value 1	value 0
x_i	value 1	α	β
	value 0	γ	δ

$\mathbf{x} = (x_1, ..., x_n)$ and $\mathbf{y} = (y_1, ..., y_n)$ have the value 1, for example.

One calculates the following metrics with that:

8. Jaccard metric

$$d_J(x, y) = 1 - \frac{\alpha}{\alpha + \beta + \gamma},$$

9. Kendall metric

$$d_K(x, y) = 1 - \frac{\alpha + \delta}{\alpha + \beta + \gamma + \delta},$$

10. Anderberg metric

$$d_A(x, y) = 1 - \frac{\alpha}{\alpha + 2(\beta + \gamma)},$$

11. Rogers/Tanimoto metric

$$d_T(x, y) = 1 - \frac{\alpha + \delta}{\alpha + 2(\beta + \gamma) + \delta}.$$

These distances can be used at the analysis of gene sequences, for example.

Metrics and mixed type data: Let

$$\mathbf{X} \oplus \mathbf{Y} = \begin{pmatrix} x_{11} & x_{12} & \cdots & x_{1r} & y_{11} & y_{12} & \cdots & y_l \\ x_{21} & x_{22} & \cdots & x_{2r} & y_{21} & y_{22} & \cdots & y_{2t} \\ \vdots & \vdots & \vdots & \vdots & \vdots & \vdots & \cdots & \vdots \\ x_{n1} & x_{n2} & \cdots & x_{nr} & y_{n1} & y_{n2} & \cdots & y_{nt} \end{pmatrix}$$

of mixed type. The x-rows are metric data related to a metric d_1, the y-rows are binary data related to a metric d_2. Then the sum

$$d_{sum}(\mathbf{O}_i, \mathbf{O}_j) = d^M(\mathbf{x}_i, \mathbf{x}_j) + d_T(\mathbf{y}_i, \mathbf{y}_j)$$

is a metric on the whole mixed type data.

The maximum of the Rogers/Tanimoto metric is 1. The Mahalanobis metric runs from zero to infinity. These are very different distance measures. Therefore the Mahalanobis metric is transformed,

$$d^M_{trans}(\mathbf{x}_i, \mathbf{x}_j) = \frac{d^M(\mathbf{x}_i, \mathbf{x}_j)}{1 + d^M(\mathbf{x}_i, \mathbf{x}_j)}$$

is a metric again. Its range is [0, 1). With that the mixed metric

$$d^\Sigma(\mathbf{O}_i, \mathbf{O}_j) = d^M_{trans}(\mathbf{x}_i, \mathbf{x}_j) + d_T(\mathbf{y}_i, \mathbf{y}_j)$$

is defined. Its range is [0, 2). Concerning the distance measuring the categorical features and the metric features have been made comparable and in a mixed metric summarized.

Data-mining methods can be adapted to the data situation by metrics of the mixed type.

It is not trivial to choose a suitable metric for a given problem.

Distance matrix: One also can use the distance matrix for data mining besides the empirical covariance matrix and the matrix of the empirical correlations. The distances of *n* objects in the p-dimensional feature space are arranged in a matrix of type (n, n). For the observations $\mathbf{x}_i = \left(x_{i1}, ..., x_{ip}\right)$ and $\mathbf{x}_j = \left(x_{j1}, ..., x_{jp}\right)$ we get the Euclidean distances

$$d_{ij}^{E} = d_{ij}^{E}\left(\mathbf{x}_i, \mathbf{x}_j\right) = \sqrt{\left\langle \mathbf{x}_i - \mathbf{x}_j, \mathbf{x}_i - \mathbf{x}_j \right\rangle} = \sqrt{\sum_{k=1}^{p}\left(x_{ik} - x_{jk}\right)^2}$$

as the elements of the distance matrix $\mathbf{D}^{E} = \left(d_{ij}^{E}\right)$ of type (n, n). A distance matrix is a symmetric matrix. The elements d_{ii} of its main diagonal are zero.

Order Structures

The order of elements of a set can be very helpful at data descriptions and data evaluations. The empirical median is the centre of the ascending ordered sample values in the descriptive statistics.

It suffices that the data are of the ordinal type. A whole group of statistical procedures is based on the idea of evaluating its rank numbers (the positions of the data in its ascending arrangement) instead of the data.

It is not a problem to order numbers. However, what shall be an order on an arbitrary set?

Let X be a set. A preorder on X is a relation R of $X \times X$ satisfying the following conditions:

1. If $x \in X$ then (xRx);
2. If (xRy) and (yRz), then (xRz).

If a preorder is given on X, then X is called a preordered set. It is more familiar to write $x \leq y$ instead of (xRy). Then $(X, \leq)$ is the notation of a preordered set.

If additionally holds

3. if $x \leq y$ and $y \leq x$, then $x = y$,

a preorder is called an order.

Two elements $x, y \in X$ of an ordered set $(X, \leq)$

are comparable if and only if either $x \leq y$ or $y \leq x$. Otherwise they are incomparable. A set X is totally ordered if and only if it is ordered and every two elements of X are comparable.

An order structure can be illustrated by a tree diagram.

Examples:

1. The set of real numbers $(\mathbb{R}, \leq)$ with the natural order is a totally ordered set.

2. The set of all English words is totally ordered by the alphabetical order (lexicographic order).

   The total order of the alphabet is transmitted to the set of the words. To be able to compare words of different length, an special letter $\varnothing$ is added to the alphabet. It is the "empty" letter, has no meaning, fills gaps and is the smallest element in the order of the letters. With that, the words "alpha" = "alpha $\varnothing \varnothing \varnothing$" and „alphabet" become comparable.

3. The system $\wp(X)$ of all subsets of a set X provided with the set theoretical inclusion $\subseteq$ is a preordered set. The empty set $\varnothing \in \wp(X)$ is its smallest element.

4. Consider the set $C\left([a,b]\right)$ of all continuous functions defined on the interval $[a,b] \subset \mathbb{R}$. This set is preordered by the definition $f \leq g$ for $f, g \in C\left([a,b]\right)$ if and only if $f(x) \leq g(x)$ for all $x \in [a,b]$. If two functions intersect, they are not comparable. Topological structure and order structure on a set are compatible in the ideal case. We consider an example: Let $\{\nabla, \Diamond\}$ be an abstract alphabet and W the set of all words of length of at most 2 over the abstract alphabet $\{\nabla, \Diamond\}$ inclusive the empty word $\varnothing$. Then W provided with the set theoretical inclusion $\subseteq$ is a preordered set. Two metrics are looked at on W, defined as

$$d_I\left(w_1, w_2\right) = \frac{WL - NI}{WL} \text{ and}$$

$$d_P\left(w_1, w_2\right) = \frac{WL - NP}{WL}$$

for words $w_1, w_2 \in W$, *WL* the maximum of the length of these two words, *NI* the number of word positions with identical symbols for these two words and *NP* the maximal length of the prefixes common to both words. The words $w_1 = \nabla\nabla$ and $w_2 = \lozenge\nabla$ are incomparable regarding the defined preorder. One calculates for these words $d_I(w_1, w_2) = 1/2$ and $d_P(w_1, w_2) = 1$. The latter is the maximal distance. The incomparable words do not have any maximum distance with respect to d_I. This metric is not compatible with the given preorder.

Structures given on a set are compatible in the ideal case. From mathematics one knows that the Euclidean space $\mathbb{R}$ is almost the only object in which the natural algebraic, topological and order structures are compatible. Consequently, if the data are not elements of the $\mathbb{R}$ special attention must be given to adequate analysis methods, peculiarities of structures and the interpretation of the results in data mining.

Metrics are needed at classification methods. Many classification methods also work besides metrics with measures which are based on similarities. Such measures usually do not fulfil the triangle inequality. The usual geometric ideas are then not valid. In the interpretation, similarity does not mean closed. Since sufficiently suitable metrics are available, one also should use these.

Probability Structure

Two reasons are mentioned to use concepts of the quantitative description of chance. Firstly, data mining shall use statistical methods. This is the case if general statements shall be derived from the data. Secondly, one studies the qualities of a chance event himself. The mathematical descriptions of chance are starting point. They are called also stochastic models.

The set X is provided with a probability structure $[X, \wp(X), P]$. It is the basic set of a probability space $[X, \wp(X), P]$. $\wp(X)$ describes the subset system of X and P a probability measure here. One calls X a population in this context. So the word has another meaning here than in the colloquial language!

One calls a function $Y: X \to \mathbb{R}$ a real-valued random variable if $\{\omega : Y(\omega) \le c\} \in \wp(X)$ for all $c \in \mathbb{R}$. The distribution function $F_Y(x)$ of a real-valued random variable Y is defined as $F_Y(x) = P(Y \le x)$. A continues random variable has a probability density function f. It is non-negative and

$$F_Y(x) = \int_{-\infty}^{x} f(t)dt.$$

Background of the mathematical modelling of chance is the abstract idea of the random experiment. The random experiment has a result. One cannot predict this result. The random experiment can be arbitrarily often repeated under identical conditions.

We look at an example. The colour of objects is a random quality. Three colours are possible, $X = $ {red, green, blue} is regarded as population. The probabilities of the appearance of these colours are P(color = red) = 3/6, P(color = green) = 2/6 and P(color = blue) = 1/6.

The elements of $\wp(X)$ are the empty set $\varnothing$, the three one-element sets, the three two-element sets and the whole population X. This way the probability space is described completely for the example.

What is the random experiment in our example? It consists in the observation of the colour of the objects. If the objects are always selected by chance and independently from the same set of objects, one has repeated the experiment under the same conditions. It can particularly happen that an object is watched repeatedly.

It is a typical task to calculate the unknown probabilities from the data. This is simple if the set of objects is small. One watches all objects. The relative frequency of a colour is taken as its probability.

If the set of objects is large, one watches a sample of the population. This is a finite number of executions of the random experiment. For our example, this means that one takes an object by chance and registers its colour. Then the object is given back to the object set. An object can be watched so repeated.

A sample does not have to be "typical". The probability that all 10 results of a sample yield "blue" is $\left(\frac{1}{6}\right)^{10} = 0.000\ 000\ 017$ and different from zero. On the other hand, a sample is representative. This means every object has the same chance to be selected for the observation.

One distinguishes the concepts "population" and "set of the observation objects"!

If the elements of a population are numbers, X is called a random variable. One can calculate with random variables. It is possible with that to establish statistical procedures. Measuring in ounces and measuring in gram yield different codes of a population of birth weights, e.g. They are two different random variables. Different results in the application of statistical methods possibly arise from the different codes.

Probability distributions of random variables are given by distribution functions or probability densities. Most popular example is the family $N\left(\mu, \sigma^2\right)$ of normal-distributed random variables $X_{\mu\sigma^2}$, characterized by the density functions

$$f_X(x) = \frac{1}{\sqrt{2\pi\sigma^2}} e^{-\frac{1}{2}\frac{(x-\mu)^2}{\sigma^2}}, \quad \mu \in \mathbb{R}, \ \sigma^2 > 0.$$

The expectation μ and the variance σ^2 are approximated by the mean value or empirical expectation and sample variance or empirical variance, respectively, derived from sample data. These are estimations of the distribution parameters μ and σ^2. There is the general question whether data are normal distributed. One must therefore carry out a statistical test of goodness of fit.

A two-dimensional normal-distributed random variable (X, Y) is looked at now. Its density reads as

$$f_{X,Y}(x,y) = \frac{1}{2\pi\sigma_X\sigma_Y\sqrt{1-\rho_{XY}^2}}$$
$$\cdot \exp\left\{-\frac{1}{2\left(1-\rho_{XY}^2\right)}\left[\left(\frac{x-\mu_X}{\sigma_X}\right)^2\right.\right.$$
$$-2\rho_{XY}\frac{x-\mu_X}{\sigma_X}\frac{y-\mu_Y}{\sigma_Y}$$
$$\left.\left.+\left(\frac{y-\mu_Y}{\sigma_Y}\right)^2\right]\right\}$$

The correlation coefficient ρ_{XY} measures the "stochastic dependence" of X and Y. Graphs of such two-dimensional density functions shows Figure 1. One can give no more graphic illustration for the higher-dimensional case.

Data mining with statistical methods is based in many cases on the supposition that the data is multivariate normal distributed. It is not a simple problem to decide whether multivariate data is normal distributed. Do the data represent at all a sample on a multivariate normal distribution?

Ontologies

If the elements of a set X are connected by a system of relations, one gets an ontology $[X, \Re]$ in the sense of information science. Ontologies are used for the knowledge representation. An application of this method in data mining is the case-based reasoning. An ontology with order character is also called taxonomy. Example is the system of Linnè for the order of the plants.

DATA-MINING PROCEDURES

Data mining is a semiautomatic interactive process of the explorative data analysis. The discovery of trends and patterns in the data is the aim. Therefore the methods of data mining shall be as general as

Figure 1. 3D-Plot of two-dimensional normal densities with $\mu_x = \mu_y = 0$, $\sigma_x = \sigma_y = 1$ and different correlation coefficients $\rho = 0.1$ (left) and $\rho = 0.9$ (right)

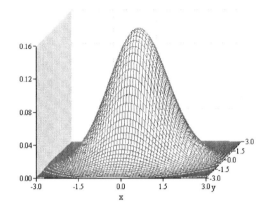 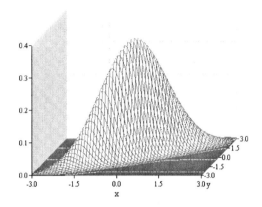

possible. In the classic data analysis one examines, on the other hand, special questions on the base more specific mathematical models.

We only want to go into two problems of the data mining here. Multivariate data of the metric type are looked at. A statistical concept of data mining is not possible if nothing is known about the a priori probability distribution of the data and about the quality of the data. It is particularly unknown whether the data represent a sample according to the statistics.

Data Visualizations

Data description is always based on a model. Statistical data descriptions are the best known. In higher dimensional data they prove, however, to be problematic.

If one asks special questions, one can generate the information being interested by an online analytical processing (OLAP) from the data. The results are given most in special tables and combinations of tables or scatter plot matrices. In the economy there are many applications of this method. There is an international market for OLAP systems.

Some of the most frequently applied methods of the visualization of higher dimensional data are discussed briefly.

Parallel coordinates presentation gives the information about an object (that is a row of the data matrix) by a polygonal line. The feature axes are arranged vertically and spaced uniformly across the plane. A row of the data matrix defines one point on each of these axes. The connecting polygonal line represents the object. One receives another representation if the order of the features is changed (cp. Figure 2).

Andrews plots (Andrews, 1992) present the feature vector $\mathbf{xr}_i = \left(x_{i1},...,x_{ip} \right)$ of an object i as trigonometric function of p summands,

$$F_{\mathbf{xr}_i}(t) = x_{i1}/\sqrt{2} + x_{i2}\sin(t) + x_{i3}\cos(t) + x_{i4}\sin(2t) + x_{i5}\cos(2t) + ...$$

plotted over the interval $[-\pi, \pi]$. The Andrew representation preserves the Euclidean distance of objects. Close feature vectors are transformed in similar functions.

Figure 2. Representation of data in parallel coordinates. The representation is dependent on the ordering of feature coordinates x_i, compare left and right illustration.

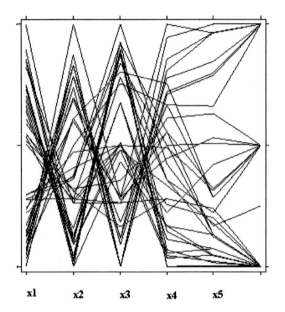 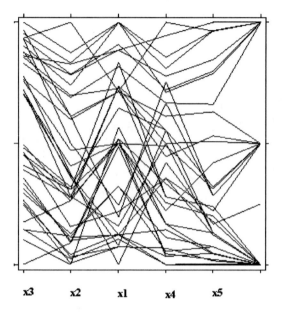

Multidimensional scaling (Borg & Groenen, 1997) transforms the feature vectors $xr_i = (x_{i1}, ..., x_{ip})$ into vectors $\widetilde{xr}_i = (\tilde{x}_{i1}, ..., \tilde{x}_{iq})$ with $q < p$ so that the distances measured in $\mathbb{R}^p$ between all pairs (xr_i, xr_j), $i, j = 1, ..., n$, and distances measured in $\mathbb{R}^q$ between all pairs $(\widetilde{xr}_i, \widetilde{xr}_j)$, $i, j = 1, ..., n$, respectively, remain the same as at once as possible. The cases $q = 2$ and $p = 3$ if possible are obviously the best choice for visualization.

Iconographic representations of information content of the data are the Chernoff faces and the star plots. Feature parameters of faces like height of faces, width of faces, curve of smile, width of nose, height of ears, width of hair etc. are calculated from the data. This way, one can immediately see similarities of Chernoff faces or the related feature vectors, for example. If a temporal change shall be represented, one looks at sequences of Chernoff faces. An expansion of the concept of Chernoff is from Flury and Rydwiel (1981). They designed asymmetrical faces.

One designs star plots as follows. The feature vector $xr_i = (x_{i1}, ..., x_{ip})$ corresponds to a star with p equally spaced radii stemming from a centre. The lengths of the radii are the respective coordinates of the feature vector. The polygonal line connecting these coordinates form a "star". Similar feature vectors yield similar stars. The idea of parallel coordinates is transformed onto radially arranged coordinates.

One finds in [http://addictedtor.free.fr/graphiques/thumbs.php] a gallery of additional graphical representations of multidimensional data for the programming language R.

Factor Analysis

Can the given metric data be reconstructed by a lower number of variables? This problem is treated algebraically. New variables are sought after, the so-called latent variables or hidden variables. The given data shall be generated as linear combina-

Figure 3. Examples of Chernoff faces

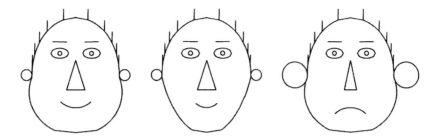

Figure 4. Examples of star plots: Two 8-dimensional feature vectors represented as "stars"

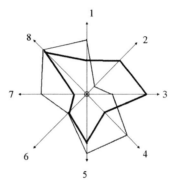

tions from them. A satisfactory solution of this problem is not successful always. In addition, a proper interpretation of the variables causes difficulties sometimes. One often judges the quality of factor analyses statistically. Software for the factor analysis can be found in many statistical packages.

Factor analysis and principal component analysis shall not be mixed up. The latter is a method of coordinate transformation. This means spoken pictorially, one goes around the data to have a better insight. The number of dimensions remains unchanged. The variables are replaced by new variables.

Classifications

A standard strategy of the explorative data mining is the identification of similar objects. This makes the answer to further questions possible: Can the number of observation features be reduced without information loss? Is a given set of observation features suitable to make a group division of the objects possible? Which quality does a diagnostic method have?

Types of classifications are explained first. As typical classification methods of data mining the cluster analysis and the discriminant analysis are then treated. There are different principles for classification methods. The statistical methods are very common. We confine ourselves to topological methods of the classification. They concern numeric data and do not require any assumptions with respect to higher dimensional probability distributions. The data do not have to be a sample according to the statistics. There is a lot of software for classification methods.

At first concepts classification are explained. Let X be the set of objects. A classification is a system $\{K_1, ..., K_S\}$ of subsets K_i of X, the classes, with the properties

1. $K_i \neq \varnothing$ for all classes,

2. $X = \bigcup_{i=1}^{s} K_i$.

A covering is a classification such that $K_i \cap K_j \notin \{K_i, K_j\}$ for all classes K_i and K_j with $i \neq j$. No class is contained in a different one.

A partition is a classification such that $K_i \cap K_j = \varnothing$ for all classes K_i and K_j with $i \neq j$.

A hierarchical classification is a sequence of partitions. This generates sequences of classes which are preordered by set theoretic inclusion. A hierarchy can be illustrated by a dendrogram, cp. Figure 5.

Classifications must be characterized in their quality. Therefore a structure is required on the data. We choose a topological structure and look at the Euclidean distance matrix $\boldsymbol{D}^E = \left(d_{ij}^{\ E} \right)$ of the data matrix as an example. The intrinsic homogeneity of a class K_i one can describe by the sum of all distances of pairs of elements $\mathbf{x}_j$ and $\mathbf{x}_k$ from K_i under use of a standardization constant c by

$$ho(K_i) = \frac{1}{c} \sum_{j<k} d_{jk}^E \ .$$

The more homogeneous the class is, the smaller is the intrinsic homogeneity.

Heterogeneity between two classes K_{i1} and K_{i2} is described by a measure $het\left(K_{i1}, K_{i2}\right)$. This measure has a high value for a good classification. Usual measures of heterogeneity are

complete linkage: $het\left(K_{i1}, K_{i2}\right) = \max_{\mathbf{x}_j \in K_{i1}, \mathbf{x}_k \in K_{i2}} d_{jk}^E$,

single linkage: $het\left(K_{i1}, K_{i2}\right) = \min_{\mathbf{x}_j \in K_{i1}, \mathbf{x}_k \in K_{i2}} d_{jk}^E$,

average linkage:

$$het\left(K_{i1}, K_{i2}\right) = \frac{1}{\left|K_{i1}\right| \cdot \left|K_{i2}\right|} \sum_{\mathbf{x}_j \in K_{i1}} \sum_{\mathbf{x}_k \in K_{i2}} d_{jk}^E ,$$

$\left|K_{i1}\right|$ is the number of elements of K_{i1} and $\left|K_{i2}\right|$ is the number of elements of K_{i2}, centroid linkage: $het\left(K_{i1}, K_{i2}\right)$ is the squared Euclidean distance of the mean vectors of the classes.

Every measure of heterogeneity defines a classification method. Instead of the Euclidean distance every metric can be used. A great variety of classification methods results with that.

Figure 5. Dendrogram of a hierarchical classification of a set of six elements

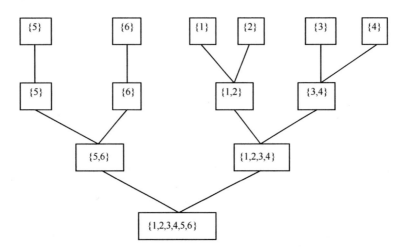

A measure of the overall quality $moq\left(\{K_1,...,K_s\}\right)$ of a classification $\{K_1,...,K_s\}$ can be composed from that, e.g.

$$moq\left(\{K_1,...,K_s\}\right)=\frac{2\cdot s\cdot\displaystyle\sum_{K_i\in\{K_1,...,K_s\}}ho\left(K_i\right)}{\displaystyle\sum_{K_i\in\{K_1,...,K_s\}}\sum_{K_j\in\{K_1,...,K_s\}}het\left(K_i,K_j\right)}$$

for $i\neq j$.

The smaller this measure the better the classification.

These measures of homogeneity, of heterogeneity and of quality of classifications are exclusively based on the chosen topological structure.

Cluster Analysis

With cluster analysis one looks for classifications in multidimensional data. Because of the "similarity" of vectors, observation units are to be clustered. Different from discriminant analysis there are no observation units with predefined class membership, which means no study sample.

A classification should be chosen in a way that the homogeneity in a class as well as the heterogeneity between classes is at maximum. These assessments can be won by a suitably defined metric and the resulting distance matrix of data.

A hierarchical cluster method can be described with reference to a metric:

1. The first step is to calculate the matrix of distances between the object data. The smallest element of distance matrix defines with the associated two vectors the first cluster. Several smallest elements of the distance matrix amount several cluster on this lowest hierarchical level.
2. A new distance matrix is determined for the set of objects and the newly formed cluster. As distance of an object to a cluster one takes, for example, the minimum of distances to

every object of the cluster. The distance between clusters can be defined in different ways, thus cluster methods with different names develop. The distance of clusters is in the single linkage process the minimum, in the complete linkage process the maximum and in the average linkage process the average of the object distances between the clusters. In the centroid process one forms the squared Euclidean distance between the averaged vectors of the cluster.

3. One continues as described in 1. A dendrogram or a table can be used to show the results. You get a tree diagram of the cluster hierarchy or a table of cluster membership at any desired level.
4. The final result is the combination of all objects in one single cluster. The tree diagram consequently has exactly one root.

However, while interpreting, one should end the hierarchical method at a particular number of classes. Another also subjective method is to end the procedure when all suspected matching objects are united in one cluster.

In the statistics system SAS are offered five procedures for the analysis of clusters (ACECLUS, CLUSTER, FASTCLUS, MODECLUS and VARCLUS). Each of these procedures makes it possible to activate with different options several cluster methods. The procedure CLUSTER, for example, offers 11 methods. In the following example the method MEDIAN is used. Details, mathematical background and required primary literature can be found in the SAS manual.

Example 1

Possibilities to recognise the high mathematical talent of pupils in lower school (lower grade area) are often discussed. Käpnick (1997) tested combinations of tests of participants of national and international mathematical Olympics. The reached score in the kth single test was interpreted as the kth coordinate of the data matrix. Each of the 28 pupils is associated with an *n*-dimensional vector. Cluster analysis shall provide clues about the possible use of the tests. As metric the Mahalanobis distance was chosen; Centroid method was the cluster method. The number of objects for this example has been artificially restricted to 28, to be still able to graphically well illustrate the process of clustering.

The calculation results of the cluster analysis can be found in Table 2 and in the tree representation of Figure 6. One clearly recognises two clusters. The right cluster formed by the pupils with the numbers 2, 15, 37, 10, 23, 18, 16 and 26 clearly stands out from the rest of pupils. Whether exactly the mathematically highly gifted pupils are characterised here cannot be answered by the cluster analysis.

One has to read the final SAS document of the Table 2 as follows: In a first step the observations of OB1 and OB22 are merged to one cluster (temporarily called CL28). They obviously show the same measurements. Their distance is valued with 0.0. The two observations – combined in one cluster (see both observations of OB1 and OB22 in Figure 6 on the left) – are continued as one line in the tree diagram.

The next distance step (d = 0.022 265) summarizes the observations of OB17 and OB20 to the cluster CL27. First in the next but one step the cluster CL27 (consisting of two observations) is combined with OB29 to CL25. The resulting cluster on the distance level d = 0.100 192 includes three observations.

First in step 14 when only 15 clusters are available two clusters are combined for the first time with now 6 observations. These are CL24 and CL16 at a distance of d = 0.258994. The procedure ends when all observations form a single cluster. This is the case at the distance level of 1.763427. There isn't any objective rule to the interim breaking off of the procedure. This additionally makes the interpretation of the results of the cluster analysis more difficult.

Besides the above-mentioned interpretation a further possibility is offered. If some objects, for example, OB26 and OB37 are part of the group of the pupils with high mathematical talent, one would end the hierarchical method, if these two objects lie in one cluster.

OB 16 and OB26 are combined to the cluster CL10. OB37 is combined with the cluster CL20 which includes OB2 and OB15. The cluster CL10 and CL6 (which includes CL21) are combined at a distance of 0.443712 to the cluster CL4. This cluster includes the two objects OB16 and OB26 which represents mathematically highly gifted pupils. Because the objects OB2, OB15, OB37, OB10, OB23, OB18 and OB16 are part of the cluster CL4 one concludes that the corresponding pupils are also members of the group of the mathematically highly gifted pupils. The three furthermore existing clusters on this level do not have to be interpreted.

With discriminant analysis one looks for classifications in multidimensional data. Because of the "similarity" of vectors, observation units are to be clustered. Different from cluster analysis there are observation units with predefined class membership. They form the so-called study sample.

The classification is carried out without reference to the class membership variable, the classification variable. One then compares the new classification with the predefined classification variable. One sees with that whether the watched features are informative for the class membership. The reduction of the number of variables is often wished. With the studying sample a method of the discriminant analysis is established. This method is then applied to objects without a previous classification.

One constructs methods of the discriminant analysis regarding algebraic, topological or probability theoretical principles. They are often explained, however, in a statistical diction. The quality of discriminant analyses is characterized with respect to the study sample mostly. For this

Figure 6. Dendrogram of the clustering of 28 objects with PROC TREE in SAS®, compare Example 1 and Table 2

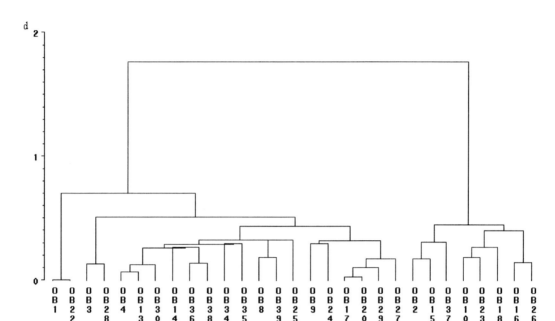

the hold-out method, the leaving-one-out method and the bootstrap method are often used. Test data designed especially offer another possibility for the studies of the qualities of a discriminant analysis.

A multivariate classification rule can be developed in various ways:

Fisher's Linear Discriminant Analysis

It is the historical example of discriminant analysis from the 1930s. A real number is assigned to every data vector x. It is the scalar product of the p-dimensional feature vector x with a certain p-dimensional column vector f. This real number decides the group membership of x. *The vector f is calculated from the study sample such that the group mean average values of the scalar products*

have the maximum distance. This algebraic discriminant procedure is not based on a probability theoretical statistical approach.

Nearest Neighbour Discriminant Analysis

An observation x is assigned to the group which contains the nearest observation of the study sample. Basis of this procedure is a metric to be chosen suitably on $\mathbb{R}^p$. One frequently uses the Euclidean distance or the Mahalanobis distance. They are standards in statistical software packages. For mixed type data the use of mixed metrics can be recommended.

The nearest neighbour discriminant analyses have a topological character and they do not require the idea of the random variable. If k nearest neighbours are considered, one gets variants of this methods.

Table 2. Results of the cluster analysis, described in the example (SAS output), median hierarchical cluster analysis, cp Figure 6

28	OB1	OB22	2	0.000000
27	OB17	OB20	2	0.022265
26	OB4	OB13	2	0.066795
25	CL27	OB29	3	0.100192
24	CL26	OB30	3	0.122457
23	OB3	OB28	2	0.127902
22	OB36	OB38	2	0.133589
21	OB16	OB26	2	0.140815
20	OB2	OB15	2	0.169564
19	CL25	OB27	4	0.172553
18	OB10	OB23	2	0.180881
17	OB8	OB39	2	0.182246
16	OB14	CL22	3	0.260604
15	CL24	CL16	6	0.258994
14	CL18	OB18	3	0.261079
13	OB34	OB35	2	0.290298
12	CL15	CL13	8	0.286606
11	OB9	OB24	2	0.292849
10	CL20	OB37	3	0.305686
9	CL11	CL19	6	0.313208
8	CL17	OB25	3	0.323224
7	CL12	CL8	11	0.321991
6	CL14	CL21	5	0.394770
5	CL7	CL9	17	0.432151
4	CL10	CL6	8	0.443712
3	CL23	CL5	19	0.508899
2	CL28	CL3	21	0.697294
1	CL2	CL4	29	1.763427

Maximum-Likelihood Discriminant Analysis

The data of the study sample are understood as samples of multidimensional distributed random variables. One derives decision rules for the solution of the classification problem from discriminant functions. One gets these discriminant functions according to the maximum likelihood principle from the data and under reference to its probability distribution.

One presupposes mostly that the data are multinomial normal distributed with common covariance over the groups.

It is not a simple problem to decide whether data on hand are samples on such multivariate random variables.

Support Vector Machines

This classification method is similar to Fisher's linear discriminant analysis in a certain way. Classes shall get separated by hyperplanes. These also can be produced from nonlinear equations. The hyperplanes are calculated from the data of the study sample.

Neuronal Nets

A neuronal net is a mathematical structure formed from electrical switching units, the neurons. The neural net is adapted to certain tasks, for example by a learning process. A neuronal net can be exercised at the study sample and then can serve as a classification method. Such classification methods have advantages if probabilistic or topological principles are not usable.

Special Mathematical Concepts

In image processing and signal processing special mathematical classification concepts are required. At first the picture or the signal is represented by certain features. One then uses these features for the classification [Shumway & Stoffer, 2000]. The Fourier analysis or harmonic analysis is a classical method for the investigation of electroencephalograms. Medical diagnostics requires discriminant analysis, for example. Developments of these methods are the wavelet analysis, the Shearlet analysis and geometric multiscale analysis. They make a better adaptation of the analyses to the respective geometric situation possible [Guo, Kutyniok, & Labate, 2006]. One cannot find these latest mathematical creations in routine applications of the discriminant analysis yet.

Discriminant analyses require effortful calculations. Computer programmes are available with a very big choice of options.

Example 2

In the search for risk factors for patients with an acute kidney failure the attention focussed on 79 amino acids and organic acids. These features were measured in the ultrafiltrate among 40 patients as concentrations. 12 of these patients are part of the forecast group 1 (reversible event), 28 to the forecast group 0 (fatal event), according to the watched course of the illness. A multivariate explorative data analysis shall give notes, whether the patients let themselves be classified so with the watched feature vectors of the dimension 79 into the two forecast groups that the result corresponds to the clinical results. Furthermore, the features which are informative for this classification had to be picked out. The study and its results are published in Jäger et al. (1999). It seems nonsensical to want to carry out a statistical data evaluation at 79 features and 40 cases. However, in consideration of the medical question and the real observation possibilities an explorative data analysis can be helpful, however.

The problem definition leads to a discriminant analysis. The data sets noticed in 40 patients form the study sample. Nothing is known about the probability distribution of the 79 dimensional feature vector. At the given case number $N = 40$ it does not appropriately to want to check distribution assumptions statistically. So whether the 40 data vectors represent a sample according to the statistics does not have to be further discussed. For these reasons, a maximum likelihood discriminant analysis is not indicated.

The discriminant analysis was carried out with SAS in two steps. With the procedure STEPDISC a variable selection was carried out first. A discriminant analysis (procedure DIS-CRIM) was then carried out with these selected variables. The procedure STEPDISC presupposes multivariate normal distributions within every group as well as equal covariance matrices of the groups. Whether these assumptions are satisfied here cannot be checked. According to a heuristic procedure STEPDISC is used, however, because the real discriminant analysis is carried out only in the second step.

The data was classified with one feature (method FORWARD) first. This feature has the name GLYSAU (see Table 3). The quality of the classification is assessed with the help of the empirical correlation (see last column 3 in Table 3). The feature THREOL thereupon is included. The data are classified once more. This procedure is continued until no more improvement in the assessment of the result occurs. This way the original set of 79 features is reduced (see column 3 in Table 3) on 15 features. The procedure exchanges a variable situated in the choice by more informative in later steps under circumstances (see Table 4, variable APFEL).

These calculations are judged to be an orientating result according to an explorative data analysis. One also pays attention to the number of the features and the small number of observations.

A discriminant analysis is carried out under reference to the select 15 features now. The procedure DISCRIM in SAS was used for it. A nonparametric discriminant analysis is chosen under the possible options. The system provides a nearest-neighbour method.

Regarding the feature GLYSAU put by STEP-DISK first an assignment of the 40 patients to the forecast groups is carried out at first. 27 of these assignments are right (see Table 4, last column). The classification is then carried out once more. The features GLYSAU and THREOL are used now. The result of 24 right assignments turns out worse in comparison with step 1. This should not confuse because the feature order according to the Table 3 makes the programme from predefined and here not verifiable distribution assumptions.

The features GLYSAU, THREOL and HPROP3 are used for the classification of the 40 patients now. This shall be explained in greater detail. Every patient is represented by a three-dimensional vector (GLYSAU, THRE-OL, HPROP3). The group average vectors $\bar{x}_0 = (0.15036, 0.04071, 0.55321)$ for forecast group of 1 and $\bar{x}_1 = (0.07417, 0.07750, 0.54917)$ for forecast group of 2 result from the measurements on hand. The empirical covariance matrix

$$C = \begin{pmatrix} 0.0132038462 & 0.0022711538 & 0.0260051282 \\ 0.0022711538 & 0.0042507051 & 0.0027425641 \\ 0.0260051282 & 0.0027425641 & 0.0942112821 \end{pmatrix}.$$

has rank 3. Therefore,

$$C^{-1} = \begin{pmatrix} 182.615 & -66.2937 & -48.4774 \\ -66.2937 & 263.825, & 10.6189 \\ -48.4774 & 10.6189 & 23.6865 \end{pmatrix}$$

can be calculated. This allows for the calculation of the quadratic Mahalanobis distance

$$\left[d^M(x, y) \right]^2 = (x - y) C^{-1} (x - y)'$$

for two arbitrary points x and y of the tree dimensional space $\mathbb{R}^3$. The quadratic Mahalanobis distance of $\bar{x}_0 - \bar{x}_1 = (0.07619, -0.03679, 0.00404)$ is

$$\left[d^M(\bar{x}_0, \bar{x}_1) \right]^2 = (\bar{x}_0 - \bar{x}_1) C^{-1} (\bar{x}_0 - \bar{x}_1)'$$

$$= (0.07619, -0.03679, 0.00404) C^{-1} (0.07619, -0.03679, 0.00404)' = 1.75619.$$

Table 3. Results of the variable selection for Example 2 with SAS, procedure STEPDISC

Stepwise Discriminant Analysis Stepwise Selection: Summary			Average Squared Canonical Correlation
Step	Variable Entered	Number In	
1	GLYSAU	1	0.09469250
2	THREOL	2	0.23358099
3	HPROP3	3	0.37821885
4	MALON	4	0.47878831
5	APFEL	5	0.58485717
6	SUBI	6	0.65698129
7	HVS	7	0.68970169
8	CITR	8	0.73560519
9	MILP3	9	0.77767783
10	GLYCOL	10	0.81522479
11	GLYAL2	11	0.85293172
12	ETHYL2	12	0.87149199
13	US121	13	0.88538491
14	HYMEBE	14	0.89484733
15	DIBU34	15	0.90497037
16	APFEL	14	0.90151036
17	MILCH	15	0.91618790

Table 4. Results of the classification with the SAS, procedure DISCRIM, at specification of identical a priori probabilities in both groups: 36 of 40 patients were classified correctly with the 5 features.

Step	Variable entered	Forecast group 0		Forecast group 1		Sum of correct classifications
		correct	false	correct	false	
1	GLYSAU	18	10	9	3	27
2	THREOL	15	13	9	3	24
3	HPROP3	23	5	8	4	31
4	MALON	24	4	8	4	31
5	APFEL	26	2	10	2	36

The Mahalanobis distances to the mean average value vectors of the classes are intended for the classification of a patient with the measurement vector. The patient with the observation vector $x = (0.14,\ 0.05,\ 0.6)$ is assigned to the forecast group to which there is the smallest distance. Because of $(d^M)^2 (x, \bar{x}_0) = 0.163217$ and $(d^M)^2 (x, \bar{x}_1) = 0.938011$ the patient is assigned to the forecast group 0.

Table 4 summarizes the result of the near neighbour discriminant analysis. 36 of 40 patients are classified correctly regarding the mentioned 5 features. An improvement in the result by consideration of broader features is not successful.

The mentioned features should be discussed as risk factors for patients with an acute kidney failure. In consideration of the low case number further examinations are required.

REFRENCES

There is an extensive literature to data mining, classification and the associated mathematics.

The reader will select from it according to his needs. Only the details on the sources used explicitly are indicated here:

Andrews, D. F. (1972). Plots of high dimensional data. *Biometrics*, 28, 125-136.

Bock, H. H., & Diday, E. (2000). Analysis of symbolic data. Berlin, Heidelberg, New York: Springer.

Borg, I., & Groenen, P. (1997). *Modern multidimensional scaling*. New York: Springer.

Chernoff, H. (1973). Using faces to represent points in k-dimensional space graphically. *Journal of the American Statistical Association*, 68, 361-368.

Cox, T. F., & Cox, M. A. A. (1994). *Multidimensional scaling*. London: Chapman & Hall.

Flury, B., & Riedwyl, H. (1981). Graphical representation of multivariate data by means of asymmetrical faces. *Journal of American Statistical Association*, 76, 757-765.

Guo, K., Kutyniok, G., & Labate, D. (2006). Sparse multidimensional representations using anisotropic dilation and shear operators. In G. Chen et al. (Eds.), *Wavelets and splines* (pp.189-201). Athens 2005. *Papers based on lectures presented at the international conference on interactions between wavelets and splines*, Athens, GA, USA, May 16-- 19, 2005. In honor of Professor Charles K. Chui on the occasion of his 65th birthday. Brentwood: Nashboro Press.

Jäger, B., Zschiesche, M., Kraatz, G., Panzig, E., Rudolph, P. E., & Guth, H. J. (1999). Which organic acids does hemofiltrate hontain in the presence of acute renale failure? *International Journal of Artificial Organs*, 22, 805-810.

Käpnick, F. (1997). Untersuchungen zu Grundschulkindern mit einer potentiellen mathematischen Begabung. Habil.-Schrift. Greifswald: Ernst-Moritz-Arndt-Universität, Math- N a t. Fakultät.

R graph gallery: Enhance your data visualization with R. Retrieved May 15, 2008, from http://addictedtor.free.fr/graphiques/thumbs.php

Shumway, R. H., & Stoffer, D. S. (2000). *Time series analysis and its applications*. Springer Texts in Statistics. New York, NY: Springer.

The R project for statistical computing. Retrieved May 15, 2008, from http://www.r-project.org/

KEY TERMS

Algebraic Structure: An abstract set equipped with addition and multiplication as algebraic operations. Example is the set of the real numbers with the usual calculations.

Classification: Elements of a set are grouped in subsets.

Cluster Analysis: This is a large ensemble of classification methods which can be based on different mathematical structures.

Discriminant Analysis: These classification methods try to reconstruct a predefined classification from the features of the objects.

Empirical Covariance: A parameter which is calculated from the multivariate numeric data. It indicates a certain kind of connection of the variables.

Empirical Correlation: A standardized parameter calculated from the empirical covariance.

Euclidean Space: A n-dimensional space ($n \geq 1$) of real numbers with the usual algebraic structure and suitable topological structure, a standard object of data analysis.

Factor Analysis: This is a method of data mining that is essentially algebraically based. The objects are represented regarding features calculated newly.

Metric Space: An abstract set equipped with a metric structure which describes the position of the elements to each other.

Mixed Metric: A metric composed from different metrics and allows for the analysis of data of mixed type.

Ordered Space: Providing an abstract set with a structure which permits comparing the elements.

Probability Space: This is a mathematical object, which describes a random variable and its probability distribution.

Topological Structure: A topological structure on a set permits the description of the position of the elements of the set to each other.

Compilation of References

23andme.com. *Consent and legal agreement*. Retrieved Feb 18, 2008, from https://www.23andme.com/about/consent/

A Chronology of Data Breaches. Privacy Rights Clearinghouse. Retrieved Oct. 25, 2007, from http://www.privacyrights.org/ar/ChronDataBreaches.htm.

Abraham, C. (2008). Click here to unlock your DNA code. *The Globe and Mail*.

Abul, O., Bonchi, F., & Nanni, M. (2008). Never walk alone: Uncertainty for anonymity in moving objects databases. In *24th International Conference on Data Engineering*, IEEE press.

Achlioptas, D. (2001). Database-friendly random projections. In *Proc. of the 20th ACM Symposium on Principles of Database Systems* (pp. 274-281). Santa Barbara, CA, USA.

Ackerman, M. S., Cranor, L. F., & Reagle, J. (1999). *Beyond concern: Understanding net users' attitudes about online privacy*. Retrieved August 31, 2006, from http://citeseer.ist.psu.edu/cranor99beyond.html

Aggarwal, C., Pei, J., & Zhang, B. (2006). On privacy preservation against adversarial data mining. In *12th ACM SIGKDD International Conference on Knowledge Discovery and Data Mining*, ACM press.

Agre, P. E., & Rotenberg, M. (Eds.). (1998). *Technology and privacy: The new landscape*. Cambridge: The MIT Press.

AgriWorld Exchange (2008). AgriWorld Exchange Web site; www.agriworldexchange.com

Aixin, S., E. L., & Ng, W. K. (2002, November). Web classification using support vector machine. In *Proceedings of the 4th international workshop on Web Information and Data Management held in conjunction with CIKM*.

Alderman, E., & Kennedy, C. (1997). *The right to privacy*. Vintage press.

Ale, J. M., & Rossi, G. H. (2000). An approach to discovering temporal association rules. In *ACM Symposium on Applied Computing*. ACM press.

Altingövde, I. S. & Ulusoy, O. (2004). Exploiting interclass rules for focused crawling. *IEEE Intelligent Systems*, (pp. 66-73).

Amin, A. (2007). Re-thinking the urban social. *City, 11*(1), 100-114.

Anagnostopoulos I., Kouzas G. Anagnostopoulos C., Vergados D., Papaleonidopoulos I., Generalis A., Loumos V., & Kayafas E., (2004). Classifying Web pages using a probabilistic neural network. *IEEE Proceedings on Software. 151*(3).

Anders, J. (2007). *U.S. student visas reach record numbers in 2007*. United States Department of State: International Information Program.

Andrews, D. F. (1972). Plots of high dimensional data. *Biometrics, 28*, 125-136.

Anton, A., Earp, J., Vail, M., Jain, N., Gheen, C., & Frink, J. (2007). HIPAA's effect on Web site privacy policies. *IEEE Security and Privacy, 5*(1), 45-52.

Ariss, S.S. (2002). Computer monitoring: Benefits and pitfalls facing management. *Information & Management, 39*(7), 553-558.

Arkin, W. M. (May 12, 2006). *NSA's multi-billion dollar Data mining effort.* Retrieved on December 15, 2007 from Washingtonpost.com

Arnold, M. (2003). Intranets, community, and social capital: The Case of Williams Bay. *Bulletin of Science, Technology & Society, 23*(2), 78-87.

Arnold, M., Gibbs, M. R., & Wright, P. (2003). Intranets and local community: 'Yes, an intranet is all very well, but do we still get free beer and a barbeque?' In M. Huysman, E. Wenger & V. Wulf (Eds.), *Proceedings of the First International Conference on Communities and Technologies* (pp. 185-204). Amsterdam: Kluwer Academic Publishers.

Asirvatham, A. P., & Ravi, K. K. (2001). Web page categorization based on document structure. *Proceedings of the ACM.*

Auer, J. W. (1991). *Linear algebra with applications.* Scarborough, Ontario, Canada: Prentice-Hall Canada Inc.,

Bagchi, K., & Udo, G. (2003). An analysis of the growth of computer and internet security breaches. *Communications of the AIS, 12*(46), 684-700.

Balz, D., & Deane, C. (January 11, 2006). *Differing views on terrorism: Americans divided on eavesdropping program.* Retrieved January 2, 2008 from http://www.washingtonpost.com

Bao, X., & Xiang, Y. (2006). Digitalization and global ethics. *Ethics and Information Technology 8,* 41-47.

Barabási, A.-L. (2003). *Linked: How everything is connected to everything else and what it means for business, science, and everyday life.* New York: Plume.

Basho, K. (2000). The licensing of our personal information: Is it a solution to Internet privacy? *California Law Review, 88,* 1507-1545.

Baskerville, R.L., & Myers, M.D. (2004). Special issue on action research in information systems: Making IS research relevant to practice. Forward. *MIS Quarterly, 28*(3), 329-335.

Benassi, P. (1999). TRUSTe: An online privacy seal program. *Communications of the ACM, 42*(2), 56-59.

Benbasat, I., & Zmud, R.W. (1999). Empirical research in information systems: The practice of relevance. *MIS Quarterly, 23*(1), 3-16.

Beresford, A., & Stajano, F. (2003). Location privacy in pervasive computing. *IEEE Pervasive Computing, 2*(1), 46-55.

Bergelson, V. (2003). It's personal but is it mine? Toward property rights in personal information. *U.C. Davis Law Review, 37,* 379-451.

Berry, M., & Linoff, G. (1997). Data mining techniques - For marketing, sales, and customer support. New York: John Wiley and Sons.

Bevan vs. Smartt, 316 F.Supp.2d 1153 (D.Utah 2004).

Bingham, E., & Mannila, H. (2001). Random projection in dimensionality reduction: Applications to image and text data. In *Proceedings of the 7th ACM SIGKDD International Conference on Knowledge Discovery and Data Mining* (p. 245-250). San Francisco.

Binmore, K. (2004). *Natural justice.* Cambridge, MA: MIT Press.

Blake, C., & Merz, C. (1998). *UCI Repository of Machine Learning Databases.* University of California, Irvine: Dept. of Information and Computer Sciences.

Blake, C., & Pratt, W. (2001). Better rules, fewer features: A semantic approach to selecting features from text. IEEE-2001, 59-66.

Bloustein, E.J. (1984). Privacy as an aspect of human dignity: An answer to Dean Prosser. In F.D. Schoeman (Ed.) *Philosophical dimensions of privacy: An anthology* (pp. 156-202) New York: Cambridge University Press.

Bock, H. H., & Diday, E. (2000). *Analysis of symbolic data.* Berlin, Heidelberg, New York: Springer.

Boeck, H., RFID Podcast. RFID Radio; June 4, 2007

Bollen, K.A. (1989). *Structural equations with latent variables.* New York: John Wiley & Sons.

Bond vs. U.S., 529 U.S. 334 (2000).

Borg, I., & Groenen, P. (1997). *Modern multidimensional scaling.* New York: Springer.

Bostwick, G. L. (1976). A taxonomy of privacy: repose, sanctuary, and intimate decision. *California Law Review, 64,* 1447-1483.

Boyd vs. U.S., 116 U.S. 616 (1886).

Brandt, A. M. (1987). *No magic bullet: A social history of venereal disease in the United States since 1880* (Expanded ed.). New York: Oxford University Press.

Brenner, S. W., & Clarke, L. L. (2006). Fourth amendment protection for shared privacy rights in stored transactional data. *Journal of Law and Policy, 14,* 211-280.

Brenner, S.W. (2005). The fourth amendment in an era of ubiquitous technology. *Mississippi Law Journal, 75,* 1-84.

Brin, D. (1999). *Transparent society: Will technology force us to choose between privacy and freedom?* Jackson, TN: Perseus Books Group.

Brissette, E. (2004, Sep 3). Personal comment. Retrieved Nov 11, 2004, from http://slashdot.org/comments.pl?cid=10147964&sid=120406

BSI. (1999). Information aecurity management – Part 1, Code of Practice for Information Security Management, BS 7799-1, BSI Group, London.

Buchanen, A. (1996). Toward a theory of the ethics of bureaucratic organizations. *Business Ethics Quarterly, 6*(4), 419-440.

Butler, B. S. (2001). Membership size, communication activity, and sustainability. *Information System Research, 12*(4), 346-362.

Butterworth, R., Piatetsky-Shapiro, G., & Simovici, D. A. (2005). On feature selection through clustering. In *Proceedings of the Fifth IEEE International Conference on Data Mining (ICDM'05).*

Cable Communications Policy Act of 1984, 42 U.S.C. § 551(2007).

Cal-Med Workshop (2007, October 26). *Traceability and incentives for food safety and quality: Implications for Mediterranean crops.* Sonoma California.

Campbell, D.T., & Fiske, D.W. (1959). Convergent and discriminant validation by the multi-trait-multimethod matrix. *Psychological Bulletin, 56*(2), 81-105.

Cannon-Bowers, J. A., Tannenbaum, S. I., Salas, E., & Volpe, C. E. (1995). Defining competencies and establishing team training requirements. In Guzzo & Salas (Eds.), *Team effectiveness and decision making in organizations,* (pp. 333-380). San Francisco: Jossey-Bass.

Capurro, R. (2005). Privacy: An intercultural perspective. *Ethics and Information Technology 7(1),* 37-47.

Capurro, R. (2007). Intercultural information ethics. In R. Capurro, J. Frühbaure and T. Hausmanningers (Eds.), *Localizing the Internet. Ethical issues in intercultural perspective.* Munich: Fink Verlag.

Carafano, J. J. (January 10, 2007). *Promoting security and civil liberties: The role of data mining in combating terrorism* (Testimony before the Senate Judiciary Committee). Washington DC: U.S. Senate.

Carroll, J. M., & Rosson, M. B. (2003). A trajectory for community networks. *The Information Society, 19*(5), 381-394.

Carvel, J. (2007). Family doctors to shun national database of patients' records. *The Guardian,* Nov. 20 2007.

Castells, M. (2001). Virtual Communities or Network Society? In *The Internet Galaxy: Reflections on the Internet, Business, and Society* (pp. 116-136). Oxford: Oxford University Press.

Center for Grassroots Oversight. (2007). *National Security Agency begins huge data mining project similar to "Total Information Awareness."* Retrieved September 10, 2007 from www.cooperativeresearch.org

Centers for Disease Control and Prevention. (2006). *BioSense: Background.* Atlanta, Georgia: CDC.

Chan, C-H., Sun, A., & Lim, E-P.(2001). Automated Online news classification with personalization. In

Proceedings of the 4th international conference of Asian Digital Library (ICADL 2001), pp. 320-329, Bangalore, India

Chaplin, C., Goddard, P., Bergman, H., Sandford, S., Conklin, C., Mann, H. et al. (1992). *Modern times* ([Version with additional material] ed.). United States: CBS-Fox Video.

Chaum, D. (1981). Untraceable electronic mail, return addresses, and digital pseudonyms. *Communications of the ACM, 24*(2), 84-88.

Chea. T. (2007 December 21). *Court deals blow to wiretapping case.* New York: The Associated Press, December 21, pp. 1-2. Retrieved November 3, 2007 from www.abcnews.com

Chen, W.-Z., & Li, L. (2004, Augusts 26-29). Correlation and MSVM-based Feature Selection. *Proceedings of the Third International Conference on Machine Learning and Cybernetics*, Shanghai.

Chen, Z. (2001). *Data mining and uncertain reasoning: An integrated approach.* New York: John Wiley and Sons.

Chernoff, H. (1973). Using faces to represent points in k-dimensional space graphically. *Journal of the American Statistical Association, 68*, 361-368.

Chow, C.-Y., Mokbel, M., & Liu, X. (2006). A peer-to-peer spatial cloaking algorithm for anonymous location based services. In *14th Annual ACM International Symposium on Advances in Geographic Information Systems.* ACM press.

Ciocchetti, C. A. (2007). E-commerce and information privacy: Privacy policies as personal information protectors. *American Business Law Journal, 44*, 55-126.

Clarke, I., Miller, S., Wong, T., Sandberg, O., & Wiley, B. (2002). Protecting free expression online with Freenet. *IEEE Internet Computing, 6*(1), 40-49.

Clarke, R. (1988). Information Technology and Dataveillance. *Communications of the Association for Computing Machinery, 31*(5), 498-512.

Clifton, C., & Marks, D. (1996). Security and privacy implications of data mining. In *Proeedings of the 1996 SIG-MOD'96 Workshop on Research Issues on Data Mining and Knowledge Discovery (DMKD'96)*, Montreal, Canada, (pp. 15-20).

CNET Forums. (2006, May 12). *Poll: Most Americans support NSA's efforts.* Retrieved January 10, 2008 from http://forums.cnet.com.

Cohill, A. M., & Kavanaugh, A. L. (Eds.). (2000). *Community networks: Lessons from Blacksburg, Virginia* (2nd ed.). Norwood: Artech House.

Combarro , E. F., Montanes, E., Dı́az, I., Ranilla, J., & Mones, R. (2005). Introducing a family of linear measures for feature selection in text categorization. *IEEE Transactions on Knowledge and Data Engineering, 17*(9), 1223-1232.

Computer Emergency Response Team (CERT). (2004). *CERT statistics.* Retrieved May 2004, from http://www.cert.org/stats/cert_stats.html#incidents

Computer Matching and Privacy Protection Act of 1988, Pub. L. No. 100-503.

Congressional Research Service. (2003). *Privacy: Total information awareness programs and related information access, collection, and protection laws* (by G. M. Stevens). Washington DC: CRS.

Congressional Research Service. (2004). *Data mining: An overview* (by J. W. Seifert). Washington DC: CRS.

Congressional Research Service. (2006, December). *USA PATRIOT improvement and reauthorization Act of 2005: A legal analysis.* Washington DC: CRS.

Congressional Research Service. (2007). *Data mining and Homeland Security* (by J. W. Seifert). An overview. Washington DC: CRS.

Congressional Research Service. (2007). *The Foreign Intelligence Surveillance Act: A brief overview of selected issues* (by E. B. Bazan). Washington DC: Congressional Research Service.

Congressional Research Service. (April, 2002). *The USA PATRIOT Act: A Sketch.* Washington DC: CRS.

Cook, J. S., & Cook, L. L. (2003). Social, ethical, and legal issues of data mining. In *Data Mining: Opportunities and Challenges*, Wang, J. (Ed.), Idea Group Publishing, Hershey, PA, 395-420.

Cooney, M. (2006, July 6). Data Mining *Report: Department of Homeland Security Privacy Office Response to House Report 108-774*

Cox , T. F., & Cox, M. A. A. (1994). *Multidimensional scaling.* London: Chapman & Hall.

Cunningham, S., & Holmes (1999). Developing innovative applications in agriculture using data mining. University of Waikato, Department of Computer Science. *SEARCC 1999 Conference Proceedings.*

Damiani, M., & Bertino, E. (2006). Access control and privacy in location-aware services for mobile organizations. In *7th International Conference on Mobile Data Management,* IEEE press.

Danielson, P. (1992). *Artificial morality: Virtuous robots for virtual games.* London: Routledge.

Danielson, P. (2002). Video Surveillance for the Rest of Us: Proliferation, Privacy, and Ethics Education. *Paper presented at the 2002 International Symposium on Technology and Society (ISTAS'02).*

Danielson, P. (2005). Ethics of Workplace Surveillance Games. In J. Weckert (Ed.), *Electronic Monitoring in the Workplace: Controversies and Solutions.* (pp. 19 - 34). Hershey PA: Idea Group Publishing.

Dave, B. (2007). Space, sociality, and pervasive computing. *Environment and Planning B: Planning and Design, 34*(3), 381-382.

Day, D., Aberdeen, J., Hirschman, L., Kozierok, R., Robinson, P., & Vilain, M. (1997). Mixed-Initiative Development of Language Processing Systems. *Fifth Conference on Applied Natural Language Processing, Association for Computational Linguistics*, 348-355.

Day, P. (2002). Designing Democratic Community Networks: Involving Communities through Civil Participation. In M. Tanabe, P. van den Besselaar & T. Ishida (Eds.), *Digital Cities II: Second Kyoto Workshop on Digital Cities* (Vol. LNCS 2362, pp. 86-100). Heidelberg, Germany: Springer.

Day, P., & Schuler, D. (Eds.). (2004). *Community Practice in the Network Society: Local Action / Global Interaction.* London: Routledge.

De Borchgrave, A. (March 16, 2005). *Likelihood of U.S. terrorist sleeper cells.* Retrieved September 3, 2007 from www.archive.newsmax.com

De Cindio, F., Gentile, O., Grew, P., & Redolfi, D. (2003). Community Networks: Rules of Behavior and Social Structure. *The Information Society, 19*(5), 395-406.

De George, R. (2006). Information technology, Globalization and ethics. *Ethics and Information Technology 8*, 29–40.

De May v. Roberts, 9 N.W. 146 (Mich. 1881).

de Tocqueville, A. (2000). *Democracy in America* (H. C. Mansfield & D. Winthrop, Trans.). Chicago: University of Chicago Press.

De Villiers, P. (1997). New Urbanism: A critical review. *Australian Planner, 34*(1), 30-34.

DeCew, J. (2002). Privacy. The Stanford Encyclopedia of Philosophy. E. N. Zalta online at: http://plato.stanford.edu/archives/sum2002/entries/privacy/ (accessed 8-31-2006).

DeFilippis, J., Fisher, R., & Shragge, E. (2006). Neither Romance Nor Regulation: Re-evaluating Community. *International Journal of Urban and Regional Research, 30*(3), 673-689.

Delanty, G. (2000). Postmodernism and the Possibility of Community. In *Modernity and Postmodernity: Knowledge, Power and the Self* (pp. 114-130). London: Sage.

DeMarco, D.A. (2006). Understanding consumer information privacy in the realm of Internet commerce:

Personhood and pragmatism, Pop-Tarts and six-packs. *Texas Law Review, 84*, 1013-1064.

Department of Homeland Security. (2007). *2007 data mining report*. Retrieved Feb. 5, 2008, from http://www.dhs.gov/xlibrary/assets/privacy/privacy_rpt_datamining_2007.pdf.

DeRosa, M. (2004). *Data mining and data analysis for counterterrorism*. Washington DC: Center for Strategic and International Studies.

DeVellis, R.F. (2003). *Scale development. Theory and applications* (2nd ed.) (Vol. 26). Thousand Oaks, CA: Sage Publications.

Dhanarajan, G. (2001). Distance Education: Promise, Performance and Potential. *Open Learning, 16*(1), 61-68.

Dhillon, G., & Backhouse, J. (2001). Current directions in IS security research: Towards socio-organizational perspectives. *Information Systems Journal, 11*(2), 127-153.

Dierks, T., & Rescorla, E. (2006). *The Transport Layer Security (TLS) protocol version 1.1.* Internet Engineering Task Force RFC 4346.

Diffie, W., & Landaw, S. (2007). *Privacy on the line: The politics of wiretapping and encryption*. Cambridge: The MIT Press.

Dingledine, R., Mathewson, N., & Syverson, P. (2004). Tor: The second-generation onion router. *Presented at 13th USENIX Security Symposium*, San Diego, CA.

Dougherty, M. (February 25, 2004). *Testimony before the House Subcommittee on Immigration, Boarder Security and Claims*. Washington DC: United States House of Representatives.

Driver's Privacy Protection Act of 1994, 18 U.S.C. §§ 2721-25(2007).

Drori, O. (2005). Using frequently occurring words to identify the subject of a document. *Journal of Information Science, 31*(3), 164-177.

Dumais, S., & Chen, H. (2000). Hierarchical Classification of Web Content. *SIGIR 2000*, ACM, pp. 256 –263.

Dunbar, R. I. M. (1996). *Grooming, Gossip, and the Evolution of Language*. Cambridge, MA: Harvard University Press.

Dwyer vs. American Express Co., 652 N.E.2d 1351 (Ill. App. Ct. 1995).

Dyckman, L. (2003). *Bioterrorism: A Threat to Agriculture and the Food Supply*. United States General Accounting Office: Testimony Before the Committee on Governmental Affairs, U.S. Senate.

Eddy, E. R., Stone, D. L., & Stone-Romero, E. F. (1999). The effects of information management policies on reactions to human resource systems: An integration of privacy and procedural justice perspectives. *Personnel Psychology, 52*, 335-358.

Eick, C. F., Zeidat, N., & Zhao, Z. (2004). Supervised Clustering – Algorithms and Benefits. *Proceedings of the 16th IEEE International Conference on Tools with Artificial Intelligence (ICTAI 2004)*.

Eisenstadt v. Baird, 405 U.S. 438 (1972).

Electronic Communications Privacy Act, Title I, 18 U.S.C. §§ 2510-22 (2007).

Electronic Communications Privacy Act, Title II, Stored Communications Act, 18 U.S.C. §§ 2701-2711 (2007).

Electronic Communications Privacy Act, Title III, 18 U.S.C. §§ 3121-27 (2007).

Electronic Frontier Foundation. (2006). *FOIA Litigation: DOJ's Investigative Data Warehouse*. Retrieved December 5, 2007 from www.eff.org

Ellison, N., Burrows, R., & Parker, S. (Eds.). (2007). *Urban informatics: Software, cities and the new cartographies of knowing capitalism. Guest editors of a special issue of Information, Communication & Society, 10(6)*. London: Routledge.

Ess, C. (2002). Computer-mediated colonization, the renaissance, and educational imperatives for an intercultural global village. *Ethics and Information Technology 4(1)*, 11–22.

Estivill-Castro, V., & Murray, A. T. (1998). Discovering associations in spatial data-an efficient medoids based approach. *In 2nd Pacific-Asia Conference on Research and Development in Knowledge Discovery and Data Mining (PAKDD '98)*. Springer-Verlag press.

Etzioni, A. (1995). *The Spirit of Community: Rights, Responsibilities, and the Communitarian Agenda*. London: Fontana Press.

Ex parte Jackson, 96 U.S. 727 (1877).

Executive Office of the President. (2008). *Privacy & Civil Liberties Oversight Board*. Washington DC: The White House.

Facteau, J.D., Dobbins, G.H., Russell, J.E.A., Ladd, R.T., & Kudisch, J.D. (1995). The influence of general perceptions of training environment on pretraining motivation and perceived training transfer. *Journal of Management, 21*(1), 1-25.

Fair Credit Reporting Act of 1970, 15 U.S.C. § 1681 (2007).

Fallows, D. (2004). *The Internet and Daily Life*. Washington, DC: Pew Internet & American Life Project.

Family Educational Rights and Privacy Act of 1974, 20 U.S.C. § 1232g (2007).

Federal Bureau of Investigation. (2007). *National security letters* (Press Release). Washington DC: Department of Justice. Retrieved December 2, 2007 from www.fbi.org

Fellegi, I. P., & Sunter, A. B. (1969). A Theory for Record Linkage. *Journal of the American Statistical Association, 64*, 1183-1210.

Ferguson, S. (2006). Study: Security Breaches Afflict Most Enterprises, Governments. *eWeek*, July 7, 2006. http://www.eweek.com/chapter2/0,1895,1986066,00.asp (accessed 8-31-2006).

Fern, X. Z., & Brodley, C. E. (2003). Random projection for High Dimensional Data Clustering: A Cluster Ensemble Approach. In *Proc. of the 20th International Conference on Machine Learning (ICML 2003)*. Washington DC, USA.

Files, J. (2006, June 29). Missing laptop with veterans' data is found. *New York Times*.

Fletcher, K. (2003). Consumer power and privacy: the changing nature of CRM. *International Journal of Advertising, 22*, 249-272.

Florida, R. L. (2003). Cities and the creative class. *City and Community, 2*(1), 3-19.

Flury, B., & Riedwyl, H. (1981). Graphical representation of multivariate data by means of asymmetrical faces. *Journal of American Statistical Association, 76*, 757-765.

Foley, R. J. (2007). Feds cancel Amazon customer ID request. Associated Press. Retrieved Nov. 28, 2007, from http://ap.google.com/article/ALeqM5gz0slCB4-SYJCVk2J3xbYHM6R55oAD8T66FAG0.

Foth, M. (2004a). Animating personalised networking in a student apartment complex through participatory design. In A. Bond, A. Clement, F. de Cindio, D. Schuler & P. van den Besselaar (Eds.), *Proceedings of the Participatory Design Conference, Toronto, Canada, July 27-31* (Vol. 2, pp. 175-178). Palo Alto, CA: CPSR.

Foth, M. (2004b). Designing networks for sustainable neighbourhoods: A case study of a student apartment complex. In G. Johanson & L. Stillman (Eds.), *Community Informatics Research Network (CIRN) 2004 Colloquium and Conference Proceedings. 29 Sep - 1 Oct 2004* (Vol. 1, pp. 161-172). Prato, Italy.

Foth, M. (Ed.). (2008). *Urban informatics: Community integration and implementation*. Hershey, PA: IGI Global.

Foth, M., & Axup, J. (2006, Jul 31-Aug 5). *Participatory design and action research: Identical twins or synergetic pair?* Paper presented at the Participatory Design Conference (PDC), Trento, Italy.

Foth, M., & Brereton, M. (2004). Enabling local interaction and personalised networking in residential communities through action research and participatory design. In P. Hyland & L. Vrazalic (Eds.), *Proceedings of OZCHI 2004: Supporting Community Interaction. 20-24 Nov 2004*. Wollongong, NSW: University of Wollongong.

Foth, M., & Hearn, G. (2007). Networked Individualism of Urban Residents: Discovering the communicative ecology in inner-city apartment buildings. *Information, Communication & Society, 10*(5), 749-772.

Foth, M., & Sanders, P. (2008, forthcoming). Impacts of Social Interaction on the Architecture of Urban Spaces. In A. Aurigi & F. De Cindio (Eds.), *Augmented Urban Spaces: Articulating the Physical and Electronic City.* Aldershot, UK: Ashgate.

Frazier, P.A., Barron, K.E., & Tix, A.P. (2004). Testing moderator and mediator effects in counseling psychology. *Journal of Counseling Psychology, 51*(1), 115-134.

Freedman, M., & Morris, R. (2002). Tarzan: A peer-to-peer anonymizing network layer. *Proceedings of the 9th Conference on Computer and Communications Security*, ACM Press, 193-206.

Freeman, L. C. (1979). Centrality in Social Networks, Conceptual Clarification. *Social Networks, 1*, 215-239.

Frentzos, E., Gratsias, K., Pelekis, N., & Theodoridis, Y. (2007). Algorithms for nearest neighbor search on moving object trajectories. In *Geoinformatica, 11*(2), 159-193.

Friel, A. L. (2004). Privacy Patchwork. *Marketing Management 13*(6), 48-51.

Froomkin, A. M. (2000). The death of privacy? *Stanford Law Review, 52*, 1461-1543.

Fukunaga, K. (1990). *Introduction to Statistical Pattern Recognition*. 2nd. Edition. Academic Press.

Fule, P., & Roddick, J. F. (2004). Detecting privacy and ethical sensitivity in data mining results. Appeared at *Twenty-Seventh Australasian Computer Science Conference* (ACSC2004), Dunedin, New Zealand.

Gabber, E., Gibbons, P., Kristol, D., Matias, Y., & Mayer, A. (1999). Consistent, yet anonymous, Web access with LPWA. *Communications of the ACM, 42*(2), 42-47.

Galal, G.H. (2001). From contexts to constructs: The use of grounded theory in operationalising contingent process models. *European Journal of Information Systems, 10*, 2-14.

Garfinkel, S. (2000). *Database nation: The death of privacy in the 21st century.* Sebastopol, CA: O'Reilly.

Garfinkel, S. (2001). *Database nation: The death of privacy in the 21st century.* New York: O'Reily Media, Inc.

Garfinkel, S. (2002). *Web Security, Privacy, and Commerce*, 2nd ed. Sebastopol, CA: O'Reilly and Associates.

Garg, A., Curtis, J., & Halper, H. (2003). The financial impact of IT security breaches: What do investors think? *Information Systems Security, 12*(1), 22-34.

Gefen, D. (2003). Assessing unidimensionality through LISREL: An explanation and example. *Communications of the AIS, 12*, 23-46.

Gellman, B. (November 6, 2006). The *FBI's secret scrutiny: In hunt for terrorism Bureau examines records of ordinary citizens.* Retrieved August, 2, 2007 from www.washingtonpost.com

Gellman, R. (2008). Personal Health Records: Why Many PHRs Threaten Privacy. Retrieved 23 Feb, 2008, from http://www.worldprivacyforum.org/pdf/WPF_PHR_02_20_2008fs.pdf

General Accounting Office. (2004). *Data mining: Federal efforts cover a wide range of uses.* Retrieved Nov. 13, 2007, from http://frwebgate.access.gpo.gov/cgi-bin/getdoc.cgi?dbname=gao&docid=f:d04548.pdf.

General Accounting Office. (2007). *Data mining: Early attention to privacy in developing a key DHS program could reduce risks.* Retrieved Feb. 5, 2008, from http://www.gao.gov/new.items/d07293.pdf.

George, J.F. (1996). Computer-based monitoring: Common perceptions and empirical results. *MIS Quarterly, 20*(4), 459-480.

Gerstein, R. S. (1984). Intimacy and privacy. In F.D. Schoeman (Ed.) *Philosophical dimensions of privacy: An anthology* (pp. 265-271). New York: Cambridge University Press.

Ghinita, G., Kalnis, P., & Skiadopoulos, S. (2007). Prive: Anonymous location-based queries in distributed mobile systems. In *16ᵗʰ International Conference on World Wide Web,* ACM press.

Ghoshal, S. (2005). Bad management theories are destroying good management practices. *Academy of Management Learning & Education, 4*(1), 75-91.

Gidofalvi, G., Huang, X., & Pedersen, T. (2007). Privacy-preserving data mining on moving object trajectories. In *10ᵗʰ ACM International Workshop on Data Warehousing and OLAP,* ACM press.

Gilchrist, A. (2000). The well-connected community: networking to the 'edge of chaos'. *Community Development Journal, 35*(3), 264-275.

Gilchrist, A. (2004). *The Well-Connected Community: A Networking Approach to Community Development.* Bristol, UK: The Policy Press.

Gillespie, A., & Richardson, R. (2004). Teleworking and the City: Myths of Workplace Transcendence and Travel Reduction. In S. Graham (Ed.), *The Cybercities Reader* (pp. 212-218). London: Routledge.

Gkoulalas-Divanis, A., Verykios, V., & Mokbel, M. (2007). A network aware privacy model for online requests in trajectory data. Technical Report, University of Thessaly.

Glaser, B.G., & Strauss, A.L. (1967). *The discovery of grounded theory: Strategies for qualitative research.* New York: Aldine Publishing Company.

Gleeson, B. (2004). Deprogramming planning: Collaboration and inclusion in new urban development. *Urban Policy and Research, 22*(3), 315-322.

Glenn, R. A. (2003). *The right to privacy: Rights and liberties under the law.* Santa Barbara, CA: ABC-CLIO Inc.

Godin, S. (2001). *Unleashing the ideavirus.* New York: Hyperion.

Goetz, T. (2007). 23AndMe Will Decode Your DNA for $1,000. Welcome to the Age of Genomics. *WIRED, 15*(12).

Golan, E., Krissoff, B., Kuchler, F., Calvin, L., Nelson, K., & Price, G. (2004). *Traceability in the U.S. Food Supply: Economic Theory and Industry Studies.* Economic Research Service, U.S. Department of Agriculture, Agricultural Economic Report No. 830.

Goldschlag, D., Reed, M., & Syverson, P. (1999). Onion routing. *Communications of the ACM, 42*(2), 39-41.

Goldsmith, R. (2002). *Viral Marketing.* London: Pearson Education.

Gopal, R.D., & Sanders, G.L. (1997). Preventive and deterrent controls for software piracy. *Journal of Management Information Systems, 13*(4), 29-47.

Gordon, A. A., & Loeb, M. P. (2002). The economics of information security investment. *ACM Transactions on Information and System Security 5*(4), 438-457.

Gordon, L. A., Loeb, M. P, Lucyshyn, W., & Richardson, R. (2004). *Ninth Annual CSI/FBI Computer Crime And Security Survey.* Computer Security Institute: Online at.

Gordon, L. A., Loeb, M. P., Lucyshyn, W., & Richardson, R. (2006). *Eleventh Annual CSI/FBI Computer Crime And Security Survey.* Computer Security Institute: Online at.

Gordon, L.A., Loeb, M.P., Lucyshyn, W., & Richardson, R. (2005). *Tenth annual CSI/FBI computer crime and security survey.* San Francisco, CA: Computer Security Institute.

Gorniak-Kocikowska, K. (1996). The computer revolution and the problem of global ethics. *Science and Engineering Ethics 2,* 177-190.

Government Accounting Office (2004). Data mining: Federal rfforts cover a wide range of uses. GAO-04-548.

Graham, S. (Ed.). (2004). *The cybercities reader*. London: Routledge.

Gramm-Leach-Bliley Act of 1999, 15 U.S.C. §§ 6801-09 (2007).

Gravano, L., Ipeirotis, P. G., & Sahami, M. (2003, January). QProber: A System for Automatic Classification of Hidden-Web Databases. ACM *Transactions on Information Systems, 21*(1), 1-41.

Greenwood, D. J. (2002). Action research: Unfulfilled promises and unmet challenges. *Concepts and Transformation, 7*(2), 117-139.

Grimmelmann, J. (2007, Dec. 10). Facebook and the VPPA: Uh-Oh. Retrieved Dec. 11, 2007, from http://laboratorium.net/archive/2007/12/10/facebook_and_the_vppa_uhoh.

Griswold v. Connecticut, 381 U.S. 479 (1965).

Gruteser, M., & Grunwald, D. (2003). Anonymous usage of location based services through spatial and temporal cloaking. In *1st International Conference on Mobile Systems, Applications and Services,* ACM press.

Gu, L., Baxter, R., Vickers, D., & Rainsford, C. (2003). Record Linkage: Current Practice and Future Directions. CMIS Technical Report No. 03/83, CSIRO Mathematical and Information Sciences, GPO Box 664, Canberra 2601, Australia.

Guo, K., Kutyniok, G., & Labate, D. (2006). Sparse multidimensional representations using anisotropicdilation and shear operators. In G. Chen et al. (Eds.), *Wavelets and splines* (pp.189-201). Athens 2005. *Papers based on lectures presented at the international conference on interactions between wavelets and splines,* Athens, GA, USA, May 16-- 19, 2005. In honor of Professor Charles K. Chui on the occasion of his 65th birthday. Brentwood: Nashboro Press.

Gurstein, M. (2001). Community informatics, community networks and strategies for flexible networking. In L. Keeble & B. D. Loader (Eds.), *Community Informatics: Shaping Computer-Mediated Social Relations* (pp. 263-283). New York: Routledge.

Gurstein, M. (Ed.). (2000). *Community Informatics: Enabling Communities with Information and Communication Technologies*. Hershey, PA: Idea Group.

Hampton, K. N. (2003). Grieving for a lost network: Collective action in a wired suburb. *The Information Society, 19*(5), 417-428.

Hampton, K. N., & Wellman, B. (2003). Neighboring in netville: How the Internet supports community and social capital in a wired suburb. *City and Community, 2*(4), 277-311.

Han, J., & Kamber, M. (2006). *Data mining: Concepts and techniques*. San Francisco: Morgan Kaufmann Publishers

Hansen, B. (2007). ADVISE data mining program by Homeland Security. *The Register,* September 6, pp. 1-3.

Harman, G. (1996). Moral relativism. In G. Harman and J.J. Thompson (Eds.), *Moral relativism and moral objectivity* (pp. 3-64). Cambridge MA: Blackwell Publishers

Harman, G. (2000). Is there a single true morality? In G. Harman, *Explaining value: And other essays in moral philosophy* (pp. 77-99), Oxford: Clarendon Press, (Orig. 1984)

Harrington, S.J. (1996). The effect of codes of ethics and personal denial of responsibility on computer abuse judgments and intentions. *MIS Quarterly, 20*(3), 257-278.

Hatch, M. (2001). The privatization of big brother: Protecting sensitive personal information from commercial interests in the 21st century. *William Mitchell Law Review, 27*, 1457-1502.

Head, B. (2004). Fresh Produce. CIO Magazine. Retrieved January 2008 from http://www.cio.com.au/index.php/id;282160542

Health Insurance Portability and Accountability Act of 1996, Pub. L. No. 104-191.

Hearn, G., & Foth, M. (2005). Action Research in the Design of New Media and ICT Systems. In K. Kwansah-

Aidoo (Ed.), *Topical Issues in Communications and Media Research* (pp. 79-94). New York, NY: Nova Science.

Hearn, G., & Foth, M. (Eds.). (2007). *Communicative Ecologies. Special issue of the Electronic Journal of Communication, 17(1-2).* New York: Communication Institute for Online Scholarship.

Hearn, G., Tacchi, J., Foth, M., & Lennie, J. (2008, forthcoming). *Action Research and New Media: Concepts, Methods and Cases.* Cresskill, NJ: Hampton Press.

Hearst, M. (1999). Trends & Controversies: Mixed-initiative interaction. *IEEE Intelligent Systems, 14(5),* 14-23.

Hendrickson, T. (2007). *Innovation: 2005 Best Practice Award Winners.* Retrieved December 10, 2007 from www.tdwi.org

Hengartner, U., & Steenkiste, P. (2003). Protecting access to people location information. In *1st International Conference on Security in Pervasive Computing,* LNCS, Springer-Verlag press.

Herold, R. (October 29, 2006). *Electronic Frontier Foundation sues the U.S. DOJ for FOIA information.* Retrieved January 2, 2008 from www.realtime.com

Heymann, P. B., & Kayyem, J. N. (2005). *Protecting liberty in an age of terror.* Cambridge, MA: The MIT Press.

Hinkin, T.R. (1998). A brief tutorial on the development of measures for use in survey questionnaires. *Organizational Research Methods, 1(1),* 104-121.

Hoffman, T. (2001). Unsupervised learning by probabilistic latent Semantic analysis. *Machine Learning Journal, 42(1),* 177-196.

Hofstede, G. (1993). Cultural constraints in management theories. *Academy of Management Journal, 7(1),* 81-94.

Hofstede, G. (2001). *Culture's consequences.* Beverly Hills CA: Sage.

Hongladarom, S. (2001). Global culture, local cultures and the Internet: The Thai example. In C. Ess (Ed.), *Culture, technology, communication: Towards an intercultural global village* (pp. 307–324). Albany NY: State University of New York Press.

Hoofnagle, C.J. (2004). Big brother's little helpers: How Choicepoint and other commercial data brokers collect and package your data for law enforcement. *North Carolina Journal of International Law and Commercial Regulation, 29,* 595-637.

Horrigan, J. B. (2001). *Cities Online: Urban Development and the Internet.* Washington, DC: Pew Internet & American Life Project.

Horrigan, J. B., Rainie, L., & Fox, S. (2001). *Online Communities: Networks that nurture long-distance relationships and local ties.* Washington, DC: Pew Internet & American Life Project.

Huang, S., & Huang, K. (2007). *Increased U.S. Imports of Fresh Fruit and Vegetables.* United States Department of Agriculture publication FTS-328-01. September 2007.

Huang, Y., McCullagh, P. J., & Black, N. D., (2004). Feature Selection via Supervised Model Construction. Proceedings of the Fourth IEEE International Conference on Data Mining (ICDM'04).

Human Rights Watch (2006). Race to the bottom. Corporate complicity in Chinese Internet censorship. *Human Rights Watch report 18(8).* Retrieved March 13, 2008, from http://www.hrw.org/reports/2006/china0806/

Huysman, M., & Wulf, V. (Eds.). (2004). *Social Capital and Information Technology.* Cambridge, MA: MIT Press.

IDTechEx Ltd. (2007). Animals and Farming. *The RFID Knowledgebase.* Retrieved January 25, 2008 from http://rfid.idtechex.com/knowledgebase/en/nologon.asp

IDTechEx Ltd. (2008). *RFID Market Projections.* IDTechEx Ltd. Retrieved February 2008 from http://www.idtechex.com/

In re DoubleClick, Inc. Privacy Litigation, 154 F. Supp.2d 497 (S.D. N.Y. 2001).

In re Order for Roving Interception of Oral Communications, 349 F.3d 1132 (9th Cir. 2003).

International Labour Organization (2007). International Labour Organization. Key Indicators of the Labour Market Programme. *International Labour Organization, 4,* 6.

ISO/IEC, Ed. (2005). ISO/IEC 17799:2005 *Information technology - Security techniques - Code of practice for information security management.* International Organization for Standardization.

Jäger, B., Zschiesche, M., Kraatz, G., Panzig, E., Rudolph, P. E., & Guth, H. J. (1999). Which organic acids does hemofiltrate hontain in the presence of acute renale failure? *International Journal of Artificial Organs, 22,* 805-810.

Jain, A. K., & Dubes, R. C. (1988). Algorithms for clustering data. Prentice-Hall, Inc.

Jankowski, N. W., Van Selm, M., & Hollander, E. (2001). On crafting a study of digital community networks: Theoretical and methodological considerations. In L. Keeble & B. D. Loader (Eds.), *Community Informatics: Shaping Computer-Mediated Social Relations* (pp. 101-117). New York: Routledge.

Jarvenpaa, S.L., & Ives, B. (1991). Executive involvement and participation in the management of information technology. *MIS Quarterly, 15*(2), 205-221.

Jasperson, J.S., Carte, T.A., Saunders, C.S., Butler, B.S., Croes, H.J.P., & Zheng, W. (2002). Power and information technology research: A metatriangulation review. *MIS Quarterly, 26*(4), 397-459.

Jesdanun, A. & Metz, R. (2007). Facebook users complain of new tracking. Associated Press. Retrieved Nov. 16, 2007, from http://ap.google.com/article/ALeqM5jktmzai0_n_sMBgH_jfy6QXNS_6gD8T299HG0.

Jingchun, C. (2005). Protecting the right to privacy in China. *Victoria University of Wellington Law Review 38(3).* Retrieved March 13, 2008, from http://www.austlii.edu.au/nz/journals/VUWLRev/2005/25.html.

John, P. M. (2001). On the Automated Classification of Web Sites. *Link¨oping Electronic Articles in Computer and Information Science. 6,* 1-15.

Johnson v. Bryco Arms, 224 F.R.D. 536 (E.D. N.Y. 2004).

Johnson, D. (2000). *Computer ethics,* 3rd ed, Upper Sadle River: Prentice Hall.

Johnson, W. B., & Lindenstrauss, J. (1984). Extensions of Lipshitz Mapping Into Hilbert Space. In *Proc. of the Conference in Modern Analysis and Probability* (p. 189-206), volume 26 of Contemporary Mathematics.

Judt, T. (2005). *Postwar: A History of Europe since 1945.* New York: Penguin Press.

Kalakota, R., & Whinston, A. B. (1996). *Frontiers of Electronic Commerce,* 1st edition. New York, NY: Addison Wesley Publishing Co.

Kalousis, A., Prados, J., & Hilario, M. (2005). Stability of Feature Selection Algorithms. *Proceedings of the Fifth IEEE International Conference on Data Mining (ICDM'05).*

Kan, M-Y., & Thi, H. O. N. (2005, October 31-November 5). Fast Webpage Classification Using URL Features. *CIKM'05,* Bremen, Germany. ACM.

Kankanhalli, A., Hock-Hai, T., Bernard, C.Y.T., & Kwok-Kee, W. (2003). An integrative study of information systems security effectiveness. *International Journal of Information Management, 23*(2), 139-154.

Käpnick, F. (1997). Untersuchungen zu Grundschulkindern mit einer potentiellen mathemati-schen Begabung. Habil.-Schrift. Greifswald: Ernst-Moritz-Arndt-Universität, Math- Nat. Fakultät.

Karahanna, E., Evaristo, R., & Srite, M. (2004). Methodological issues in MIS cross-cultural research. In M.E. Whitman & A.B. Woszczynski (Eds.), *The handbook of information systems research* (pp. 166-177). Hershey, PA: Idea Group Publishing.

Karas, S. (2002). Privacy, identity, databases. *American University Law Review, 52,* 393-445.

Kaski, S. (1999). Dimensionality Reduction by Random Mapping. In *Proc. of the International Joint Conference on Neural Networks* (p. 413-418). Anchorage, Alaska.

Katz vs. U. S., 389 U.S. 347 (1967).

Kavanaugh, A. L., Reese, D. D., Carroll, J. M., & Rosson, M. B. (2003). Weak Ties in Networked Communities. In M. Huysman, E. Wenger & V. Wulf (Eds.), *Proceedings of the First International Conference on Communities and Technologies* (pp. 265-286). Amsterdam, NL: Kluwer Academic Publishers.

Keen, P. G. W. (1999). *Competing in chapter 2 of internet business: Navigating in a new world.* Delft, The Netherlands: Eburon Publishers

Kerber, R. (2007, Oct. 24). Court filing in TJX breach doubles toll. *Boston Globe*, p. A1 (Business).

Kerr, N. L. (1983). Motivation losses in small groups: A social dilemma analysis. *Personality and Social Psychology, 45*, 819-828.

Kesdogan, D., Reichl, P., & Junghartchen, K. (1998). Distributed temporary pseudonyms: A new approach for protecting location information in mobile communication networks. In *5th European Symposium on Research in Computer Security.* Springer-Verlag press.

Kido, H., Yanagisawa, Y., & Satoh, T. (2005). An anonymous communication technique using dummies for location based services. In *International Conference on Pervasive Services,* IEEE press.

Kilcullen, D. (2007). *New paradigm for 21st century conflict.* Retrieved February 2, 2008 from www.smallawarsjournal.com

Kitiyadisai, K. (2005). Privacy rights and protection: Foreign values in modern Thai context. *Ethics and Information Technology 7*, 17–26.

Klaebe, H., Foth, M., Burgess, J., & Bilandzic, M. (2007, Sep 23-26). *Digital Storytelling and History Lines: Community Engagement in a Master-Planned Development.* Paper presented at the 13th International Conference on Virtual Systems and Multimedia (VSMM'07), Brisbane, QLD.

Klimoski, R., & Jones, R. G. (1995). Staffing for effective group decision making: Key issues in matching people and task. In *Team effectiveness and decision making in organizations,* Guzzo & Salas (Eds.), Jossey-Bass, San Francisco, 292-332.

Klimoski, R., & Zukin, L. (1999). Selection and staffing for team effectiveness. In *Supporting work team effectiveness: Best management practices for fostering high performance,* E. Sundstrom & Associates (Eds.), Jossey-Bass, San Francisco.

Kobsa, A. (2007). Privacy-enhanced personalization. *Communications of the ACM, 50*(8), 24-33.

Kollock, P. (1998). Transforming Social Dilemmas: Group Identity and Co-operation. In P. Danielson (Ed.), *Modeling Rationality, Morality, and Evolution 7.* New York: Oxford University Press.

Kopytoff, V. (2006, Jan. 20). Google says no to data demand. *San Francisco Chronicle*, p. A1.

Kotulic, A.G., & Clark, J.G. (2004). Why there aren't more information security research studies. *Information & Management, 41*(5), 597-607.

Kozlowski, S. W. J., & Ilgen, D. R. (2006). Enhancing the effectiveness of work groups and teams. *Psychological Science in the Public Interest, 7,* 77–124.

Kristol, D. (2001). HTTP cookies: standards, privacy, and politics. *ACM Transactions on Internet Technology, 1*(2), 151-198.

Küng, H. (2001). *A global ethic for global politics and economics.* Hong Kong: Logos and Pneuma Press.

Kuper, P. (2005). The state of security. *IEEE Security and Privacy, 3*(5), 51-53.

Kwon, O-H., & Lee, J-H. (2000). Web Page Classification Based on k-Nearest Neighbor Approach. *Proceedings of the 5th International Workshop Information Retrieval with Asian Languages*, 2000, ACM, pp. 9-15

Landwehr, C. E. (2001). Computer security. *International Journal of Information Security 1*(1), 3-13.

Langley, P. (1994). Selection of Relevant Features on Machine Learning. *Proceedings of AAAI conference on Relevance-1994.*

Larsen, B., & Aone, C. (1999). Fast and Effective Text Mining Using Linear-Time Document Clustering. In *Proceedings of the 5th ACM SIGKDD International Conference on Knowledge Discovery and Data Mining* (p. 16-22). San Diego, CA, USA.

Last, M., & Maimon, O. (2004, February). A Compact and Accurate Model for Classification. *IEEE Transactions on Knowledge and Data Engineering, 16*(2), 203-215.

Law, M. H. C., Figueiredo, M. A. T., & Jain, A. K. (2004, September). Simultaneous Feature Selection and Clustering Using Mixture Models. *IEEE Transactions on Pattern Analysis and Machine Intelligence, 26*(9), pp1154-1166.

Lawrence vs. Texas, 539 U.S. 558 (2003).

Lazer, D., & Katz, N. (2000). Putting the Network into Teamwork. Presented at the Academy of Management annual meeting, Toronto, Canada.

Leach, J. (2003). Improving user security behavior. *Computers & Security, 22*(8), 685-692.

Lee, S.M., Lee, S.G., & Yoo, S. (2004). An integrative model of computer abuse based on social control and general deterrence theories. *Information & Management, 41*(6), 707-718.

Levchuk, G. M., Feili, Y., Pattipati, K. R., & Levchuk, Y. (2003). From hierarchies to heterarchies: Application of network optimization to design of organizational structures. *Proceedings of the 8th International Command and Control Research and Technology Symposium,* Washington, DC.

Li, J. (2006, August). Robust Rule-Based Prediction. *IEEE Transactions on Knowledge and Data Engineering, 18*(8), 1043-1054.

Liang, J-Z. (2003). Chinese Web Page Classification Based on Self-organizing Mapping Neural Networks. *Proceedings of the Fifth International Conference on Computational Intelligence and Multimedia Applications (ICCIMA'03),* IEEE.

Lieberaman. J. K. (1999). *A practical companion to the constitution: How the Supreme Court has ruled on issues from abortion to zoning.* CA: University of California Press.

Linn, J. (2005). Technology and Web user data privacy. *IEEE Security and Privacy, 3*(1), 52-58.

Liu, H. & Yu. L. (2005). Towards Integrating Feature Selection Algorithms for Classification and Clustering. *IEEE Transactions on Knowledge and Data Engineering, 17*(4), 491-502.

Lo, V. S. Y. (2002). The True Lift Model - A Novel Data Mining Approach to Response Modeling in Database Marketing. *SIGKDD Explorations, 4*(2), 78-86.

Loaharanu, P. (2006). *Don't Fear Spinach – Irradiate It.* American Council on Science and Health. Health Facts and Fears.com. Retrieved from http://www.acsh.org/factsfears/newsID.865/news_detail.asp

Long, L. K., & Troutt, M. D. (2003). Data mining for human resource information systems. In *Data Mining: Opportunities and Challenges,* Wang, J. (Ed.), Idea Group Publishing, Hershey, PA, 366-381.

Loving vs. Virginia, 388 U.S. 1 (1967).

Lu, H., Sung, S. Y., & Lu, Y. (1996). On preprocessing data for effective classification. *Workshop on Research Issues on Data Mining, Proceedings of ACM.*

Lü, Yao-Huai (2005). Privacy and data privacy issues in contemporary China. *Ethics and Information Technology 7,* 7–15.

Lung, J-Z. (2004, August 26-29). SVM multi-classifier and Web document classification. *Proceedings of the Third International Conference on Machine Learning and Cybernetics,* pp. 1347-1351.

MacKinnon, D.P., Krull, J.L., & Lockwood, C. (2000). Mediation, confounding, and suppression: Different names for the same effect. *Prevention Science, 2,* 15-27.

Macqueen, J. (1967). Some methods for classification and analysis of multivariate observations. In *Proc. of the 5th Berkeley Symposium on Mathematical Statistics and Probability, 1,* 281-297). Berkeley: University of California Press.

Maloney-Krichmar, D., Abras, C., & Preece, J. (2002, Jun 6-8). *Revitalizing an Online Community.* Paper presented at the International Symposium on Technology and Society (ISTAS) – Social Implications of Information and Communication Technology, Raleigh, NC.

Margulis, S. T. (2003). On the status and contribution of Westin's and Altman's Theories of Privacy. *Journal of Social Issues, 59*(2), 411-429.

Martin, D., Wu, H., & Alsaid, A. (2003). Hidden surveillance by Web sites: Web bugs in contemporary use. *Communications of the ACM, 46*(12), 258-264.

Marx, G. T., & Reichman, N. (1984). Routinizing the Discovery of Secrets: Computers as Informants. *American Behavioral Scientist, 27,* 423 - 452.

Matignon, R. (2007). *Data mining using SAS Enterprise Minor.* New York: Wiley-Interscience.

McClurg, A. J. (2003). A thousand words are worth a picture: A privacy tort response to consumer data profiling. *Northwestern University Law Review, 98,* 63-143.

McCoy, S., Galletta, D.F., & King, W.R. (2005). Integrating national culture into IS research: The need for current individual-level measures. *Communications of the Association for Information Systems, 15,* 211-224.

McCue, C. (2006). *Data mining and predictive analysis: Intelligence gathering and crime analysis.* New York: Butterworth-Heineman.

McDougall, B., & Hansson, A. (eds.) (2002). *Chinese concepts of privacy.* Leiden: Brill Academic Publishers.

Medill School of Journalism. (August 16, 2006). *Commercial data use by law enforcement raises questions about accuracy, oversight* (by N. Duarte). Retrieved December 19, 2007 from http:// newsintiative.org

Melvin vs. Reid, 297 P. 91 (Cal. 1931).

Meredyth, D., Ewing, S., & Thomas, J. (2004). Neighbourhood Renewal and Government by Community. *International Journal of Cultural Policy, 10*(1), 85-101.

Meregu, S., & Ghosh, J. (2003). Privacy-Preserving Distributed Clustering Using Generative Models. In *Proc. of the 3rd IEEE International Conference on Data Mining (ICDM'03)* (p. 211-218). Melbourne, Florida, USA.

Minnery, J., & Bajracharya, B. (1999). Visions, planning processes and outcomes: Master planned communities in South East Queensland. *Australian Planner, 36*(1), 33-41.

Mitchell, T. M., (1999). The Role of Unlabeled data in Supervised Learning. *Proceedings of the Sixth International Colloquium on Cognitive Science.*

Mizutani, M., Dorsey, J., & Moor, J. (2004). The Internet and Japanese conception of privacy. *Ethics and Information Technology 6*(2), 121-128.

Moores, T. (2005). Do consumers understand the role of privacy seals in E-Commerce? *Communications of the ACM, 48*(3), 86-91.

Morgan, B. B., & Lassiter, D. L. (1992). Team composition and staffing. In *Teams: Their training and performance,* R. Sweezy & E. Salas (Eds.), Kluwer, Norwood, Mass., 75–100.

Murphey, Y-L., & Guo, H. (2000). Automatic Feature Selection - A hybrid statistical approach. *IEEE-2000,* 382-385.

Naamani-Goldman, D. (2006). *Revealing terror* (Medil School of Journalism). Retrieved December 17, 2007 from http://newsinitiative.org.

Naamani-Goldman, D. (2007). *The IRS war on terrorism: How it work.* The Los Angeles Times, January 15, p. 1-7.

Nakada, M., & Tamura, T. (2005). Japanese conceptions of privacy: An intercultural perspective. *Ethics and Information Technology 7,* 27–36.

Nakashima, E. (2007, Nov. 23). Cellphone tracking powers on request. *Washington Post,* p. A1.

Nakashima, E. (2007, Nov. 30). Feeling betrayed, Facebook users force site to honor their privacy. *Washington Post*, p. A1.

National Commission on Terrorist Attack Upon the United States. (2005). *The 9/11 Commission Report.* Washington DC: Government Printing Office.

National Intelligence Council. (2004). *Mapping the global future: Report of the National Intelligence Council's 2020 Project.* Washington DC: Government Printing Office.

Nelson vs. Salem State College, 845 N.E.2d 338 (Mass. 2006).

New York Times. (2006). *Education dept. shared student data with F.B.I* (by J. D. Glater). September 1, pp.1-2.

Norman, D. A. (2005). *Emotional design: Why we love (or hate) everyday things.* Basic Books.

NSTISSC (1999). National Information Systems security (INFOSEC) Glossary. *National security Telecommunications and Information Systems security Committee (NSTISSC), 4.*

Nunnally, J. (1978). *Psychometric theory.* New York: McGraw-Hill.

O'Connor vs. Ortega, 480 U.S. 709 (1987).

O'Harrow Jr., R. (2005). *No place to hide.* New York: Simon & Schuster, Inc.

Oliveira, S. R. M. (2005, June). *Data Transformation For Privacy-Preserving Data Mining.* PhD thesis, Department of Computing Science, University of Alberta, Edmonton, AB, Canada.

Oliveira, S. R. M., & Zaïane, O. R. (2007). Privacy-Preserving Clustering to Uphold Business Collaboration: A Dimensionality Reduction-Based Transformation Approach. *International Journal of Information Security and Privacy (IJISP), 1*(2), 13-36.

Olmstead v. U.S., 277 U.S. 438 (1928).

Orlikowski, W. (1993). CASE tools as organizational change: Investigating incremental and radical changes in systems development. *MIS Quarterly, 17*(3), 309-340.

Orwell, G. (1949). *Nineteen eighty-four, a novel.* New York: Harcourt Brace.

Pant, G., & Srinivasan, P. (2006). Link contexts in classifier-guided topical crawlers. *IEEE Transactions on Knowledge and Data Engineering, 18*(1), 107-122.

Papadakis, M. C. (2004). *Computer-mediated communities: A bibliography on information, communication, and computational technologies and communities of place* (SRI Project Report No. P10446.004). Arlington, VA: SRI International.

Parker, D.B. (1981). *Computer security management.* Reston, VA: Reston Publishing Company.

Patterson, S. J., & Kavanaugh, A. L. (2001). Building a sustainable community network: An application of critical mass theory. *The Electronic Journal of Communication, 11*(2).

Peace, A.G., Galletta, D.F., & Thong, J.Y.L. (2002). Software piracy in the workplace: A model and empirical test. *Journal of Management Information Systems, 20*(1), 153-177.

Pedrycz, W., & Sosnowski, Z. A. (2000, March). Designing Decision Trees with the Use of Fuzzy Granulation. *IEEE Transactions on Systems, Man, and Cybernetics—Part A: Systems and Humans, 30*(2 151-159.

Pelekis, N., & Theodoridis, Y. (2006). Boosting location-based services with a moving object database engine. In *5th ACM International Workshop on Data Engineering for Wireless and Mobile Access (MobiDE)*, ACM press.

Penenberg, A. (1999, Nov. 29). The end of privacy. *Forbes*, p. 182.

Perez, J. C. (2007, Nov. 30). Facebook's Beacon more intrusive than previously thought. *PC World*. Retrieved Dec. 4, 2007, from http://www.pcworld.com/article/id,140182-c,onlineprivacy/article.html.

Perner, P. (Ed.). (2002). *Advances in data mining: Applications in e-commerce, medicine, and knowledge management.* New York: Springer.

Peuquet, D., & Wentz, E. (1994). An approach for time-based analysis of spatiotemporal data. In *6th International Symposium on Spatial Data Handling*, Advances in GIS Research.

Pinkas, B (2002, December). Cryptographic techniques for privacy-preserving data mining. *SIGKDD Explorations, 4*(2), 12-19.

Pinkett, R. D. (2003). Community technology and community building: Early results from the creating community connections project. *The Information Society, 19*(5), 365-379.

Podsakoff, P.M., & Organ, D.W. (1986). Self-reports in organizational research: Problems and prospects. *Journal of Management, 12*(4), 531-544.

Podsakoff, P.M., MacKenzie, S.B., Lee, J.Y., & Podsakoff, N.P. (2003). Common method bias in behavioral research: A critical review of the literature and recommended remedies. *Journal of Applied Psychology, 88*(5), 879-903.

Polanyi, M. (1966). The tacit dimension.

PollinREport.Com. (2007). *War on terrorism: Nationwide surveys of Americans.* Retrieved January 5 from http://www.pollingreport.com/terror.htm

Ponemon, L. (2005). Lost Customer Information: What Does a Data Breach Cost Companies? Tucson, Arizona, USA: Ponemon Institue (online at: http://www.securitymanagement.com/library/Ponemon_DataStudy0106.pdf) (accessed 8-31-2006)

Ponemon, L. (2005). The National Survey on Data Security Breach Notification. Tucson, Arizona, USA: Ponemon Institute (online at: http://www.whitecase.com/files/Publication/bdf5cd75-ecd2-41f2-a54d-a087ea9c0029/Presentation/PublicationAttachment/2f92d91b-a565-4a07-bf68-aa21118006bb/Security_Breach_Survey%5B1%5D.pdf) (accessed 8-31-2006)

Posner, R. A. (1984). An economic theory of privacy. In F.D. Schoeman (Ed.) *Philosophical dimensions of privacy: An anthology* (pp. 333-345). New York, NY: Cambridge University Press.

Power, R. (2002). CSI/FBI computer crime and security survey. *Computer Security Issues & Trends VIH,* (1), 1-22.

Preece, J. (2000). *Online communities: designing usability, supporting sociability.* Chichester: John Wiley.

Preimesberger, C. (2006). Hackers Hit AT&T System, Get Credit Card Info. *eWeek,* August 29, 2006, http://www.eweek.com/chapter2/0,1895,2010001,00.asp?kc=EWNAVEMNL083006EOA (accessed 8-31-2006).

Priest, L. (2008). Your medical chart, just a mouse click away. *The Globe and Mail,* p. 6.

Primus (2008). Primus Labs Web site; www.primuslabs.com

Privacy Act of 1974, 5 U.S.C. § 552a (2007).

Privacy Protection Act of 1980, 42 U.S.C. § 2000aa (2007).

Priyantha, N., Chakraborty, A., & Balakrishnan, H. (2000). The cricket location-support system. In *6th Annual International Conference on Mobile Computing and Networking,* ACM press.

Produce Marketing Association (2005, May). *ASAP Implementation Guide/* Produce Marketing Association publication. Newark Delaware USA.

Produce Marketing Association (2008). *GTIN – A Case for Streamlining the Supply Chain.* Publication of the Produce Marketing Association.

Prosser, W. L. (1960). Privacy. *California Law Review, 48,* 383-423.

Putnam, R. D. (2000). *Bowling Alone: The Collapse and Revival of American Community.* New York: Simon & Schuster.

Quan-Haase, A., Wellman, B., Witte, J.C., & Hampton, K. N. (2002). Capitalizing on the Net: Social Contact, Civic Engagement, and Sense of Community. In B. Wellman & C. A. Haythornthwaite (Eds.), *The Internet in everyday life* (pp. 291-324). Oxford: Blackwell.

Quirk, M. (2005). The Best Class Money Can Buy. *The Atlantic, 17.*

R graph gallery: Enhance your data visualization with R. Retrieved May 15, 2008, from http://addictedtor. free.fr/graphiques/thumbs.php

Rawls, J. (1971). *A Theory of Justice.* Cambridge Mass: Harvard University Press.

Reay, I., Beatty, P., Dick, S., & Miller, J. (2007). A survey and analysis of the P3P protocol's agents, adoption, maintenance, and future. *IEEE Transactions on Dependable and Secure Computing, 4*(2), 151-164.

Reddick, C. G. (2004). A two-stage model of e-government growth: Theories and empirical evidence for U.S. cities. *Government Information Quarterly 21*(1), 51-64.

Reidenberg, J. R. (2003). Privacy wrongs in search of remedies. *Hastings Law Journal, 54,* 877-898.

Reiter, M., & Rubin, A. (1999). Anonymous Web transactions with Crowds. *Communications of the ACM, 42*(2), 32-48.

Remsburg vs. Docusearch, Inc., 816 A.2d 1001 (N.H. 2003).

Rennie, S. (2008). Day tried four times to get Arar off U.S. no-fly list. *The Globe and Mail,* p. A8.

Restatement (Second) of Torts (1976), § 652B.

Restatement (Second) of Torts (1976), § 652C.

Restatement (Second) of Torts (1976), § 652D.

Restatement (Second) of Torts (1976), § 652E.

Rezgui, A., Bougeuettaya, A., & Eltoweissy, M. (2003). Privacy on the Web: Facts, challenges, and solutions. *IEEE Security & Privacy, 1*(6), 40-49.

Rheingold, H. (2002). *Smart Mobs: The Next Social Revolution.* Cambridge, MA: Perseus.

Riboni, D. (2002). Feature Selection for Web Page Classification. *Proceedings of ACM Workshop (EURASIA-ICT 2002).*

Riboni, D. (2005). Feature Selection for Web Page Classification. *Proceedings of International Conference on Data Mining, ICDM'05.*

Richardson, R. (2003). Eighth Annual CSI/FBI Computer Crime And Security Survey, Computer Security Institute: Online at. http://www.reddshell.com/docs/csi_fbi_2003. pdf#search=%22Eighth%20Annual%20CSI%2FFBI%2 0COMPUTER%20CRIME%20AND%20SECURITY% 20SURVEY%22 (accessed 8-31-2006)

Right to Financial Privacy Act of 1978, Pub. L. No. 95-630.

Roberge, B. (September, 2004). New research center focuses on IT and the intellectual community. *The MITRE DIGEST,* pp. 1-4. Retrieved November 10, 2007 from www.mitre.org/news/digest

Roe vs. Wade, 410 U.S. 113 (1973).

Romano Jr., N. C., & Fjermestad, J. (2001-2002). Customer relationship management research: An assessment of research. *International Journal of Electronic Commerce 6*(3 Winter)), 61-114.

Romano Jr., N. C., & Fjermestad, J. (2003). Electronic commerce customer relationship management: A research agenda. *Information Technology and Management, 4,* 233-258.

Rosen, J. (2000). *The unwanted gaze.* New York: Random House.

Rosenzweig, P. S., & Ahern, J. P. (2007). *Testimonies before the Senate Subcommittee on Terrorism, Technology, and Homeland Security.* Washington DC: United States Senate.

Rouse, W. B., & Morris, N. M. (1986). On looking into the black box: Prospects and limits in the search for mental models. *Psychological Bulletin, 100,* 350-363.

Rouse, W., Connon-Bowers, J., & Salas, E. (1992). The role of mental models in team performance in complex systems. *IEEE Trans. On Sys., man, and Cyber, 22*(6), 1296-1308.

Roy, J. (1999). Polis and oikos in classical Athens. *Greece & Rome, 46*(1), 1-18.

Roychowdhury, S. (2001). Feature Subset Selection using Granular Information. *IEEE-2001*, 2041-2045

Rule, J. B. (2007). *Privacy in peril*. New York: Oxford University Press.

Rykwert, J. (2001). Privacy in Antiquity. *Social Research, 68*(1), 29-40.

Saban, K. (2001). The data mining process: At a critical crossroads in development. *Journal of Database Marketing, 8*, 157-167.

Salas, E., Burke, C. S., & Cannon-Bowers, J. A. (2002). What we know about designing and delivering team training. In *Creating, implementing, and managing effective training and development: State-of-the-art lessons for practice*, K. Kraiger (Ed.), Jossey-Bass, San Francisco, 234–259.

Satchell, C. (2003). The Swarm: Facilitating Fluidity and Control in Young People's Use of Mobile Phones. In S. Viller & P. Wyeth (Eds.), *Proceedings of OZCHI 2003: New directions in interaction, information environments, media and technology. 26-28 Nov 2003*. Brisbane, QLD: Information Environments Program, University of Queensland.

Saul, P. L. R. (1994). Automated Feature Extraction for supervised Learning, 674-679.

Scherf, M., & Brauer, W. (1997). *Feature Selection by Means of a Feature Weighting Approach*. Technical Report No. FKI-221-97, Forschungsberichte kunstliche Intelligenz, Institut fur Informatik, Technische Universitat Munchen, http://citeseer.ist.psu.edu/scherf97feature.html

Schoder, D., & Madeja, N. (2004). Is customer relationship management a success factor in electronic commerce? *Journal of Electronic Commerce Research, 5*(1), 38-53.

Schuler, D. (1996). *New Community Networks: Wired for Change*. New York: ACM Press.

Schwartz, N. (2007, Dec. 9). Blogger threatens LA campus shooting. *Denver Post*. Retrieved Dec. 9, 2007, from http://www.denverpost.com/breakingnews/ci_7674486.

Schwartz, P. M. (1995). Privacy and participation: Personal information and public sector regulation in the United States. *Iowa Law Review, 80*, 553-618.

Schwartz, P. M. (2004). Property, privacy, and personal data. *Harvard Law Review, 117*, 2055-2128.

Seaphus vs. Lilly, 691 F. Supp. 127, 132 (N.D. Ill. 1988).

Sebastiani, F. (2002). Machine learning in Automated Text categorization. *ACM Computing Surveys, 34*(1), 1-47.

Segars, A.H., & Grover, V. (1998). Strategic information systems planning success: An investigation of the construct and its measurement. *MIS Quarterly, 22*(2), 139-163.

Seifert, J. W. (2004). Data mining and search for security challenges for connecting the dots and databases. *Government Information Quarterly, 21*(4), p. 461-480.

Seitz, K. (2006). Taking Steps To Ensure CRM Data Security. *Customer Inter@ction Solutions 24*(11), 62-64,66.

Selamat, A., Yanagimoto, H., & Omatu, S. (2002). Web News Classification Using Neural Networks Based on PCA. *SICE* 2002 Auk 57, Osaka

Setino, R., & Liu, H. (1997). Feature Selection via Discretization. *IEEE Transactions on Knowledge and Data Engineering, 9*(4),642-645.

Sharma, R., & Yetton, P. (2003). The contingent effects of management support and task interdependence on successful information systems implementation. *MIS Quarterly, 27*(4), 533-555.

Shaw, M. (2008). Community development and the politics of community. *Community Development Journal, 43*(1), 24-36.

Sheth, J. N., Sisodia, R. S., & Sharma, S. (2000). The antecedents and consequences of customer-centric marketing. *Journal of the Academy of Marketing Science, 28*(1 Winter), 55-66.

Shibley vs. Time, Inc., 341 N.E.2d 337 (Ohio Ct. App. 1975).

Shou-Bin, D. (2004). The Hierarchical Classification of Web content by the combination of Textual and Visual Features. *Proceedings of the Third International Conference on Machine Learning and Cybernetics*, Shanghai, 26-29 August 2004,1524-1529.

Shukla, S., & Nah, F. (2005). Web browsing and spyware intrusion. *Communications of the ACM, 48*(8), 85-90.

Shumway, R. H., & Stoffer, D. S. (2000). *Time series analysis and its applications.* Springer Texts in Statistics. New York, NY: Springer.

Siegel, B. (2007). State-secret overreach. *Los Angeles Times*, September 16, pp. 1-2.

Singel, R. (2007, Nov. 6). FBI mined grocery store records to find Iranian terrorists, CQ reports—Updated. Retrieved Nov. 10, 2007, from http://blog.wired.com/27bstroke6/2007/11/fbi-mined-groce.html.

Skyrms, B. (2003). *The Stag Hunt and the Evolution of Social Structure.* Cambridge ; New York: Cambridge University Press.

Slobogin, C. (2005). Transaction surveillance by the government. *Mississippi Law Journal, 75*, 139-190.

Smailagic, A., & Kogan, D. (2002). Location sensing and privacy in a context-aware computing environment. *IEEE Wireless Communications, 9*(5), 10-17.

Smith vs. Maryland, 442 U.S. 735 (1979).

Smith, S. W., & Spafford, E. H. (2004). Grand challenges in information security: process and output. *IEEE Security and Privacy 2*(1), 69-71.

Smith, S., & Jamieson, R. (2006). Determining Key Factors In E-Government Information System Security. *Information Systems Management, 23*(2), 23-33.

Sniffen, M. J. (2007). DHS ditches data mining program over privacy woes. *The Associated Press,* September, 5, p. 1-3.

Solove, D. (2006). *The digital person: Technology and privacy in the information ag*e. New York: New York University Press.

Solove, D. J. (2001). Privacy and power: Computer databases and metaphors for information privacy. *Stanford Law Review, 53*, 1393-1462.

Solove, D. J. (2002). Access and aggregation: Public records, privacy and the Constitution. *Minnesota Law Review, 86*, 1137-1218.

Solove, D. J. (2002). Digital dossiers and the dissipation of Fourth Amendment privacy. *Southern California Law Review, 75*, 1083-1167.

Solove, D. J. (2006). A taxonomy of privacy. *University of Pennsylvania Law Review, 154*, 477-564.

Solove, D. J., Rotenberg, M., & Schwartz, P. M. (2006). *Privacy, information and technology.* New York: Aspen Publishers.

Sookhdeo, P. (2007). *Global jihad: The future in the face of militant Islam.* New York Isaac Publisher: W. W. Norton & Company.

Spector, P.E. (1994). Using self-report questionnaires in OB research: A comment on the use of a controversial method. *Journal of Organizational Behavior, 15*, 385-392.

Spinellis, D., Kokolakis, D., & Gritzalis, S. (1999). Security requirements, risks and recommendations for small enterprise and home-office environments. *Information Management & Computer security, 7*(3), 121-128.

Srinivasan, A. (1985). Alternative measures of system effectiveness: Associations and implications. *MIS Quarterly, 9*(3), 243-253.

Stanley vs. Georgia, 394 U.S. 557 (1969).

Story, L., & Stone, B. (2007, Nov. 30). Facebook retreats on online tracking. *New York Times*, p. C1.

Straub, D.W. (1990). Effective IS security: An empirical study. *Information Systems Research, 1*(3), 255-276.

Straub, D.W., & Nance, W.D. (1990). Discovering and disciplining computer abuse in organizations: A field study. *MIS Quarterly, 14*(1), 45-60.

Straub, D.W., & Welke, R.J. (1998). Coping with systems risk: Security planning models for management decision making. *MIS Quarterly, 22*(4), 441-469.

Straub, D.W., Boudreau, M.C., & Gefen, D. (2004). Validating guidelines for IS positivist research. *Communications of the AIS, 13*(24), 380-427.

Straub, D.W., Limayem, M., & Karahanna-Evaristo, E. (1995). Measuring system usage: Implications for IS theory testing. *MIS Quarterly, 41*(8), 1328-1342.

Strauss, A., & Corbin, J. (1998). *Basics of qualitative research. Techniques and procedures for developing grounded theory* (2nd ed.). Thousand Oaks, CA: Sage.

Strickland, L.H. (1958). Surveillance and trust. *Journal of Personality, 26*, 200-215.

Stuckenschmidt, H., Hartmann, J., & van Harmelen, F. (2002). Learning Structural Classification Rules for Web-page Categorization. *Proceedings of Fifteenth International conference on Artificial Intelligence*, Flairs-2002 , American Association for Artificial Intelligence,(www. aaai.org)

Supreme Court of the United States. (2004). *Rasul et al. v. George W. Bush, President of the United States, et al.* (No. 03-334). Washington DC: The U.S. Supreme Court.

Suresh, K., Jitender, C., Deogun, S., Vijay, V., Raghavan, & Sever, H. (1996). A comparison of Feature Selection Algorithms in the context of Rough Classifiers. *Proceedings of Fifth IEEE conference on Fuzzy Systems, 2*(8-11), 1122-1128.

Sweeney, L. (2002). K-Anonymity: A Model for Protecting Privacy. *International Journal on Uncertainty, Fuzziness and Knowledge-Based Systems, 10*(5), 557-570.

Sylvers, E. (2008). Privacy on hold in cellphone business. *International Herald Tribune.*

Tanner, M. (October, 16, 2003). *Foreign Terrorist Tracking Task Force* (Testimony before the House Judiciary Subcommittee on Immigration, Border Security and Claims). Washington DC: United States House of Representatives.

Tapscott, D. (1999). *Growing up digital: The rise of the net generation.* New York, NY: McGrow Hill.

Thai, J. T. (2006). Is data mining ever a search under Justice Stevens's fourth amendment? *Fordham Law Review, 74*, 1731-1757.

The Pew Research Center. (January 11, 2006). *Americans taking Abramoff, Alito and domestic spying in stride.* Retrieved January 5 from http://people-press.org

The R project for statistical computing. Retrieved May 15, 2008, from http://www.r-project.org/

The White House. (2006). *Strategy for winning the war on terror.* Washington DC: The Office of the President

The White House. (2006). *President visits National Security Agency* (Press Release). Washington DC: The White House.

The White House. (2007). *Fact sheet: The Protect America Act of 2007.* Washington DC: The White House.

The White House. (April, 2004). *Biodefense fact sheet: President Bush signs Biodefense for the 21st century.* Washington DC: The White House.

The White House. (October, 29, 2001). *Homeland Security Presidential Directive-2.* Washington DC: The White House.

Thomson, J. J. (1975). The right to privacy. *Philosophy and Public Affairs, 4*, 295-314.

Tian, L., Bullock, D., & Westervelt, J. (2001). *Developing an Agricultural Remote Sensing Program at the University of Illinois.* Illinois Laboratory for Agricultural Remote Sensing.

Tien, L. (2004). Privacy, technology and data mining. *Ohio Northern University Law Review, 30*, 389-415.

Tindall, C. D. (2003). Argus rules: The commercialization of personal information. *Journal of Law, Technology & Policy, 2003*, 181-202.

Tolkien, J. R. R. (1966). *The Lord of the Rings* (2nd ed.). London: Allen & Unwin.

Tönnies, F. (1887). *Gemeinschaft und Gesellschaft* (3rd ed.). Darmstadt, Germany: Wissenschaftliche Buchgesellschaft.

Tureen vs. Equifax, Inc., 571 F.2d 411 (8th Cir. 1978).

Turow, J., Feldman, L., & Meltzer, K. (2005). Open to Exploitation: American Shoppers Online and Offline. Retrieved Jan 30, 2008, from http://www.annenbergpublicpolicycenter.org/04_info_society/Turow_APPC_Report_WEB_FINAL.pdf

U.S. Constitution, amendment IV.

U.S. Constitution, amendment XIV.

U.S. vs. D'Andrea, 497 F. Supp.2d 117 (D. Mass. 2007).

U.S. vs. Forrester, 495 F.3d 1041 (9th Cir. 2007).

U.S. vs. Karo, 468 U.S. 705 (1984).

U.S. vs. Knotts, 460 U.S. 276 (1983).

U.S. vs. Miller, 425 U.S. 435 (1976).

United States Census. (2003). *History.* Washington DC: Bureau of the Census, Department of Commerce.

United States Court of Appeals for the Ninth Circuit. (November 16, 2007). *Al-Haramain Islamic Foundation et al. v. George W. Bush, President of the United States et al.* (No. 03-36083).

United States Court of Appeals for the Sixth Circuit. (July 6, 2007). *American Civil Liberties Union et al. v. National Security Agency et al. (Nos. O6-2095.2140).*

United States Department of Defense. (2004). *Safeguarding privacy in the fight against terrorism* (Report of the Technology and Privacy Advisory Committee). Washington DC: DOD.

United States Department of Defense. (2006). *Quadrennial Defense Report.* Washington DC: Office of the Secretary of Defense, DOD.

United States Department of Homeland Security. (2007). *2007 Data Mining Report* (DHS Privacy Office Response to House Report 109-699). Washington DC: DHS.

United States Department of Homeland Security. (August, 2006). *Survey of DHS data mining activities.* Washington DC: DHS.

United States Department of Justice. (2002). Statement regarding today's filing in *Sibel Edmonds v. Department of Justice.* Washington DC: DOJ.

United States Department of Justice. (2007). *Report on data mining activities* (Submitted to the Congress Pursuant to Section 126 of the USA PATRIOT Improvement and Reauthorization Act of 2005). Washington DC: DOJ.

United States District Court for the District of Columbia. (2004). *Sibel Edmonds v. United States Department of Justice et al.* Washington DC (Case No. 02-1448).

United States General Accounting Office. (2003). *Results and challenges for government program audits and investigation* (Testimony of D. Katz before the Subcommittee on Technology, Information Policy, Intergovernmental Relations and the Census). Washington DC: United States House of Representatives.

United States General Accounting Office. (2004). *Data mining: Federal efforts cover a wide range of uses.* Washington DC: GAO.

United States General Accounting Office. (2005). *Data Mining: Agencies have taken key steps to protect privacy in selected efforts, but significant compliance issues remain.* Washington DC: GAO.

United States General Accounting Office. (2006). *Personal information: Key federal privacy laws do not require information resellers to safeguard all sensitive data.* Washington DC: GAO.

United States General Accounting Office. (2007). *Data mining: Early attention to privacy in developing a key*

DHS Program could reduce risk. Washington DC: GAO.

United States General Accounting Office. (February, 2004). *Aviation security: Computer Assisted Passenger Prescreening System faces significant implementation challenges.* Washington DC: GAO.

United States Government Printing Office. (2004). *The 9/11 Commission Report (Executive Summary).* Washington DC: GPO.

United States Government Printing Office. (2006). *Congressional reports* (H.RPT. 108-796—Intelligence Reform and Terrorism Prevention Act of 2004). Washington DC: GPO.

United States Senate. (January 10, 2007). *Balancing privacy and security: The privacy implications of government data mining programs* (Hearing before the Committee of the Judiciary). Washington DC: U.S. Government Printing office.

Vaidya, J., & Clifton, C. (2003). Privacy-Preserving K-Means Clustering Over Vertically Partitioned Data. In Proc. *of the 9th ACM SIGKDD Intl. Conf. on Knowledge Discovery and Data Mining* (p. 206-215). Washington, DC, USA.

van Wel, L., & Royakkers, L. (2004). Ethical issues in Web data mining. *Ethics and Information Technology, 6*(2), 129 - 140.

VandenBos, G., Knapp, S., & Doe, J. (2001). Role of reference elements in the selection of resources by psychology undergraduates. *Journal of Bibliographic Research, 5,* 117-123. Retrieved October 13, 2001, from http://jbr.org/chapters.html

Vara, V. (2007, Dec. 6). Facebook rethinks tracking. *Wall Street Journal,* p. B4.

Varchaver, N. (2004). Scanning the Globe. Fortune Magazine May 31, 2004.

Venkatraman, N., & Ramanujam, V. (1987). Measurement of business economic performance: An examination of method convergency. *Journal of Management, 13*(1), 109-122.

Verykios, V. S., Bertine, E., Fovino, I. N., Provenza, L. P., Saygin, Y., & Theodoridis, Y. (2004). State-of-the-art in Privacy Preserving Data Mining. *ACM SIGMOD Record, 33*(1), 50-57.

Video Privacy Protection Act of 1988, 18 U.S.C. §§ 2710-11(2007).

Vikki, G. (2007). *The law: Unilateral shaping U.S. national security policy: The role of National Security Directives.* Presidential Studies Quarterly, http://goliath.ecnext.com

Volonino, L., & Robinson, S. R. (2004). Principles and Practice of Information Security. Upper Saddle River, NJ, USA: Pearson Prentice Hall.

von Solms, R., & von Solms, B. (2004). From policies to culture. *Computers & Security, 23,* 275-279.

Wahlstrom, K., & Roddick, J. F. (2001). *On the Impact of Knowledge Discovery and Data Mining.* Canberra.

Walmsley, D. J. (2000). Community, Place and Cyber-space. *Australian Geographer, 31*(1), 5-19.

Wang, J. (2003). *Data mining: Opportunities and challenges.* London: Idea Group Publishers.

Wang, W., & Yang, J. (2005). *Mining sequential patterns from large data sets.* New York: Springer.

Wang, Y., Hodges, J., & Tang, B. (2003). Classification of Web Documents Using a Naive Bayes Method. *Proceedings of the 15th IEEE International Conference on Tools with Artificial Intelligence (ICTAI'03),* 2003 IEEE.

Wareham, J., Zheng, J. G., & Straub, D. (2005). Critical themes in electronic commerce research: a meta-analysis. *Journal of Information Technology 20*(1), 1-19.

Warner, R. (2005). Surveillance and the self: Privacy, identity, and technology. *DePaul Law Review, 54,* 847-871.

Warren, S., & Brandeis, L. (1890). *The right to privacy. Harvard Law Review, 4*(5), 193-220.

Wasserman, J.J. (1969). Plugging the leaks in computer security. *Harvard Business Review, 47*(5), 119-129.

Watters, E. (2003). *Urban Tribes: Are Friends the New Family?* London: Bloomsbury.

Watts, D. J. (2003). *Six Degrees: The Science of a Connected Age.* New York: Norton.

Weeks, C. (2007, September 24). *Army of little brothers as bad as Big Brother: Privacy czar Technology turning citizens into unintended spies, federal commissioner warns ahead of conference.* Edmonton Journal.

Wellman, B. (2001). Physical Place and Cyberplace: The Rise of Personalized Networking. *International Journal of Urban and Regional Research, 25*(2), 227-252.

Wellman, B. (2002). Little Boxes, Glocalization, and Networked Individualism. In M. Tanabe, P. van den Besselaar & T. Ishida (Eds.), *Digital Cities II: Second Kyoto Workshop on Digital Cities* (Vol. LNCS 2362, pp. 10-25). Heidelberg, Germany: Springer.

Wellman, B., & Haythornthwaite, C. A. (Eds.). (2002). *The Internet in Everyday Life.* Oxford, UK: Blackwell.

Wellman, B., Quan-Haase, A., Boase, J., Chen, W., Hampton, K. N., Díaz de Isla Gómez, I., et al. (2003). The Social Affordances of the Internet for Networked Individualism. *Journal of Computer-Mediated Communication, 8*(3).

Westin, A. (1967). *Privacy and Freedom.* New York: Atheneum.

Westin, A. (1967). *The Right to Privacy.* Boston: Atheneum Press.

Westin, A. F., & Baker, M. A. (1972). *Databanks in a free society: Computers, record-keeping and privacy.* New York: Quadrangle Books.

Whalen vs. Roe, 429 U.S. 589 (1977).

Whitaker, R. (1999). *The end of privacy: How total surveillance is becoming a reality.* New York: New Press.

White, B. (2007, Dec. 6). Watching what you see on the web. *Wall Street Journal,* p. B1.

Widmeyer, G. R. (2004). The Trichotomy Of Processes: A Philosophical Basis For Information Systems. *The Australian Journal of Information Systems, 11*(1), 3-11.

Williams, L.J., Cote, J.A., & Buckley, M.R. (1989). Lack of method variance in self-reported affect and perceptions at work: Reality or artifact? *Journal of Applied Psychology, 74,* 462-468.

Willson, M. A. (2006). *Technically Together: Rethinking Community within Techno-Society.* New York: Peter Lang.

Winkler, W. E. (1993). *Matching and record linkage.* Washington, D.C.: Bureau of the Census.

Winkler, W. E. (2002) *Methods for Record Linkage and Bayesian Networks.* Washington, D.C.: Statistical Research Division, Bureau of the Census.

Wong, D. (1984). *Moral relativity.* Berkeley, CA: University of California Press.

Wong, D. (1993). Relativism. In P. Singer (ed.), *A companion to ethics* (pp. 442-450). Cambridge MA: Blackwell.

Wong, D. (2006). *Natural moralities: A defense of pluralistic relativism.* Oxford: Oxford University Press.

Wu, F., Zhou, Y., & Zhang C. (2004). Relevant Linear Feature Extraction Using Side-information and Unlabeled Data. *Proceedings of the 17th International Conference on Pattern Recognition (ICPR'04).*

Yan, J., Zhang, B., Liu, N., Yan, S., Cheng, Q., Fan, W., Yang, Q., Xi, W., & Chen, Z. (2006). Effective and Efficient Dimensionality Reduction for Large-Scale and Streaming Data Preprocessing. *IEEE Transactions on Knowledge and Data Engineering, 18*(3),320-333.

Yang, K.S. (1986). Will societal modernization eventually eliminate cross-cultural psychological differences. In M.H. Bond (Ed.), *The cross-cultural challenge to social psychology.* Newbury Park, CA: Sage.

Ye, N. (Ed.). (2003). *The handbook of data mining.* Mahwah, NJ: Lawrence Erlbaum Associate Publishers.

Young, F. W. (1987). *Multidimensional Scaling.* Lawrence Erlbaum Associates, Hillsdale, New Jersey.

Yu, H., Chen-Chuan Chang, K., & Han, J. (2002). Heterogeneous Learner for Web Page Classification. *Proceedings of International Conference on Data Mining 2002.*

Zanasi, A. (2007). *Data Mining and Information Engineering Conference 2007. Wessex Institute of Technology.* Retrieved January 2008 from http://www.wessex.ac.uk/conferences/2007/data07/index.html

Zarsky, T. Z. (2002-2003). "Mine your own business!": Making the case for the implications of the data mining of personal information in the forum of public opinion. *Yale Journal of Law & Technology, 5,* 1-56.

About the Contributors

Ephrem Eyob is a professor in the Department of Engineering and Engineering Technology and co-ordinator of the Logistics Program at Virginia State University. Prior to that he was professor and chair for the Department of Computer Information Systems in the School of Business. His research interest is in information systems and decision sciences areas primarily on Web based functional integration of operations, logistics, optimization of supply chain networks, and information technology applications in supply chain management. He served as the guest editor for the *International Journal of Management and Decision Making* in 2006. Currently, he is serving as a member of the editorial board member for *International Journal of Services and Standards*, and *International Journal of Electronic Government* among others. He has published over 70 articles and proceedings in major journals and conferences in international and national venues.

* * *

Karl-Ernst-Erich Biebler studied mathematics at the Friedrich-Schiller-University in Jena, Germany and dealt with problems of functional analysis and topology in his thesis. After that he turned to the topics of biomathematics and medical computer science. He is now director of the Institute of Biometry and Medical Computer Science at the Ernst-Moritz-Arndt-University in Greifswald, Germany. Professor Biebler teaches biometry for students of medicine, human biology and biomathematics. He has published monographs, book contributions and journal articles concerning different fields of mathematics and its applications.

Philip Brey (PhD, University of California, San Diego, 1995) is professor of philosophy of technology and chair of the Department of Philosophy, University of Twente, The Netherlands. He is also director of the Centre for Philosophy of Technology and Engineering Science (CEPTES) of the University of Twente and a member of the management team of the Centre of Excellence for Ethics and Technology of the Universities of Twente, Delft and Eindhoven. His research is in philosophy and ethics of technology, with special attention to ethical issues in information technology.

Tanya Candia is president of Candia Communications, an international marketing and strategic consulting company. She has served as vice president of marketing for F-Secure, Sigaba and several other software startups, and held executive positions at IBM/Tivoli, and Amdahl. She is the published author of a series of comprehensive marketing guidebooks, co-author of research published in the *Encyclopedia of Digital Government*, and has served as editor-in-chief of three scholarly journals. Candia holds an MS in systems management from the University of Southern California and an MA in communications from the Monterey Institute of International Studies.

Thomas Chen is an associate professor in the Department of Electrical Engineering, Southern Methodist University in Dallas, Texas. Prior to joining SMU in 1997, he was a member of the technical staff at GTE (now Verizon) Laboratories in Waltham, Massachusetts. He was the former editor-in-chief of *IEEE Communications Magazine* (2006-2007) and former founding editor-in-chief *of IEEE Communications Surveys*. He is a co-editor of *Broadband Mobile Multimedia: Techniques and Applications* (CRC Press, 2008) and co-author of *ATM Switching Systems* (Artech House, 1995). He was co-recipient of the IEEE Communications Society's Fred W. Ellersick best paper award in 1996.

Peter Danielson is the Mary & Maurice Young professor of applied ethics and director of the Centre for Applied Ethics at the University of British Columbia. His research program aims to understand how various agents – rational, moral, and ethical – interact using methods from evolutionary game theory, agent-based computer modeling, and ethical theory. His Norms Evolving in Response to Dilemmas (NERD) research group for a series of Genome Canada/BC funded projects has designing an innovative web-based survey experiments to gather data on ethical decision-making.

M.Indra Devi received the BE degree in computer science and engineering from Madurai Kamaraj University in 1990 and the ME degree in computer science and engineering from Madurai Kamaraj University in 2003. She is currently a lecturer at Information Technology Department at Thiagarajar College of Engineering, Madurai. She has published ten papers in national and international conferences. Her research interests include machine learning applications and web mining. She is a life member of Computer Society of India, Institution of Engineers, India and Indian Society for Technical Education.

Jerry Fjermestad is an associate professor in the School of Management at NJIT. He received his MBA and PhD from Rutgers University in management information systems. His current research interests are in collaborative technology, decision support systems, data warehousing, electronic commerce, global information systems, customer relationship management, and enterprise information systems. Jerry has published in the *Journal of Management Information Systems, Communications of the ACM, Group Decision and Negotiation*, and several other journals and conference proceedings. He also serves as an associate editor for *Journal of Information Science and Technology*, the *International Journal of Electronic Collaboration*, and the *International Journal of Information Security and Privacy*.

Nelson Ford is associate professor and coordinator of MIS programs in the Department of Management, Auburn University. Dr. Ford has published in a wide range of journals including *MIS Quarterly, The Journal of Management Information Systems, Decision Support Systems, Interfaces, Database, Information Management and Computer Security*, and *Information & Management*.

Marcus Foth is a senior research fellow at the Institute for Creative Industries and Innovation, Queensland University of Technology (QUT), Brisbane, Australia. He received a BCompSc(Hon) from Furtwangen University, Germany, a BMultimedia from Griffith University, Australia and an MA and PhD in digital media and urban sociology from QUT. Dr Foth is the recipient of an Australian Post-doctoral fellowship supported under the Australian Research Council's Discovery funding scheme. He was a 2007 visiting fellow at the Oxford Internet Institute, University of Oxford, UK. Employing participatory design and action research, he is working on cross-disciplinary research and development at the intersection of people, place and technology with a focus on urban informatics, locative media and mobile applications. Dr. Foth has published over 40 articles in journals, edited books, and conference proceedings in the last four years. He is a member of the Australian Computer Society and the Executive Committee of the Association of Internet Researchers.

Zhi (Judy) Fu is a principal staff researcher at Motorola research labs. She received her PhD from the Computer Science Department of North Carolina State University in 2001 and since then joined Motorola Labs focusing on wireless network security research. Her research interests include wireless AAA, protocol vulnerability analysis, security policy, Web security and intrusion detection, etc. She is inventor on more than 10 pending patents and has published over 20 papers in premier conferences and journals.

Alexandra Geyer is a cognitive scientist in Aptima's Advanced Training Systems Division. Ms. Geyer's expertise is in the areas of psychophysiology and language processing. At Aptima, her work focuses on training system design and human language technologies. Ms. Geyer holds an MS in cognitive neuroscience and a BS in biology and psychology from Tufts University. She is a doctoral candidate in cognitive neuroscience at Tufts University. She is a member of the Cognitive Neuroscience Society and the Eastern Psychological Association.

Aris Gkoulalas-Divanis received the Diploma degree in computer science from the University of Ioannina, Greece, in 2003, ranked 2nd best out of 80 students. He was accepted as a graduate student in the Computer Engineering Department, University of Minessota, where he received his MS degree in 2005. He was then admitted as a PhD candidate to the Department of Computer and Communication Engineering, University of Thessaly, Greece. Gkoulalas-Divanis has served as a research assistant in the University of Minnesota and in the University of Manchester. His research interests are in the fields of privacy preserving data mining, information retrieval and document clustering.

Andrew Duchon is a lead scientist on the Communications and Cognition Team at Aptima, Inc. He is a project manager, researcher, and software engineer on projects related to automatic communications analysis, analyzing news trends to predict terrorist activities, automatically matching resumes to mission descriptions, and cognitive computing architectures. Dr. Duchon holds a PhD in cognitive science from Brown University, and a BA in psychology and the Integrated Science Program from Northwestern University. He is a member of the Association for Computational Linguistics.

Mokerrom Hossain, is an associate professor of criminal justice in the Department of Sociology, Social Work, and Criminal Justice, Virginia State University, Virginia. He received his MA and PhD in sociology from the University of California-Riverside. His major fields of research include global illegal drug trades, global terrorism, homeland security, criminal justice policy, and ethics in criminal justice. Dr. Hossain was the chair of the Department of Sociology, Social Work, and Criminal Justice from 1999-2007.

Bernd Paul Jäger studied mathematics and geography and was a research assistant at the Institute of Mathematics and Computer Science of the Ernst-Moritz-Arndt-University in Greifswald, Germany. At present, he is a senior research assistant at the Institute of Biometry and Medical Computer Science of the same university. Dr. Jäger is author of several books and papers dealing with the application of mathematical methods in medicine.

Kenneth J. Knapp is an associate professor of management information systems at the U.S. Air Force Academy, Colorado. His works have been published in numerous outlets to include the *Communications of the Association for Information Systems, Information Systems Management, Information Management & Computer Security, International Journal of Information Security and Privacy* and *Information Systems Security*. Dr. Knapp was the 2008 recipient of the General Robert F. McDermott Award for excellence in research in the social sciences and the humanities.

Thomas E. Marshall is an associate professor of management information systems at Auburn University, Auburn, Alabama. He has published in journals such as *Omega, Information & Management, Information Systems Security, Information Management & Computer Security, Journal of Computer Information Systems, Journal of End User Computing, Information Resource Management* and *Journal of Database Management*.

Robert McCormack is an applied mathematician at Aptima, Inc., where he applies the techniques of mathematical modeling to complex dynamic systems. He is particularly interested in the modeling of biological and epidemiological systems, and the impact of human decision-making and policies on dynamic and emergent behavior. Dr. McCormack has expertise in creating both deterministic and stochastic differential equation models to describe complex systems, as well as applying numerical techniques to simulate and analyze these models. Dr. McCormack received a PhD and MS in mathematics from Texas Tech University, and a BA in mathematics and computer science from Austin College.

Stanley R. M. Oliveira has worked as a researcher in computer science at the Brazilian Agricultural Research Corporation (Embrapa) since February 1995. He obtained his master's degree in computer science from the Federal University of Campina Grande, Brazil, in 1995, and his PhD in computer science from the University of Alberta, Canada, in 2005. His PhD thesis work focused on privacy-preserving data mining. Dr. Oliveira is also a collaborator professor at the UNICAMP/FEAGRI (State University of Campinas / Agricultural Engineering Faculty) in Brazil where he teaches graduate courses on data mining. He has published several papers, most of them in refereed journals and international conferences. His main research interests include privacy-preserving data mining, database security, bioinformatics, text mining and feature selection.

Kara Orvis is an industrial-organizational psychologist at Aptima, Inc. with expertise in the areas of team leadership, dispersed team collaboration, dispersed leadership, and training technologies. At Aptima, she works on projects dealing with issues of team and leadership development. Dr. Orvis holds an MA and a PhD in industrial-organizational psychology from George Mason University and a BA in psychology from Ohio Wesleyan University. She is a member of the American Psychological Association, the Academy of Management, and the Society for Industrial and Organizational Psychology.

R. Kelly Rainer, Jr. is George Phillips Privett professor of management information systems at Auburn University, Alabama. Dr. Rainer has published in leading academic and practitioner outlets and is associate editor of *Communications of the Association of Information Systems*. He is co-author, with Efraim Turban and Richard Potter of *Introduction to Information Systems* (Wiley).

R. Rajaram is the dean of computer science and information technology, Thiagarajar College of Engineering. Madurai has a BE (1966) in electrical and electronics engineering from University of Madras. He secured the MTech Degree (1971) in electrical engineering from IIT Kharagpur and the PhD degree (1979) from Madurai Kamaraj University. He and his research students have published nearly 45 papers in journals, seminars and symposia. His areas of interest are data mining, machine learning, neural networks, network security, fuzzy systems and genetic algorithms. He attended the International Symposium on Solar Energy at the University of Waterloo, Canada, during August 1978. He served at the Makerere University, Kampala, Uganda during 1977 – 79, and at the Mosul University, Iraq during 1980 – 1981. He studied at Malaysia and has traveled to London, Paris, New York, Toronto, Nairobi and Colombo.

Nicholas C. Romano, Jr. is assistant professor of management science and information systems at Oklahoma State University. Romano received a PhD in MIS from the University of Arizona in 1998 and worked for IBM. He was ranked 3rd in the world in electronic commerce research journal articles from 1998-2004 in the *2006 Business Research Yearbook*. He has published papers in several journals and proceedings including: *Journal of Management Information Systems, International Journal of Electronic Commerce*. He serves as associate editor for *Journal of Information Systems Technology* and reviews for *ISR, JMIS, IJEC, Management Science, DSS* and others. He is active in the HICSS and AMCIS conferences.

K.Selvakuberan received the BTech degree in IT from Anna University in 2007. He is currently an associate in Tata Consultancy Services. He is working in Innovation Labs(Web 2.0) in Chennai and his research interests include data mining, web mining and machine learning. He has published 10 papers in national and international conferences.

Shahid M. Shahidullah is an associate professor of criminal justice in the Department of Sociology, Social Work, and Criminal Justice, Virginia State University, Virginia. He received his MPIA (Master in Public International Affairs) and MA and PhD in sociology from the University of Pittsburgh. Westview Press published his first book *Capacity-Building in Science and Technology in the Third Word* in 1991. His second book *Globalization and the Evolving Society* (with P. K. Nandi) was published by E. J. Brill of The Netherlands in 1998. American University Press will publish his book on *Crime Policy in America* in 2008. Dr. Shahidullah's major fields of research interests are criminal justice policy, crime policy and the constitution, global crimes, and global terrorism.

Robert Sprague is an assistant professor in the Department of Management & Marketing, University of Wyoming College of Business. He teaches upper-division legal studies courses covering commercial law, employment, business formation, and corporate governance. Professor Sprague's research interests derive from a convergence of law, business, and technology, with an emphasis on privacy and cyberspace issues. He also just completed a two-year Kauffman Foundation grant researching the impact of securities laws on new ventures. Prior to joining academe, Professor Sprague provided legal counseling to small businesses, primarily in high-tech industries, and served as senior manager in various start-up ventures.

Arlin Torbett serves as chairman and founder of AgriWorld Exchange. He was formerly chairman/ CEO of mobileID, and held executive positions at GWcom (now mTone) and byair.com USA. At SRI International, Dr. Torbett led DARPA-funded research on packet-radio, packet-switching technology, and Department of Defense efforts on fourth-generation computer architectures. He holds a PhD in management science & engineering from Stanford University, an MA in mathematics from the University of Maryland, and a BS in applied mathematics from Georgia Tech. Dr. Torbett holds four patents on packet data systems for mobile Internet communications.

Vassilios S. Verykios received the Diploma degree in computer engineering from the University of Patras, Greece, in 1992 and the MS and PhD degrees from Purdue University in 1997 and 1999, respectively. In 1999, he joined the Faculty of Information Systems in the College of Information Science and Technology at Drexel University, Pennsylvania. Since 2005 he is an assistant professor in the Department of Computer and Communication Engineering at the University of Thessaly, Volos, Greece. Dr. Verykios has published over 40 papers in major referred journals and in the proceedings of international conferences and workshops, and he has served in the program committees of several international scientific events.

Michael Wodny is a senior research assistant at the Institute for Biometry and Medical Computer Science at the Ernst-Moritz-Arndt-University of Greifswald, Germany. Dr. Wodny studied mathematics and is especially engaged in numeric methods and its applications. His publications are related to classification methods and pharmacokinetics. He teaches biometry.

Osmar R. Zaïane is an associate professor in computing science at the University of Alberta, Canada. Dr. Zaïane joined the University of Alberta in July of 1999. He obtained a master's degree in electronics at the University of Paris in 1989 and a master's degree in computer science at Laval University, Canada, in 1992. He obtained his PhD from Simon Fraser University, Canada, in 1999 under the supervision of Dr. Jiawei Han. His PhD thesis work focused on web mining and multimedia data mining. He has research interests in novel data mining algorithms, web mining, text mining, image mining, and information retrieval. He has published more than 80 papers in refereed international conferences and journals, and taught on all six continents. Osmar Zaïane was the co-chair of the ACM SIGKDD International Workshop on Multimedia Data Mining in 2000, 2001 and 2002 as well as co-Chair of the ACM SIGKDD WebKDD workshop in 2002, 2003 and 2005. He is the program co-chair for the IEEE International Conference on Data Mining 2007 and general co-chair for the conference on Advanced Data Mining Applications 2007. Osmar Zaïane is the ACM SIGKDD Explorations associate editor and associate editor of the *International Journal of Internet Technology and Secured Transactions*.

Index